A NEW
HISTORY
OF
CHRISTIANITY

A NEW HISTORY OF CHRISTIANITY

HANS J. HILLERBRAND

Abingdon Press
Nashville

A NEW HISTORY OF CHRISTIANITY

Library of Congress Cataloging-in-Publication Data

Hillerbrand, Hans Joachim.
  A new history of Christianity / Hans J. Hillerbrand.
    p. cm.
  Includes bibliographical references and index.
  ISBN 978-0-687-02796-5 (pbk : alk. paper)
  1. Church history. I. Title.
  BR145.3.H55 2011
  270.09—dc23

                                                            2011025508

Photo credits:

Jesus as the Good Shepherd, Scala/Art Resource, NY.

St. Augustine of Hippo, V&A Images, London/Art Resource, NY.

Canterbury Cathedral, copyright 2012 iStockphoto LP.

Statue of St. Francis of Assisi, copyright 2012 iStockphoto LP.

Mary and the Infant Jesus, copyright 2012 iStockphoto LP.

Martin Luther, Scala/Art Resource, NY.

John Calvin, Snark/Art Resource, NY.

Ecstasy of St. Theresa, Scala/Art Resource, NY.

Nikolaus Copernicus holding a compass and armillary sphere, copyright 2012 iStockphoto LP.

John Wesley. Used by permission of the Arthur Moore Methodist Museum, Library, and Archives of the South Georgia Conference of the United Methodist Church, Epworth by the Sea.

Cathedral of Mary's Assumption into Heaven, copyright 2012 iStockphoto LP.

Camp Meeting, courtesy of the New Bedford Whaling Museum.

River Baptism, Unidentified Photographer [River baptism, Pibel, Nebraska], 1913 International Center of Photography, Museum Purchase, 2005 (440.2005).

12 13 14 15 16 17 18 19 20—10 9 8 7 6 5 4 3 2 1

MANUFACTURED IN THE UNITED STATES OF AMERICA

For Dylan and Johannes

CONTENTS

Preface xiii

By Way of Introduction—*Reflection 1: Whose Story?* xv

1. The First Four Centuries 1

    The Beginning 4

    Early Expansion 7

    The Christian Assemblies 10

    Persecution 14

    The Triumph 21

    The Emergence of Christian Writings 25

        Apostolic Authority 29

    Theological Clarification 31

    The Theologians 37

        Irenaeus 37

        Tertullian 38

        Origen 41

        Augustine 43

    The Creeds 52

Contents

Diversity and Heresy 59

    Gnosticism 64

    Marcion 68

    Arius 71

    Donatism 76

The Monastic Impulse 79

    Origins 81

    Christian Monasticism in the Middle Ages and Beyond 84

Reflection 2: Church and Society in the Shadow of Constantine 89

2. The Medieval Church in the West 93

    The Heavenly and the Earthly Kingdom: Church and State . . . 100

    The Medieval Church: Structure and Practice 103

    The Renewal of the Monastic Vision 109

    The Saint: Francis of Assisi 113

    The Theological Maturing of the Faith: Scholasticism 121

    The Church in the East 124

        Spread and Expansion of the Church in the East 124

        The Rivalry between the Eastern and Western Churches . . 125

        Theology 130

    The Crusades 134

    The Christian Faith in Asia 142

Contents

Reflection 3: Jews and Christians 145

3. The Western Church Divides: The Protestant Reformation 149

    The Controversy 152

    The Consequences 157

    The Issues 167

    The Divided House 170

    The Anabaptist Dissent 172

    The Reformer of Geneva: John Calvin 177

    The Catholic Church in the Sixteenth Century 182

    The Reform in Europe 189

    Kings, Queens, and Bishops: Reformation in England 191

    The Puritan Dissent 196

    Success and Failure in France 198

    The Age of Confessionalism 201

Reflection 4: Studying the Faith of the People 205

4. The New Challenge: Modernity 209

    The New Science 213

    Religions of the Heart 222

        German Pietism 222

        The Wesleyan Revival in England 233

    The Turbulent Nineteenth Century 239

Roman Catholicism Enters Modernity 248

The Modern Missionary Impulse 255

Christianity in the Twentieth Century 263

Reflection 5: Women in Christianity 277

5. Christianity in the Americas 281

The Colonial Period 281

The Protestants Arrive 284

New Churches 290

The Revivals 296

Protestantism and the Social Order 299

The Conservative Reaction 300

The Catholic Story 302

African American Christianity 302

Reflection 6: Christianity as a Global Phenomenon 305

By Way of an Epilogue 309

Appendix A: Theological Currents in the Early Twenty-first
Century 309

Appendix B: Recurrent Themes in the History of Christianity . . . 311

Appendix C: On the Gap between Ideals and Practice 314

Appendix D: The Church Moves into the Future 316

Appendix E: The Houses of God: Christianity and Material
Culture 323

Contents

Chronology of the Christian Religion 335

Glossary of Terms 351

Bibliography 353

    General Surveys and Narratives 353

    For Early Christianity 353

    For the Medieval Church 354

    For the Reformation of the Sixteenth Century 354

    For Christianity in the Modern Period 355

    For Christianity in North America 355

    For Christianity in the Global Era 356

    Audiovisual Materials 356

    Internet Resources 357

Selections from Christian Sources 358

Scripture Index 403

Subject Index 405

PREFACE

I have not sought to calculate how many times I have taught an introductory course on the history of Christianity. As my notes began to yellow (I had to make sure that I would not use the word *recent* when describing a book published in the 1970s), I began to experiment with a variety of approaches, even at one time attempting to teach the course backwards, starting with the twentieth century and ending with the first. Needless to say, there were no textbooks for that kind of approach. I did resist the temptation to make this approach permanent, but I made other changes, for example, integrating extensive primary sources into the course syllabus. Basically, however, the course has remained the same: to tell the story of Christian self-understanding and action during the past two thousand years. I tried to write the book for readers with little background in the theology and history of the Christian tradition, keeping technical vocabulary and the description of happenings simple.

The reader will notice that I devote considerable space to the telling of the story of women and men. This was done because in many instances this will allow us to encounter a rich cluster of facets—commitment and desertion; conversion and new life; obstacles and opposition. It will also confront us with the awareness that the Christian story surely is above all the story of individuals—men and women—who took the call of the gospel seriously.

A great deal of the scholarly discourse during the past decades was devoted to the assertion that objectivity is impossible to attain and that the voice of the historian will thus reflect certain presuppositions and preconditions. The point was well taken, though perhaps not as novel as some intimated. This book will quickly make evident that I write about the Christian religion as someone who is very much part of it. I should like to think, however, that my appreciation of the Christian tradition is tempered by a commitment to the highest standards of the historical profession, which compels me to be critical and even judgmental when that is called for. To make the difference between personal opinion and scholarly values explicit, I chose the vehicle of end-of-chapter musings, which I titled "Reflections."

A word also about some tricky semantic issues. Following established precedent, I have capitalized *God*, but not the divine pronouns, throughout the book, even as I have used the ancient but Christian designation *anno Domini* (A.D.) whenever I was referring to dates in a Christian context. Likewise, I refer to the Old Testament whenever the context is Christian; in non-Christian contexts I use the terms "Hebrew Bible" or "Hebrew Scriptures."

Several colleagues read parts of the manuscript—Caroline Bruzelius, Ruth Homrighaus, Peter Kaufman, Gregory Lee, Volker Leppin, Warren Smith, Orval Wintermute, Grant Wacker—and it is assuredly better for their helpful suggestions. I record my special appreciation to J. Samuel Hammond, librarian and carillonneur at Duke University, also a true expert on Christian history and thought. His many suggestions (and criticisms!) have improved the book. Gratitude is also due Flynn Cratty, whose painstaking reading of the manuscript removed many an error. I record my public thanks to both Robert Ratcliff and Susan Cornell of Abingdon Press. Especially Ms. Cornell was unfailingly helpful and constructive, qualities an author dearly cherishes in an editor.

Given the objective I had in mind for this book, I turned to my two grandsons, Dylan and Johannes Hillerbrand, to benefit from their notions of what makes history readable when writing for an audience of nonprofessionals. They both are bright college students; both read the draft of the manuscript carefully and made a host of suggestions and criticisms, virtually all of which I incorporated. The book would not be what it is without them. I therefore gratefully dedicate this book to them. They are of a new generation that will face its own new challenges in relating the faith of the past to the present.

Hans J. Hillerbrand
Duke University

BY WAY OF
INTRODUCTION

Reflection 1: Whose Story?

A note to the reader: At particular points throughout the book I will include brief sections in which to ask what the history of Christianity can tell us about contemporary Christianity and its relationship to culture, society, politics, and the like. What follows is the first of these "reflections."

All chroniclers of the Christian tradition have to deal with methodological issues that need to be settled, explicitly or implicitly, before they ever put down the first word on paper. Foremost is the issue of the subject matter: what is the subject matter of a history of Christianity? That seems a strange and bewildering question, for on the face of things it should be simple enough. But through the centuries what one interpreter has called true Christianity, another has labeled heresy—Martin Luther and his followers being the most obvious illustration. The Christian story is exceedingly complex. A variety of views has vied for acceptance as the authentic teaching of Jesus of Nazareth. How does one make sense of this variety of assertions and claims?

Traditional nomenclature complicates matters as well. What does it mean to speak of "church" history? Where and what exactly is the "church" whose story is to be recounted? In North America, a brief glance at the local telephone directory or online search will demonstrate this diversity of claims. Numerous "churches" have claimed to be *the* church. And this multiplicity of competing or rivaling "churches" has not been altogether irenic, as each church frequently employed verbal abuse and, at times, even oppression and violence to vindicate correct belief. What is the chronicler of the past to do with these competing claims? One obvious answer is to define "church" according to one's criteria and find it (and only it) in the past, while another is to follow the *Alice in Wonderland* exclamation that "everyone has won, and all must have prizes," including all movements and individuals that in one way or another have claimed to be Christian. It seems best that when speaking of the "history of Christianity" to include in that history all interpretations and manifestations of the meaning of Jesus of Nazareth. In that context, then, the Jehovah's Witnesses or the Mormons become as important to the story as do Calvinism and the Great Awakening in New England.

In recent years some scholars have also become uncomfortable with the theological implications of the word *church* and have proposed substitutes to avoid what they perceive as a terminological and theological dilemma. They prefer to speak of the "history of Christianity." However, that term, too, has found detractors, who have argued that it fails to acknowledge that there has never been a single "Christianity" but always "Christianities," that is, multiple and diverse interpretations of the Christian faith. The demurrer about the diversity of "Christianities" is well taken but has led to a distorted conclusion. The fact of the matter is that all of these diverse streams and separate interpreting communities have understood themselves as interpreters and followers of Jesus of Nazareth, to whom they pledged their allegiance. In that sense, they form through the centuries, therefore, a single entity. The history of Christianity may thus be defined as the story of the interpretation of the gospel by those who sought to apply it in daily life.

An even more far-reaching proposal has been to employ the term "religious history." That, assuredly, is a generically neutral term. If properly used, it entails the inclusion of non-Christian religious history, which in Europe needs to include both Judaism and Islam; in North America, all those religions brought here by immigrants. "Church history" then becomes a subsection of a broader historical narrative—at which point the question of the particular identity of the Christian narrative will come to the fore again.

No matter what the nomenclature, the fact of the matter is that the historical story of the Christian religion has been typically told from the perspective of a particular tradition, often at the expense of competing traditions. Thus, Catholic historians recounted the authentic Christian story as the history of the Catholic Church, while Eastern Orthodox historians declared the story of the Western church to be one of perversion. In some accounts Martin Luther was seen as a heretic—immoral and ignorant to boot—in others, however, as the most insightful interpreter of the faith since John wrote the book of Revelation on the island of Patmos. While this parochial perspective has largely disappeared in the last half-century in favor of what has been called "ecumenical" history, the problem of how to adjudicate divergent views and positions remains. While this is a problem faced by all chroniclers of the past, it receives particular poignancy when it comes to religious values and convictions.

Something else. The story of the Christian religion is also rather complex. It includes the lofty theological notions and ideas that may be seen as either unimportant theological squabbles or as a consistent drawing out of the meaning of Jesus of Nazareth. It includes the stories of leaders and followers, of the high and mighty in church and state, and of the marginalized and outcast. It includes the stories of personal courage and cowardice. It includes the stories of wide geographic parameters, of Christian believers in Africa and New Guinea no less than in England and Sweden.

The question becomes one of selection and emphasis. What should the focus of the narrative be? Essentially, the answer boils down to two alternatives: a theological or a historical narrative.

Which brings us to the related topic of an overall unifying theme, a cohesive perspective, of the two thousand years of the Christian faith. There are several themes in Christian history that possess a striking timelessness as they are found in all periods of the past. Related is the challenge of ascertaining which of the several strands of the Christian story of the past should be prominent. After all, there are the sophisticated delineations of theological issues in conjunction with the trinitarian controversy in the fourth century or the groping of a variety of biblical scholars in the nineteenth century to come to grips with the findings of modern science. But there are also the stories of heroes of the faith, of Francis of Assisi, of John Calvin, or Charles Wesley and Dietrich Bonhoeffer. And finally, there are the people in the pews, the men, women, and even children, who appear neither in the annals of theological reflection nor in the accounts of heroism and martyrdom. Should their stories not be prominent, no matter how difficult the sources?

The pages that follow will seek to answer these questions and in so doing provide a coherent narrative of two thousand years of Christian history.

CHAPTER ONE

THE FIRST FOUR CENTURIES

Around the year 110, the Roman provincial governor of Bithynia in Asia Minor requested instructions of Emperor Trajan about what to do with a group of people called "Christians." Wrote Governor Pliny:

> I have never been present at the trial of Christians, and I do not know what to ask or how to punish: I have been very much at a loss to know whether to make any distinction for age or strength, whether to excuse those who have renounced Christianity, whether the name itself, lacking other offense, or the crimes associated with the name, should be punished. In the meantime this is what I have done. I have asked the accused whether they were Christians. If they confessed, I asked a second and a third time, threatening with a penalty. Those who persisted I ordered to be executed, for I did not doubt that, whatever it was they professed, they deserved to be punished for their inflexible obstinacy. There were others of equal lunacy who, because they were Roman citizens, I sent to Rome. (Pliny, *Letters* 10.960)

Obviously, the governor was puzzled, and his request for a directive from the emperor marked the first official recognition of the existence of "Christians" in the Roman Empire. There obviously was trouble of some sort in Bithynia, to which Pliny obliquely referred by mentioning "the trial of Christians," but at the same time he did not think these Christians to be a big issue (though he clearly did not like them). They were a concern of his, however, though we are left in the dark about exactly what that concern was. Nonetheless, echoing the concern of bureaucrats of all times and places, Pliny the bureaucrat wanted to make sure that the matter was handled properly.

1

Neither governor nor emperor could have had the slightest inkling that some nineteen hundred years later more than two billion men, women, and children would be the successors to those "Christians" who pledge allegiance to Jesus of Nazareth. In the early years of the twenty-first century, millions of Christians gather for worship, devotions, and study around the globe. In some places the gospel of Jesus has been proclaimed for almost two millennia, while in others this gospel is altogether new. Christianity has become the largest of the world's religions.

The beginning of this religion was even more modest than Pliny may have imagined. It started, some two thousand years ago, when Jesus of Nazareth, a Jew, walked the Palestinian countryside preaching and teaching. He had followers, male and female; propounded a striking religious message about an imminent kingdom; ran into conflict with the religious and political authorities of his day; and died an ignominious death as a criminal outside Jerusalem. While this might well have been the end of his story, his followers—convinced that after his death he had risen from the dead, thereby vindicating his mission—continued to gather and eventually followed his exhortation to go "into all the world" and make disciples. As the centuries passed, they were stunningly successful.

At the core of Jesus' first followers' beliefs stood their conviction that he had been the "Christ" (in Greek, *Christos*), the Anointed One, the Messiah, promised to bring deliverance to Israel. According to the New Testament book of Acts (11:26), these followers were called "Christians" to express their affirmation of Jesus as the Messiah.

The Roman authorities were not particularly fond of this emerging religious movement, which was so different from the other religions that populated the Roman Empire. For two centuries they repeatedly did everything they could to remove the Christians and their strange religion from the face of the earth. Nonetheless, little by little the movement gained adherents in all parts of the "known world," the Roman Empire, and even beyond. And somehow the Christians and their religion did not fit into the otherwise tolerant religious culture of the Roman Empire. Before long Christians found themselves on the receiving end of intermittent governmental oppression and persecution. The reason for this tension between the Christian movement and the Roman state is not altogether clear, though it may well have been the Christian deliberate aloofness from the culture of Roman society, particularly the Christian unwillingness to pay homage to the Roman emperors and serve in the civic offices of the powerful empire. Aloofness tended to create suspicion; suspicion tended to create fear; and fear tended to trigger intolerance.

Roman governmental action proved unsuccessful. In the early fourth century a dramatic change occurred in this story of suspicion, suppression, and persecution. In the year 313, Emperor Constantine formally declared Christianity to be a "recognized" religion in the Roman Empire; the days of persecution were over. Soon, however, the decline and eventual disintegration of this empire posed new challenges, since they caught the Christian religion in the maelstrom of a changing political and social order. The mighty Roman Empire began to show signs of weakness and collapse. The Christian religion, however, survived. Indeed, it flourished. Its initial expansion eastward into Asia Minor was followed by a vigorous expansion throughout Europe, and by the end of the millennium virtually all of Europe was (in name, at least) Christian. For centuries to come, the Christian faith and church united the people of Europe.

And when European explorers and adventurers from the late fifteenth century onward began to travel across the oceans and encountered other continents and cultures and peoples, they took the Christian religion with them. Little by little the Christian religion became a global movement. By the early twenty-first century, it had ceased being a European faith—as a matter of fact, it appears to be liveliest and most dynamic not in its traditional European (and North American) locales but in Africa and Asia.

The Christian journey through the centuries is thus a dramatic story, again and again dripping with unexpected turns and developments. This was particularly true of the first several centuries, for in the beginning the Christian journey was neither smooth nor simple. Rather, it was complex and difficult, as the small band of persecuted outsiders turned into a powerful church. For believers, the eventual triumph of the Christian faith is a poignant manifestation of divine Providence; for cynics, it is a story of serendipity and chance. Scholars, in turn, have looked for rational explanations for this striking development.

Telling this story is more complicated than it may appear at first glance, for its features are manifold akin to the strands of a tapestry, with rich and overlapping features and themes. Theological developments, the relationship of the new religion to the Roman Empire, the formulation of statements of belief, and the determination of right and false teaching, of heresy and orthodoxy, are important facets of the story.

The account here will, therefore, not attempt to compress this story into a single chronological narrative. Rather, it will traverse the first half-millennium of the Christian religion several times, with each narrative focusing attention on one particular aspect of the larger story.

THE BEGINNING

At the beginning stands Jesus of Nazareth. This is both to be expected (after all, the Christian religion is named after the title "Christ" ascribed to Jesus) and also surprising, for we know so little about him from contemporaneous sources. Indeed, some have argued that the Apostle Paul, rather than Jesus, should be seen as the true founder of the Christian religion, not only because his extensive travels throughout the eastern Mediterranean as a missionary for the new faith led to a network of Christian congregations but also for the impressive way he proclaimed the meaning of the "good news" of Jesus. Either way, a dynamic religion developed, testifying to the vibrant power of the slender sources that are the basis for the Christian message. What we do know about Jesus and his earliest followers comes from Christian documents, notably the four Gospels and the book of Acts in the New Testament, together with ruminations in the writings of the Apostle Paul. No other valuable historical sources exist, though some documents, such as the Gospel of Thomas, are useful in that they tell us of the eccentricities of some of the earliest followers of Jesus and the initial absence of a clear notion of what Jesus had all been about.

For the better part of the two millennia of Christian history, it was taken for granted that the four Gospels—Matthew, Mark, Luke, and John—were reliable documents that offered an accurate historical record of the birth, life, teachings, and death of Jesus. Of course, readers through the centuries were aware that this record was of a special sort. After all, it included accounts of uncommon and supernatural events, such as Jesus feeding a crowd of five thousand, Jesus raising Lazarus from the dead, or Jesus' own return to life after his crucifixion. However, these accounts of supernatural happenings caused no problem from Late Antiquity onward and certainly did not call into question their historical accuracy. Believers and nonbelievers alike accepted the Gospels and their accounts as authentic. Disagreement among the theologians (and outsiders) about these sources—and there was plenty—had to do with the theological interpretation of the happenings.

This certainty about the historical accuracy of the biblical accounts began to be challenged some three hundred years ago. Under the impact of the new critical stance of the European Enlightenment, the biblical narratives were subjected to the same scrutiny as were other texts from antiquity. The traditional notion that the biblical narratives of supernatural events were historically accurate and reliable was called into question and, with increasing frequency, rejected outright. This questioning of the historical facticity of the events described in the Bible, and particularly in the four Gospels, brought about a radical turn in the perception of Jesus. At the same time, a new way of understanding the ancient texts found increasing acceptance. It was soon labeled "liberal," has persisted since the eighteenth century, and has encompassed a variety of interpretations.

Accordingly, during the past three centuries, diverse interpretations of the nature of the biblical narratives have been offered, ranging from the reaffirmation of the traditional reading to the charge that the Gospels are forgeries or accounts of fictitious events. A conciliatory perspective has argued that the Gospels are documents of faith and not of history—that they do not tell us much about actual happenings, not even about Jesus' self-understanding, but tell us a great deal about the disciples' perceptions of Jesus and his ministry.

This diversity of scholarly views has persisted to the present, though there now appears to be a consensus that holds that the Gospels do indeed contain useful historical data about Jesus alongside the views of the Gospel writers. Thus, the "historical" Jesus can be reconstructed in meaningful fashion. Consensus also exists on another point: the writers of the four Gospels wished to share their conviction that God had been uniquely at work in Jesus, who had risen from the dead and energized his followers to boldly spread the word about him.

This diversity of understanding the biblical records has divided Christians into two factions, not at all denoted by traditional ecclesiastical labels, such as Catholic, Lutheran, Anglican, or Reformed-Calvinist, but by the acceptance or rejection of the new naturalistic understanding of the Gospel records and the entire supernatural biblical narrative. "Conservative" Christians have continued to affirm traditional notions of the historicity of events in the Bible, including the Gospels, while "liberal" Christians have seen them as bereft of meaningful historical information. Both perspectives entail theological consequences.

So what can be said about Jesus?

To begin with, the overwhelming notion found in the Gospels is Jesus' claim to be singularly authorized to proclaim the divine will—even if this meant a reinterpretation of the Jewish Law (Torah). Repeatedly, the Gospels tell how Jesus reminded his hearers of a traditional stipulation of the Law and then added, "but I say unto you..." From this claim came Jesus' insistence of a special filial relationship with God, whom he called his father.

Second, Jesus' followers used a number of terms to describe him, always drawing on the rich vocabulary of the Hebrew Scriptures. They spoke of him as Rabbi, Master, Son of Man, Teacher, the Anointed ("Christos"), Son of God. Indeed, the latter appellation—Son of God—became over time the most prominent way Jesus was understood by Christians. Behind all of these terms, each trenchant with theological meaning, stood the conviction that Jesus had been the promised Messiah of Israel, who would set all things new.

Third, Jesus proclaimed that the Kingdom of God, when all will be made right, was an imminent reality. Indeed, he asserted that in him, this kingdom had already begun and manifested itself in a radical concern for the marginalized of society—the poor, the suffering, the downtrodden. The rule of God was about to begin. Jesus called upon people to become members of this kingdom as his followers and disciples.

Finally, Jesus proclaimed that God, before whom all humans are sinners, accepts the repentant sinners in love and mercy.

As matters turned out, the catastrophic end of Jesus' public activity— his crucifixion outside Jerusalem—did not mark the final chapter of the story, for three days after his death his followers experienced his return from the dead and after another forty days they received his exhortation to go beyond the Jewish cradle into all the world and make disciples. Jesus' followers did not disperse into the four directions of the wind but returned to Jerusalem, the place of their master's catastrophe. They stayed together and affirmed that Jesus was alive among them, because he had risen from the dead as he had told them he would. And he would soon return.

No doubt, the notion of Jesus' resurrection from the dead was the critically important affirmation of his followers. Needless to say, proof of this startling claim lies beyond the province of the historian. What the historian can record, however, is that the New Testament writings cannot be understood apart from the conviction of Jesus' disciples that he rose on the third day after his death and then appeared to two women, then to the disciple Peter, then to two other disciples, and finally to many more. The notion that Jesus was alive and would return in due time to judge the living and the dead and make all things new explains the startling dynamic of the Christian message.

Before long, the motley group of Jesus' followers turned into a movement, the Jesus movement, with diverse emphases and interpretations. Eventually, however, this diversity fed like little brooks turning into a mighty stream, a mainstream which, in turn, evolved into the Christian church.

EARLY EXPANSION

The story of Jesus took place in Palestine, one of the border provinces of the Roman Empire, which ruled the lands from the southern part of the British Isles to the Euphrates River and from the northern coast of Africa to the Rhine and Danube. It has been pointed out that this empire was most congenial for the budding Christian movement. The world of this empire was enjoying an unprecedented time of peace, the famous *pax Romana*, the Roman Peace. A well-organized communications and administrative system, strategic roads, a single official language, and a common legal system made the Roman Empire not only powerful but also cultured and efficient. The expansion of the message of Jesus from its Palestinian cradle into other regions of the empire took place in that setting. The evangelists of the message of Jesus traveled the Roman roads to regions distant, unhindered by either turbulence of war or civil unrest, even as Latin, the official language of the empire, aided by Greek, the language of the intellectuals, allowed easy communication with those they met along the way.

According to the account in the book of Acts, the first Christian community had its beginning on the day called Pentecost, ten days after Jesus had "ascended into the heavens," fifty days after his resurrection. The place was Jerusalem, and the event was a gathering of Jesus' followers, who, according to the account, suddenly experienced the ability to speak in a variety of foreign languages, much to the astonishment of bystanders, who assumed that they were drunk already early in the day. Jesus' followers, however, saw their ability to speak in foreign tongues as evidence of the pouring out of the divine spirit, confirming their conviction that these were the last days.

Jesus' followers, who were convinced that he was the Messiah of Israel, might well have continued as a Jewish sect, confined to Palestine, had it not been for the appearance of Saul, a rabbi from the Diaspora of Tarsus. Saul forced the issue whether the significance of Jesus extended beyond the Jewish people. He became the pivotal figure in the spread of the message of Jesus into the Gentile (non-Jewish) world. His importance for the Christian faith is underscored by the fact that his epistolary writings—letters to Christian assemblies—make up much of the New Testament. These writings, together with references in the book of Acts, provide us with information about the man, his thought, and his role in the transformation of a Jewish sect into a Gentile church.

Saul took the name "Paul," and one may well see this name change as symbolic for the commitment with which he proclaimed the message of Jesus. He was a most unlikely choice to assume the mantle of leadership of the emerging movement. He himself acknowledged that he had not known Jesus as had the other disciples, but he also asserted that while traveling on the road from Antioch to Damascus, probably in the year 49, a transforming religious experience had brought him face-to-face with Jesus. This conversion changed everything. Saul became Paul and joined the fledgling group of followers of Jesus, convinced that Jesus had spoken directly to him—more than that, that Jesus had called him to be an apostle, a claim he made frequently throughout his letters.

Paul gave the message of Jesus its universal human dimension and appeal. It was he who took Jesus out of his Jewish context and argued for his cosmic relevance. Paul saw the life and message of Jesus as grounded in a unique filial relationship with God, and he advocated a revolutionary religion of conversion and commitment to this Jesus, the creative force of the universe. The Christian profession "Christ is Lord" meant that Jesus was lord of humankind but also—and even more important—lord of the universe.

Paul proclaimed the message that the one God had revealed himself in his son, Jesus. Through this son, both Jews and Gentiles could be saved to everlasting life and be spared in the Last Judgment. Paul's message of salvation in the world to come was proclaimed against the backdrop of his understanding of the Law, which he saw, not altogether correctly, not only as the core of what it means to be Jewish (ignoring the role of the

Covenant) but also as leading to despair because it was impossible to fulfill it. Paul replaced the Law with faith in Jesus. He challenged the followers of Jesus to reconsider their relationship to Judaism, the mother religion. To the question whether the movement of the followers of Jesus was a Jewish sect, Paul retorted with a resounding no. Categorically asserting the cosmic significance of Jesus, Paul reasoned that the proclamation of Jesus, the Christ, the Jewish Messiah, had to be taken to the Gentile world and the Law no longer needed to be observed.

The decision to proclaim the message of Jesus to Gentiles was truly revolutionary. The closing verses of Matthew's Gospel, in which Jesus commanded his disciples to make disciples "of all nations" and baptize them in the name of the Father, Son, and Holy Spirit, express this dramatic expansion, which was anything but undisputed. The Book of Acts tells the story of Paul's advocacy of taking the good news of Jesus to the Gentile world with all of its attendant disagreements in the Jerusalem assembly. In particular, it offers an account of a meeting in Jerusalem, known as the Apostles' Council, and its startling decision—following Paul's urgings—that Gentile believers in Jesus' message need not obey the Jewish Law, which mandated circumcision and dietary restrictions.

The decision to spread the word about Jesus among the Gentiles disrupted the Jewish homogeneity of the Jesus movement. As the story continued, a minority of followers of Jesus saw themselves as a Jewish sect, while the growing Gentile church spread throughout the Mediterranean. Freed from the obligation to observe the full stipulations of the Law, as had been mandated for Gentile converts to Judaism, Christianity, despite its Jewish connections, presented itself as an attractive alternative, and Gentiles gained ever greater importance in the evolving church. As one consequence, the term "Christ" was no longer understood by Christians in its Jewish meaning of "Messiah," but became Jesus' second name.

Paul's contribution was the message of Jesus' universal significance. His extensive missionary travels throughout the eastern Mediterranean grew out of this conviction. The book of Acts records his incessant travels to spread the message of Jesus and indicates that the synagogue was his point of contact in when he arrived to proclaim the message about Jesus—though this focus on the synagogue came not without difficulties and strife. Paul came to understand how the Jewish religion had proved deeply attractive to Gentiles for its strict monotheism and its firm moral code as expressed in the Ten Commandments. These "God-fearing" Gentiles failed to take the ultimate step, however, of converting to

Judaism because they found the observance of the Mosaic Law, particularly the requirement of circumcision, an insurmountable obstacle. For these individuals, Paul's message was one of liberation, because it conveyed that through faith in the good news of the gospel and through baptism, one became part of the people of God and was redeemed from the present evil world, without having to be circumcised and observe the Law.

The Christian message was a call to repentance and entailed a fervent expectation of the return of the Son of God. The Torah (Law) did not need to be observed any longer, but the centrality of repentance was affirmed because the Last Judgment was imminent. Wherever they went, Christian missionaries parlayed visions of a liberated present and a glorious future for those redeemed in Christ; it clearly proved to be an electrifying message. It meant freedom and release from all fears, taboos, and restraints. The Law could no longer terrify. As Paul himself had written: "All things are lawful" (1 Corinthians 6:12).

THE CHRISTIAN ASSEMBLIES

We know little about earliest Christianity. The New Testament suggests that groups of Christians gathered regularly to acknowledge Jesus as Messiah and Lord. They assembled in homes, for churches—special buildings dedicated to Christian worship—came only at a much later stage. Buildings intimated permanence and were inappropriate for men and women who expected Christ's imminent return and the end of all history. The Apostle Paul called the Christian assemblies *ecclesia*, a Greek word meaning "called out," without exactly defining what this term was to denote, other than that Christians are "called out" of the world.

Worship of the Christian assemblies followed the pattern of the synagogue. Christians read the Hebrew Scriptures, taking from them the ardent messianic prophecies fulfilled in Jesus, and the longing anticipation of the return of Jesus. They were challenged, in their gatherings, to ignore existing social distinctions between male and female, free and slave, Jew and Gentile.

No uniform pattern of organizational structure and liturgical practice seems to have prevailed. Paul's letters to the churches in Rome, Galatia, and Corinth are full of advice, instruction, and exhortation, for example, that there were (or ought to be) certain congregational offices, such as

10

healers, prophets, speakers of "various kinds of tongues" (1 Corinthians 12:10), administrators, and teachers, together with apostles, bishops, elders, and deacons. This suggests diversity and, at the same time, a striving for uniformity of belief and practice. The exact nature and purpose of all the offices and functions mentioned by the Apostle Paul are not altogether clear.

The rite of initiation into the Christian community was baptism. Paul seems to have understood it as expressing the believer's participation in Christ's death and resurrection, as noted in Romans 6 and Colossians 2 and 3. At the same time, baptism evidently was also understood as the present seal of future salvation. It was accompanied by the gift of the Holy Spirit, which provided the ability to live a life of Christian discipleship. Whether infants were baptized in the apostolic church—that is, the assemblies led and guided by the apostles—and the early postapostolic church has been much disputed in New Testament scholarship. Probably some infants were baptized as part of the baptism of entire households, even though the general practice appears to have been to baptize adult converts to the faith.

A second practice gave identity to the coalescing of the Jesus movement and the beginnings of the Christian church. This was the meal Christians shared together in memory of Jesus' last meal with his disciples, the Last Supper. This, one of the most familiar episodes in Jesus' life, had undoubtedly been a Passover Seder, observed by Jesus and his disciples after he had apprised them of his intention to go to Jerusalem to confront the authorities with his messianic claims. According to the Gospel accounts and the virtually verbatim account offered by the Apostle Paul in 1 Corinthians 11, Jesus told his disciples toward the end of the supper that they should "do this in remembrance" of him and, according to the Gospel of Matthew, that he would "not drink again of the fruit of the vine" until the day when he drank it anew in the kingdom of God. With these words, Jesus obviously sought to impress on his disciples that the events about to ensue in Jerusalem—possibly catastrophe and death— would not be the end, but a beginning that would eventually usher in the fullness of the kingdom of the Messiah. Importantly, Jesus challenged his disciples, "Do this in remembrance of me." Even though he would be no longer with them, they should stay together and repeat the meal. When observing the Seder in future years, his followers should remember their master's last meal with them.

This "last supper" carried special meaning for Jesus' followers because Jesus had attached particular significance to the sharing of bread and wine in the meal, its key features. He had said, "This is my body" (Matthew 26:26; Mark 14:22; Luke 22:19; 1 Corinthians 11:24) and again, "This cup is the new covenant in my blood" (1 Corinthians 11:25)—words whose meaning at first glance is not altogether clear, though generations of theologians and biblical exegetes have striven to remove the lack of clarity. The Apostle Paul speaks of bread and wine as the body and blood of Jesus, but what he meant, and what the churches to which he wrote understood, has remained controversial. Some have suggested that the meal was understood as spiritual communion of the recipients of bread and wine with the exalted Jesus.

Only the baptized members of the Christian assemblies shared in this communal meal, where bread was eaten and wine drunk as body and blood of Christ. This nonpublic aspect of the Christians' meetings caused the rise of a damaging slander: Christians were accused of cannibalism for eating flesh and drinking blood. They were charged with eating their God in their secret ceremonies, a charge that gained credence because of the Christians' tendency to keep to themselves and celebrate their weekly memorial meal without outsiders present. Rumors, misunderstandings, and distortions were bound to result.

By the final decade of the first century, the apostles who had known Jesus "after the flesh" had passed from the scene. Three prominent leaders of the Jesus movement—James, Peter, and Paul—had suffered martyrdom, and new leaders and new challenges emerged. While this generational change was taking place in the Christian communities, an event of dramatic importance for Christians occurred: the First Jewish War (66–70), triggered by a Jewish uprising against Roman domination. The uprising led to Jewish defeat, the destruction of the Temple in Jerusalem, and the dispersal of the Jews from the Holy Land. This fateful event had bearing on the Christian story, as Jewish Christians refused to join their fellow compatriots in their uprising against Rome. While it is pointless to speculate about their reason (it might have been the notion of peacemaking Jesus elaborated in the Sermon on the Mount), by their passivity Jewish Christians severed their emotional and cultural ties with their people, thereby surrendering their civic identity as Jews. Religiously, however, they continued to see themselves as Jews and were convinced that the promised Messiah of Israel had come in the person of Jesus of Nazareth. The religious catastrophe of the destruction of the Temple left these Jewish Christians unfazed. They survived the catastrophe and continued with only the loosest of contacts with either Gentile Christians or the Jewish community, or both.

By the year 100, two related but different understandings of the meaning of the Hebrew Scriptures, Gentile Christianity, and Jewish Christianity, existed side by side. The mainstream Christian religion had long ceased being a Jewish sect, even though the Ebionites, the Nazarenes, and other Jewish Christian groupings continued to emphasize the "Jewishness" of the Christian religion. In turn, Jews, who had survived the catastrophe of the destruction of the Temple in Jerusalem and had fled to various regions of the Roman Empire, were even more determined to distance themselves from the Christian communities, which they saw as heretical. They drew a sharp line against the Christian "heretics," this all the more so because the Gentile converts to Christianity, while called upon to acknowledge Jesus as the Jewish Messiah, were told that they need not observe the Torah Law. The same applied to the Jewish Christians who, despite their confession of Jesus as the Messiah, who had freed them from the Law, could not remain in the synagogue. The bond between the Jewish matrix and Christianity was dissolving. This "divorce" meant that diversity turned into uniformity.

At about the same time, this new epoch in Christian history, labeled the postapostolic period, brought further changes. It was characterized by the first attempts to safeguard the memory of Jesus by collecting the literary sources about him and the apostles. There were also the first efforts to offer theological interpretations of the meaning of these documents. The first treatises offering a cohesive theological understanding of the nature of the faith were written at this time. In the generation between 95 and 150, a number of theologians, the so-called Apostolic Fathers, put their understanding of the Christian faith into writing and exerted considerable influence as its first normative interpreters. Theologians such as Justin Martyr, Polycarp, Irenaeus, and Ignatius influenced the thinking of the church in the decades and centuries to come.

Curiously, in some instances the authors seem to have lacked self-confidence, as they attributed their narratives to an apostle rather than to themselves. (Or they displayed exquisite public relations skills with such name-dropping.) This name-dropping to sanction writings was not new. The so-called Pseudepigrapha, such as the Wisdom of Solomon or the Psalms of David, had been around for a long time; attributing the "Wisdom" to Solomon gave greater authority to the document. Now such figures as the apostles Thomas or Peter began to be invoked as authors of important documents.

Christian congregations, small in size, were found in Persia, Syria, Greece, Italy, and North Africa as missionary efforts accelerated. Antioch and Ephesus (both located in present-day Turkey) became major Christian centers. Three emphases increasingly characterized the Christian gatherings. One was a focus on congregational structure and order. Since the return of Jesus had not occurred as expected, Christians were forced to think in long-range terms, putting such topics as Christian belief, worship, and congregational authority on the table. Clear notions of authority and structure in a local congregation had to be formulated, a concern found in such New Testament writings as 1 and 2 Timothy and Titus. The leaders of congregations, such as bishops, presbyters, and deacons, had to be shown to have clearly defined responsibilities. For example, one of the earliest Christian leaders and theologians, Ignatius (ca. 50–98/117), the third bishop of Antioch, argued strenuously that the role of the bishop was divinely instituted to assure proper order and faith in the Christian assemblies. He wrote: "It is not lawful to baptize or give communion without the consent of the bishop. On the other hand, whatever has his approval is pleasing to God" (Ignatius, *Letter to the Smyrneans* 8). Ignatius's argument offered the first inkling that a hierarchical structure of the church, and thereby a distinction between clergy and laity, was in the making. In the process, the leadership roles played by women in local assemblies in the postapostolic age decreased until they were exclusively exercised by men.

The Christian mandate of living exemplary moral lives became ever more explicit during this time as well. Again, there are inklings of this concern already in such writings as the New Testament Letter of James, but now theologians and church leaders understood the Christian faith to mean a daily life of impeccable moral standards. By all accounts, the high moral standards of Christians soon was a distinguishing feature of the Christian communities. Outsiders stood in embarrassed awe.

PERSECUTION

In a way both understandable and enigmatic, the story of the Christian faith quickly became a story of oppression and persecution. The plain fact of the matter was that Christians and their church clashed with the reli-

Figure 1A

Jesus as the Good Shepherd. While the shepherd theme, based on John 10, enjoyed wide popularity in early Christianity, the personification of Jesus as the Good Shepherd was a late development. Christian sarcophagus. Church of S. Francesco, Urbino, Italy.

gious value system of the Roman Empire. Initially, the Roman authorities viewed the Christian communities as a Jewish sect, and since Judaism was a licensed religion in the empire, Christians were tolerated. Before too long, however, something happened and toleration was replaced with suspicion and suppression.

At the core of the emerging conflict between the church and the state probably lay the absolutist religious claims put forward by Christians and their aloofness from society. In the setting of the religiously tolerant atmosphere of the Roman Empire, Christians did not consider their religion as one among many equals. Quite the contrary, they claimed their religion alone to be authentic and true—indeed, the final divine revelation to humankind. Needless to say, this was taken as a shocking and arrogant claim, bound not to go over so well with the Roman authorities. The Roman Empire had allowed the people in the conquered provinces to keep their language and customs, as well as their religion. No suppressive measures were taken against a religion unless it was deemed to be a threat to the public order—and that was precisely the problem with those Christians and their sect.

Governor Pliny's query to the emperor about how to handle the Christians allows only intimations as to why Christians gained the unfavorable attention of the Roman authorities. Christians, so Pliny informed the emperor, did not "supplicate the gods nor place wine and incense" before the emperor's image. The implication was that Christians were disloyal to the emperor and the Roman state. If that much seems clear, Pliny's report remains tantalizingly cryptic. What "crime" stood behind the phrase "whatever it was they professed"? And, for that matter, what were the "crimes associated with their [the Christians'] name"? People came to detest the Christian religion. The historian Tacitus (56–120) remarked that Christians were hated "for their abominations," while Suetonius (75–after 160) found that Christians were "given to new and wicked superstitions." Perhaps those enigmatic phrases were to denote the Christians' aloofness from Roman cultural values. Christians eschewed the "circuses," the standard entertainment venue of Roman society, thereby invoking apprehension, if not fear, about a subversive threat to the body politic.

The issue that brought the Christians' civic trustworthiness to the fore was the increasingly prominent emperor cult, or emperor worship. The problem was not so much Christian belief in general as it was the demand of the Roman state for absolute loyalty. Things got tricky for Christians when, toward the end of the first century, Emperor Domitian ordered that the emperor will be called "our Lord and God." Subjects of the Roman Empire had to swear a loyalty oath. In Ephesus, for example, a monumental statue of the emperor was erected to provide a place to pay homage. The refusal of Christians to do so prompted their oppression and persecution. Since the Apostle Paul had advised Christians in Romans 13 to accept all government as ordained by God, they might have been willing to swear such an oath. But the problem ran deeper than the oath to the emperor. Contemporary sources tell us the cause of irritation and suspicion on the part of Roman society was the way Christians showed themselves unwilling, by refusing to serve in the military and in governmental offices, to assume their responsibilities as citizens. Christians saw themselves as citizens of the heavenly kingdom, and not of the Roman Empire. They were outsiders, pilgrims, opposed to the values and customs of society. The symbolic gesture of paying homage to statues of the emperor was deemed abhorrent and tantamount to a denial of their faith.

It was in this setting that the most puzzling of the earliest Christian writings offered a commentary on how persecution was to be understood. John the Divine wrote his apocalyptic book of Revelation, with its vivid images of the several kinds of churches, offering his vision of both things present and things to come. In language at once striking and profound, he sought to assure the churches in Asia Minor that the horror and terror of the present were part of God's plan, and he challenged his readers to anticipate the imminent return of the Lord of lords and King of kings.

The allegations levied against Christians were many and complex. To the charge of civic disloyalty were added those of sexual perversion, magic, and cannibalism. Christians became scapegoats when catastrophes, such as epidemics or floods, defeats in battle, or a fire in Rome shook the tranquility of the empire. Obviously, those mysterious and enigmatic Christians had to be the cause. Calamities of all kinds were attributed to the machinations of Christians or indirectly to the Christian rejection of traditional Roman values. Emperor Nero's famous indictment of Christians for the fire in Rome in 64 was only the beginning of a long line of such accusations. Early in the third century, Tertullian sized up the situation: "If the river Tiber rises to the walls; if the river Nile does not rise to the fields; if the sky does not rain; if there is an earthquake, a famine, a plague, immediately the cry arises 'the Christians to the lion!'" (Tertullian, *Apology*) Suspicion led to suppression, and suppression was followed by persecution. Beginning early in the second century and lasting until the fourth, the Roman state sought ways to deal with the steadily growing, dynamic, and yet deeply enigmatic Christian movement. Three stages characterized official Roman policy toward Christians and their church.

A first stage, beginning late in the first century and lasting intermittently until the third, was characterized by anti-Christian governmental action to enforce political and societal loyalty. However, the suppression was sporadic and geographically restricted. The Roman political authorities had become aware of the existence of Christian assemblies in society and anything unusual in a community or region triggered adverse action. Outright persecution lasted only for brief periods of time.

The middle of the third century brought a second phase of governmental action, the systematic suppression of the church and especially its leaders. This phase occurred in the context of an increasing presence of the Christian religion in society, as well as broader political and social developments in the Roman Empire. By the third century, Christian congregations were found throughout the Roman Empire, and the number of adherents of the Christian faith had continued to grow. Even a few church buildings were beginning to be erected, providing evidence that the new religion was staking out a claim for a public presence in the midst of Roman society. By the early fourth century, the Christian church had become an impressive organization. It possessed an empire-wide administrative structure, a hierarchy of skillful, even charismatic, leaders, and a throng of committed followers. The church proclaimed a message that reverberated in the communities in which Christian assemblies were established. It also affirmed a set of strict moral values to which its members were committed. The church was a state within the state, a body in the body of the empire, and yet not part of it. The ultimate loyalty of the Christians was not to the Roman Empire but to the heavenly Kingdom.

The same period brought formidable external challenges to the military power of the Roman Empire. The successful invasions of Gothic tribes raised the question of why the mighty empire seemed so powerless in the face of these incursions. In the search for answers and explanations, Christians were once again blamed for the distressing turn of affairs, a painful public demonstration of the loss of Roman strength and power. When, in October 249, Decius, a popular army general, became emperor, he attempted to stem the adverse tides of the body politic with policies that sternly demanded a return to traditional Roman values. Sacrifices had to be offered to the ancient Roman gods and all citizens were ordered to swear what amounted to a loyalty oath; Christians were explicitly included in this stipulation. The external threat from the Gothic tribes was the catalyst for a second wave of Christian persecution.

During the years of the Decian persecution and the difficult years that followed, the church almost collapsed. Many of its leaders were put to death. Property of the church was confiscated. Christians throughout the empire faced the dreadful choice of affirming their faith and suffering or forsaking their faith and being left unharmed. As matters turned out, however, the Decian persecution was short-lived, and the church was able to recover quickly from the tragic vicissitudes—and continued to flourish.

The final challenge to the church came when Emperor Diocletian (245–313) decided to rid the empire of the church once and for all. Again, the underlying determination was that in times of external and domestic strain and stress the Empire needed to be unified. A new wave of persecution began in 303, when a Christian priest refused to divine the future from chicken entrails and some Christians were seen publicly making the sign of the cross. That was too heavy a medicine for Diocletian, an otherwise mild-mannered individual. He decided to act. Early on in his imperial rule, Diocletian had not been at all hostile to the church, since he understood the problem of attempting to crush the religion of a substantial minority of his subjects. Christians had lived peacefully during most of Diocletian's rule, and some historians have suggested that Galerius—his deputy and a fierce advocate of the old ways and old gods— prodded him into a policy of persecution by secretly having the imperial palace torched and then blaming the deed on the Christians. Regardless of who was at fault for the fire, Diocletian's rage was aroused, and he began the most severe religious persecution of the church in its history.

In February 303 an imperial edict ordered the destruction of Christian houses of worship because they were serving—so it was stated—as secret meeting places for political sedition. Christian worship was outlawed, Christian writings burned, and liturgical vessels demolished. Numerous bishops were arrested, since Galerius shrewdly meant to deprive the Christian church of its leaders and thereby sap its intellectual and organizational strength. When Diocletian retired to his country home, Galerius took over as emperor and continued his fierce determination to crush the church, even if it meant carrying out a most violent persecution, especially in the eastern part of the empire.

Galerius's determination to suppress Christianity knew no bounds. Christians were tortured, crucified, drowned, beheaded, burned, and put to the lions, echoing what Ignatius of Antioch had already lamented some two hundred years earlier that "fire, crucifixion, wild beasts, hacking and quartering, breaking of bones and mangling of limbs, indeed, pulverizing my whole body" (Ignatius, *Letter to the Romans* IV) were only paths to Jesus' presence. The historian Eusebius, who provided the most vivid account of the Diocletian persecution and claimed to have been an eyewitness ("I was there and saw many of the persecutions myself"), told his readers that on some days more than one hundred Christians— "not counting women and small children"—suffered martyrdom (Eusebius, *Church History*). It was by far the most serious assault on the church, even though Eusebius, under the impact of the horrible suffering of Christians, may well have overly dramatized his account.

Galerius continued this policy of repression when he succeeded Diocletian as emperor until, apparently during the last stage of a fatal illness, he had a change of heart and issued a general edict of toleration in April 311. He did so both in his own name and those of his co-rulers Licinius and Constantine. The Christian writer Lactantius printed the text of the edict in his moralizing chronicle titled *De Mortibus Persecutorum* (*On the Deaths of the Persecutors*) in order to demonstrate the horrible end of all who persecuted the church and the faithful. Galerius's edict meant that the persecution of Christians ended.

What had happened? The persecutions after all had been far more than expressions of the disapproval of a particular religion by the Roman state. They were part and parcel of the effort to restore cohesiveness to the empire at a time when that empire was in a period of decline, crumbling ever more noticeably on the fringes. During this same period, "barbarians" (noncitizens) were allowed to serve in the Roman army, and economic problems brought a radical debasement of Roman currency. Generals feuded with one another, and bickering prevailed as to what ailed the body politic—and what should be done about it. Diocletian undertook the last-ditch effort to straighten things out and at the same time undo the damage that the Christian religion had allegedly done to the empire and to Roman unity. His decrees were calculated to remove the Christian religion from the face of the earth, destroy the churches, degrade its leaders, and force rank-and-file Christians to denounce their beliefs or be sent into slavery.

Diocletian's effort failed. He succeeded neither in destroying the administrative structure of the church nor in driving a wedge between ordinary Christians and their leaders. Nonetheless, his policies caused considerable turmoil in the church. Some Christians were hardly determined would-be martyrs for the faith under persecution and had found ways to weasel their way out of oppression and martyrdom. After persecution had ended, seemingly endless debates took place in the church about what to do with those—clergy or laity—who for fear or cowardice had forsaken the faith during persecution, had offered sacrifices to Roman gods, or had handed over Christian books of worship and faith to the authorities. The fierceness of these debates suggests that lack of steadfastness was not confined to a few. The formal Roman records about the administration of the various anti-Christian edicts suggest that there was a great deal of collaboration and acquiescence on the part of Christians, understandable perhaps, since not all women and men are cut out to be martyrs. During the harsh days of persecution some Christians cooperated with the authorities and forsook the faith; in fact, their number may well have been embarrassingly large.

But there was another side to this story of persecution and suffering for the faith. Many Christians exhibited remarkable commitment and loyalty, evoking the admiration and esteem of their fellows. Tertullian, the theological firebrand never at a loss for words, coined the phrase that would become a hallmark in Christian history, invoked again and again: "The blood of the martyrs is the seed of the church" (Tertullian, *Apologeticum*). What he expressed was that the martyrdom of the Christians, their steadfastness under suffering, their willingness to give up everything society considered precious, invigorated the church. Such esteem for the martyrs of the faith was especially shared in the church, and before long, martyrs were seen as Christians of a special kind, venerated, with their lives and labors piously studied, their intercessory prayers devoutly solicited.

In the end, there was an emperor's signature on an edict of toleration. Why did the Galerian persecution fail and usher in the formal recognition of the Christian religion in the Roman Empire? Simply put, it was the awareness by the Roman rulers that the persecution was not successful in achieving its goal. Despite the adversity, and the weakness of members, the church remained intact. Galerius's toleration edict rationalized the recognition of the Christian church by claiming that some Christians did not really believe in their God, but then went right on and asked them to pray to their God for the welfare and salvation of the empire.

After the waves of persecution had run their course, the church rebounded, and at the end of the first decade of the fourth century, it was a force to be reckoned with in the Roman Empire. Numerically, Christians were a minority, perhaps no more than 10 percent of the population, but they inspired awe and esteem, however grudging, far out of proportion to their actual numbers.

THE TRIUMPH

To speak of the "triumph" of Christianity simply expresses the fact that the Christian religion was made a "licensed" and then the "official" religion in the Roman Empire. We must ask the question, what did that mean? That the majority of the people in the empire had become Christians? Assuredly not. The formal recognition of the Christian religion as the official religion meant the end of discrimination and persecution as well as the beginning of an era of governmental support and privilege. The policy determination of the Roman state to cease persecution and favor the Christian religion was remarkable—indeed, revolutionary—considering the humble beginnings of this faith and church only three and a half centuries earlier. One wonders what Governor Pliny would have queried the emperor in 311.

By that year, Christianity had attained the status of a quasi-recognized religion in the eastern part of the empire, and Galerius's edict of that year stipulated that Christians were to be tolerated unless they explicitly threatened the societal order. Soon thereafter, the empire was torn by the strife of two contenders for the imperial crown, Constantine and his rival,

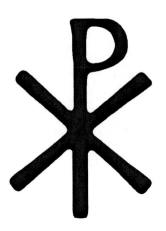

Figure 1B

The two Greek letters chi and rho were the first two letters of the Greek word Christos, Christ; superimposed on each other they had become by the early fourth century a widely used reference to Jesus, the Christ.

Maxentius, a usurper. Conflict had broken out between these two, and in October 312 their armies were poised to face each other in decisive battle. Constantine later confided to the historian Eusebius, who made a great deal of this story, that just before the fighting began, he prayed that Christ would reveal himself. Promptly, the heavens opened, Christ appeared and assured him that "with this sign you will be victorious"—the sign being the monogram *chi-rho*, the first two Greek letters of the word *Christ*. Constantine's soldiers hurriedly affixed the emblem on their shields. Not surprisingly, scholars have cast great doubt on this account.

When at daybreak the armies of Constantine and Maxentius went into battle, Constantine's soldiers, with Christ's monogram on their shields, forced the ranks of Maxentius to retreat across the Milvian Bridge, the stone bridge that carries the Via Flaminia across the Tiber River into Rome. In the confusion of a hasty retreat, Maxentius drowned in the Tiber. Constantine was now the unchallenged emperor of the Roman Empire, even as the empire remained divided.

It is difficult to say what prompted Constantine, politician and realist, brutal and bloody ruler, who had both his eldest son and wife killed, to embrace the Christian religion at this point, unless it was his hope that the Christian God could intervene in the fate of the two armies. The triumphal arch erected after his victory depicted the pagan gods Apollo, Diana, and Hercules, but included no references to the Christian faith. Constantine had not been baptized at that time and thus was not formally a member of the Christian church, even though an ancient mosaic depicts him standing squarely (and prominently) in the midst of the twelve apostles. The artist meant to depict the emperor as the protector of the church, and in the years that followed Constantine did indeed shower the church with political attention and financial support, both highly welcomed, of course, by the church. Together with his sister he financed the construction of churches, according to legend even the first Church of Saint Peter's in Rome. In 325, he played a pivotal role in the deliberations of the Council of Nicea. And eventually, when on his deathbed, Constantine was baptized.

In February 313, Constantine issued the Edict of Milan (the Edict of Toleration), which formally made Christianity a "licensed" religion in the empire and ordered the return of all church property confiscated during the Galerian persecution. Sundays were made legal holidays, and the Christian clergy received the privileges of Roman priests. Jesus of Nazareth, who had been executed by the Roman Empire, was now worshiped as the very savior of that empire. The church that had been tried by fire became privileged beyond fondest dreams.

Did Constantine ever have a vision of Christ before that fateful battle at the Milvian Bridge? Who can know? One may assume that Constantine did know what would make for a stable empire and what the Christian Church might contribute to it. He was a reformer—gladiatorial games were outlawed, as was execution by crucifixion, the killing of unwanted infants, and the abuse of slaves. The real challenge (and Constantine was surely very much aware of this) was the utilization of the church as an ally for the reforms he envisioned. The Christian religion, with adherents throughout the vast ranges of the Roman Empire, with poignant moral principles, not to mention an empire-wide administrative structure, seemed to offer what Constantine was looking for. It could undergird a new cohesiveness of an empire that was facing all sorts of unsettling challenges. Constantine, in favoring Christianity, sought support for the traditional values of the empire. Thus, the new faith was co-opted for the purpose of political integration. And Constantine may well have been convinced that the God of the Christians had been the source of his political and military achievements.

For a while, Christianity and other religions existed side by side in the empire, not altogether harmoniously. Increasingly, however, the Roman state handed favors to the church and imposed restrictions on traditional Roman religion. Constantine's immediate heirs endorsed his benefactions, which included separate church courts, return of confiscated church property, and significant privileges for the clergy. And at least on three occasions—in 340, 351, and in 391—stern governmental mandates against pagan rituals and sacrifices further enhanced the place of the Christian faith in society.

This march to prominence was rudely disrupted in 361, when Emperor Constantius II was succeeded by his nephew Julian, a self-declared pagan. Julian had been a Christian but had rejected Christianity, a turnabout that earned him the hardly complimentary label "the Apostate." Like the emperors before him, Julian was concerned about restoring the vitality and resilience of the empire, and he was convinced that reestablishing the traditional religion of Rome would do so. Accordingly, Julian revoked some of the privileges his two immediate predecessors had bestowed on the Christian religion. He advocated a strident religious pluralism; he did not intend to persecute the Christian religion as much as to drive Christianity out of "the governing classes." An edict of 362 stipulated full freedom of religion in the empire: all religions were equal. As it turned out, Julian did not reign long enough to allow the success of his policies; he died one year later, and his successors, Jovian and Valentinian, were both Christians who not only favored the Christian role in society but also took active sides in theological controversies besetting the church.

Eventually, toward the end of the fourth century, Emperor Theodosius (r. 379–95) made Christianity the sole official religion of the empire both East and West. He was a firm partisan of the Nicene Council's side in the Trinitarian controversy, labeled the remaining Arians (who opposed the Nicenes in that controversy) "demented and insane," and found ways to suppress them. His support of the church took the form of closing or destroying pagan temples and confiscating their property and art. The Olympic Games were outlawed and pagans prohibited from occupying governmental or military offices. In 448 all non-Christian and anti-Christian literature was ordered to be burned, an order that was carried out with stunning success; virtually none of these anti-Christian writings survived, much to the regret of latter-day scholars who lost out on crucial sources and must reconstruct, say, the thought of Marcion, from quotations in the writings of his antagonists.

Since, as we already noted, by the early fourth century only an estimated 10 percent of the population of the Roman Empire were Christians (indeed, more skeptical scholars have suggested 4 to 5 percent), one must be careful not to dramatize the "triumph" of the Christian faith. Yet the new role of the Christian faith meant that an important shift did occur, especially if one recalls that in the beginning of the Christian religion there were no more than a few dozen followers of a migrant preacher in Palestine.

The spread of the Christian message into the Mediterranean world had occurred quite unevenly. The geographic center of the Christian religion continued to be the eastern part of the Mediterranean, where most Christian assemblies were located in urban areas. Initially, the expansion of Christianity was slow and hardly impressive, but a significant increase in members appears to have taken place around the middle of the third century. The growing political instability of the empire has been cited as an important element in the appeal of the Christian message; one needs to remember that the empire was ruled by no less than twenty-seven different emperors in the span of roughly seventy years to understand the yearning for stability and the concomitant appeal of the Christian religion.

If Christians were a mere 5 to 10 percent of the population of the empire when their religion was officially recognized, the increase in adherents from the days of the Jerusalem congregation is significant but not stunning. It must not have been its numerical strength that made the Christian religion so impressive. Other forces must have played a role. The Christian view of the good and moral life and the message of a better life in the world to come appealed to a society that had become unsure of its vigor and values. The exemplary suffering of the Christian martyrs during periods of persecution has also been mentioned, though one must wonder why unbelievers would be attracted to a religion that led to persecution and death.

The legal triumph of the Christian religion thus grew out of an intriguing interweaving of the cogency of its message and the needs of the Roman Empire. Toward the end of the third century, religion, understood as a set of civic values, had become a crucial element in the politics of the empire, whose power and authority were increasingly taxed by challenges to its military might and its finances. There was a yearning for common values that would hold the disintegrating empire together. A universal empire needed universal values. The formal recognition of the Christian religion was a means to co-opt Christianity and to utilize its cohesive and extensive authority to bind the empire together.

THE EMERGENCE OF CHRISTIAN WRITINGS

The early Christians wrestled with the question of what it meant to be a follower of the "way," as they described their commitment to Jesus. At the beginning the apostles provided the answers, but as they passed from the scene other authentic statements were necessary. What was the significance of the life and work of Jesus? Since all sorts of competing explanations were making the rounds, which one was authentic? Above all, on what authority were the affirmations about Jesus made?

Initially, Christians appealed to "scripture." That meant, of course, the Hebrew Scriptures, in which they found the prophetic anticipation of the coming of the Messiah and the details of the story of Jesus—his birth by a virgin, his suffering, his ignominious death, his resurrection from the dead. This appeal to the authority of the Hebrew Scriptures to vindicate Jesus as the Messiah promised to Israel promptly ran into problems when it became evident that certain notions in the Hebrew Scriptures, such as polygamy, were deemed incompatible with Christian values.

The solution was to turn the Hebrew Scriptures into the Christian Old Testament. The Hebrew Scriptures were read allegorically, as one grand anticipation and foreshadowing of Jesus. The literal meaning of a text gave way to a symbolic (or allegorical) meaning that was related to the life and work of Jesus. For example, the Christian truth to be derived from the practice of polygamy by many of the patriarchs in the Hebrew Scriptures was not that the followers of Jesus should also have many wives. Rather, the patriarchs, the heroes of the faith, such as Jacob and David and Solomon, were "married" to more than one virtue. The slaughter of Amalekites, hardly an edifying story about a people who, according to the book of Exodus, attacked the Israelites on their exodus but were eradicated by Saul on God's command, was turned into a story about the eradication of vices. Virtually all of the legislative mandates in the book of Deuteronomy—for example, 23:1, which specified that "no one whose testicles are crushed . . . shall be admitted to the assembly of the LORD"— were declared to have been overcome by the new "law" proclaimed by Jesus. The universal Christian view was to insist that the Old Testament had been replaced by the Good News, the gospel, of Jesus.

Christians, of course, were eager to learn more about the one whom they called their Lord and Savior. Initially they seemed to have had recourse to oral accounts of Jesus' life and message for their knowledge and edification. Later, this oral tradition gave way to written documents, the Gospels, and ever since the eighteenth century, biblical scholars have debated how this happened. Some have suggested that at the beginning, the tradition about Jesus consisted of remembered sayings of Jesus, that these individual sayings became a written collection (the "Q" text, so called from the German word *Quelle*, "source"), and that Matthew, Luke, and Mark used this source as the point of departure for writing their respective Gospels. This theory has not remained uncontested, even as the question as to what was the "first" Gospel—nowadays assumed by many scholars to have been the Gospel of Mark—continues to generate debates, with some scholars emphatically opting for the chronological priority of Matthew's Gospel.

However the Gospels came into being, before too long written documents existed and were widely circulated. They described Jesus' life and ministry, and Christians drew spiritual edification as well as understanding from accounts that summarized his life and death. While none of the four Gospels in the New Testament can be properly considered a biography (for example, nothing is recorded of the time between Jesus' appearance in the Temple as a teenager and the beginning of his public ministry some twenty years later), they do provide important accounts of his teaching and message. They contributed solid historical facts about Jesus.

As time passed, the writings of the "new covenant," consisting of the Gospels and Paul's epistolary writings, were considered to be on par with the Hebrew Scriptures and eventually deemed superior to them. Indeed, one of the first major theological dissenters in the church, Marcion, caused considerable agitation when he declared that the Hebrew Scriptures did not portray the loving, fatherly God of Jesus and must therefore be removed from use in Christian worship. The church did not follow his advice, but insisted uniformly on the superiority of the New over the Old Testament. Symbolically, this notion of theological superiority can be found in the liturgical practice in some churches to have the worshipers rise for the reading of the Gospel passage as a gesture of esteem but remain seated for the reading from the Old Testament.

In addition to the four Gospels that eventually found their way into the canonical New Testament, other "gospels" were in circulation by the early second century, such as a Gospel of Judas or a Gospel of Peter. Until recently, many of these apocryphal gospels were known only through references to them in the writings of hostile theologians. In the writings of Irenaeus, for example, are extensive references to "gnostic gospels." When the actual copies of these writings surfaced in Egyptian caves half a century ago, they changed our understanding of the theological scene around the end of the first century. To the surprise of some (and the dismay of others) these gnostic writings conveyed an understanding of Jesus different from that of the four Gospels. In the Gospel of Thomas, for example, the

27

boy Jesus causes a dried sardine to come back to life and swim in the water. Other accounts of Jesus' childhood, for example, told how he breathed life into a bird made of clay, while yet another described his journey "to those below" between his death on the cross and his resurrection.

Importantly, these writings revealed that in the early second century some Christians embraced an understanding of Jesus heavily influenced by tenets of what has been called Christian Gnosticism (there was also a non-Christian Gnosticism). These Christian Gnostics grounded their message on the notion that there were "secret" sayings and teachings of Jesus, which the church at large had ignored and obfuscated. Gnostic Christians insisted that it was possible to lead a sinless life once one had attained knowledge (*gnosis*) of God's will. This gnostic understanding of Jesus' message evidently found widespread acceptance, and brought about the further delineation of an understanding of Jesus' life and work based on the four canonical Gospels.

The challenge confronting the church was to decide which of the numerous writings in circulation conveyed the authentic apostolic understanding of the life and work of Jesus. If there had only been the four Gospels now found in the New Testament, the answer would have been easy enough. Equally simple would have been the situation if the multiplicity of Gospels essentially conveyed the same theological understanding. But such was not the case. This pluralism of theological perspectives in early Christian writings explains the process of clarifying the views that took place in the church. And it was not until the third century that the church confronted the question of which of the numerous writings more or less in circulation conveyed the authentic apostolic understanding of the life and work of Jesus? If there had only been the four Gospels now found in the New Testament, the answer would have been easy enough. It would have been easy as well if the multiplicity of other Gospels all conveyed the same theological understanding. But such was not the case. This pluralism of theological perspectives in early Christian writings explains the process of clarification of views and affirmations in the church. It was not until the late third century that the point was reached where a widespread consensus throughout the church began to emerge about which writings properly should be included in a collection, or canon, of apostolic writings for which the term New Testament was coined. Long discussions in both the Western and Eastern church had taken place.

It is noteworthy that Christians came to agree, without too much discussion and debate, which of the plethora of allegedly apostolic writings offered the authentic message. Disagreement prevailed only over a few. It is not correct to say that the church made an authoritarian determination of the New Testament canon or that Emperor Constantine's charge to Eusebius, in 336, to prepare fifty Bibles with the writings that became the New Testament forced the issue of the normative Christian writings. Little by little a universal consensus was universally accepted. The Gospels of Matthew, Mark, and Luke and several letters attributed to the Apostle Paul had never posed real questions of authenticity, and a fourth Gospel, that of John, was also deemed to be written by an apostle. Uncertainty, however, prevailed about several writings that claimed to be apostolic in origin, namely, the Letter to the Hebrews, 2 Peter, Jude, James, and 2 and 3 John. The book of Revelation, with its strange metaphors and picturesque language, indictments of lukewarm churches and misshapen beasts, failed to elicit much enthusiasm as conveyor of the good news of Jesus. But these were minor demurrers and the book gained real, if grudging, acceptance. Eventually, all these books found acceptance and became the New Testament. The so-called Apocrypha of the Hebrew Scriptures, however, were not included in the canonical writings used in worship. Importantly, the establishment of a canon of "apostolic" writings meant that all the other writings claiming to be of apostolic origin were rejected.

Apostolic Authority

The authority of some Christian writings—as those were circulating toward the end of the first century—was predicated on the assumption that apostles (or contemporaries of apostles) had been their authors and that they, therefore, expressed the authentic apostolic faith. The true Christian faith was the "apostolic" faith because the eyewitnesses of Jesus' life and work could be relied on for accuracy and authenticity in their accounts of the story. This notion of seeking to go back to the time of the apostles gave rise to the concept of apostolicity as the norm and hallmark of the proper understanding of Jesus. This yardstick proved to be of little value when apostolic claims were made for writings of much later origin. The church responded by emphasizing that alongside the notion of "apostolic writings" had to be the notion of "apostolic succession." The authentic Christian faith was found in the teaching of the apostles as passed on by them to their disciples, who in turn passed it on to their disciples. And so the chain continued, from bishop to bishop to bishop to the present. An unbroken continuity of ecclesiastical leaders was traced from the present back to the time of the apostles, where each new bishop received the true and authentic apostolic faith from his predecessor and faithfully passed it on.

Around the year 160 the Christian historian Hegesippus compiled a historical list of bishops, from those of his own time all the way back to the apostles: "And when I was in Rome, I made a succession up to Anicetus, whose deacon was Eleutherus" (Eusebius, *Church History* IV). His list—not altogether accurate—was of the Roman bishops, but his point was a universal one to encompass all bishops. "And in each succession and in each city all is according to the ordinances of the law and the Prophets and the Lord." They all proclaimed the same doctrine, he declared, and he made it clear that this formal line of succession vouchsafed the authentic maintenance of apostolic truth. The development of the notion of apostolicity, expressed in apostolic writings, apostolic creed, apostolic tradition, and apostolic succession, meant that the initial period of diversity characteristic of the earliest church was coming to an end. Formal criteria replaced a free-for-all. All along, the organization of the church had been characterized by flexibility—Justin Martyr called the leader of his assembly simply "chairman"—but it became increasingly dominated by the model of declaring the bishop the pivotal office in the church, both local and universal.

Eventually, the concepts of "apostolic writings" and "apostolic succession" were augmented by two additional notions, "apostolic tradition" and "apostolic creed." A summary or compendium of the Christian faith, to be used in a variety of ways but notably as the "confession" of those who had indicated their desire to join the church, suggested itself as the means to sharpen the meaning and teaching of Jesus. The Apostles' Creed was the eventual outcome. Apostolic tradition, in turn, referred to the sum of the teachings and mandates of the apostles as found in the New Testament.

Thus, four hallmarks defined the meaning of "apostolicity," with that of the apostolic writings pivotal. The apostolic creed was secondary, a derivative of apostolic succession and apostolic tradition. The latter was a somewhat evasive category that referred to various "traditions," practices, and affirmations that were part and parcel of the liturgical life of the churches. Tradition determined which of the numerous Christian writings in circulation deserved to be used in worship.

THEOLOGICAL CLARIFICATION

The increasing appeal of the Christian message in the Roman Empire was paralleled by a process of an increasing clarification and elaboration of that message. This development took place slowly and tediously and took some five centuries to reach conclusion (if it indeed has ended even in our time). The challenge was that from the very beginning, disagreements existed among those who claimed to proclaim Jesus' authentic message. The key figures in this development were the theologians, men (and women) who pondered the meaning of the teachings of Jesus and sought to put them into coherent form.

Theologians, alongside church leaders, have dominated the history of the Christian faith, particularly during its first centuries. Theologians clarified, sorted, determined, elaborated, and authenticated the faith, sometimes to restate affirmations already part of a prevailing consensus, sometimes to offer new interpretations and perspectives of established truths. Theologians sought to understand the faith intellectually, and even though theological opinion was also influenced by the worship of the Christian community (in the opinion of some scholars dramatically so), the theologians' importance in defining the faith can hardly be overestimated. Alongside the pronouncements of popes, metropolitans (bishops of major ecclesiastical provinces), and bishops, theologians put their imprint on the faith and life of the Christian community.

Theologians are a special breed. Their contribution to the Christian story lies not so much in an exercise of leadership in the church, though in the early church quite a few of them—for example, Ignatius, Irenaeus, Cyprian, Hippolytus, Athanasius, the Cappadocian Fathers, and Ambrose—were bishops or presbyters. Augustine was a bishop as well, and there were popes, such as Gregory I, who made incisive theological contributions to the church. In our own day, Pope Benedict XVI was (as Joseph Cardinal Ratzinger) prior to his papal elevation one of the most influential theologians in the Roman Catholic Church.

Theologians reflect on the faith, write treatises about it, sometimes highly sophisticated, sometimes bereft of formal learning yet with startling religious intensity, and they vie to have their notions accepted by believers and the church at large. They are also not to be equated with the men and women in the pews, often simple and uneducated people who have neither interest in nor understanding of the sometimes complex theological issues being debated.

The profound truth of the matter is that any reflection on the faith, no matter whether erudite or uneducated and no matter how naive or sophisticated, is theologizing in a real sense. Though some theologians by all accounts have been pretty mushy in their thinking (one thinks, for example, of Joachim of Fiore in the Middle Ages), most have been insightful men and women, and not at all necessarily so because of formal schooling. Many—for example, Saint Teresa of Avila in the sixteenth century—were uneducated, yet theologically profound.

Several stages marked the theological development of early Christianity. A first phase encompassed the generation of the apostles and their immediate followers; it lasted roughly until the end of the first century. The major issue was the relationship of the emerging Christian community to Judaism. The key figure, as we have seen, was the Apostle Paul, and the primary topic was the continued relevance of the Law for Christians. The several missionary journeys of Paul had resulted in Gentile converts, increasingly changing the Jesus movement from a Jewish sect into a broad Gentile phenomenon.

A second phase—the era of the Apostolic Fathers, so-called since the eminent theologians and church leaders were male—lasted until the middle of the second century. Certain issues, such as the appropriateness of taking the message of Jesus to the Gentiles, had been decided, and the ties to the synagogue had been cut. Christians were Gentiles rather than Jews. But new issues had arisen, for example, the organizational structure of the congregation and matters of worship and liturgy. The nature of the Lord's Supper, increasingly called "Eucharist," became the focus of discussion, and a distinctive "eucharistic" piety developed. The outcome was a focus on the function of the "priest" as the one who officiated alongside the more prominent role of the bishop, whose stature increased significantly, both as administrator and as theologian and spiritual leader.

A third phase left its imprint on the second half of the second century. If the preceding period had been marked by considerable homogeneity of Christian thought and practice, the new phase brought extensive restlessness and disagreement. The continuing expansion of the Christian religion and its acceptance by individuals from all classes of society brought new issues, problems, and impulses to the fore.

Some saw the growth of the church accompanied by a loss of the striking moral standards that had characterized earlier Christians. This, in turn, made for the notion that there were, in fact, two kinds of Christians: those determined to attain spiritual perfection and those who, for whatever reason, were unable to pursue this goal. Christian monasticism had its beginnings in this setting, and over time numerous communities of monks and nuns would come into being for women and men who sought to live lives of spiritual perfection.

This development had a theological corollary: the identification of some Christians as "saints," for their extraordinary spirituality or having suffered martyrdom during persecution. From the earliest days of the Christian community, it was customary to speak of "saints," a term found in the New Testament, as the collective appellation for all those, male or female, free or slave, who were followers of Jesus. As time passed, this general use of the term gave way to a more restricted use. It came to be reserved for select Christians who, because of their special aura of holiness, were admired, then revered, for their spiritual perfection.

For a long time, however, the Catholic Church had no prescribed official process by which such extraordinary spiritual women and men were formally declared to be saints of the church. Popular approval often sufficed. This procedure had the disadvantage of depending on local whims and preferences, not to mention the possibility that it produced a verdict of sainthood at times too quickly and too casually. Indeed, when the Roman Catholic Church in 1969 subjected its long roster of saints—more than five thousand of them—to critical scrutiny, it discovered that some of the early saints were legendary rather than historical figures. None other than Saint Christopher, who was said to have carried the young Jesus safely across turbulent waters and had become the patron saint of travelers, was one of them. Millions of Saint Christopher medals in cars driven by faithful Catholics lost their spiritual meaning as a result—at least officially.

The theological issues accompanying (and at times plaguing) the church through the first four hundred years differed markedly over time and place. Theology developed differently in the Eastern church, which geographically comprised the Greek-speaking eastern Mediterranean from Alexandria to Constantinople, than it did in the Latin-speaking Western church, which centered in Italy and North Africa. Eastern theologizing tended to be speculative and mystical, while Western theology focused on juridical and institutional issues. However, virtually all the theologians who made a major impact on Christian self-understanding during the first four centuries, such as Origen (d. 254), John Chrysostom (d. 407), and Jerome (d. 420), lived and taught in the East; Jerome after a substantial sojourn in Rome.

In the East, the burning theological issue had to do with the proper understanding of the Trinity, while in the West the focus was on understanding Jesus. The theologizing in the East began with the confession that Jesus was God, but precisely that assertion raised a quandary for the profession that God was one. Christianity claimed to be monotheistic (to affirm only one God). How, then, could it be that there was a second God, namely, Jesus? The theologians' challenge was to find a way to synthesize these two assertions. A long series of suggestions and notions was put forward, but as matters turned out, each seemed to raise more questions than it answered. A view called Adoptionism, for example, held that Jesus was born an ordinary human who at his baptism was "adopted" by God and took on God-like qualities. The difficulty with this understanding of Jesus was that the opening sections of Matthew's and Luke's Gospels (and especially that of John) had to be ignored, since they affirmed the divine in Jesus from the very beginning. Modalistic Monarchianism, another notion, held that the designation "son" for Jesus was merely a different name (or mode) for the Father, the monarch. That notion, too, could be challenged on the grounds that the Gospels clearly speak of the Father and Jesus as separate beings. It took several centuries for the church to sort out this Babel of opinions and to formulate definitive affirmations.

A surprisingly fierce controversy took place over the day Christians should gather for worship. Early on, Christians had taken their cue from the account in the Gospels that Jesus had risen from the dead on a Sunday. Sunday was therefore considered the proper day to gather for worship in commemoration of Jesus' resurrection. They did so with Scripture readings, the singing of psalms, and the celebration of the Last Supper. Gathering on Sundays meant the rejection of those who insisted that the (Jewish) Sabbath should be observed as also the day of Christian worship.

The determination when to celebrate Easter, the day of Jesus' resurrection, brought heated tempers and pointed disagreement. Two positions vied for acceptance by the church at large: the observation of Easter on the fourteenth day of the (Jewish) month of Nisan, the day of the Passover (the Christians observing this date were promptly labeled "Quartodecimans" from the Latin *quarta decima*, meaning "fourteen") or the observation on the first Sunday after the fourteenth of Nisan. In other words, the issue was whether the commemoration of the resurrection should be on the day of the Jewish Passover, no matter what day of the week, or on a Sunday. The larger issue was whether the date of the celebration should be set according to the Jewish calendar or independently of it. Christians in Asia Minor took the former position, while Christians everywhere else insisted on the latter.

On the face of things, this was hardly a major theological issue—certainly not one for which Christians were prepared to suffer martyrdom—but nonetheless the controversy was severe, a telling first instance of the potential ferocity of theological disagreements even over relatively unimportant topics. Except, of course, the issue had a public face, so to speak: when did Christians gather for worship to commemorate the resurrection of their Lord? In the ensuing controversy Pope Victor I (r. 189–98), who became heavily involved in the issue, employed a simple method of attaining theological uniformity. He threatened to excommunicate all Christians who observed Easter according to the Jewish calendar. His decision was hardly calculated to resolve the disagreement or ease tensions between Christians in Syria and those in Asia Minor, who observed Easter on the day Victor found unacceptable. Eventually, the storm caused by Victor's pronouncement blew over, but the issue remained unresolved. Numerous suggestions were made, but two parts of the church, separated by both geography and culture, remained in conflict.

It was Emperor Constantine who forced the church to resolve the issue. Constantine insisted that the topic be on the agenda of the council to convene at Nicea. Not surprisingly, the council fathers rendered a decision. The council declared that Christians would henceforth observe Easter on the first Sunday after 14 Nisan. The issue was settled.

There were further developments. The quest to safeguard the authentic message of Jesus not only led to the delineation of the formal criterion of apostolicity and standardized patterns of worship but also inspired the effort to demonstrate to the pagan intellectual world the cohesiveness and cogency of the Christian message. The latter effort was particularly important for a group of theologians living and writing between 130 and 200 who collectively came to be known as "Apologists." As the term suggests, the Apologists wanted to expound the Christian faith, in an intellectually cogent manner "apologetically." At a time of intense theological disagreements within the church, the Apologists addressed the outside world to argue that the Christian faith was intellectually persuasive.

Until that time, theological reflections had taken place largely apart from the intellectual world of Late Antiquity. Christians did not particularly care what outsiders thought of them and their beliefs. This changed when some church leaders became concerned to demonstrate that Christian teachings lent themselves to be argued on rational, philosophical grounds. After all, Christianity was the true and natural religion of humankind. The Apologists undertook their task by employing the language and categories of Greek philosophy for the formulation of Christian truth. Christianity was the perfect philosophy, and there was no reason for a true philosopher not to embrace Christianity.

Many Apologists had been converted to Christianity after having found the notions of philosophy wanting. They were determined to demonstrate that their new faith possessed intellectual vitality and that it was superior to the best of philosophical reflection. Justin Martyr, for one, sought to dispel the notion that Christianity was a ridiculous religious sect without proper philosophical grounding. He and the other Apologists had experienced otherwise.

The foremost objective of the Apologists was to lay out a rational and judicious concept of God, the proper worship of this God, and the ideal of a community marked by virtue, love of fellow humans, and peacefulness. The Apologists wanted to achieve the goal of philosophy to give even the most ordinary individuals access to ultimate truth. They offered salvation history plain and simple, though their telling was not so much the story of the people of Israel as the story of the Greek philosophers. Socrates became the prototype of the Christian martyr, and Christ the fulfillment of all human wisdom and philosophy.

In their own way the Apologists were the founding fathers of Christian systematic theology, since they engaged in systematic reflection to probe the meaning of the faith. But there was a negative aspect to their ventures: the Apologists, like theologians ever since, faced the temptation to slide into esoteric discussions of little interest to either the church at large or its individual members.

Justin Martyr, the archetype of these Apologists, was born of Greek parents in Samaria around the year 100. His was the life of a perpetual student. His interest was philosophy, and over the course of years he pursued virtually every philosophical school of thought in order to find meaning in his own life and the universe. In his autobiographical reflections, the main source for his life story, Justin recounted how he had sought meaning in the various schools of Greek philosophy, until—altogether dissatisfied with them all—he discovered Christianity, which he found intellectually impressive and cogent. He became a Christian and hailed the Christian faith as the "only truly trustworthy and practical philosophy." The Hebrew Scriptures, as interpreted by Christians, had won him over to the Christian faith. He also confessed that he had been deeply affected by the serene bravery of Christians enduring martyrdom, but the decisive factor in his embracing the Christian faith was the cogency of its thought. Not surprisingly, Justin was the first to delineate a systematic Christian theology. After moving to Rome, he established a school of philosophy, where he debated supporters of Marcion and the gnostic understanding of the faith. During the rule of Emperor Marcus Aurelius, he suffered martyrdom in Rome.

THE THEOLOGIANS

No other period in Christian history has had an equal to the plethora of eminent theologians who expounded the meaning of the Christian faith from the third century of the Christian era onward. The lineage began with Irenaeus (d. ca. 200), continued with Tertullian (d. 222), and reached a crescendo in the fourth century with Athanasius (d. 373), Cyril of Jerusalem (d. 386/7), Ambrose (d. 397), John Chrysostom (d. 407), and the three Cappadocian Fathers—Basil of Caesarea (d. 379), Gregory of Nazianzus (d. 389/90), and Gregory of Nyssa (d. after 394). Then there was Augustine (d. 430), overshadowing them all in influence—and disagreement—though judgments of this kind are tricky. In no other period of the Christian faith, with the exception perhaps (at least as Protestants are concerned) of the sixteenth century, did so many prominent theologians live and write at almost the same time.

A few deserve special mention.

Irenaeus

Irenaeus, who hailed from Smyrna in Asia Minor and eventually served as bishop of Lyons, was the first of the so-called "church fathers" because he was the first to speak of the "universal" or "catholic" church as a definable entity and the first also to denounce those as "heretics" who did not accept the views of this church. He categorically affirmed (against Marcionite thinking) the Hebrew Bible as an integral part of Christian Scripture. He introduced a novel vocabulary into the Christian discourse, labeling his opponents with intriguing epithets, such as "jokesters," "empty sophists," or "sick." As matters turned out, he was to have many faithful imitators through the centuries.

Tertullian

Tertullian has been called the "Father of the Latin Church," a rather prominent appellation of importance. He was born ca. 160 and even though no less than thirty-eight of his writings have survived, we know very little about him. Apparently, he was a North African, raised in Carthage, his father a Roman centurion. Tertullian converted to Christianity, but that did not alter his "sharp and violent temperament," and before long he turned into an ardent, if vigorous, not to say abrasive theological and ethical hard-liner. He belonged to that cadre of humans for whom offense is always the best defense. The aggressiveness of his denunciation of unbelievers and of his indictment of heretics knew no bounds; one would not have wanted to be at the same dinner party with him. He never really relinquished his legal background (he was thoroughly schooled in law), for his writings reveal a keen analytic mind, as well as passion and personal engagement. Most of his writings were polemical in nature, addressing specific opponents or specific points of theology. Not surprisingly, contemporaries described him as a hotheaded lawyer.

Tertullian was impressed by the Christians' steadfastness in the face of persecution. His treatise *Apologeticum*, or *Defense*, addressed the recurrent accusations against the Christians—that they were guilty of contemptible crimes, such as ritual incest and cannibalism; that their religion combined superstition and ignorance; that Christians, by their unwillingness to defend the Roman Empire and their contempt for traditional Roman religion, were guilty of high treason. Tertullian refuted all of these charges as nonsense or vile slander and asserted the superiority of the Christian religion, because it was based on divine revelation. In the *Apologeticum* he identified Christianity as the "true religion" (*vera religio*) and called the traditional religion of Rome and the other religions of antiquity nothing but "superstitions."

Tertullian had little sympathy for Christians who combined the Christian profession with the easy life instead of being witnesses to the faith in times of persecution. That was true of some of the gnostic Christians, who maintained that Christians could worship the pagan gods without sin, for it was after all only the body that conformed to the demand for pagan worship and not the soul. Tertullian had harsh words for Christians on the other end of the spectrum as well, those who deliberately sought martyrdom, hoping that in so doing they would speed the return of Jesus. He related with sardonic disgust how in one instance several Christians in Asia Minor voluntarily appeared before the civic authorities to be given the death sentence for their faith, only to be told that if they were so eager to die, they could always jump off a cliff or hang themselves.

Tertullian's greatest scorn was, however, reserved for the Roman state. He wrote:

> Christians are persecuted without due process for they are not allowed to defend themselves. As long as they can be called "Christians," they can be executed. Real criminals are given the opportunity to deny their offences, defend themselves, and are tortured so that they confess. Christians, on the other hand, are not allowed to ask for evidence of the crimes of which they are accused and are tortured to make them stop confessing. Christians are denied the opportunity to vindicate themselves, nor do the magistrates try to produce any evidence of crime—the name "Christian" is enough.

Tertullian told the accusers: "You know very well that Christians are moral and upright people. It has happened that a wanton wife has become chaste on becoming a Christian; a useless slave has become faithful. Apparently their crimes only matter once they have abandoned them" (Tertullian, *Apologeticum*).

Tertullian was the first theologian of importance who wrote in Latin (though even he could not desist from writing occasionally in Greek). As an apologist for the Christian faith, he endeavored to make a rational, juridical case. He was the first theologian (of whom we know) to use the term "Trinity" to express that the Godhead consisted of three persons yet was one being. He was the first, too, to refer to the Hebrew Scriptures as "Old Testament" and to the Gospels and the writings of the Apostle Paul as "New Testament."

Late in his life came a not altogether unexpected personal and theological turn. About the year 202, he joined the Montanists, a faction labeled as schismatic by the church at large. Their founder, Montanus, together with two women, Priscilla and Maximilla, had claimed a century earlier to be mouthpieces of the Holy Spirit and had supported the claim with the practice of glossolalia (speaking in tongues) as a sign that the end times were imminent. Even though the Montanists did not seem to reject any formal church teaching, their claim of receiving new divine revelations filled the church at large with dismay. They announced that the end (and Jesus' return to a one-thousand-year rule) was near, a

conviction that may well have prompted them to affirm a rigorous ascetic morality that included fasting and celibacy. Not surprisingly, the rigor
of Montanism appealed to Tertullian's sense of the proper Christian life,
which for him meant categorical ascetic denial of the body. After all, he
was a moral purist, a Puritan, the first of the huge throng of "puritans"
through the centuries, who identified the Christian life with the most rigorous ethical positions.

Tertullian's writings turned into bitter indictments of the church hierarchy, which he believed consisted of gluttons and adulterers who
despised the exhortation to fasting and condoned remarriage. His catalog
of unacceptable behavior for Christians was endless. As far as he was concerned, the moral failure of the church-at-large was fundamental, and he
pronounced judgments on female fashion, fasting (or rather, many
Christians' lack of it), marriage, modesty, and popular entertainment, to
name but a few of his favorite targets. He despised all worldly show. What
is the point in being fashion conscious, he argued, when the accessory
may turn out to be the fur of a lion that had maimed a Christian? A foot
that wore an anklet, he wrote, could not bear the pain of the torturer, and
the neck adorned by a necklace would not face the ax of the executioner.
After all, Christians were in training for martyrdom. Tertullian detested
women who blackened their eyelids or rouged their cheeks, men who
sprayed perfume on their bodies and shaved hair from their faces (or their
chests). Tertullian found it horrible that such men and women claimed to
be Christian. The attire of Christians should be simple, he said, its fabric
both plain and undyed, for if God wished people to have colorful clothes,
he would have made the sheep purple. No difference should there be in
the clothes of men and women: a simple white robe sufficed. Wigs were
an abomination, for when the priest laid hands on someone wearing a
wig, he would bless the wig and not the person. Soft bed linen did not
induce sleep, nor did tables require ivory legs. Jesus had not come down
from heaven with a silver foot basin to wash his disciples' feet.

It was all quite simple. The Christian faith was to lead women and men
to new lives of exceptional morality and rigid discipline, to a change of
life in repentance and obedience. Tertullian unsurprisingly referred to the
Christian message as "law" and to the Christian life as "discipline."
Salvation was attained by the fulfillment of the law. The church-at-large
rejected this dire moralism, and the Montanists who embraced it
remained a small North African splinter group. Tertullian, though
tainted by his association with the Montanists, became the exemplar par

excellence of Western theologizing and of the moral rigor of the early church.

Origen

Origen of Alexandria (d. ca. 253), by all counts the most important theologian of the Eastern church, was a near contemporary of Tertullian but cut from an altogether different cloth. Born in Alexandria of Christian parents, he was one of the few prominent theologians of the early centuries who had not become a Christian through conversion; he was brought up a Christian. His teacher was Clement of Alexandria (d. 215), who argued the Apologists' line that the Christian faith was not just for the uneducated and the ignorant, for uncouth men and women of the lower classes. It was equal to the best of Greek philosophy, validated by self-evident truths. In the process Clement had written a kind of daily guide for Christians, which combined spiritual and mundane advisories, including the rather worldly advice not to talk with a full mouth.

His pupil Origen turned into a universal genius, a theological Leonardo da Vinci, a third-century "Renaissance man." Origen shared Tertullian's moralism, and it was said that he had himself castrated in order to avoid all temptations of the "flesh" and to be able to engage in spiritual conversation with women but not be erotically aroused. From his youth, he was determined to live such an ascetic life of utter commitment, with a minimum of material comfort and "things." He slept on a bare floor, and had only the barest necessities, which allowed him to be single-mindedly devoted to theological and intellectual pursuits.

Origen's fame as a theologian became widespread, even though he was not an ordained priest and earned his livelihood by tutoring students. These students adored him and even wrote an encomium for him (a practice nowadays described with the German word *Festschrift*, a celebratory set of essays in honor of an individual). Nor did he write much of anything until he was more than forty years old (an age nowadays when some theologians and intellectuals begin to repeat thoughts and ideas from earlier years), and then he burst forth with a flood of writings. A friend, Ambrose, paid for a stenographer and scribes, and it was said when Origen was done, he had written some six thousand tomes on theology and the Bible, mostly biblical commentaries—though that figure, spread over roughly thirty active years, would mean some two hundred books a year, which may well be a pious exaggeration. Jerome, another eminent divine and biblical scholar, remarked that no one would be able to read

Origen's writings in a lifetime, a remark that may have as much to do with the content of Origen's publications as with their quantity. One wonders, of course, how Origen could have written them all in his lifetime if it was not possible to read them. Alas, most of his writings are lost.

Origen wrote a great deal about practical issues of daily living that affected Christians. Like many theologians of those days, he had much to say about human sexuality, not much of it positive, undoubtedly prompted by the Apostle Paul's rather ambivalent views on the matter. He had opinions on many other topics as well. Some of his theological views suggest that he was not altogether orthodox—he affirmed reincarnation, for example.

Origen meant to be a faithful expositor of the Bible, so that its message, from the first chapter of the book of Genesis to the last chapter of the book of Revelation, could be understood by even the simplest Christians. His most notable achievement undoubtedly was the *Hexapla*, a Hebrew and Greek edition of the Old Testament, by all accounts the most formidable textual work of Late Antiquity. Origen sought to create an authoritative text of the Old Testament in order to dispel, once and for all, the confusion about its text. The church had adopted the Septuagint, the Greek version of the Hebrew Scriptures, but there were problems, not only because several books of dubious merit had somehow been added to the Hebrew Scriptures but also because the Hebrew and Greek texts in circulation had innumerable variants. These were due mainly to errors in the transcription of ancient manuscripts, the result of human frailty. But some textual variants resulted from the "culpable temerity," as Origen called it, of scribes who made corrections, additions, and deletions rather freely, convinced that they knew best how the text should read—an understandable assertion of editorial authority in light of the mistakes in previous transcriptions.

The Septuagint had been made from a Hebrew text that differed from that fixed at Jamnia by rabbis under Akiba ben Joseph, the founder of rabbinical Judaism. Origen collected both the texts and the variants of the entire Old Testament into one book, arranging them in six (in Greek, *hexa*) parallel columns. It was the work of a genius, carried out with patience and devotion. In it, he attempted to demonstrate the relationship of the Septuagint to the existing variants and to the Hebrew text. Sadly, the work has perished; our knowledge of it is based on secondhand accounts.

Origen was the first to offer a systematic understanding of the Hebrew Scriptures as the Christian "Old Testament." The Hebrew Scriptures had been part of the biblical canon for worship and reflection. Indeed, in the beginning of the Christian movement they were the sole Scripture used in Christian worship. The challenge was to find the proper method of interpreting them as sacred Christian texts.

Origen's solution was to employ allegory. From Clement he derived the notion of an allegorical interpretation of biblical texts, while from Philo, the Hellenistic Jewish philosopher, he adopted the notion of a threefold exegesis of biblical passages: the literal, psychological (moral), and spiritual. In this scheme, for example, "Jerusalem" was not only an earthly city but also a heavenly city that signified values and principles. Origen's interpretative method rescued Christians from embarrassment about the spiritual meaning of biblical passages when they appeared to be devoid of spiritual meaning and dealt with embarrassingly mundane matters. This allegorical interpretation of Scripture dominated Christian biblical exegesis until the Protestant Reformation in the sixteenth century.

Augustine

A fourth theologian overshadowed all the others. Without minimizing the contributions made by the myriad of theologians in the first four centuries of the church, Augustine (354–430) deserves primacy of place. Arguably one of the most seminal minds of Western Christianity, his influence extended far beyond his time and place, and the history of Christian theology in the Western church since Augustine may well be seen as but a series of footnotes to his thought.

In contrast to many other theologians of Late Antiquity about whom we know very little aside from their writings, we know a great deal about Augustine: his early life, his personal development, his spiritual journey. The explanation is that in midlife, Augustine recorded the story of his life, the famous *Confessions*, to lay it all out before the reader, but like most writers of autobiographies, he carefully selected what he shared about himself, about his childhood, about his story. While the *Confessions* is a work of deep spirituality and keen psychological insight, the reader must realize that Augustine wanted to project a certain image of himself, for example, painting a rather dismal picture of his adolescence, surely in order to make his conversion appear all the more splendid.

Tellingly, Augustine's autobiographical account ends shortly after his conversion. In later years Augustine wrote a book titled *Retractions* (not as well known nor as frequently read as the *Confessions*), which summarized his writings and interspersed a few autobiographical observations; however, we do not learn much more about him from this sequel and we remain dependent on the *Confessions*, which in a striking way offer both episode and reflection. It is the latter—the almost endless ruminations on the motivations and feelings behind specific acts and deeds—that reveal uncommon introspection and explain the work's timeless significance. Of course, it was all related to fundamentals of Christian self-understanding—the need to confess one's sins called for precisely the reflections that Augustine offered in his *Confessions*.

Augustine grew up in the small town of Thagaste (now Souk) in modern Algeria, the son of a pagan father and a Christian mother. The family was well-to-do, and so he received the education appropriate for someone of his social status. After his mother, Monica, made unsuccessful entreaties on behalf of the Christian religion, Augustine turned to Manichaeism, the religion founded by Mani in the third century that sought to reconcile Christianity and Zoroastrianism. Mani's followers lived in self-chosen poverty and celibacy, but Augustine (only a seeker, after all) was freed from both obligations, which allowed him to have a concubine, whom he mentions but never identifies by name in his *Confessions*. She made him, at age nineteen, the father of a son who received the intriguing name Adeodatus, "Gift from God."

Figure 1C

St. Augustine of Hippo, as sculpted by the French neo-classicist artist Augustin Pajou (1730–1809). No authentic representation of St. Augustine exists. Undoubtedly this depiction, which resembles a person of European descent, does not accurately represent Augustine, the son of North Africa.

Augustine's adolescence was marked by promiscuity and irresponsibility; that, at any rate, is what Augustine wants the readers of his *Confessions* to know. He vividly describes those early years with disarming candor. Realizing his spiritual emptiness, he became fascinated by Manichaeism but, finding it unsatisfactory, turned to Neo-Platonism, the dominant philosophical school of the time, which disciplined the "flesh" through asceticism and ventured through contemplation to attain union with God. In 382, Augustine left his native North Africa for Rome, the capital and destination of young men with ambition and determination. Augustine was persuaded that he could successfully pursue a vocation as teacher. He soon discovered that his pupils did not share his enthusiasm for intellectual pursuits, perhaps a timeless characteristic of most pupils, while he in turn developed an intense dislike of Rome. With the help of a well-placed friend, he moved northward to Milan, then a thriving metropolis and residence of the Western Emperor. Despite his unhappy experience with teaching in Rome, he resumed teaching and, at age thirty, became a teacher of rhetoric.

In Milan, his life dramatically changed, and Augustine faithfully recorded the happening in his *Confessions.*

> I heard the voice of a boy or girl, I know not which, coming from the neighboring house, chanting, and repeating several times, "Take up and read: take up and read." Immediately my countenance was changed, and I began most earnestly to consider whether it was usual for children in any kind of game to sing such words; nor could I remember ever to have heard the like. So, restraining the torrent of my tears, I rose up, interpreting it no other way than as a command to me from heaven to open the book and to read the first chapter I should come across. . . . I grasped, opened, and in silence read that paragraph on which my eyes first fell—"not in rioting and drunkenness, not in chambering and wantonness, not in strife and envying; but put on the Lord Jesus Christ, and make no provision for the flesh." (Book 8)

It was August of the year 386. An affluent friend provided a retreat in the country as a place for study and meditation, but eventually Augustine returned to North Africa, became a monk, was ordained to the priesthood (in 391 at age thirty-seven), and became bishop of Hippo five years later. Thirty-four years later, in the year 430, he died, without ever having advanced in the hierarchy of the church beyond the rather unimportant bishopric of Hippo. His ecclesiastical career was less than distinguished, for Hippo was hardly a power center of the church. From the time he arrived back in North Africa, he had his vocation: he became an ardent writer.

Augustine's writings left a deep imprint on Western theology. To be sure, not all of his notions were accepted and embraced by the church, especially since some tended to become more one-sided and extremist as their author got older. The theological term "semi-Augustinianism" describes what the church appropriated from the bishop of Hippo—some parts of his thought, but not others.

Augustine serves as a perfect illustration of a type of theologian that might be called "polemical," in distinction from the "systematic" theologian. While the systematic theologian, such as Origen, approaches his or her task by laying out the basics (and details) of the Christian faith in a coherent and systematic fashion, making it easy to follow and understand the notions advanced, the polemical theologian writes (and rails) against a specific opponent in a specific controversy. One might see the systematic theologian as reflective and thoughtful; one might see the polemical theologian as explosive. Such was the case with Augustine: most of his writings are directed against a rival theologian or an erroneous (in Augustine's mind) view. There are a few exceptions in Augustine's writings, such as his book on the Trinity. It is thus not easy to discern a cohesive theology in the bishop of Hippo's thought.

The work for which Augustine is often noted took a long time to write: he titled it *De Civitate Dei* (*Concerning the City of God*), and it was a comprehensive statement of Christian salvation history. The book offered a grandiose sweep of human history, not as poetic as John Milton's *Paradise Lost* or Dante's *Inferno* but thoughtful nonetheless. Augustine's reflections were triggered by the Goths' Sack of Rome in 410, a traumatic event that profoundly shook Roman self-confidence and was widely understood to have resulted from the abandonment of the ancient Roman gods, principles, and values. The formal acceptance of the Christian religion, many non-Christians believed, had undermined the resilience and vigor of the ancient Roman tradition.

Not so, responded Augustine. Well before Christianity became a force in the empire, he pointed out, Rome showed weaknesses and disintegration. If anything, the fall of Rome was the doing of the Romans themselves, for they had become too complacent, too self-confident, and too arrogant.

Augustine informed his readers that there was a historical and theological context for what was taking place in the Roman Empire. From the beginning of time, two forces, two powers, have faced and contested each other, Augustine argued: the "City" of God and the "City" of Satan. The beginnings of this struggle are described in Genesis 1:4, with its reference to the forces of light and darkness. And this struggle has continued ever since, though not so much as an empirical struggle between two political foes, but rather a metaphysical confrontation between two sets of values, the divine and the satanic. Two principles, the Eternal and the Transient, operate in human affairs. They are constantly in tension and opposition. At times the one is holding the upper hand; at other times the other holds the upper hand, but neither is able to enjoy such glory for very long. These principles do translate into empirical reality of power politics among nations and empires. God allows empires to rise and become powerful and mighty, but then God also permits these empires to fall and disappear from the face of the earth. This struggle of the forces of darkness against the forces of light is elemental in human history.

It is in this context that Augustine's enduring contribution to Christian self-understanding must be considered: his concept of the "just war" and the legitimacy of Christians' participation in the exercise of force. In early Christianity, most Christians had interpreted several sayings of Jesus—particularly the Sermon on the Mount about loving one's enemies and turning the other cheek—to mean that there was no place for a follower of Jesus to serve as a soldier in the Roman army or to exercise governmental positions that employed force, such as executioner or judge. Indeed, as we have noted, this Christian aloofness quickly became a factor in the suspicion and hostility that many Romans felt toward Christians and their communities.

A shift occurred when Emperor Constantine decreed the formal toleration of the Christian religion. The new status of a "state" religion forced a reappraisal of the traditional view of the Christians' relationship to the social and political order. Augustine took on the challenge, and his response to the new societal circumstances has been the normative Christian view through the centuries. In so doing, he emphasized the importance of Romans 13 (where Paul writes that all governments are ordained by God) and appropriated Cicero's notion that wars vindicating justice and restoring peace are moral and legitimate. Echoing this sentiment, Augustine argued that for a war to be just from a Christian perspective, it had to have a just cause, which meant, for example, a country's self-defense against aggression. Also, a war had to be waged by a legitimate authority, that is, by a ruler, king, or queen and could not be a wanton exercise of force. Finally, a war had to have a just objective; the use of force must have as its immediate objective the restoration of peace. If these criteria were fulfilled, Augustine concluded, a war was just, and Christians could affirm it and participate in it by serving as soldiers.

Augustine's understanding was a compromise between the "pacifist" orientation of the early church, when serving in the Roman military or serving as judges was frowned upon by Christians, and what might be called the "crusader" mentality, which assumed that rulers could engage in any war and demand the loyal participation of the citizenry, including the Christians. No longer were faith and society seen to be in tension or even opposition; the whole range of societal affairs was declared to be proper for Christians, including participation in war. Augustine baptized Cicero's notion of "just wars" by giving it a Christian meaning. In the millennium and a half since, Augustine's notion has been the lodestar that allowed rulers and potentates to call on Christians to go to war, secure in the awareness that the moral theologians and church leaders would proclaim that their side had a "just" cause. That, for example, was the sentiment of Francisco de Vitoria about the Spanish conquest in the Americas. And that German soldiers in World War II had the inscription "God with us" on their belt buckles derived from the same source.

Of course, for a war to be just for one side, it has to be unjust for the other side. Therein lay the problem, since in what came to be called "Christendom," neither side of an armed conflict was ever willing to concede that its pursuit of military force was selfish and therefore morally wrong. Viewing the history of warfare in Europe since the fifth century quickly forces the conclusion that both belligerent sides declared to be fighting for a just cause. Thus, no matter how theologically (and biblically) profound, Augustine's notion of the just war may be said to have offered little practical guidance to Christians and their leaders. In fact, until the 1960s, when churches and individual Christians in the United States and other countries protested the involvement of the United States in Vietnam, hardly any mainstream Christian voice in Europe or North America ever judged their side of a particular war to be unjust. There were, of course, Christians on the margins, such as the Quakers and the Mennonites, who argued for a categorical pacifism, but their voices were seldom heard over the sound of battle.

A corollary of Augustine's thought on the Christian and the political order was his advocacy of coercion to make individuals conform to (and accept) the Christian religion. The bishop of Hippo had no empathy for what we today call religious liberty. Religious dissent could not be allowed in a Christian society, he argued, for to do so meant that blasphemy was tolerated and allowed to spread. Augustine insisted that there was Old Testament precedent for harsh punishment for blasphemers. Individuals could be compelled to accept the faith, just as Jesus in his parable had indicated that some were forced to come to the banquet table.

Augustine's view on the treatment of those outside the church (and even that of dissenters in the church) was a fateful insight, for it provided the moral and theological rationale for all those who in subsequent centuries sought to compel individuals to be Christians. Augustine's vision bespoke a new understanding of the relationship of the Christian faith to society, and while we must not make him the forerunner of the Inquisition, he must be numbered among those who were deeply convinced that a society had to be homogeneously Christian.

Augustine's other commanding contribution to the Christian theological heritage was his view of human nature. At issue was the simple but profound question that had been asked many times before: are humans intrinsically good or evil? What did it mean when Christian theologians and churchmen defined humans as "sinful"? Indeed, were humans free to do good? Theologically this raised the issue of the relationship between divine grace and human freedom. At the end of the fourth century, the views on the matter of an English monk named Pelagius evoked Augustine's irate and fierce response. A controversy ensued, in which Augustine succeeded in silencing Pelagius both theologically and politically (in the process stating Pelagius's views not altogether correctly).

The bishop and the monk confronted each other over the specific issue of human moral prowess, but their disagreement ran deeper. Ever since the Christian religion had become the official religion of the Roman Empire, some Christians had lamented that many faithful were no longer committed to the moral standards that had earlier characterized the members of the church. It had become all too easy to become a Christian. Pelagius shared this sentiment and bewailed the unwillingness of the church to enforce the highest moral standards for its members. Instead it had become commonplace for the church to assert that it was impossible to fulfill the mandates of the law. Pelagius argued that to be a Christian meant the commitment to the highest moral standards (at that point Augustine agreed with him), and he insisted that the Law was given by God so that it would be fulfilled. Fulfillment of the Law was not some sort of unattainable ideal. Humans were able to live moral lives, and were not born into this world totally corrupted. While moral perfection was not attainable, baptism restored the freedom of human moral action. Jesus was the role model for the Christian; humans were free to choose the good and were judged by their choices.

The ensuing controversy that pitted Augustine against Pelagius and his eloquent supporter Julian, bishop of Eclanum, hinged in a way on the interpretation of Romans 7, in which the Apostle Paul bemoans his inability to do good. Did that chapter describe the apostle's understanding of the moral capabilities of the unredeemed, who found themselves unable to control their sinful disposition? Or did the passage describe the moral struggles even of believers? Augustine's answer was to view the words of the apostle as his own, as the agonizing plea of the believer overwhelmed by the conjunction of will and act. Adam's sin had put all future generations into the chains of moral powerlessness.

Augustine's skillful antagonist, on the other hand, insisted that God acts rationally and fairly, so that it must be possible to fulfill the commandments he has given. Humans must rally their will to do good. They can act morally—if they only are determined to do so. Pelagius believed that Adam's fall in the Garden of Eden had no bearing on posterity, a view radically different from Augustine's notion of an "original" sin, that fundamental inclination of each human being to be inclined to do evil.

When Pelagius propounded his views in Rome, Augustine (who had initially found no fault with Pelagius's emphasis on the moral life) concluded that if accepted they would destroy the edifice of Christian belief. He decided to act, and his astute political intervention with the powerful in Rome brought about Pelagius's formal condemnation by no less than two popes—and his lasting infamy as a theological heretic and biblical lightweight. His writings were relegated to oblivion. Yet the bishop of Hippo had scored a Pyrrhic victory, for he had let his relentless castigation of Pelagius drive him to extremist views, which the church at large never embraced.

Augustine's views on human sexuality were related here, leaving a permanent and fateful impact on the Western church. Was human sexuality a wonderful gift of God or a troublesome stain on humankind's higher spiritual calling? Christians seeking guidance were not particularly helped by the Bible, which had much to say about adultery and fornication but little about human sexuality as such. Nor was it easy to discern the teachings of Jesus on the matter, for he, too, focused his comments on adultery and divorce. And the Apostle Paul hardly improved matters with his clear preference for celibacy and sexual renunciation, while at the same time not rejecting marriage in the process. "It is better to marry than to be aflame with passion," he wrote (1 Corinthians 7:9), hardly a rousing endorsement of marriage. Of course, the expectation of an imminent return of Jesus relativized the issue, though Paul and many other churchmen shuddered at the thought of being found in the marriage bed at Christ's victorious appearance in the clouds.

Augustine's reflections began with a cultural reality. In all human cultures, he observed, the private body parts are covered and hidden, even as sexual intercourse occurs in private. Augustine elucidated this cultural reality by arguing that, in a mysterious way, humans are deeply ashamed about their sexuality. Probing the cause of this "shame," he concluded that the sexual act revealed a profound disjuncture between mind and body. Sexual passion did away with rationality and control. The "lower" body exerted itself against the "higher" will. Humans, when sexually aroused, were no longer controlled by mind and rationality; they had a "half maimed will."

Augustine found this "disjunction" between body and will prefigured in the story of Adam and Eve in the garden of Eden. It was a telling paradigm of all men and women who experience in their sexuality a perturbing reminder of Adam's and Eve's rebellion against God, which was a rebellion of the lower (Adam and Eve) against the higher (God). The disjunction experienced by humans offered a clue to the nature of the sin of Adam and Eve, and indeed of all humanity: disobedience and rebellion. The human body became a symbol of a profound spiritual truth.

It was easy to conclude from all of this that human sexuality was sinful as such, and generations of theologians after Augustine reached precisely that conclusion. Sexuality and the Christian faith were seen as incompatible. Augustine was too subtle a theologian, however, to allow such categorical pronouncements. He simply meant to point out that the mystery of human sexuality is a powerful reminder of the mystery of the Garden of Eden and its lasting legacy for humankind. Of this, Christians were to be mindful.

THE CREEDS

Whatever else may be said about Christianity, it is also a religion of creeds, statements of faith, and confessions. Its belief system can be expressed in intellectual propositions that demand acceptance and concurrence from Christian "believers," a term that in itself underscores the importance of belief. The followers of Jesus are to "acknowledge" ("confess") him, a notion that in the Gospel of Matthew is related to Jesus' declaration that he will confess them before his Father. When the earliest Christians paid homage to Jesus by speaking of him as Christ, the Anointed One, as Son of God, as Lord, they were in fact making a confession.

Creeds and confessions served to repudiate erroneous teachings about Jesus, and before long simple declarations about Jesus—such as "Jesus is Lord"—were augmented by facts of his life deemed important for understanding his mission, and both became the core of confessional declarations, particularly of those wanting to become members of the church. Requiring new Christians to make a "confession" accelerated from the middle of the second century onward, when increasingly more precise affirmations about Jesus were required and added. The crucial question of the nature of Jesus' divinity received a clarification at the Council of Nicea. And through the centuries Christians have not hesitated to put their core convictions about their faith into the form of confessions and statements of faith. There are hundreds of such statements; a recent encyclopedic scholarly edition of Christian creeds comprises three hefty tomes.

In Christian theological parlance the term "creed" tends to be reserved for three important statements of faith formulated in the early church: the Apostles' and the Nicene/Constantinopolitan creeds, together with the Athanasian Creed, a lesser-known statement of faith with an uncertain date of origin. These creeds were meant to summarize the faith of the church. In turn, the parallel term "confession" (or "statement of faith") refers to more extensive statements to be affirmed. They express that the Christian faith is not only a way (or walk) of life but also a system of belief. A Christian, so the ancient creeds and confessions assert, is someone who affirms certain propositional truths, mainly about Jesus of Nazareth—that he was born of a virgin, that he rose from the dead, and that he is equal in substance to God, the "Father." All corollary affirmations in the New Testament—about God, about the Holy Spirit, about a Last Judgment, for example—emanate from this central affirmation.

The confession about Jesus was understood to articulate the witness of the apostles expressed in apostolic writings. The affirmations of the creeds thus summarized apostolic truth, and whatever was not specified in the creeds remained matters concerning which differing opinions could be held; Christians could interpret those aspects of the faith as they chose. This freedom allowed competing and differing views to exist side by side, albeit not always harmoniously. Departure from the explicit confessional norms evoked suspicion and censorship. The affirmation of one set of propositional truths, moreover, implicitly entailed the rejection of diverging truth claims. Eventually the departure from norms found in the creeds was labeled "heresy" and meant not only theological stricture but also often incarceration and the loss of life.

While creeds and confessions are understood to be summaries of the teachings of the Bible, their vocabulary and idiom are not necessarily scriptural; rather, creeds and confessions are formulated in the language of their time, if doing so facilitates the resolution of theological controversy. Generally, creeds and confessions seek to be statements of the community of believers. Confessions and creeds are church documents, formal, concise, authorized statements of the belief of the church. They call on individual believers to express their concurrence with the corporate identity of the larger Christian community. Tertullian in the second century employed the label "Rule of Faith" (in Latin, *regula fidei*) as an individual's witness of what the entire church "immovably and irreformably" confessed. Consequently, statements of faith use the plural pronoun "we," the one major exception being the Apostles' Creed that came into prominent usage, with ever greater detail and specificity, stating what individuals had to affirm in order to be admitted to baptism and church membership. What was to be affirmed was intensely personal: it was "my" affirmation about Jesus, "my" confession. At the same time, confessions were also communal pronouncements. "I" confess what "we," the church, also confess.

While creeds are documents of the church, their formulation and acceptance have not been altogether free from outside involvement. Governmental authorities, beginning with Emperor Constantine at the Council at Nicea, have played at times an important role in the delineation of confessional norms by favoring one theological position over another. Constantine, while not yet baptized, took his theological and ecclesiastical role with great seriousness, referring to himself on one occasion as "the bishops' brother." Similarly, in the age of the Reformation, the Lutheran Augsburg Confession of 1530 and the Lutheran Book of Concord of 1580 would not have come about without the involvement of the political authorities. The same holds true for some of the confessional pronouncements in the English Reformation, such as the Six Articles of 1539, which have no other explanation than Henry VIII's Catholic disposition.

Early on, a basic characteristic of theological reflection emerged. Whenever a specific theological affirmation (or "confession") was made, questions immediately arose about that affirmation, and once those questions had been answered, the answer triggered a new question. Thus, the affirmation "Jesus is Lord" raised the question of the meaning of "Lord." What does it mean to speak of Jesus as "lord"? That Jesus is Lord over me? That he is Lord over Israel? Lord over the universe? Likewise, the affirmation that Jesus was the son of God raised questions about his divinity and his divine uniqueness. A theological statement always tended to call forth a new question.

The clarification of affirmations about Jesus may be said to have had its beginnings in the Apostle Paul's declaration in his letter to the Church in Rome: "If you confess with your lips that Jesus is Lord and believe in your heart that God raised him from the dead, you will be saved" (Romans 10:9). Over time, this simple affirmation was expanded in order to include a variety of additional affirmations about Jesus. A document titled "The Dialogues of Jesus with his Disciples after his Resurrection," probably originating in Egypt in the middle of the second century, called for the "confession" of God, the Father, as the ruler of the universe, of Jesus Christ, of the Holy Spirit (the "Paraclete"), the Holy Church, and the forgiveness of sins. None of these affirmations spelled out details.

Somewhat later, in the year 165, a personal confession of faith—a creed-like formula—was incorporated into the account of Justin Martyr's martyrdom. Specific affirmations about Jesus had grown longer. The *Witness of Justin* affirmed belief in "the Lord Jesus Christ, the servant of God, who had also been proclaimed beforehand by the prophets as about to be present with the race of men, the herald of salvation, and the teacher of good disciples." At about the same time, Irenaeus recorded as the "Rule of Faith" the belief

> in one God, the Father Almighty, who made the heaven and the earth
> and the seas and all the things that are in them; and in one Christ Jesus,

the Son of God, who was made flesh for our salvation; and in the Holy Spirit, who made known through the prophets the plan of salvation, and the coming, and the birth from a virgin, and the passion, and the resurrection from the dead, and the bodily ascension into heaven of the beloved Christ Jesus, our Lord, and his future appearing from heaven in the glory of the Father to sum up all things and to raise anew all flesh of the whole human race (Irenaeus, *Against Heresies*, I:10).

A quarter-century later, the *Interrogatory Creed* of Hippolytus, a theologian who wrote in the first half of the third century, was meant as a baptismal confession for those seeking to become members of the Christian community; it extended Justin Martyr's formulation. In question-and-answer format the future member of the church was asked: "Do you believe in Jesus Christ, the son of God, who was begotten by the Holy Spirit from the Virgin Mary, who was crucified under Pontius Pilate, and died and was spirit and rose the third day living from the dead, and ascended into the heavens and sat down on the right hand of the father, and will come to judge the living and the dead?"

As these statements over decades and centuries inched ever closer to the wording eventually found in the Apostles' Creed, an intense controversy erupted over the phrase that Jesus "descended to the dead," an obvious effort to explain what happened to Jesus between his crucifixion and his resurrection.

Ambivalence about this phrase lingered for a long time, so much so that some churches recite the Apostles' Creed without it. Part of the problem has been the ambiguity of meaning: does the phrase mean that Jesus' pain on the cross was comparable to the pain experienced by those in hell? Or does it suggest that Jesus carried the sins of the world to hell? Or that Jesus carried the good news of salvation to the godly dead, such as Lazarus the beggar and the repentant thief? A third-century Syrian creed sought to be specific: it affirmed that Jesus was "crucified under Pontius Pilate and departed in peace, in order to preach to Abraham, Isaac, and Jacob and all the saints concerning the end of the world and the resurrection of the dead." (*Didascalia Apostolorum*).

A new controversy demonstrated that the confessions in circulation did not address a fundamental question, namely, the precise nature of Jesus' divinity. The "Christological," or "Trinitarian," controversy began to divide the Eastern church and called for a sharper formulation of orthodox belief. When the controversy broke out, both factions acknowledged Jesus as "God's only Son" and "our Lord," but they pointedly disagreed about the meaning of this affirmation. Different views of the relationship between God the Father and God the Son were at stake. Indeed, more than that, Athanasius, the leader of one of the factions, declared that the disagreement was, in the final analysis, over salvation itself. Eventually a council was to resolve the disagreement.

Deeply disappointed that the religion to which he had conferred legal status was engaged in such acrimonious debate, and so divided, Emperor Constantine decided to convene a council (the bishops traveled to Nicea at his expense) and played a major role in its deliberations. Famous is Constantine's letter to the chief antagonists, Alexander, bishop of Alexandria, fierce proponent of the full deity of Jesus, and Arius, elder of the church in Alexandria, the equally fierce proponent of the notion that there was a time when the Son did not exist:

> When you, Alexander, inquired of your presbyters what they thought of a certain inexplicable passage of the written Word, a subject improper for discussion, and when you, Arius, rashly expressed a view of the matter that should have never been expressed, or when thought of, should have been buried in silence. This dispute having arisen among you, destroyed your fellowship. And the people of God, divided into two factions, have departed from the harmony of the common body. Wherefore let each one of you show consideration for the other and listen to the impartial exhortation of your fellow-servant. What counsel does he offer? It was neither prudent to raise such a question, nor to reply to it when it was raised. No law demands the investigation of such subjects, but the idle useless talk of leisure occasions them. And even if they should exist for the sake of exercising our natural faculties, we ought to confine them to our own consideration, and not carelessly bring them forth in public assemblies. Indeed, few are capable of adequately expounding, or even accurately understanding, the significance of matters so vast and profound! (Constantine, *Letters*, Book 2)

The emperor was annoyed at the theological hairsplitting of the antagonists, but having reprimanded them, he was determined to resolve the controversy. The majority of the council fathers evidently had no strong opinion one way or another: the controversy had passed by them or they had little interest in this subtle theological issue. One account of the council called them "simpletons." At the outset, the council rejected a proposed Arian confession of faith, as well as a mediating statement proposed by Eusebius of Caesarea, the "father" of church history. The council inserted several anti-Arian phrases into Eusebius's moderate document, affirming that Jesus was "begotten, not made" and "of one essence" with the Father. "The divine and sacred First Ecumenical Council of three hundred and eighteen God-inspired fathers...attached the term 'consubstantial' to the Holy Trinity, [and] fixed the time of the divine and mystical Passover," wrote Eusebius (Eusebius, *Historia Ecclesiastica*). But that was not all. The council "set forth the divinely inspired teaching of the Creed" against a long list of heretics, most of whom history has forgotten, but who did include Sabellius, Photinus, Paul of Samosata, Manes, Valentinus, Marcion, and their respective followers.

With the emperor taking sides, the majority of the bishops opted for Athanasius's view, and so the formal document adopted by the council was not a compromise but affirmed the Athanasian position. The creed drawn up by the council replicated the basic structure of the Apostles' Creed but added a lengthy set of affirmations dealing with Jesus' divinity. Thus, the creed affirmed that Jesus was

> One Lord, Jesus Christ, the Son of God, only begotten of the Father, that is to say, of the substance of the Father, God of God and Light of Light, very God of very God, begotten, not made, being of one sub-stance with the Father, by whom all things were made, both things in heaven and things on earth; who, for us men and for our salvation, came down and was made flesh, was made man, suffered and rose again on the third day, went up into the heavens, and is to come again to judge both the quick and the dead.

As matters turned out, the council notwithstanding, the controversy did not die down. The Arian party quickly rebounded from its defeat at Nicea and for a while gained the upper hand, in good measure because Constantine's son Constantius II weighed in mightily on the Arian side. He succeeded in reuniting the divided empire but failed to unite the church divided over the issue. His *Declaration of Sirmium* of 357 prohibited any discussion of the Athanasian position, though the new political intervention did as little to end the disagreement as had the previous (and contrary) pronouncement of the Council of Nicea. No less than fourteen councils met between 340 and 360 to resolve the issue, leading the pagan observer Marcellinus to comment sarcastically: "The highways were covered with galloping bishops," galloping, one suspects, from one council to the other.

Ultimately, the Athanasian party won. The tedious controversy had made its partisans doubt, however, whether the language of the Nicene Creed was specific enough and they concluded that the Athanasian position, as stated in the Nicene Creed, needed more precise formulation to express the proper understanding of Jesus' deity. A council in Constantinople in 381 augmented the Nicene wording. Jesus was described as "the *only* begotten Son of God" and declared to be "begotten of the Father before all worlds." On the face of things, these changes seemed to be rather modest, but theologically they were significant. The lengthy addendum of the Nicene Creed was deleted ("those who say: 'There was a time when he was not,' and 'He was not before he was made,' and 'He was made out of nothing,' or 'He is of another substance' or 'essence,' or 'The Son of God is created,' or 'changeable,' or 'alterable'— they are condemned by the holy catholic and apostolic Church").

The Nicene Creed answered the question of Jesus' humanity only by implication; an open issue remained, and it was addressed decades later by the Council of Chalcedon in 451. The "Definition of Chalcedon" elaborately affirmed the humanity of Jesus. Jesus possessed two full natures, human and divine, in one person. This was bitterly opposed by the "Non-Chalcedonians," who embraced various forms of monophysitism. But the answer triggered new questions: did Jesus have both a human and a divine will? How were they related? The issue was not resolved until the closing years of the seventh century with the declaration that even as Jesus possessed two natures, so he possessed two wills.

By the year 600, the important Christian beliefs were in place and had found expression in statements of faith. They are known as the four ecumenical creeds (or three, if the virtually identical creeds of Nicea-Constantinople are considered a single creed), and became the creeds affirmed by most Christians: the Apostles' Creed, the Creed of Nicea, the Creed of Constantinople, and the Definition of Chalcedon. But that did not mean complete unanimity. Coptic (Egyptian) Christians and others known today as the Eastern Orthodox churches embraced a different Christology, particularly of Jesus' human nature, and accordingly did not affirm the Definition of Chalcedon.

These creeds avowed a Trinitarian theology. Jesus was declared to be equal to the Father in all respects or, as the Creed of Constantinople expressed it, Jesus is of the same "substance" as the Father. The Constantinopolitan version of the Nicene Creed belabored the point by adding the phrase "begotten of the Father before all worlds" so as to assure clarity about Jesus' divinity, and the phrase "he was crucified for us under Pontius Pilate, and suffered, and was buried, and the third day he rose again, according to the Scriptures" to assure the full humanity of Jesus as well. Alternate points of view were understood to challenge the centrality of Jesus for human redemption, and were rejected.

Also, the creeds clearly focused their attention on Jesus. The Apostles' Creed lengthily described the salient features of the earthly life of Jesus— his birth of the Virgin Mary, his suffering under Pontius Pilate, his death, and his resurrection. So did the Creed of Nicea. By comparison, the affirmation about God, the Father, is brief, as is the statement about the Holy Spirit (in the Nicene Creed, the simple affirmation "I believe in the Holy Spirit"; in the Constantinople version, slightly larger "the Lord and Giver of life, who proceeds from the Father, who with the Father and the Son together is worshiped and glorified, who spoke by the prophets").

Finally, the creeds offer what might well be considered a commentary on the meaning of all of this, poignantly expressed again in the Nicene Creed with the affirmation of "one holy catholic and apostolic Church; we acknowledge one baptism for the remission of sins; we look for the resurrection of the dead, and the life of the world to come"). All creeds also speak of a time of judgment of the living and the dead, which will take place at the second coming of Jesus and the end of history. Jesus will return to earth as the ultimate judge.

DIVERSITY AND HERESY

It is tempting to view the early history of Christianity as the story of a church that ever more precisely delineated the meaning of Jesus, with a modest sprinkling of dissenters on the fringes. Alas, this winsome picture does not exactly correspond to historical reality. The fact of the matter is that during those centuries the Christian religion was buffeted by competing interpretations and groupings within the church, all of which claimed to proclaim the authentic gospel of Jesus.

This should not come as a surprise for two reasons. One, no matter how efficient the road and communication systems of the Roman Empire, the Christian assemblies that had spread throughout the eastern Mediterranean region tended to be isolated, so that particular emphases of life and thought were easily established in a community or a region, regardless of what was believed and lived in another community or region. Universally affirmed creeds and confessions were only slowly coming into use; parameters of what Christians must believe were virtually nonexistent. And there was no dearth of strong charismatic leaders, who absent such parameters propounded their particular understanding of the gospel with the result that divergent interpretations of what it meant to be a Christian existed side by side. That in Antioch a different theology was propounded than in Alexandria was known and accepted. The fact that the Western part of the church wrote in Latin while the Eastern part wrote in Greek (a bit also in Syriac) also complicated matters and helped ensure disagreement.

In short, the early Christian religion was not a single, uniform movement. Beginning with the story of the church recorded in the book of Acts, continuing with the exhortations to unity in the letters of Paul, and ending (at least for now) in the twenty-first century with divisions in churches along liberal and conservative lines, the Christian story has been one of disagreement and division. Despite this diversity of theological sentiment, one must not conclude that the Christian faith was hopelessly divided and that the Christian self-understanding during the first three centuries was a chaotic juxtaposition of opinions. There was a "mainstream" church, affirming an implicit majority consensus, and a process of clarification eventually turned what was affirmed and believed by a major part of the church into normative belief of the entire church. As that clarification occurred, two words entered the Christian vocabulary: *orthodoxy* and *heresy*. Both words came from the Greek, with *orthodoxy* denoting "right teaching," while *heresy* meant deviation from such orthodox belief.

This distinction between "right" and "wrong" teaching is by no means confined to the Christian religion. In one way or another, all religions have normative principles, which must be affirmed by their adherents in order to be an authentic part of the tradition. To be sure, intellectual assent is not always the core affirmation. Judaism, for example, urges obedience to the Law. However, all religions (and, for that matter, political movements) that claim specific truth propositions have "heresy" and "heretics" on their hands whenever there is dissenting sentiment in the ranks, a characteristic that seems to be chronic. In the New Testament, the term *heresy* is found as a value judgment. The Second Letter of Peter applied it to certain Christians: "There will be false teachers among you, who will secretly bring in destructive opinions" (2:1). The Jewish historian Josephus applied the term *heretics* in his *History of the Jewish Wars* to factions within Palestinian Judaism, the Sadducees, Pharisees, and Essenes, not at all pejoratively, but in keeping with the Greek root meaning of "sect" or "party" or "choice."

Later, in the thirteenth century, Thomas Aquinas provided a definition of heresy that became normative in the Western church. Heresy represented, so he stated, "a species of infidelity in man who having professed faith in Christ corrupts its dogmas." (*Summa Theologica* II, 11,1) A heretic, in other words, is a Christian who deviates from the approved teaching of the church. While orthodox believers accept the entire range of the church's teaching, the heretic accepts parts and rejects others. Thomas also offered the explanation for the causes of heretical views held by individuals. In his judgment, they were ignorance, flawed understanding of church teachings, and errors of judgment. For good measure, however, Thomas added intellectual pride, religious zeal, the lure of political power, and personal ambition. In other words, the heretic merged theological opinion or biblical interpretation and personal flaws and defects. In fact, Thomas implied that were it not for these personal qualities, there would be neither heresy nor heretics. Martin Luther was chided in 1521 that it was his haughtiness, rather than his biblical understanding, that kept him from acknowledging (and recanting) his errors.

The "heretics," of course, saw things altogether differently. As far as they were concerned, it was the church at large that had fallen from biblical truth and had perverted the gospel. They had discovered, or rediscovered, orthodox truth. The verdict of heresy entails, accordingly, the element of subjectivity. One person's heretic is another person's saint. A good case in point once again is Martin Luther, excommunicated as a heretic by the Catholic Church in 1521 but honored as a godly and authentic preacher of the gospel by countless followers through the centuries.

The subjective element in the definition of heresy has been pointed out by critics, foremost by the German Lutheran Gottfried Arnold (1666–1714), whose *Unpartheyische Kirchen- und Ketzergeschichte* (*Impartial History of the Church and of Heretics*), published in 1699, first argued poignantly that the two terms *church* and *heretic* were blatantly partisan. Arnold insisted on an "impartial" inclusion in the Christian universe of all who claimed to be Christian, for example, the much-despised (and persecuted) Anabaptists. His point was well taken and, indeed, has influenced the writing of the history of Christianity ever since. For most historians in the field, it has become commonplace to be inclusive rather than restrictive in the "Christians" and ideas covered.

From the early centuries of the Christian faith the consequence of holding false beliefs, called "heresy," was an act known as "excommunication." This meant exclusion from the fellowship of the church and the Eucharist, the Lord's Supper, and even more seriously the grave judgment that those excommunicated were eternally damned. Initially, there were no further societal or legal consequences for the individuals involved. This state of affairs began to change in the fifth century when Christianity became the official state religion of the Roman Empire and theological deviation from orthodoxy was also defined as the crime of blasphemy to be punished by the state. Heresy was, so the argument went, a form of public blasphemy that disrupted civic law and order in addition to violating the mandates of the Old Testament. Governmental power was employed to safeguard the moral and religious order of Christian society. Government imposed penalties, including being burned at the stake, based on the theological verdict rendered by the church, and it did so quite willingly because of its concern for law and order in society.

The church's role was to supply the indictment and the judgment, while government pronounced and executed the sentence. Thus, the sixteenth-century Anabaptists, who in a striking consensus were deemed heretics by Catholics and Protestants alike, found themselves thrown into dungeons, tortured, and executed by the political authorities. It was not until the late eighteenth century that this intimate collaboration between church and state ceased in Europe and the execution of ecclesiastical verdicts became once again, as it had been in early Christianity, solely a matter of theological judgment and condemnation within the church.

For a millennium theological dissent was taken to have a political component (which it sometimes had); theological dissenters were politically suspect. In the eyes of the authorities, the sixteenth-century Anabaptists were revolutionaries as well as theological heretics. This traditional system of church and state working hand in hand depended, of course, on the willingness of government—for reasons selfish or noble—to act as handmaiden of the church. The moment such willingness disappeared, the system crumbled; this began to take place in the eighteenth century. The increasing determination of governments, such as in France, to pursue the separation of the churchly and the political realms meant that those labeled heretics by a church remained untouched by government. The heretics were able to shrug their shoulders and leave the church that had so labeled them, join another church, or even found a new one. This happened, for example, in the aftermath of the promulgation of the dogma of papal infallibility by the First Vatican Council in 1870. Those Catholics unwilling to accept this new dogma left the Catholic Church and formed the Old Catholic Church. While a few of the leaders of this new church suffered adverse professional consequences, no governmental intervention followed. Because European governments did not play a role in this theological conflict, the dissenting Catholics escaped being punished by the government for their views. By the same token, these "heretics" could not count on governments for support either. An illustration of the second type of response—leaving the old church and joining another one—comes from our own time. When the Presbyterian Church (U.S.A.) agreed to ordain women to the ministry, opponents left the church and joined a variety of conservative Protestant denominations.

Theological dissent is triggered in one of two ways. In some instances, a dogmatic decision has been promulgated by the church and is on the books, so to speak, and the dissenters reject the decision. At issue is the unwillingness to accept what the church enjoins. Rejection of the Roman Catholic position on abortion is a relevant contemporary illustration. A second type of dissent occurs when there is no formal declaration on a specific issue, but a process is under way to clarify the matter. Ambivalence and lack of clarity prevail. In the ensuing process of doctrinal clarification, some find it impossible to accept the emerging position. This was the case when Arius and Alexander formulated their Christologies, when Martin Luther drafted his famous *Ninety-five Theses*, or when the First Vatican Council began its discussion on papal infallibility. In all of these instances, no normative position on these topics existed. Once the process of clarification has been concluded, however, the decision must be made whether to agree or disagree with the new formalized teaching of the church.

The significance of theological topics rises and falls over time. What is important at one time is not so important at another. Dissent or heresy, in other words, are not only theological judgments, they also reflect specific circumstances that might even pertain more to society at large than to biblical or theological insight. In the fifth century, for example, the pivotal question was whether Jesus was fully human; in the early twenty-first century, the question centers on whether Jesus was fully divine.

Heresy is only one of several types of dissent from mainstream affirmations. There is also apostasy, which is the rejection of the faith of the church after having earlier accepted it. While a heretic retains faith in Christian truth but defines that truth differently from the church, apostates reject all Christian belief, having once professed it. Christians who, during the Decian persecution, abandoned the faith are one illustration for apostasy, as is Emperor Julian in the fourth century, who not surprisingly was labeled "the Apostate." Heresy also differs from schism: schismatics separate themselves from the life of the mainstream church without necessarily rejecting a dogma or doctrine. Tellingly, Jerome observed in the early fifth century "heresy perverts dogma, while schism separates from the church." All heretics are schismatic, though not all schismatics are heretics, at least at the outset. The Donatists in the early fourth century, for example, submitted their grievances to both the emperor and Miltiades, the bishop of Rome; when their concerns were dismissed, they rejected the authority of Rome and became schismatics.

Given its long history, it is not surprising that the Roman Catholic Church (and, to some extent, also the Eastern Orthodox churches) has formally codified the various categories and distinctions described. Thus, Catholic canon law stipulates who is authorized to issue the verdict of excommunication, which incidentally continues to be issued in the early twenty-first century, though generally without notoriety or public controversy. Protestant churches historically also employed the category of "heresy" for views contrary to commonly held belief. No formal processes delineated, however, a way to deal with individuals who held beliefs condemned as heretical. In one way or another, the distinction between acceptable and unacceptable belief continues to be made in the early twenty-first century, though mainly by conservatives. Here the category "heresy" has found a new intensity of meaning, even if the term is rarely used.

Gnosticism

The story of theological dissent in the emerging Christian movement began late in the first century, when a view of the Christian faith subsequently labeled "gnostic" found followers in a large number of Christian assemblies. While scholars have known of the existence of such gnostic Christians and their communities for a long time, a dramatic turn in our understanding of the phenomenon occurred in December 1945, when a peasant from the village of Nag Hammadi in southern Egypt in a cave of the nearby mountains stumbled upon a large, three-foot-high, sealed earthenware jar. Assuming that he had come upon a hidden treasure, he smashed the jar, only to find, undoubtedly to his great disappointment, thirteen leather-bound papyrus books. To make at least some use of his find, he brought the books back to his village, to be used as kindling. Fortunately, not all the books suffered this fate. It took a few years and a few harrowing turns before the true significance of the find became clear. The books became the source for an exciting reinterpretation of early Christianity.

The books, as they began to be examined, revealed the significance of the discovery. The very beginning of the first book inspected had a startling, even radical, sentence: "These are the secret words which the living Jesus spoke, and which the twin, Judas Thomas, wrote." Was this another Gospel? One that somehow had been overlooked in the formation of the New Testament canon? It was the Gospel of Thomas. Scholars had known about such a gospel for a long time and were even familiar with a few passages from quotes in writings of theologians. Now the entire gospel was available. It included both familiar and unfamiliar sayings of Jesus, such as "If you bring forth what is within you, what you bring forth will save you. If you do not bring forth what is within you, what you do not bring forth will destroy you."

The Gospel according to Thomas was not the only text found at Nag Hammadi; what made the discovery so dramatic and even sensational was that a whole trove of previously unknown writings of a gnostic Christian bent became available. There was a Gospel of Philip, a Gospel of Truth, a Gospel to the Egyptians, a Secret Book of James, and an Apocalypse of Paul, to name but a few. In short, the discovery of an earthenware jar yielded an enormous treasure of previously unknown early Christian literature. The traditional understanding of early Christianity was called into question as the find showed a significantly richer diversity of readings of Jesus.

The key question of the Nag Hammadi discoveries had to do with the date of the texts. The scholarly consensus quickly declared them to be late fourth-century Coptic copies, but dating the composition of the original texts proved to be more controversial. Most scholars came to agree, however, that the texts were written around the middle of the second century, at the latest.

The Nag Hammadi discoveries offered further proof, if such was necessary, that Christian writings around the turn of the first century were far more extensive than had been known, and more diverse than those eventually collected in the New Testament. The writings underlined the theological diversity of early second-century Christianity. Most important, the documents suggested the importance of the gnostic interpretation of the Christian faith within the larger church. It was obvious that this gnostic interpretation was at odds with that propounded by the church-at-large, forcing an understanding of the early second century as a time when two fundamental perspectives of the meaning of Jesus vied for acceptance. In the end, the anti-gnostic church carried the day, and those who propounded gnostic views were labeled heretics by that church, and their teachings called heresy, notwithstanding that these gnostic Christians saw themselves as true followers of Jesus.

The phenomenon of gnosticism, especially Christian gnosticism, has generated much controversy and disagreement over the years. The word *Gnosticism* itself comes from the Greek word *gnosis* and is generally translated as "knowledge." An "agnostic," therefore, is someone who does not know. However, a better translation of *gnosis* might be "insight" or "wisdom," denoting that the gnostics claimed to possess true insight and wisdom. Second-century gnostic ideas flourished as a movement, both inside and outside Christianity; its followers saw themselves as having retained the true "knowledge" and "wisdom" about Jesus.

Accordingly, scholars view Gnosticism as influencing a second-century Christian movement that sought to interpret Christian faith with Greek philosophical categories. Gnosticism was a religion in its own right, older than Christianity and of Greek or Jewish origins. It was a mass movement, and not merely a fringe phenomenon on the edges of the mainstream church. It was also utterly diverse: one observer identified no less than sixty different gnostic theological views, making generalizations about the movement precarious and difficult. Reading any gnostic text tends to shatter prior generalizations.

By the early second century gnostic notions had made inroads into the church. The Christian gnostics saw their views as authentically Christian and as the genuine biblical alternative to the theology proclaimed by the mainstream church. They seemed to take it for granted that they held a higher and deeper understanding of the faith than did other Christians, who, for example, were foolish enough to claim that Jesus was conceived by the Holy Spirit and born of a virgin. How could the (feminine) spirit impregnate a woman? The cogency of arguments and the rigor of the prescribed lifestyle made Christian Gnosticism a serious challenge to the mainstream church, even though most Christian gnostic writers had what we nowadays call an "attitude problem," exhibiting an exceptionally heavy dose of self-confidence and arrogance. They saw themselves as more enlightened and more knowledgeable than the ordinary folks in the church. They were the ones who possessed saving knowledge. When one compares gnostic writings with those of the Egyptian Desert Fathers, who reflected endlessly on the minutiae of the propriety of sleeping on a pillow or on escaping the wiles of women, the intellectual brilliance of the big picture drawn by Christian gnostic writers becomes evident.

At the beginning of gnostic Christianity stood the question asked by all religions: what is true enlightenment, and how can one attain perfection? Gnostic Christians chided the mainstream church for being too worldly, too materialistic, and too neglectful of the spiritual, higher, and secret meaning of biblical truth that could be fathomed by a careful reading of biblical texts. The conclusions were shocking: the biblical God was called into question. He was regarded as limited, because he did not know where Adam and Eve were when they hid in the garden of Eden. And he was arrogant to boot, saying "I am God and before me there has been no other." Theologically, the Christian gnostics affirmed a divine spark in humans and the possibility of discovering within oneself the mysteries of existence and the universe, truths that needed no mediation by any church.

Gnosticism was an intellectual religion, committed to understanding and perceiving mysteries while at the same time challenging its followers to live on a higher spiritual plane. A key gnostic belief was the notion of a cosmic dualism, which made a distinction between a transcendent God and a lesser god, a Demiurge. Gnostics believed that the universe was not created by the transcendent God of light and truth (the *logos*) but by the Demiurge. Since humans have a spark of the divine, they are not completely at the mercy of the Demiurge. In order to be able to live a spirit-filled life, nonetheless, the soul must be freed from its earthly bondage. The redeemer is thus a teacher, and redemption thus consists in the acknowledgment of the divine spark that liberates individuals from the limitations of material things and allows the believer to participate in the divine.

This intriguing perspective succeeded in entering Christian self-understanding, and a number of eminent theologians of the time, such as Basilides in Egypt or Valentinus in Rome, offered a gnostic interpretation of biblical salvation history. In support of their contention that their views were authentically "apostolic," the gnostics claimed that secret writings from the time of Jesus and the apostles had been unacknowledged, even suppressed, by the church and that these writings supported the gnostic interpretation of the meaning of Jesus' message. The Nag Hammadi documents were a library of such "secret" writings, suppressed by the mainstream church. The mainstream church reacted to this challenge by proceeding to use the category of "apostolicity" to identify and define the authentic writings.

The gnostic interpretation gave Jesus a central place in the cosmic story of salvation: he was the heavenly redeemer who came to this evil world and took on the appearance of human form in order to lead humans back to true enlightenment. If some gnostic notions showed a keen understanding of certain biblical passages, others were in fatal conflict with mainstream affirmations, notably the radical contrast between creator and creation, good and evil, body and spirit. Also, the gnostics' denial of Jesus' humanity, his suffering, and his death did not seem to account for key affirmations in the canonical Gospels.

Gnostic sentiment, as found in gnostic assemblies and congregations, lasted, and centuries were to pass before the challenge of the Christian gnostics had completely subsided. In the twenty-first century, however, it has made a new appearance.

Marcion

At about the same time, the churches in the eastern Mediterranean were perturbed by another theological challenge. An outsider by the name of Marcion, who may well be called the first Christian reformer (or the first Christian heretic), tested the emerging theological understanding of the Christian faith. As far as we know, Marcion was the first of a long line of theologians whose theological dissent led to the formation of a new "church." Since Marcion succeeded in gathering a movement, he presented a major threat to the mainstream church.

We know little about him and little also about his thought. After Emperor Constantine had given the Christian religion a legal place in the Roman Empire, the church, in its newfound self-confidence, undertook to destroy the memory of all heretical adversaries by committing their writings to the oblivion of fire. Accordingly, the writings of Marcion and his followers were destroyed so that his name and teachings would be expunged from human memory. Not a single word from Marcion's pen is extant; his thought must be reconstructed from quotations or summaries found in the polemical treatises of his mainstream opponents. Naturally, this creates a good deal of uncertainty as to what he actually taught, since relying on what his opponents wrote suggests the likelihood of misunderstanding, misrepresentation, and even caricature. One fundamental Marcionite position seems clear, however: Marcion was convinced that Jewish influences had distorted the true Christian faith.

Marcion, the son of a Christian bishop, was born in Sinope, near the Black Sea, though we can only guess the year of his birth, probably around the year 85. After attaining prosperity as a shipping magnate, he moved to Rome around 139, became a member of the Christian congregation there and—an indication of his affluence or his commitment or his yearning for recognition—made a huge donation to the church, which easily allowed him freedom to propound his idiosyncratic notions.

After five uneventful years in Rome, the commotion began. In 144, Marcion challenged the leaders of the Roman congregation to a debate over the interpretation of certain Scripture passages. He was a gifted and well-educated theologian and became an ardent student of Scripture, meaning the Hebrew Scriptures and the new Christian writings in circulation. He was eager to share his own newfound insights. Alas, those insights struck the congregation in Rome as altogether bizarre, and before long came the inevitable break with the congregation. Ill feelings seem to have prevailed on both sides, and the congregation decided to return the donation that Marcion had earlier so generously given.

This is about all the evidence we have of the man. One source records that after his unsuccessful confrontation in Rome he founded a congregation that shared his views. He remained adamant in his understanding of the Hebrew Scriptures, and somewhere along the line a Marcionite church came into existence that lasted until the tenth century.

What exactly triggered Marcion's clash and the parting of the ways with the congregation in Rome? Like all reformers, Marcion did not want to be understood as the propagator of a new theology, but as a faithful Christian who called attention to the genuine and original message of Jesus. If nothing else, he deserves credit for having noted the tensions between the God of the Hebrew Scriptures and the God of Jesus as depicted in the Gospels. Marcion's theological concern can best be understood with the fundamental Christian question, from what exactly did Jesus redeem humankind? According to the Apostle Paul's argument in the Letter to the Galatians, Christ redeemed humankind from the curse of the Law. A similar assertion is made by Paul in his Letter to the

Romans, where he notes that "the law of the Spirit of life in Christ Jesus has set you free from the law of sin and of death" (8:2).

Evidently, the study of Paul, especially the Letter to the Galatians, deeply impressed Marcion and provided him with a set of dualisms that defined his theology—law and gospel, justice and love, the God of justice in the Hebrew Scriptures, and the God of love of the Christian writings. Marcion found that the new order of Jesus was based on love, in contrast to the teachings of the Hebrew Scriptures, which were based on justice. He concluded that Christians must reject the Hebrew Scriptures and the God of the Hebrew Scriptures, the creator God, and accept the other God, the God of Jesus, the God of love. Marcion acknowledged that the Demiurge God of the Old Testament did exist. However, he judged that god to be a lowly and ignorant god—weak, helpless, disobedient, virtually a mortal creature. This God created and chose a people, Israel, to whom he gave the Law, the land, and the promise of the Messiah. In a way, Marcion's notion could be called a milder version of what was advocated by the gnostics, who also held to a divine dualism, the existence of two "gods." A "good" God could not have created matter that was evil; accordingly, there must be more than one God.

In contrast, Marcion argued, the gospel of Jesus teaches the reality of another God: a God of love who had pity on humankind and its miserable condition under the Law. This God sent his Son, who appeared on earth, revealing the one true God and exhorting people everywhere to believe in him. When the creator God of the Hebrew Scriptures learned of the existence of the unknown God, he persecuted Jesus and had him die an ignominious death. The resurrection of Jesus vindicated the victory of the Christian God of love.

Marcion searched the biblical basis of the Christian faith and rejected the Hebrew Scriptures. He took the writings of Paul to be the key for understanding Jesus, but rejected the Letter to the Hebrews (which he presumed to have been written by Paul) as well. He also felt free to make changes—"corrections"—in the biblical manuscripts whenever the text failed to confirm his notions.

To buttress his case, he compiled a canon of what he considered the authentic apostolic writings—the first effort at compiling a "New" Testament, in other words—and it consisted of one Gospel, that of Luke, and ten writings of the Apostle Paul. Even in these writings, Marcion boldly edited out everything that smacked of Judaism and its God. His version of the Gospel of Luke, for example, began with verse 32 of the fourth chapter. This allowed him to ignore the accounts of Jesus' birth, his presentation in the Temple, his temptations in the wilderness— accounts that bolstered the notion of Jesus' divinity from his very birth.

In the broad context of Christian theological self-understanding, Marcion occupies an important place. He was a clarifier, the kind of theologian dissatisfied with the traditional answers to theological issues—who then ventures to provide a novel answer. The problem that Marcion sought to resolve has continued to agitate Christianity through the centuries: the distinction between the God described in the Hebrew Scriptures and the God described in the New Testament. Numerous explanations were offered; Marcion found the answer in the writings of the Apostle Paul, whose categorical repudiation of the Law was tantamount for Marcion to the repudiation of the God who had decreed that Law. More than any other theologian in Christian history, Marcion understood the radical gap between Paul and the Hebrew Scriptures. He failed to understand, however, how the apostle had succeeded in keeping the two together. The German historian Adolf von Harnack quipped that in the entire history of Christianity, only Marcion truly understood Paul, and he misunderstood him!

Arius

A century later the church was rattled by yet another major theological controversy, which primarily agitated the Eastern church. Again, a theologian stood at the center of the controversy, and no other theologian of Christianity, with the exception perhaps of Martin Luther and John Calvin, caused as much controversy, disagreement, emotion, and division as did Arius, the pastor of a large church in Alexandria. The time: the late third century. Arius was an eloquent preacher of impeccable learning and character. To be sure, his enemies (and he had many) called him vain, arrogant, opinionated, and proud; they not only noted his erroneous theological opinions but also shuddered at his flair for public relations as yet another indication of his theological shallowness. He put his theological notions into jingles and set them to simple tunes, which were sung, so the story goes, by dockworkers and schoolchildren. But that he was a brilliant theologian can hardly be doubted.

Arius was born around the year 260. After a distinguished church career and rather late in his life (he was by then in his sixties), he got hooked into a theological squabble. As is often the case in fierce controversies and disagreements, there was a personality factor: if it had not been for Arius's rigidity and unfailing self-confidence (traits which his chief antagonists in the squabble, Alexander and Athanasius, fully shared), the disagreement might well have reached a quick theological compromise. But Arius and Alexander, bishop of Alexandria, were much alike in personality and temperament. Neither was prepared to yield an inch; neither was willing to compromise. Both were convinced that the stakes were too high to do so. But Arius also had a deep mistrust of the church authorities who, he was convinced, were all too eager to negotiate compromises. And when it was all over, the controversy had created a division in the church that took centuries to heal, and Arius had become the most infamous heretic of all centuries.

What got Arius going was his conviction that God, the Father, and Jesus were not fully equal. For example, he noted that Jesus had acknowledged not knowing the time of the end of all things; only the Father knew. Also, according to the gospel, the boy Jesus grew in stature and wisdom. Arius put this understanding into the phrase that, whatever exalted statements one might make about Jesus' divinity, there must have been a time "when Jesus was not." Jesus was, in other words, a creature, a creation, of God. To declare this was, of course, to lessen Jesus' stature. At issue was thus the nature of Christ's divinity. All along, Christians had referred to God as "Father" and to Jesus as his "Son." Understandably, this raised the question of whether these terms, "father" and "son," had theological significance. If they were taken seriously, they meant a measure of subordination of the son to the father and the ultimate inequality of the two.

Arius affirmed this subordination and found it also, for example, in Jesus' interceding for sinners with his Father. If this was the case, Arius argued, Jesus was not God in the fullest sense of the word. The Son was the highest of all creatures, even divine, but still a creature. He was not fully God except in some approximate sense. The Son had a beginning, but the Father was without beginning—that was the battle cry of Arius and his followers. The persuasiveness of Arius's position lay in its logic.

In the ensuing controversy, two Greek words, *homoousios* and *homoiousios*, were employed to express the difference between Arius and his antagonist Athanasius, who fiercely advocated the full equality of Father and Son. Both *homoousios* and *homoiousios* were new words in the theological vocabulary, borrowed from the vocabulary of Greek philosophy. They certainly were not part of the traditional theological discourse. They were coined by theologians who sought to put the theological issue into crisp terms. The two words differed only in one single *i* and meant, respectively, "of identical substance" and "of like substance." Those who used the word *homoousios* to define the relationship between the Father and the Son emphasized the fact that Jesus, the Son, was divine in just the same way that the Father was divine. Those who employed *homoiousios* to define the relationship believed that, while Jesus was divine, his divinity was different from (and lesser than) the Father's. In the East, where the language of society and of theology was Greek, the two Greek words, neither of them actually found in the Bible, made sense. Edward Gibbon's famous *Decline and Fall of the Roman Empire* sneered that in the controversy Christians fought each other over a diphthong, a vowel mark over a single Greek letter. So it was, but the diphthong held profound theological meaning.

The West, the Latin Church, was by and large unaware of the raging controversy until it was virtually over. Ever since the fourth century, some have looked at the war of words, as Emperor Constantine had done, with incredulity, if not outright scorn. But the matter in dispute dealt with an important theological issue, namely, how to understand Jesus, and little by little the fundamental notions became obvious.

The argument over how Jesus related to the God whom he called Father did not stand alone. It had ties to another theological issue, namely, how humans are saved to eternal life. Jesus' death on the cross had been an atoning death, and Athanasius argued strenuously that only God himself could offer the sacrifice that would reconcile humans with him.

Arius's view of Jesus was modeled on the Synoptic Gospels of Matthew, Mark, and Luke and focused on the passages in which Jesus appears to make a distinction between himself and his heavenly Father. This view of Jesus minimized the Gospel of John and the writings of the Apostle Paul, with their exalted descriptions of Jesus, and completely ignored the Letter to the Hebrews. Arius used scriptural passages to support his position, though the ultimate strength of his views lay in their clarity, the simple notion of a difference between a "God the Father" and a "Son of God." Arius charged that his opponents held positions "unworthy of men of understanding." But those who opposed him centered their argument on a broader spectrum of texts of the New Testament, which, while suggesting the subordination of the Son to the Father, at the same time affirmed the fundamental unity of the two. Again and again, Arius sought to make his case, pointing to the passage in the Letter to the Colossians that Christ was "the firstborn of all creation" (1:15).

Athanasius, eventually Arius's formidable antagonist, was much younger and served as secretary to the bishop of Alexandria. He, too, was an individual of strong and unshakable convictions, and accordingly held his views with fervor and intensity. As far as he was concerned, those who disagreed with him were not simply mistaken; they were evil. Not surprisingly, he made few friends. Nonetheless, he became involved in the dispute with a considerable advantage: his views agreed with those of the bishop of Alexandria, who had been Arius's first antagonist.

When Arius sensed that the opposition to his views was widespread, he appealed to his friend, the bishop of Nicomedia, for support, raising the matter beyond a local disagreement. At this point, the long-standing rivalry between the bishoprics of Alexandria and Nicomedia came to the fore. Nicomedia was the political capital and Alexandria the intellectual capital of the Eastern Empire. Each was important in the church. Arius received support from Nicomedia, but that meant that the local Alexandrian controversy began to engage the entire Eastern church; more and more theologians wanted to be part of the action, convinced that they had something to say.

In the controversy, neither Scripture nor tradition appeared to be of much help. The Gospel of John, for example, seemed to support the Athanasian position, as it called Jesus the "Word," the *logos*, who was "in the beginning with God" (1:2) and was God. And while theologians had uniformly affirmed Jesus' divinity, they had not spoken with equal unanimity about the nature of that divinity. Tertullian, for example, had given the Son a beginning in time, while Origen declared Jesus to have been timeless. The disagreement between Arius and Athanasius became increasingly severe, to the point that their followers took to the streets of Alexandria in demonstration, even though it is unclear if they did so purely for theological reasons.

Enter Emperor Constantine. Soon after he licensed the Christian religion to contribute to the tranquility of the realm, this major theological disagreement among theologians and bishops posed a formidable threat to the cohesiveness and stability of the empire. Accordingly, in the second year of his rule, Constantine took it on himself to summon the bishops of the church to the town of Nicea, not too far from his imperial palace in Constantinople, to meet and to resolve the issue. Not all of the bishops of the church heeded the summons; allegedly some 318 attended, a somewhat mystical number of symbolic significance, for it equaled the number of servants the Bible assigned to Abraham. The emperor had astutely summoned only those of whose sentiment he was certain or who could be swayed in Athanasius's favor. Most bishops came from the eastern Mediterranean; less than a dozen came from the Western church. The bishop of Rome was not a player. And the emperor presided in person over the pivotal sessions.

At the opening of the council, Constantine addressed the assembled bishops and declared himself deeply shocked by the controversy—a timeless illustration of lay sentiment about the often esoteric doings of the theologians. In his own way, of course, the emperor was right, but he seems not to have appreciated that behind the controversial words—*homoousios* and *homoiousios*—stood fundamental theological disagreement.

At the outset, the bishops seemed evenly divided, but increasingly Constantine let it be known that he, for one, favored the Athanasian position. His chief advisor was a committed follower of Athanasius. Constantine wined and dined the bishops, many of whom had experienced (and survived) not too many years earlier the persecution under Emperor Diocletian. For them, it was miraculous to be taken seriously by the emperor of the realm. One of the bishops had lost an eye during the persecution: Constantine kissed the empty spot. Another bishop wondered if the Kingdom of God had come or whether he was dreaming. But not all bishops were delighted. Gregory of Nazianzus left the council in disgust and dismay, uttering the famous words "There has not been a single instance where bishops did any good in a council."

In the end, Arius and his views were condemned as heretical. A creed, named the Nicene Creed after the site of the council, expressed the position of Alexandria and Athanasius. However, the decision of Nicea was not the end of the story. Arius's views continued to influence the churches in the eastern Mediterranean. The Eastern church remained deeply divided. And in the Balkan Peninsula, Arianism became the version of the Christian religion of the ever more important Goths.

Of course, the controversy was more than a conflict between a priest and his bishop; rather, many bishops and many priests disagreed about what was understood to be a fundamental aspect of the Christian faith. Arius was the straw that broke the camel's back. Long-standing uncertainty and disagreement as to how to understand the deity of Jesus came to the fore and needed to be resolved.

Equaling the importance of the decision of the council fathers was the fact that the council had not been convened by church leaders but by the emperor. At the time, it seemed wondrous that the ruler of the empire would show such interest in the theological well-being of the church. Nonetheless, it was an ominous beginning of a long and fateful story. For some fifteen hundred years, political authorities attempted, sometimes successfully, sometimes unsuccessfully, to determine the decisions and the agenda of the church. To be sure, in some cases, emperors and kings were motivated by the best of spiritual intentions, but often a lust for power over the church appears to have been a motivating factor. Emperor Constantine, for one, was anything but a theologian; in fact, he formally was not even a member of the church.

Soon after the adjournment of the council, Constantine had to realize that the decision of Nicea had neither ended the controversy nor restored tranquility to the church. Since his main objective was harmony in the empire, he was willing to reopen the issue that Nicea had seemingly resolved. In 335, a council convened at Tyre, and this time an Arian majority carried the day. Arius was rehabilitated and Athanasius exiled. Thus, two diametrically opposed conciliar decisions stood side by side. The conflict remained unresolved.

The lingering uncertainty meant that the Athanasian position was by no means universally accepted, and Athanasius himself was sent into exile no less than five times. Later emperors proved not particularly helpful either. Constantius II favored Arianism; Julian, called "the apostate," was more concerned about the neutrality of the Roman state in matters of religion; Jovian cared little about the issue. Moreover, the Arians promptly divided into factions, of which one denied that Jesus was in any way "like" the Father, while the so-called "semi-Arians" argued that Jesus was of like substance with the Father. It was not until the end of the century that the Council of Constantinople reaffirmed the original Nicene decision and made Athanasius the orthodox theologian in both East and West.

Donatism

At the very time the Eastern church was beset by the Arian controversy, the Western church had an issue of its own: the challenge of the Donatist movement. It was triggered by the Diocletian persecutions, the most severe attempt to crush the church in what proved to be the last persecution. When Diocletian in 303 ordered Christian books confiscated to be burned, churches to be razed, and the bishops to be arrested, most leaders and the rank and file of the church steadfastly faced suppression and persecution. But some were unprepared to bear the brunt of persecution and abjured their belief, often surrendering voluntarily their Christian books to the Roman authorities.

The persecution triggered a theological controversy: how should the church treat those members who, under the threat of persecution, had renounced the faith or had "handed over" Christian books to the Roman authorities? Intriguingly, the Latin verb for "to hand over" (*tradere*) became the root word for the English word *traitor*. Was it sufficient for those "lapsed" Christians, as they were called, to repent of their renunciation of the faith in order to be restored to the fellowship of the church? Or was the renunciation of the faith one of the misdeeds and sins that could never be forgiven? These questions divided the Western church.

Understandably, the line in the sand was drawn between those who had abjured their belief and those who had remained faithful. And once the persecution had abated, the question facing the church was what to do with those "traitors" whose faith had been weak during the time of persecution but who now asked to be readmitted to the church. Some argued that the traitors were no longer members of the church; others were prepared to forgive and forget upon the evidence of genuine repentance. Both hard-liners and those who favored compromise agreed that these Christians had sinned; but was theirs the unpardonable sin, the sin against the Holy Spirit, which, so it was held by many, could not be forgiven? The answer seemed relatively easy with respect to laity: there was agreement that, after due penance, lapsed lay Christians could be restored to full membership in the church. The lapsed clergy, however, were taken to pose an altogether different problem: more was to be expected from the leaders of the church and eventually the sentiment carried the day that priests (and bishops) who had denied the faith during the persecution could never be restored to membership. A bishop, priest, or teacher who had so sinned could not be forgiven.

The lingering uncertainty broke out into the open in the year 311 when a certain Caecilius was consecrated bishop of Carthage. Uproar ensued. Many were unwilling to accept him as bishop because Felix, one of the bishops who consecrated him, was known to have turned over Christian writings to the governmental prosecutors. Things got even more complicated when it turned out that the evidence against Felix was untrustworthy and that some of those who objected to Caecilius's consecration had themselves been fickle during the persecution. Nonetheless, adamant opposition against church leaders who had been weak during the Diocletian persecution became the mark of the hard-line party named after Donatus, who was consecrated bishop of Carthage in 313. Donatus had not been prominently involved in the controversy at the outset, but quickly became the leader of the rigoristic party. The church in North Africa divided over the issue; in many places one church was Donatist, the other not. There were rival bishops.

More than theology was at stake in the controversy: Emperor Constantine showed himself a generous supporter of the construction of new churches, and the controversy in Carthage raised the question of whether Donatists or non-Donatists were to be the beneficiaries of his continued largesse. And there was a social dimension to the Donatist movement as well. The Christian faith in North Africa drew its members from diverse classes—Romans; Punics; Berbers. The prosperous landowners, the elite of North African society, had moved from Rome to North Africa. Their cultural background was Latin, and they enjoyed and displayed their newfound prosperity. They had little inclination for the kind of ethical rigor propounded by the Donatists. The Punics, the native underclass, served their landowning masters, and they turned out to be the most adamant Donatist hard-liners. They established their own congregations and consecrated their own bishops, as did the third social group in the church, the Berbers, who lived in the countryside, were culturally and ethnically distinct, and pointedly anti-Rome to boot. They had aligned themselves with the church during the persecution. In all three groups, religious conviction was mixed with political and social concerns.

Repeated efforts to resolve the "Donatist" controversy proved unsuccessful. Two churches existed alongside each other in North Africa, hardly distinguishable in liturgy, organization, and theology. The difference lay in the rigorist moral code demanded by the Donatists. Initially, the Donatists hoped (much against Donatus's own sentiment) that the resolution of the controversy (in their favor, of course) would come from the emperor, prompting Donatus to exclaim, "What does the emperor have to do with the church?" Constantine responded to the Donatist entreaties by convening a council, which decided in favor of the Caecilian faction. Understandably, that decision did not assuage the Donatists, and so a second council at Arles in southern France, in 314, reconsidered the issue and reaffirmed the decision of the earlier council. The preservation of church unity lay at the heart of the decisions of these councils. The theological mind behind the anti-Donatist position was

Cyprian (d. 258), who wrote a famous essay on the unity of the church. Cyprian argued that a bishop who had committed the sin of apostasy and had thus denied the faith during persecution, had placed himself outside the church. He could no longer administer the sacraments. However, a truly penitent bishop could be restored to the full functions of his office.

While the church at large favored a lenient view, the Donatists adamantly argued that the denial of the faith was the unpardonable sin. At that juncture, Augustine, who had closely followed the controversy from his vantage point in Hippo, weighed in with a distinction that became normative for the Western church. Sacraments do not receive their efficacy from the faith and life of those who administer them, he argued (that was not in fact the Donatist position). Rather, the efficacy of the sacraments derived from their proper administration. As long as, for example, the priest used water and the Trinitarian formula in baptism, the sacrament had been validly administered. The special status of the priest and the proper understanding of the sacraments combined to make the personal demeanor of the priest a secondary issue. Augustine's view proved to be normative for the Catholic Church.

The Donatists, in turn, were labeled heretics. Nonetheless, they continued to flourish. Provincial councils held in Carthage in 400 and 401 sought in varying ways to explore reconciliation, but no reconciliation occurred. A council in 404 concluded that pacification had proved to be impossible, leading the Catholic party to petition the emperor that the penalties against the heretics be restored. Even though now the whole power of the state was now used to suppress theological opinion, many Donatist congregations survived until, in 697, the Muslim Arabs swept across North Africa and conquered Carthage. While in other places of Muslim conquest Christian communities were more or less tolerated by the new lords, in North Africa the Muslim conquest heralded the end of Christianity. Donatism as a movement disappeared, as did the anti-Donatist church in North Africa so skillfully defended by Augustine. The banner of moral rigor, however, so characteristic of Donatist sentiment, persisted through the centuries.

THE MONASTIC IMPULSE

At the heart of Christian monasticism lies the Gospel story of the encounter of Jesus and a rich young ruler. The young man had expressed his desire to become a follower of Jesus, but when Jesus conveyed to him that in order to be perfect he had to sell all his possessions and give the proceeds to the poor, he went away, as the Scripture account has it, "sad; for he was very rich" (Luke 18:23). This Gospel story came to be understood to demonstrate that the path to Christian perfection meant the letting go of all worldly desires, values, and goods. It was a path for the committed few, but not mandatory for all.

Monasticism is thus the means to attain Christian perfection. The word *monasticism* itself has its roots in the Greek word *monos*, meaning "alone." The word denotes that an individual's decision to live a perfect Christian life entails living alone in a solitary life, unencumbered by the temptations of the world. Accordingly, the earliest Christian monks lived in solitude, for they were convinced that in isolation perfect union with God was possible. Jesus' exhortation to his followers not to conform to this world was understood as a mandate for radical separation from a spiritually distractive world. After all, the exhortation was, "Do not love the world or the things in the world" (1 John 2:15). Christians committed themselves to live in penance, simplicity, and abstinence; in short, in total disregard of the body, away from the distractions of human communities. The extraordinary commitment of these men and women evoked awe and amazement from other Christians, and before long monks became role models for ordinary Christians, who, for whatever reason, would not live in noble dedication as did monks and nuns.

While Christian monasticism evolved over time, its basic notion that spiritual perfection may be attained through a higher level of commitment was present early on. It received its dynamic energy from the tension of being called to flee from the world in pious renunciation on the one hand, and carrying out the mandate to Christianize the world on the other. The story of Christian monasticism is the story of both—of monastics disappearing into the Egyptian desert to live in utter isolation and of monastics who remained in their communities to care for the sick, the hungry, and the homeless or left these communities to take the message of Jesus to those who had never heard it.

From the beginning, monasticism was based on the premise that different Christians will manifest different levels of spiritual commitment. Some will be weaker, while others will be determined to pursue an ever-higher level of spiritual discipline. This distinction was expressed in the biblical notion that Jesus had given his followers both commands and counsels: while following the former was mandatory for all Christians, the latter would be followed only by a few. Origen, for example, insisted that whoever keeps the simple commandments of the Bible, follows the Golden Rule, is faithful to the church and the sacraments, and leads an upright life is a Christian. But Origen also claimed a higher path for himself and others, a more difficult rule, which entailed accepting the counsels of the Gospels and turning them into commandments. The counsels, as they were taken from the Sermon on the Mount or Jesus' exhortation to the young, rich ruler, mandated poverty, celibacy, and obedience. Later, as Christianity became an integral part of the larger society, a new dynamic enhanced the monastic appeal: the desire to be separate from the multitude of spiritually lukewarm Christians who flocked to the church in ever-greater numbers.

Monasticism called for the disavowal of the body and of society, the withdrawal from human contact, including family, friends, and even fellow believers, to "abscond" or "withdraw." The Greek word for "to withdraw" is *anachorein*, from which is derived the term *anchorites*, those in early Christianity who sought out inhospitable and forlorn places to live and to spend their days in prayer and meditation. The temperate climate in the regions of upper Egypt or Syria made it possible for the anchorites to forego contact with society at large and live completely engulfed by nature.

The monks removed themselves from human contact to live in total devotion and commitment to God. The renunciation of the body, expressed in numerous ways—fasting, silence, sexual abstinence, sleep deprivation—lay at the core of the monastic vision. The body was to be treated in such a way that it ceased being a hindrance to the communion with God. This renunciation of the body requires the acceptance of a division between creation and creator, body and spirit, the physical and the spiritual—and the renunciation of the former. Monasticism of all shapes and varieties—it is not an exclusively Christian phenomenon, for monks are important in other religions as well—is always dualistic at its core. The body and its needs are seen as a hindrance to true spirituality and the communion with the divine. The body and bodily needs are to be disciplined, subjugated, to allow the spiritual side of individuals to flourish. Abstinence from bodily needs in all forms, such as food or sex, is the hallmark of the monastic phenomenon.

Origins

By all accounts, the fourth-century call to the monastic life as a means living fully committed to God triggered one of the greatest social movements in Christian history. As decades and centuries passed, monastic communities sprang up wherever there were Christians, first in the Mediterranean region of Egypt, then in Palestine, Syria, and Asia Minor, and eventually in Greece and Italy. According to the glowing biography of Antony written by Athanasius, that pivotal figure of the Arian controversy, the origins of Christian monasticism were to be found in Lower Egypt toward the end of the third century, when Antony first separated himself from society and its seemingly corrupting influences to live a solitary yet perfect Christian life. There had been Christian ascetics before, so Athanasius's encomium of Antony's primacy is more an encomium than it is history, but Antony does deserve recognition for having been the first to take to the desert there to live the committed spiritual life.

Antony came from a well-to-do family in Egypt. After losing his parents at an early age, he came under the spell of Jesus' words about discipleship, particularly the story of the encounter between Jesus and the rich young ruler. According to Athanasius's biography, that story changed Antony's life. He gave away his parental estate, leaving a small part for the support of his sister and of the poor. He himself took to the desert, where he lived in solitary isolation, spending his days in manual labor and a disciplined life of prayer and meditation. Even if Athanasius's claim that Antony lived to be more than a hundred years old (he died in 356) is doubtful, his was indeed a long life and Antony exerted enormous influence on his contemporaries.

Athanasius's adulatory biography of Antony became a stellar public relations success. Antony was given the status of founder of Christian monasticism, and his special kind of spirituality was seen as normative for all who wished to take the message of Jesus seriously. "Even though they hide themselves and are desirous of withdrawing from the world," Athanasius wrote about monks, Jesus "makes them illustrious and well-known everywhere on account of their virtue and the help they render others." Antony was the exemplar of true sainthood.

Antony's commitment must be placed into the context of the church in the fourth century. The legal recognition of the church by the Roman Empire drastically influenced the development of the monastic ideal: the Christian religion had become increasingly popular, and eventually church membership encompassed everyone, since every individual in the empire was baptized in infancy and thereby became part of the church. This turn of affairs prompted some Christians to conclude that the church had become too worldly, that too many Christians were lukewarm in their belief and commitment, and that serious Christianity had to be lived in a special way, separate from the church at large. Christians had two choices: to live as lukewarm, nominal church members or to become monks or nuns and thereby aspire to a higher level of spiritual commitment. Intriguingly, many Christians responded to the latter challenge, and beginning in the fourth century Christian monasticism flourished. It was the golden age of the "Desert Fathers," monastics who lived apart from human communities, by themselves, sometimes with one or two others, in a hut or cave, supporting their minimal physical needs with small vegetable patches.

Some of the early monks in Egypt went to great lengths to live simply and in isolation. Anchorites, increasingly renowned for their perceived godliness and spirituality, sought to demonstrate their aloofness from the world and their abrogation of all physical needs by living on small platforms on top of columns several feet high. They became known as "pillar saints." While most of them have remained nameless, the heroics of some have stood the test of time. Simeon Stylites (390–459) lived in the Syrian desert and offered prayer and counsel. His advisories must have been found helpful, for his fame spread, crowds came to seek him out, and before long they disturbed his solitude and hampered his devotional life. Simeon found refuge on top of a pillar, at first nine feet high, eventually no less than fifty feet high, with a small platform on top and a crossbar to keep him from falling in his sleep. Disciples of his would ascend on a ladder from time to time to bring food and remove waste. There he lived for thirty years. Other monks exhibited different eccentricities, such as standing for the entire period of Lent or constantly bowing in reverence during meditation. One practitioner of the latter discipline quit counting the monk's bows after he had reached twelve hundred.

A second type of Christian monasticism emerged alongside these anchorite monks. Communities of men (and women) came into being, committed to the principle that living in a disciplined community was the most meaningful expression of spiritual commitment. In the course of the fourth century, monastics increasingly decided to live not in isolation but in community—and communal (or "cenobite") monasticism was born. Before long, it became the normative form of monastic life, aided by the excesses of anchorite monasticism. Its key feature was living, eating, working, worshiping, and praying together as a community; wearing the same attire; and following the same daily routine as the best way of enhancing the spiritual life. This understanding of the monastic ideal was decisively influenced by Pachomius (d. ca. 347), who showed himself an administrative genius and headed an Egyptian monastic community of more than a thousand monks. His vision of monasticism included the notion of a "rule," that would spell out in some detail the ordered daily life of the community.

Obviously, communal life required guidelines or rules for living together, lest the community lapse into confusion. Thus monastic "rules" were written, the first one drawn up in Cappadocia by Basil of Caesarea. His ideas provided the guidelines for Eastern monasticism through the centuries—an important consideration, since in the East monasticism came to be more closely integrated into the life of the larger church than was the case in the West, where monasteries and monastic orders were often removed from the life of the larger church. Basil energetically promoted the establishment of monasteries, wrote rules for monastic communities, and made them part of the larger church.

In the West, monks and monasteries tended to go their own way, apart from the hierarchical structures of the church, even though many monasteries were founded with the support of bishops and as far north as Ireland and Scotland. Augustine, himself a monk, placed great importance on the notion that monks (and nuns) be an integral part of the church. Tensions existed, not only because the monastic houses seemed to live apart from the hierarchical structures but also because the monastic ideal suggested the possibility of reaching spiritual perfection apart from the church, the priesthood, and the sacraments.

The story of early Christian monasticism cannot be told without reference to the importance of societal forces facilitating its growth. Many early monastic recruits came from impoverished families. For peasants, the monastic life offered, alongside spiritual growth, economic security and the possibility of education. For women, the same held true as well, perhaps even more strikingly so than for men. Monasticism was a high-minded spiritual renunciation of worldly wealth, but the *Lives of the Fathers*, a fairly reliable account of early monasticism, reveals that it was rare to see someone from the privileged class become a monastic. When, on one occasion, monks in a monastery were angered because one of these wealthy recruits was sleeping on a pillow, they were told that a pillow was a small concession to someone who had given up so much to become a monk, while other monks had given up nothing.

Christian Monasticism in the Middle Ages and Beyond

In the Western church, monastic houses were supported and nurtured by local bishops, who were pleased to have communities of men and women in their midst committed to living serious religious lives. In Italy, where more and more religious houses were established, the early sixth century brought the formulation of two monastic rules that exerted lasting influence on Western monasticism. In Rome, it was the "rule of the master," the *regula magistri*, which derived its name from its question-answer format, while to the south of Rome, in the monastery of Monte Cassino, Benedict of Nursia (ca. 480–545) wrote his enormously influential guidelines for the monastic life that was to become known by his name, the Rule of Benedict.

Benedict is the eminent figure of monasticism in the Western church. He was puzzled as well as aggrieved that no meaningful practical guidelines or rules existed for the daily round of the monks. In 529, he began to have the opportunity to put his ideas into practice. In the mountainous wooded region some eighty miles south of Rome on the site of a former pagan temple dedicated to Apollo, Benedict founded a monastery. A millennium and a half later, the monastery still exists: Monte Cassino has the distinction of being the oldest active monastic community in Europe, even though all its buildings were destroyed in World War II and had to be rebuilt.

Benedict drew up a "rule" for the Monte Cassino community, and this rule became the paradigm of the rules of most other monastic orders. Its brevity made it practical and workable, especially since it was flexible in its physical demands. It is full of spiritual insight as well as practical wisdom. Its genius is its down-to-earthiness and its moderate tone; it was not designed for religious fanatics. One observer remarked about it that "a lamb can bathe in it without drowning, while an elephant can swim in it;" in other words, its hallmark was flexibility. The rule acknowledged the diversity of monastic life and the multiplicity of practical issues and chores in a community. Its seventy-three brief chapters are filled with biblical references as well as practical guidelines, such as the daily ration of wine and strictures about excessive laughing.

Benedict was blessed with uncanny administrative insights, and his rule sought to combine practical instruction with spiritual guidance. By the early ninth century, it became the mandatory template for the rules of all monastic communities. Underlying its success was the conviction that external regimentation can be a vehicle for spiritual growth.

A monastery, as Benedict envisioned it, had to be self-contained and self-supporting. It was to be ruled by an abbot (an abbess in women's communities), elected by the monks of the monastery. The daily round prescribed periods of work, eating, and sleeping. They were filled with diverse responsibilities and assignments calculated to make the community run smoothly, harmoniously, and self-sufficiently. Understandably, that involved menial kitchen and household duties. The rule prescribed silence at meals, with one monk delegated to read aloud to the assembled community from a devotional book. The religious day was structured around the seven canonical hours, beginning with Lauds at daybreak and followed by the services of Prime, Terce, Sext, None, Vespers, and the concluding office of Compline. An eighth office, the Vigil, was celebrated at night. The time spent in prayer reflected not only a belief in the efficacy of prayer but also a concern for society at large: monks and nuns were exhorted to pray for the community.

Initially, monasteries were lay communities. Benedict himself was a layman, as were all of the early abbots. The need for a priest to celebrate Mass for the community led to the ordination of monks to serve their monastery in this way. Later, in the ninth century, monks began to view ordination as the pinnacle of the committed Christian life. Lay communities became priestly communities, which meant that the nature of the common life changed, especially when priests began to celebrate private Masses (Masses celebrated because of bequests and legacies). This drove a wedge into the community, since there were now two classes of monks, those ordained and those not.

The increasing prominence of ordained priests as members of monastic communities marks the major difference between male and female monasticism. While initially the monastic impulse was a male phenomenon, soon the monastic ideal was understood to apply to women no less than it did to men. Female monastic communities came into being, initially as female parallels to male orders but later as independent female orders. In their function and role in their communities the female monastic orders did not differ much from their male counterparts—except that nuns could not publicly preach and, of course, could not celebrate Mass; outside priests were needed to hear confession and celebrate Mass.

In the centuries after its emergence, monasticism in the Western church, both male and female, flourished and served the dynamic arm of the church. It is no overstatement to say that the "Christianization" of Europe resulted from the labors and commitment of countless monks who endured hardships and at times oppression to carry the Christian message to new places and regions in central and northern Europe. Once this mission of evangelism had been concluded, the monastic communities became important features not only of the church but also of society. Monks and nuns cared selflessly for the poor and destitute, fed orphans and widows, healed the sick, and comforted the aged. Monasteries took on cultural functions. Monks copied ancient manuscripts, invented reading glasses, brewed beer, and distilled liqueurs—"Benedictine" and "Chartreuse" are produced and enjoyed (by some) to this day. In the process, monastic orders and monasteries became wealthy as the centuries passed, especially by steadily increasing, through pious bequests, their ownership of land, the most valued possession of medieval society. In the early sixteenth century, monasteries were the largest landowners in England and Sweden.

The mandate of Christian monasticism was expressed in the Latin phrase "ora et labora," pray and work, an imperative applied to all monastic communities. Once monasticism had matured, each order was identifiable by its distinctive monastic habit, as well as by its distinctive spiritual and societal emphasis. Some orders focused on teaching, others on evangelism, yet others on education. Some orders focused on the care of the sick in hospitals, while others emphasized caring for the marginalized in society, the widows and orphans. Monks and nuns demonstrated great diversity in the way they exercised their societal engagements and in the way they understood religious commitment. In the Western church, both contemplative and activist monastic orders have formed the face of monasticism, while in the Eastern church the contemplative approach, embedded in a stunningly rich liturgical life, has carried the day.

There are a few monastic communities in both the Lutheran and Anglican traditions, but monasticism is foremost an Orthodox and Roman Catholic phenomenon. Particularly in the Roman Catholic Church, a multiplicity of monastic orders was founded over the centuries, each with a distinctive style of piety and mission. Different orders emphasize different notions of spirituality and of "being in the world." These orders are identified by their official Latin names, though that is not always the way they are popularly known. Franciscans, for example, are actually the "Order of Friars Minor" (*Ordo Fratrum Minorum*), while the Dominicans are the "Order of Preachers" (*Ordo Praedicatorum*) and the Jesuits are the "Society of Jesus" (*Societas Jesu*). These and the other monastic communities are called "orders" because, with the notable exception of the Jesuits, they follow a rule ("order") that structures their daily rounds and must be followed by the members.

All monastic orders have in common the notion of a probationary period during which those who aspire to join a monastic community (called "postulants" or "novices") are given the opportunity to discern whether they are prepared to take on the monastic commitment, in early years with the Benedictine vows of stability, "conversatio" (fidelity to monastic life), and obedience, later with vows of celibacy, poverty, and obedience (to the monastic superior, the abbot or abbess of the monastery or convent). In general, postulants are eligible to be admitted to an order, though there are exceptions. The seventeenth-century Saint Joseph of Cupertino, for example, was refused acceptance by several monastic orders because of his academic "ignorance." His determination, all the same, eventually made him succeed, and he did become a monk. Not surprisingly, Joseph is the patron saint of students taking exams.

The head of the monastic community is the abbot, who administers the affairs of the monastery and supervises its members. This office was crucial, as the abbot administered the abbey's lands, estates, and business affairs, and also had to deal with litigation pertaining to the monastery. The abbot was the spiritual "head" of the community, the shepherd leading the flock.

Catholic monasticism was rich and varied, a vibrant tapestry of spiritual emphases and practical options. It gave men and women the avenue to live committed lives in the setting of a community of like-minded individuals. It played an important role in the establishment and maintenance of medieval Christendom. At the same time, the powerful sway of the monastic world also held the seed for problems—of wealth, of form over substance, of neglect of spirituality. That the Protestant reformers of the sixteenth century were able to level ridicule and polemic against the monastic life suggests that by that time, at any rate, dramatic changes had occurred.

Reflection 2: Church and Society in the Shadow of Constantine

In a strange way, October 28, 312, may well have been the most significant date, and Emperor Constantine the most significant individual, in all of Christian history. On that day Constantine defeated his rival Maxentius with the help of the Christ monogram *chi-rho* painted on the shields of his soldiers. Constantine's Edict of Milan of the following year ended the suppression of the Christian religion in the Roman Empire. But Constantine did more than allow Christians to worship publicly. By giving the Christian church an unending series of privileges, he initiated a model of church-state relationship that lasted in Europe until the twentieth century and brought about an impressive flourishing of the Christian faith. Church and state were linked in an intimate bond, making it often impossible to say where the principles, the authority—and the power—of the one ended and those of the other began. For more than a millennium and a half every individual born in Europe was baptized into the church. Birth was followed by baptism as certainly as night followed day, and no religious alternative was publicly allowed. For Christians, this new public status of their religion necessitated a readjustment of certain beliefs, in particular of those that pertained to the Christian understanding of the social and political order. Until Constantine, the Christian understanding had been one of separation. As the "state religion," however, the Christian religion was called upon to assume responsibility for the public order. A new understanding of the relationship to state and society developed, as protector, guide, and at times as master.

This was the "Constantinian Revolution," the turn of the Christian religion from a persecuted movement to the official religion of the realm. The church began to have a hand in the laws and statutes promulgated by society; church principles, such as the declaration of Sunday as the day of rest, became matters of law. Theological dissent, labeled heresy, became a public crime, and churchly indifference a manifestation of civic disloyalty. To be sure, as time passed there were chronic conflicts of primacy between church and state, even as there were voices, such as those of the sixteenth-century Anabaptists, who discovered in Scripture a categorical tension between the ways of the world and the ways of Jesus. Nonetheless, the notion of a society unified by religion ruled supreme until the coming of modernity.

More than that. Until the eighteenth century and the French Revolution, the political authorities exercised real authority in ecclesiastical affairs, sometimes formidable, sometimes mild. In turn, the church sometimes acquiesced and sometimes put up fierce resistance. The Middle Ages turned into a veritable battlefield of competing claims of authority, and by the time the Protestant Reformation came around, the political authorities made sure that their voices counted. King Henry VIII dramatically demonstrated that in England, and even small German principalities followed suit. Thus, the 1654 church order for Liegnitz, now Legnica, stipulated on what holidays sermons should be preached, ordered the substitution of catechetical instruction for sermons during the winter months, ordered cursing, blaspheming, and violating the Sabbath to be punished by putting the perpetrators into the stocks, and penalized agricultural and domestic work on Sundays with a monetary fine. Explicitly theological matters were excluded from rulers' interference.

Something else was to characterize the church and society through the centuries. Christians and their churches showed themselves not any more tolerant of other beliefs than the Roman state had been of the Christians. The memory of the Roman government enforcing religious uniformity by force must have remained vividly on the Christians' minds, not as repulsive memory, however, but as a policy to be emulated. When Christians gained the upper hand in society, they were intolerant, unwilling to offer to pagans and Jews the kind of free exercise of their religion that oppressed and persecuted Christians had demanded for themselves.

The term used to justify the enforcement of religious conformity was "blasphemy." Picking up Old Testament notions, the church declared that all non-Christian belief was blasphemy, which meant that alternate religious views disrupted order in society, in addition to leading souls to hell. To be sure, the authorities, both religious and secular, jealously watched uniformity of belief, yet the fear of theological dissent was always accompanied by fear of political disorder, which may well have been paramount time and again.

Not surprisingly, in their effort to assure religious uniformity Christians first turned their attention to the Jews in their midst. The Second Jewish-Roman War (132–35) brought the dispersal of the Jewish people, made them homeless, and settled them elsewhere in Roman lands. Until the succession of Emperor Constantine, Jewish-Christian relations were marked by fierce mutual incriminations and charges, but no sooner had Christianity become the sole authorized public religion in the Roman

Empire than the fateful history of Christian hostility toward Jews began. The initial theological tensions between the two religions turned into a policy of confrontation and legal discrimination that increasingly imposed restrictions on Jewish life and activities.

Strikingly, neither theologians nor church dignitaries raised their voices in protest of such oppression and persecution. Amnesia befell a church that no longer remembered the fate Christians had endured for almost two centuries. Christians probably did not act out of angered revenge, but took seriously the stipulations in the Hebrew Scriptures about blasphemy. Christians fondly uttered triumphalist notions, how Jesus had been the fulfillment of God's eternal purposes, where "at the name of Jesus / every knee should bend... / and every tongue should confess / that Jesus Christ is Lord" (Philippians 2:10-11). The church's intolerant triumphalism was thus based on a sense of fidelity to Scripture, though it also intertwined with society's fear of dissent.

The Protestant Reformation did little to change the intimate relationship between church and state. If anything, it would not have been successful (King Henry VIII of England serves as splendid illustration) without the tangible support of governments. Only the ideals of the European Enlightenment began to effect change, and both the American and the French revolutions began the first steps toward what in modern language we have come to call the "separation of church and state." However, not until the end of the twentieth century did the tradition of automatic church membership in Europe begin to change.

CHAPTER TWO

THE MEDIEVAL CHURCH IN THE WEST

Ironically, the decline and fall of the Roman Empire in the fifth century took place during a period of increasingly vigorous Christian expansion. As Rome broke apart and new ruling dynasties emerged in Europe, the Christian religion became ever stronger and more resilient, while itself undergoing at the same time a dramatic metamorphosis. The church enjoyed various privileges in society and entered into an intimate relationship with the political elites. Emperor Constantine had set a precedent with his vigorous personal engagement in church affairs, all the way from presiding over the sessions of the Council of Nicea to providing funds for the construction of churches. In the centuries following, emperors and kings took a leaf out of Constantine's book and declared themselves guardians of the faith—with attendant claims of both authority and power in the church. Their claims carried weight, because, after all, the political powers had made possible the missionary advance into central and northern Europe by providing support and military pressure; it was natural for them to reason that they were entitled to be involved in church affairs.

The geographic center of the Christian faith changed as well in the early Middle Ages, as it moved from the eastern Mediterranean to points north. This change was triggered by the success in spreading the gospel; Germanic peoples turned to the Christian faith throughout Europe. Monks took the Christian message to those called "Barbarians" and brought about mass conversions of entire tribes, sometimes by brutal force, however, rather than by religious persuasion.

But Christianity's northward shift grew out not only from the successful conversion of the Germanic tribes, such as the Saxons, the Celts, and the Norse, but also from the rise of Islam, the powerful new religion that, much like the Christian religion, linked itself to political interests. Driven by an expansionist momentum in which politics and religion intertwined, Muslim forces little by little took control of Palestine, Egypt, Asia Minor, and the North African coastline. Even though the new Muslim rulers showed amazing, if fickle, toleration, ancient and important Christian centers, such as Antioch, Alexandria, and Carthage disappeared, as did the church in most of Spain and the southeast Balkans—previously all sites of dynamic and vital Christian communities. The pivotal place of the church in those places was gone. These political developments also meant that the Christian communities in Ethiopia and India, already distant by geography and theology, became even more distant. The cultural (and theological) diversity of Christianity, as it existed from Rome to India, gave way to an increasing centering in Europe.

Geography thus marked an incisive difference between the Christian religion of Late Antiquity and that of the Middle Ages. In antiquity, the Christian centers were nestled around the eastern Mediterranean and beyond, while by the early Middle Ages they were located in areas that later became France, Germany, and England. Had it not been for the conversion of the Germanic peoples, the Christian religion would have been confined to Italy and the remaining parts of the eastern Byzantine Empire.

Theologically, by the middle of the fifth century and the time of the Council of Chalcedon the basic creedal affirmations of the church were in place. To be sure, the determination of Chalcedon concerning the two natures of Christ was not shared by all, especially not by the Monophysite faction, and so the issue remained unresolved in the church at large and the theological skirmishes continued. Eventually Chalcedon did win out, not the least because Monophysite regions came under Muslim control and ceased to participate in the theological discussion. It took time to resolve the theological battle, for Emperor Zeno (425–91) wrote a "letter" that completely ignored the decisions made at Chalcedon and declared that the acceptance of Nicea was all that was necessary to be a good Christian, a notion bitterly opposed in turn by Pope Leo I. Once the issue of Jesus' humanity was settled, however, neither the Latin nor the Byzantine churches faced major internal "heretical" challenges that threatened fierce controversy and schism. The triumphant energies of the church were devoted to expansion against the backdrop of the steady disintegration of the Roman Empire and the waves of invasions by the Vandals, Visigoths, Goths, and Lombards.

Much has been written about the "decline and fall of the Roman Empire," before and after the Englishman Edward Gibbon put his thoughts on paper and wrote his monumental if biased account. The disappearance of the once-powerful empire has fascinated as well as puzzled historians. The causes of the fall were complex, though eventually the inability to match its imperial aspirations with its fiscal resources proved to be a major factor. At the time some related this decline and fall also to the new role of the Christian religion, and ever since, prophets of doom have seen in their own days and times the unfolding of the same forces that led to the demise of Rome.

Importantly, the church offered an explanation for the catastrophic turn of Roman society. Early in the fifth century, in the face of the fall of Rome to the Gothic invaders, Augustine argued in his monumental treatise on the meaning of history, the *City of God*, that the empire of the "world" had not disappeared. According to the book of Daniel, it will last until the coming of the Antichrist. For the time being, the church had taken the place of the City of God so that the Kingdom of God could make its appearance on earth. This view of the meaning of history highlighted the importance of the church as an earthly institution. The message of the church was about the tentativeness of all earthly pursuits; it found ever-greater numbers of listeners.

No matter how the disappearance of the Roman Empire was interpreted, clearly a new era had begun. Later, in the fourteenth century, Italian Renaissance Humanists coined the term *medium aevum* ("middle age") to encompass the time between the end of antiquity and the present. The term was a slap in the face of the Christian understanding, designating as "middle" the epoch in which the church (almost) ruled supreme. Two centuries later, the *philosophes* of the Enlightenment appropriated the term, now even more pointedly separating human and salvation history. The term was meant as more than a historical label: it expressed the judgment that not much worthy of note had taken place in the years between 500 and 1500.

And to add insult to injury, a second, even more pejorative term was used, "Dark Ages," to designate roughly the first half of the medieval millennium. In part, this unenthusiastic assessment stemmed from a pointed dislike of the hegemonic Christian presence during that period, a time of ubiquitous Christian splendor, when churches and cathedrals and monasteries, some magnificent, some modest, rose all over Europe, symbolically expressing the triumphant Christian worldview, with priests ubiquitously performing the rites of the church, and monks and nuns serving as living symbols of Christian spirituality, while also caring for the needy, the sick, and the orphans, and providing education to the young.

The Middle Ages were the remarkable undertaking to translate the message of Jesus into mature reality, even though at the time, and since, there were critical voices about the possibility of such harmonization. Christianity and society intertwined in a myriad of ways, as year after year the Christian faith and the political powers vied with one another for control and the imposition of its will on society. Both claimed to be committed to the enhancement of the spiritual and material well-being of the people.

Even the incessant power struggle between popes and emperors for control symbolized the prominence of the church, which was an all-encompassing presence in society and often blurred the line between religion and politics. The ventures of the crusades to reconquer the Holy Land illustrate the intermingling of committed spirituality and political power.

Chronologically, the "Middle Ages" began roughly in 476, when the last Roman emperor was removed from office. A new era was dawning, and the church began to be caught up in the complex and vacillating political fortunes of Europe. The Visigoth and Ostrogoth invaders were militarily superior to the Roman Empire, but they respected (and even were awed by) Roman culture and religion, so that the political turbulence of the time had few repercussions for the Christian religion. Moreover, for the Goths, Christianity was not a new religion, since Byzantine missionary efforts in the Balkan Peninsula had brought conversions to Christianity, much of it Arian in orientation.

During this era of invasion, decay, and disintegration of political institutions, the church proved to be a fairly stable and important institution. More and more people became Christians, and more and more men opted for the priesthood. Bishops exercised spiritual and political influence; the bishops of Rome claimed a special primacy in the entire church, which was ever more widely, if grudgingly, accepted. The church became prosperous. It received bequests from the high and the lowly, and the acquired wealth meant power as well as the ability to engage ever more in works of Christian mercy.

The high esteem of the church helps explain the conversion of the French king Clovis (466–511) to the Catholic faith. At the time, Clovis was the most powerful monarch in Europe, having expanded his rule over all of the old Roman province of Gaul (roughly modern France). According to legend, when Clovis began to worship the God of his wife, Clotilda, who had abandoned her Arian beliefs in favor of orthodoxy, he scored a decisive military victory over the Germanic tribes. The queen had persistently urged him to acknowledge the only true God (the God of the Catholic Church) and to forsake all idols.

> The God who should be worshiped is he who by his word created from nothingness the heavens and the earth, the sea and all that in them is; he who made the sun to shine and adorned the sky with stars; who filled the waters with creeping things, the land with animals, the air with winged creatures; by whose bounty the earth is glad with crops, the trees with fruit, the vines with grapes; by whose hand the human race was created; whose bounty has ordained that all things should give homage and service to man, whom he created. (Gregory of Tours, *History of the Franks*, chaps. 30–31)

Clovis became a champion of orthodox Catholic Christianity against Arianism. In turn, the church vigorously supported his military exploits. His own conversion laid the foundation for the expansion of the faith northeastward to the Germanic tribes, pursued with his support and power.

The first missionary successes, though, were scored in Ireland and England. In Ireland, Christianity had found a home as early as the fourth century, and when Irish missionaries subsequently took the gospel to England, they brought with them the Irish version, which was much influenced by the monastic ideal. Patrick (ca. 389–461), an English monk whose Celtic name was Naomh Pádraig, played the decisive role in bringing Christianity to Ireland. Little is known about him (and much of what is ascribed to him in folklore appears to be about another cleric by the name of Palladius). Nonetheless, Patrick's story made him the patron saint of Ireland and one of the best-known Catholic saints. Other than his remarkable religious accomplishments, there was not much that was striking about him, but his feast day, March 17, has allowed Catholics everywhere, but especially in Ireland, to combine religious devotion and worldly frolic, an intriguing combination given that the day always falls into the somber season of Lent, when the faithful are exhorted to engage in penitential acts. The Catholic Church, knowing what it was up against, centuries ago waived the prohibition against eating meat on Patrick's feast day.

As a youth, Patrick had been sent to Ireland as an indentured slave. While tending sheep one day, an apparition instructed him to return to England—a rather precarious and even dangerous assignment given his enslavement in Ireland, not to mention the hazards of a two-hundred-mile journey to be made on foot. After a few years in England, a second apparition informed him that "the unbaptized babies of Ireland . . . plead with him to tell them about Jesus." The apparition changed his life:

> I saw a man coming, as it were from Ireland. His name was Victorius, and he carried many letters, and he gave me one of them. I read the heading: "The Voice of the Irish." As I began the letter, I imagined in that moment that I heard the voice of those very people who were near the wood of Foclut, which is beside the western sea—and they cried out, as with one voice: "We appeal to you, holy servant boy, to come and walk among us." (Saint Patrick, *Confession*, 37).

Aware that he lacked the learning necessary to respond to the challenge of this plea, Patrick went to a monastery that offered him a place to study. He was ordained to the priesthood and, later, Pope Celestine I sent him to evangelize Ireland and England. Patrick accepted the assignment and was stunningly successful. When he died, converts by the thousands, churches by the hundreds, were found all over Ireland. His resting place was Saul, where many years earlier he had built the first church.

Roughly a century later it was not a humble monk but an august pope who left his mark on the church. Pope Gregory I (r. 590–604) is called "the Great," for his contributions to the church were many and profound. Born of wealthy parents, Gregory used his inheritance to establish no less than seven monasteries in Sicily and to convert his parental home in Rome into a monastery. When he was to be elected pope, he fled Rome in haste, not wanting to accept the office; he eventually agreed and returned. Gregory was also the first monk to occupy the Throne of Saint Peter, an indication of the growing importance of the monastic orders in the Roman church.

The fourteen years of Gregory's pontificate were a time of remarkable papal activity and achievement. Though plagued by a variety of physical ailments, Gregory was a bundle of energy. He adroitly managed the extensive landholdings of the church in Rome, Italy, and North Africa.

He reiterated the Roman bishops' claims for primacy in the church and exercised political and religious leadership in Italy, despite theological troubles in northern Italy and the irritating claim of Patriarch John of Constantinople to be an ecumenical patriarch.

Gregory addressed issues of liturgy and church music—so much so, as a matter of fact, that the new type of liturgical music he introduced is known as "Gregorian chant." His empathy for the monastic ideal led him to give greater autonomy to monasteries and convents from their bishops, a policy that, no matter how important at the time, proved to be counterproductive in the long run, because exact supervision of monasteries often got lost in the shuffle.

To top it all, Gregory was a humble individual, who wanted to be known as "servant of the servants of God." An impressive theologian, he was influenced by Augustine, and he was more of a popularizer than a seminal mind. No matter. His reflections on purgatory, for example, influenced the thinking of the church for centuries to come. And it was Gregory who fashioned a compromise between the extreme theological positions of Augustine and Pelagius, the one radically emphasizing human dependence on divine grace, the other stressing the human ability to do good. The compromise became known as "Semi-Augustinianism" and declared that grace and human will need to cooperate in the process of salvation; it formed the matrix of the acceptance of Augustine in the medieval church.

Gregory had set a high standard for the holders of the papal office, but, alas, not all of his successors rose to the challenge. Between the late ninth and the mid-eleventh centuries, the papacy became caught up in the power struggles of powerful Italian families. At issue was the role of the papacy as a political entity in Italy—it ruled the so-called Papal States, which encompassed most of central Italy—and this responsibility meant a preoccupation with Italian political issues and a concomitant if understandable neglect of spiritual concerns. The popes during this time, beginning with Pope John VIII, were a sorry lot. One of them, Pope Stephen VI (r. 896–97), performed the weird feat of exhuming the body of his predecessor, Pope Formosus, in order to put the dead man on trial. Stephen had the body clad in the full papal regalia, and shouted the indictments at him, then removed the papal insignia, and cut off the two fingers with which Formosus had blessed the faithful. The corpse was thrown into the Tiber River, only to resurface promptly and be said to perform miracles.

Such strange turns notwithstanding, the church continued to consolidate its self-understanding, theologically as well as organizationally. Thus, the church was prepared for the great showdown in the Middle Ages: the confrontation between pope and emperor, between political and ecclesiastical authority.

THE HEAVENLY AND THE EARTHLY KINGDOM: CHURCH AND STATE

The increasing weakness of the papacy in the tenth century (in the ten years between 893 and 903 there were no less than seven popes) created a vacuum that was eagerly filled by the political powers. Commanding and ambitious monarchs sought to assume the crucial role in church affairs and, in fact, claimed authority over the church and its bishops. Otto I, "the Great" (r. 936–73), the first emperor of the Holy Roman Empire, declared that the church must be under the king's jurisdiction. Practically, this meant a two-way street: the church and its leaders received all sorts of privileges from the monarchs, or had traditional privileges affirmed, for example, exemption of the church from royal taxation. In the process, however, the church lost a great deal of autonomy and freedom, signaled by the monarchs' claim to possess the authority to name bishops—loyal to them, of course—and even to preside over their installation. This practice was known as "investiture," the royal privilege to "invest" the bishop with the emblems of the episcopal office.

Otto personified the intriguing relationship between church and state. Crowned emperor by the pope in 962, he nonetheless insisted that popes swear an oath of loyalty to the emperor before they could be installed in office. Otto's successor, Henry III, deposed three competing popes in 1046, when their feuds had made a spectacle of the papal office. Pope Leo IX (1049–54) set himself to the task of reforming the structures of the church, which he saw as pivotal for reforming its spiritual life. He changed the process of papal elections, putting them in the hands of the College of Cardinals, thereby curtailing the influence of the emperors (and the Roman populace), who had previously played a major role in the papal elections.

In 1073, Leo's banner of reform was taken up by Hildebrand, a monk and abbot who upon his election as pope assumed the name of Gregory VII. He was a seasoned churchman and no less than five popes had benefited from his advisories. His election gave him the opportunity to exert his influence directly and mold the church into the form he was persuaded it should be. He turned out to be, in the words of a contemporary, a "holy Satan." Controversial already in his own time, Gregory has continued to be so to this day. Deep humility and otherworldly resignation characterized him, as did harshness and an autocratic temper.

Gregory understood the need for church reform, and he was determined to accomplish it. He was horrified that there were married priests, and he took stern measures to enforce clerical celibacy. He was dismayed that important offices of the church could be bought, and he set out to end that practice. He despaired over the influence of the political authorities in church affairs, and he was determined to end that as well.

The opportunity to deal with powerful political influences in the church presented itself quickly enough. Two years after his election as pope, Gregory threw down the gauntlet to clear the air: any ruler who claimed the authority to appoint or invest bishops or abbots would be excommunicated. Gregory made the point in a rather radical document titled *Dictatus Papae* ("Notes of the Pope"), which consisted of some twenty-seven assertions about the place of church and pope in society. The document, Gregory's personal notes and jottings, possessed no legal standing, though it revealed the pope's thinking: it argued not only that church and pope could never err but also that the popes had the authority to depose political rulers, that the pope alone had the right to use the imperial insignia, and that the pope had the authority to absolve people from allegiance to wicked and sinful rulers. The grand conclusion of the document was that "the Roman church has never erred nor ever shall to all eternity."

That was heavy medicine, even though most of Gregory's assertions had been propounded by previous popes in one way or another without too much adverse fallout. Now the assertions caused a major conflict, for within a year, Gregory had the opportunity to decide if action was going to follow his words. In accord with established practice (which Gregory found so despicable), the German King Henry IV had named a new archbishop of Milan, then part of Henry's domain. Gregory protested the king's move and quickly demonstrated that he meant business. He threatened to excommunicate the king and his supporters if the king did not desist, Henry rallied to a counterattack, insisting that Gregory had overstepped the bounds of his office, was no longer the legitimate incumbent on the Throne of Saint Peter; he was nothing other than "Hildebrand, a false monk." He was told to resign from the papal office.

The opposite happened. Gregory responded by excommunicating Henry and relieving his subjects (including the nobility, who had not been altogether pleased with their arrogantly powerful ruler) of their obligation of loyalty to him. The move had the intended effect. Henry's political support from the nobility slipped, and the king eventually was forced to conclude that he had no choice but to yield to the pope. In the worst winter in decades, Henry and a small entourage made their way southward across the Alps to Italy, to a castle near Canossa, south of Reggio, where Gregory was staying on his way to Germany to crown a new king. Henry was traveling to plead directly for the pope's forgiveness, receive his pardon, and have his excommunication lifted. According to tradition, the king stood barefoot in the snow outside the castle gate, a humble penitent begging for the pope's mercy. Gregory took three days to relent, finally granting an audience in which the proud king had to throw himself at the pope's feet. Only then did Gregory lift the excommunication. The pope and church had won. That was not the end of the story, however, for before long Henry regained his political equilibrium and muscle, occupied Rome, sent Gregory into exile, and installed a new pope, Clement III, who crowned him emperor.

Despite Henry's success, the image of a humiliated king seeking the pope's mercy in the cold of winter has reverberated through the centuries. When, for example, late in the nineteenth century the German chancellor Otto von Bismarck found himself in a fierce struggle with the Catholic Church, he uttered the sentence, "I will never go to Canossa!" to denote that he would never surrender to the Catholic Church. Before long, however, Bismarck had to realize that, much like Henry, he, too, had to yield and that conciliation with the papacy was the most prudent course of action.

A similar conflict between church and state broke out in England a century later. The Norman kings—such as William the Conqueror—had long insisted on controlling the church, often driven by a concern for church reform and the improvement of spirituality among the people. In turn, the leaders of the English church had jealously guarded their independence, and at times they seemed to make headway, as during the reign of King Stephen, a rather weak monarch. The succession of King Henry II in 1154 put a monarch on the English throne who was determined to gain control over the church. He assumed (mistakenly, as it turned out) that he would be aided in his efforts by having his friend, Thomas à Becket, appointed as archbishop of Canterbury, the highest ecclesiastical position in England. The king conveniently overlooked that Becket had no qualifications whatsoever for the august office (Becket did not even have priestly orders) other than being his crony. Henry's push prompted Becket's ecclesiastical career to experience a meteoric rise: he rose from layperson to archbishop in the span of two days, during which time he was ordained, consecrated bishop, and enthroned as archbishop.

Alas, Henry had failed to consider that there might be a measure of integrity in his friend, who, once in high office, turned into a jealous defender of the prerogatives of the church. Becket ran into conflict with his friend the king when he refused to restore, at the king's urging, two bishops whom he had excommunicated. The king decided to resolve the conflict by having Becket assassinated—a rather unusual way to resolve conflict—in, of all places, Canterbury Cathedral. Though Henry sought to distance himself from the heinous deed, he was promptly implicated and hardly four years later he had to realize that he would not win against the church, and much like the other Henry, the German King Henry IV, he had to yield. He did public penance at Becket's tomb in Canterbury Cathedral. Subsequent events were to show, nonetheless, that the balance of power between church and state in England continued to favor the kings.

THE MEDIEVAL CHURCH: STRUCTURE AND PRACTICE

The New Testament may be said to be vague and general about how Christian assemblies should be structured and governed (though some scholars and theologians would beg to differ), and not surprisingly, over time different notions were propounded as to how this should be done, both on the local level and in the church at large. No aspect of authority and structure was more important than the increasingly central role vested in the office of the bishop.

The earliest Christian writings made reference to "bishops," but only as one of a number of other congregational offices whose exact definition is not altogether clear. Initially, "priest" and "bishop" may well have referred to one and the same function. The First Epistle of Clement of Rome, toward the end of the first century, mentioned *episkopoi* (superintendents, bishops) and *presbyteroi* (elders, presbyters) as an "upper class" of clergy, and emphasized their pivotal importance. Ignatius of Antioch advanced weighty claims for the office of bishop, insisting that Christians should view the bishop as "the Lord himself," adding, "Without the bishop you may not do anything." In his polemic against the Gnostics and their claim of a secret tradition of Jesus, Ignatius articulated the centrality of the bishop as the guarantor of the apostolic faith. He counseled, "Where your bishop is, there follow him like sheep," and "Make sure that no step affecting the church is ever taken by anyone without the bishop's sanction." (Ignatius, *Letter to the Smyrneans* 8:2). Of course, Ignatius himself was a bishop, so there may have been a bit of pleading on his own behalf here, but his theological reasoning was based on the notion of apostolic succession. The knowledge that each bishop had received the faith from a line of predecessors stretching all the way back to the original apostles vouchsafed the perpetuation of the true apostolic faith.

In earliest Christianity, the bishop probably was the "overseer" of a congregation—the designation possibly another term for the local office of "elder," as one might glean from the New Testament—but soon the bishop became a regional overseer, not merely the administrator or overseer of the churches in a region, soon referred to as a diocese, but also a spiritual and theological leader. This authority was seen to be based on scriptural mandates.

By the third century, the writings echoing Clement and Ignatius in extolling the importance of the bishop seemed endless. Cyprian, bishop of Carthage, a zealous convert to the Christian faith and an equally zealous advocate of the pivotal authority and power of the episcopal office (his maxim was "*Ecclesia in episcopo*" ["The church is in the bishop"]), insisted that all bishops in the church were equal: none had authority over another. Such sentiment seems to have been more or less universally shared until the fourth century. This meant, of course, that no representative body with authority over the entire church existed.

Cyprian's egalitarian views were in conflict, however, with the claims of one set of bishops, the bishops of Rome, who held that they had greater authority than the other bishops of the church. They were not exactly shy about asserting this claim, which they based on Jesus' identifying the Apostle Peter, to whom he would give "the keys of the kingdom" as "the rock" on which he would build the church. This Gospel passage (Matthew 16:18-19) was taken to have conferred the status of primacy on the apostle and all his successor bishops. According to tradition, Peter was the first bishop of the Christian assembly in Rome, and as his successors all the subsequent Roman bishops claimed the priority Jesus had bestowed on Peter. The apostle had suffered martyrdom in Rome, and according to tradition he, too, was put to death on a cross, except that he did not consider himself worthy to be crucified as Jesus had been, so he was crucified upside down. Through the centuries, Catholic Christians have stood in awe at the apostle's gravesite, directly under the high altar of Saint Peter's Basilica in Rome.

By the third century, the Roman bishops had established their primacy over the churches in Italy, though the bishops of other regions, notably the patriarchs (leading bishops) of such Christian centers as Antioch, Alexandria, Jerusalem, and Constantinople, contested any claim of Roman primacy over the universal church.

The Council of Nicea in 325 recognized four "metropolitan" bishops: those of Antioch, Alexandria, Constantinople, and Rome. These metropolitan bishops exercised final jurisdiction over the bishops in their regions. Two decades later, the Council of Antioch (341) created a structure that challenged Rome's claim to universal primacy. The bishop of the major city of a region had precedence over the bishops in the region, so that they could "do nothing extraordinary without him." As archbishop, a bishop governed a diocese of his own while also presiding over the bishops of his district.

The details of the process by which the Roman bishops became the head of Latin Christianity by the fifth century are not altogether clear, and the exact nature of the pope's primacy was even then far from having been fully worked out. Importantly, the popes were bystanders in the great christological controversies of the fourth and fifth centuries. But as the centuries passed, the papal claim to primacy was strengthened by a variety of biblical, theological, and even historical arguments, such as the "Donation of Constantine," a document that claimed that Emperor Constantine, on his deathbed, had transferred to the popes all his imperial possessions and dignities, which they in turn had conferred to the stewardship of the secular authorities. The Donation espoused an understanding of the papal office that entailed not only ecclesiastical primacy but political primacy as well.

Papal authority and power grew in the Western church in the context of an increasingly intense rivalry between Rome and Constantinople, as both heads of the churches claimed primacy: the metropolitan bishop of

Constantinople because he resided in the capital of the (Eastern) Empire and the bishop of Rome because of the promise made by Jesus to Peter. The third canon of the first Council of Constantinople (381) still acknowledged the Roman primacy when it asserted: "The Bishop of Constantinople, however, shall have the prerogative of honor *after* the Bishop of Rome because Constantinople is New Rome." But this canon turned out to be merely a first step in the increasing claims of the bishops of the new imperial capital, then barely fifty years old. Eventually, the Council of Chalcedon in 451 declared the bishop of Constantinople equal to the bishop of Rome. The claims of Rome to primacy won out only in the Western, but not the Eastern church. The Roman bishops lacked the strong political backing enjoyed by the bishops of Constantinople because of their close proximity to the emperor; however the Roman bishops were able to speak on moral and theological issues with greater freedom and independence from political powers.

Pragmatically, the quest of the Roman bishops for primacy of authority in the church is not at all surprising. Alongside the biblical claim of the Apostle Peter's special status, there also was the increasingly obvious need—given the diversity of theological opinion, the multiplicity of monastic orders, the complexity of guidelines for moral living—for an authoritative voice that spoke for all, for an arbiter to render verdicts whenever there was disagreement and controversy. Emperor Constantine had used church councils to render a definitive judgment on contested issues, but as history was to show, councils had a way of contradicting one another, and thus complicated rather than resolved controversial issues. And the appeal to the Bible hardly settled matters either, since interpretation and opinion stood against interpretation and opinion. An authoritative voice was necessary, and the office of the supreme pontiff in Rome filled that need of which the logical conclusion occurred in 1870 with the promulgation of the dogma of papal infallibility.

In the Western church the popes were aided in their duties by the highest dignitaries of the church, the "cardinals," an office that evolved slowly over the centuries. The word itself is derived from the Latin *cardo* ("hinge") to denote that the holder of the office occupies a "hinge" position of authority in the church. Initially, all clergy at the major churches in Rome held the title "cardinal." This changed in the Middle Ages, when the number of priests who could be so designated had become increasingly unwieldy; a surplus of cardinals existed in Rome. In the eleventh century, the number of cardinals was reduced to twenty-five, subsequently raised to twenty-eight. Later, seven regional deacons and seven bishops from the vicinity of Rome were added to form the College of Cardinals; all were appointed by the pope. To this day, cardinals residing in the Vatican are responsible for administrative affairs, such as the maintenance of theological standards and of the liturgy. Ever since 1059, cardinals have also had the authority to elect the popes, who had previously been elected by the Roman populace (at times amid turmoil, bribery, and scandal).

The everyday representative of the church was the priest. The pivotal office of the bishop in the church notwithstanding, the priests were the face of the church to the people. Until the third century, the priestly office was not clearly defined, and, indeed, until the High Middle Ages, the terms *clergy* or *cleric* were rather loosely employed. At various places and at various times, choirmasters, janitors, bell ringers, and even gravediggers were all considered "clergy," who were separated by different "vocations." Later, clergy received the tonsure (the partially shaved head) to express visibly that they were set apart from the laity.

Figure 2A
Canterbury Cathedral, site of the assassination of Archbishop Thomas Becket in 1170. The construction of the cathedral took centuries and was not completed until the late 1400s.

One became a member of the clergy upon having been examined in the faith and having rendered an oath of obedience to the ecclesiastical superiors. Ordination followed. Clergy, no less than laity, had to uphold a virtuous life: sodomy, bestiality, adultery, and the rape of nuns were considered cardinal sins that called for the imposition of punishments, generally suspension from office for a period of time, removal from an income-producing ecclesiastical position known as a "benefice" (called "privation"), or permanent removal from office (called "deposition"). Capital crimes were punished with "degradation," which involved removal from the priestly office and return to lay status. Sins considered so serious as to call for removal from the clerical office included murder, sexual crimes, perjury, marriage, heresy, idolatry, and simony (paying to obtain an ecclesiastical office), as well as improper election to the office and delinquency in priestly responsibilities. In turn, the office of deacon, based on the narrative in Acts 6, was created to administer church funds for the needy, to provide for orderly worship services, to read the gospel lesson in the service, and to help with the distribution of the elements in the Mass.

This broad understanding of the meaning of "clergy," buttressed by the absence of a stern rule of clerical celibacy in the early centuries of the church, increasingly gave way to a definition of the clerical office that restricted the designation "clergy" to priests and established the priesthood as a special order reflecting special spiritual gifts and functions. The understanding of the nature of the priesthood in the twenty-first century stems from developments that culminated in the ninth and eleventh centuries. It was then that the distinction between clergy and laity became pronounced. Priests became economically independent from their parishes, as they acquired the privilege of accepting legacies and donations. Moreover, since Emperor Constantine had granted the church sole jurisdiction over legal disputes within the church and over civil disputes involving clergy that did not involve criminal charges, priests became exempt from the general legal processes in society. When charged with a crime, they enjoyed the privilege—to use this term loosely—of being tried in an ecclesiastical rather than a secular court. Priests also were exempt from most taxation.

The ordination to the priesthood was performed by a bishop, and since the bishops stood in apostolic succession, ordination was understood as the safeguard of the theological purity of the faith. Ordination bestowed upon the priest an "indelible character," which not even despicable moral demeanor could remove; Augustine had resolved that issue in the Donatist controversy. As the priest was the intermediary between God and humans, the priest's function was to administer the sacraments, foremost to celebrate the Mass. Neither of those two obligations called for much formal theological training, with the result that most clergy were altogether oblivious of the fundamentals of the faith and theologically illiterate. By the late Middle Ages, priests had become ubiquitous in communities large and small. Their number was large, often excessively so, constituting 5 to 10 percent of the total population was not at all unusual. Even though Augustine had delineated the church's distinction between the personal qualities of a priest and his proper exercise of the office, it seemed that the church tended to be judged by the moral stature of its local representatives, the priests. So it is not at all surprising that the call of reform for the church was first of all a call for reform of the priesthood and also, initially even more tellingly so, of the monastic life of the church.

THE RENEWAL OF THE MONASTIC VISION

The exuberance connected with the rise of monasticism was not to last. To be sure, as the centuries passed, monasticism became firmly established in the church, both East and West. Monasteries and convents were found throughout European Christendom, and they were taken to be manifestations of the highest ideals of the faith. But with such esteem had come influence, and with influence had come wealth, and with wealth had come priorities that tended to neglect the spiritual center of the monastic vocation. Monasticism had become settled and complacent, and sensitive leaders pleaded for reform.

This call for reform took on momentum in the tenth century and found a voice in the monastery in the small town of Cluny in Burgundy. That monastery had been founded in 910 when William, by the grace of God Duke of Aquitaine, gave his favorite hunting lodge and surrounding land near Cluny to the Benedictine Order to establish a monastery. There the monks should "ardently engage in heavenly discourse and painstakingly offer prayers and intercession" for the donor. It was a generous benevolence, for William relinquished all feudal rights to the land, thereby curbing outside influences in the affairs of the monastery, including the important elections of the abbot. Since the gift came with the tillers of the soil, the bonded serfs, the Cluniac monks were free from the manual labor necessary for the smooth functioning of the community.

The Cluny monastery developed its own distinctiveness, with unusual independence from even papal control and supervision. Cluny grew in importance as it benefited from the leadership of a string of gifted and reforming abbots, beginning with Odo (served 926–42), who worked tirelessly to have the monastery observe Benedict's original order. Odo and the abbots following him tirelessly stressed the monastery's liturgical responsibility and the pivotal importance of cultivating the spiritual life. An increasingly elaborate liturgical life came to characterize the Cluny community. The monastery church was claimed to be the largest in all of Christendom. For centuries it stood, a magnificent symbol of monastic splendor, until the French Revolution found it a quite different symbol, namely, of everything despicable in the Christian religion. Stone by stone the structure was dismantled. Today the visitor sees a few Gothic pillars that seem to rise to the heavens, but they are torsos—parts of a magnificent undertaking brought to fruition, and then humbled.

The engagement in this rich liturgy meant that the Cluny monks had little time to move out of their monastery walls into their community and beyond, perhaps even little time to undertake the mundane labors necessary in a community. A large number of lay brothers was needed to do the menial chores in the kitchen, where soup had to be cooked and pots cleaned; in the garden, where weeds had to be pulled and vegetables harvested, while the serfs tilled the lands, affording the monks the time to immerse themselves in the liturgy.

The richness of the Cluniac liturgy, together with the pursuit of reform, prompted other monasteries to follow the Cluniac lead. Around the turn of the millennium, the Cluny abbots began to focus their attention on broader issues of the Benedictine order. A major objective had to do with greater centralized control. New Benedictine monastic houses in England, France, Germany, and Italy found that they enjoyed little independence. Under the dynamic leadership of several Cluny abbots, the Benedictine order was divided into "congregations," or geographic clusters of monasteries. And Cluny dominated the congregations; Odilo became the "abbot of abbots," to whom the other abbots rendered obedience. Before long, Cluny was the vibrant center of European monasticism, with its roughly one thousand monasteries, some large, many small. Cluniac reform meant, however, that monasteries were removed from the oversight and jurisdiction of the local bishops: they were placed directly under the supervision of the pope, which effectively gave Cluny the leading role and afforded monasteries considerable freedom from both local barons and bishops. This arrangement worked well as long as the monastic houses sought to live up to the spirit of monasticism; it spelled trouble as soon as deficiencies of one form or another set in.

There were other manifestations of a renewal of the monastic vision. The Cistercians, originating in Citeaux, France, toward the end of the eleventh century, were committed to simple living and strict poverty and to a rigid observance of Saint Benedict's rule. They battled endlessly against what they perceived to be the Cluniac perversion of Saint Benedict's ideals, the centrality of rich liturgical celebrations. On feast days, the lengthy and elaborate liturgy of the Cluny monastery would keep the community glued to their choir stalls for the entire day. Cistercians emphasized liturgical simplicity.

And yet the energetic institutional reforms associated with Cluny were paralleled by several new mendicant ("begging") orders that introduced new values and commitments, different than the established monastic orders. Since these new orders had in common that they rejected not only individual property, a common feature of all existing orders, but also communal property, their members depended on begging to sustain their common life.

The Second Council of Lyons (1274) recognized five "great" mendicant orders, Servites, Dominicans, Carmelites, Augustinians, and Franciscans. These orders had come into existence in the early thirteenth century, characterized by the prominence given to "begging" for their daily food and livelihood: the Carmelites (Brothers of the Order of Our Lady of Mount Carmel), founded at Mount Carmel in Palestine early in the thirteenth century; the Servites (Order of Friar Servants of Mary), founded in 1304; and the Augustinians (Hermits of Saint Augustine, founded in 1256). Most important, two new monastic orders overshadowed them all: the Franciscans and the Dominicans.

The Dominican Order, the "Order of Preachers" (*Ordo Praedicatorum*), grew out of the vision of Dominic de Guzmán, who was born around 1170 in Calaroga, Old Castile, the fourth child of a town official. Dominic received an unremarkable and routine education and undoubtedly was destined to the career of a minor ecclesiastical official had it not been for an accidental journey. He accompanied his bishop, Diego de Acevedo, to a region in southern France heavily populated by the heretical Cathari, the "pure ones." This dissenting movement had emerged in the eleventh century in the Languedoc region of France, the area between Toulouse and Marseille. It propounded a kind of gnostic dualism and emphasized living a pure and sinless life. Dominic's trip became a life-changing event. He was overwhelmed by the religious illiteracy of the people among whom the Cathari had made such dramatic inroads. As he saw it, blatant religious ignorance was the cause of the success of the heretical communities. The common people simply were not conversant with the teachings of the church and so became easy prey of heretics. He was convinced that the menace of heresy was best countered by churchmen characterized by spiritual commitment, erudition, holiness, and love. They would sap the strength of the heretical movement.

Dominic set out to put his conviction into practice. In 1215, he obtained a house in Toulouse, where he gathered a group of like-minded individuals who shared his vision of theological learning and exemplary living. A few years later, he traveled to Rome, boldly seeking the pope's approval for a new monastic order comprised of the group that had first gathered in the house in Toulouse. Reluctantly, Pope Innocent III gave his approval, and when Dominic died in 1221, some sixty "Dominican" monasteries had been established.

The Franciscans were cut from a different cloth. They are a particularly striking case in point, because their hallmark, commitment to absolute poverty, rejected the distinction made by other monastic orders between private and communal property (forbidding the former but affirming the latter). For Franciscans poverty meant absolute poverty of the entire monastic community. A second distinctive feature followed: Franciscans had to obtain their food by growing it with their own hands. If that was not possible, they had to beg for their daily bread. Of course, the Franciscans were not the first monks who resorted to begging; other orders had done so as well, but the Franciscans begged not so much for themselves as for the support of the sick, the destitute, and orphans. They made begging socially respectable and spiritually meritorious in European society—until, in the sixteenth century under the influence of the Protestant Reformation, communities concluded that to have beggars in their midst, whether in rags or in monastic habits, was a blot on their common life.

The Franciscans introduced another innovation: administrative centralization of the order. Houses of other monastic orders were more or less autonomous. Aside from a common commitment to the rules of the particular order, each monastery was free to go its own way. The Franciscans, however, emphasized not so much the individual monastery as the province of the order. This administrative streamlining meant that the objectives of the order, such as the care of the sick, could be pursued more efficiently.

Intriguingly, much connects the order founded by Saint Francis with that founded by Saint Dominic. Both were mendicant ("begging") orders, and both were committed to poverty; probably Dominic was influenced by Francis in this regard. Both orders were concerned to make the faith relevant for the common people, but there was an enormous difference in the strategies the two orders pursued to reach their goals. The Franciscans sought to make their appeal through their own radical discipleship and devotion to the needs of the people; the Dominicans, in turn, were committed to a strategy of educating the people in order to make them loyal to the church. They stressed the education of their own members and insisted that each monastery had to be a school, with a doctor of theology as teacher. Later, the Dominican brothers' disposition to counter heresy with theological learning made them eager collaborators with the Inquisition, which likewise was committed to proper doctrine through the suppression of heresy, a turn that gave the Dominicans the hardly complimentary appellation "*domini canes*," the dogs of the Lord. In the early Reformation some thought that the controversy was simply a rivalry between the Dominican and the Augustinian orders.

THE SAINT: FRANCIS OF ASSISI

Saint Francis of Assisi personified both the spirit of monastic reform and the ability of the church to accept new ways of spirituality.

Of all the saints in the huge pantheon of the Catholic Church, Francis "out-saints" them all. He is everybody's saint—for Catholics and non-Catholics alike, reminiscent of Mother Teresa in our own day, whose devotion to India's outcastes evoked universal esteem. Francis himself would be mortified by his posthumous fame, which derived from the winsome legends that sprung up around him and have been told and retold through the centuries—his preaching to the birds, his love of animals, his tender reference to "Brother Sun and Sister Moon," the cadences of his prayer, "Lord, make me an instrument of your peace. Where there is hatred, let me sow love. . . ."

Figure 2B
Statue of St. Francis of Assisi by an anonymous artist. Assisi, Italy.

The story of Saint Francis of Assisi is part of a larger mosaic of a time when sensitive souls in the church became convinced that the church had fallen from its professed ideals. They called for reform, and the concern became official, so to speak, when Pope Gregory VII joined the phalanx of would-be-reformers. He had likeminded forerunners—Popes Clement II and Leo IX—and successors, such as Innocent III, an energetic and youthful pope (he was in his thirties at the time of his elevation in 1198), who turned the vision of a reformed church and papacy into reality. Innocent left a lasting imprint on both church and papacy. He detested heresy as much as political interference in church affairs. Before his elevation to the papal throne, he had written a treatise on asceticism, so when he and Francis eventually met face to face, he understood Francis's concerns.

Francis was in his teens when this dynamic individual became pope. Born Giovanni Francesco di Bernardone in Assisi, Umbria, in 1181 or 1182, Francis did not look for sainthood, nor did he set out to found a new monastic order. He was the son of a prosperous Assisi cloth merchant, and as he grew up he displayed the qualities of a youth blessed with affluence and intellect: a ready wit and a delight in fine clothes and showy display. Handsome, gallant, and courteous, he was a natural fit among the young elites of Assisi.

Francis received a rudimentary education and later assisted his father in his business. But there was little harmony between father and son, for Francis showed no liking for a merchant's career. Legend has it that even at this time Francis showed uncommon sympathy with the poor. One day, as he was selling cloth at a booth in the town square, a beggar approached him for alms. Francis ignored the beggar, but moments later, when the man had disappeared, he was overcome by the conviction that he should have helped. Deserting his booth of cloth and embroidery, he hurried through the narrow streets of Assisi, frantically looking for the beggar. When he found him, he showered him with coins. And he swore, so the story goes, that he would never again refuse to help a person in need.

When he was twenty, Francis went out with other Assisi townsmen to fight the neighboring town of Perugia in one of the petty skirmishes between rival Italian city-states so frequent at that time. The warriors from Assisi were defeated on that occasion, and Francis, having been taken prisoner, was held captive for more than a year. Illness incapacitated him, providing endless time to ponder his future—with visions of fame, conquests, and victorious battles. Eventually, his thoughts turned to things religious.

He trailed back to Assisi, forlorn, uncertain how his life would sort out. His illness persisted, but when it was over, he had resolved to become a follower of Jesus. A conversion had taken place. It occurred at La Portiuncula, an abandoned chapel some three miles outside Assisi, where a Benedictine monk came regularly to celebrate Mass. It was the dawn of February 24, 1208. Afterward Francis made himself a tunic of coarse peasant material, cutting it in the form of a cross, as a reminder of the savior to whose service he had committed himself.

And so the son of the prosperous merchant in Assisi, known throughout town as a careless and indulged youth, turned into a shockingly different person. He began to preach a message of radical discipleship, and the townspeople in Assisi were perplexed and puzzled by this change in the young man-about-town into an apostle of radical commitment and poverty. There was something enticing and magnetic about Francis's preaching and life, however, for his exuberance stood in poignant contrast to the routine (and boring) exhortations of the local priests.

Then a pivotal event occurred. A well-to-do Assisi citizen, Bernard de Quintavalle, invited Francis to be his houseguest so that he could understand better his motivation. That night, Quintavalle discreetly observed that Francis prayed until dawn, and this sight so moved him that he told Francis that he would "abandon the world and follow [him]." When the two, after Mass, opened a Bible at random, they found it opened to the nineteenth chapter of the Gospel of Matthew, the story of Jesus' encounter with a young rich ruler, whom Jesus challenged to sell all that he had and give it to the poor. It was the same passage that had deeply moved Antony in the early centuries of the Christian faith to make a commitment to spiritual perfection by becoming a monk.

Francis found his calling; with Quintavalle's decision to join him, there were a few others who were inspired by him. The central motif in Francis's understanding of the gospel became the commitment to the simplest lifestyle, in effect, to poverty. It was both an end in itself—after all, Jesus had commanded it—and it was a means toward an end—the way to dismiss all worldly cares that came with having and owning things. Francis was a radical on the topic of poverty. On one occasion, he said that letting a friar have a Psalter would make him wish for a breviary, and once he owned a breviary, he would demand that friars bring it to him. Faithful followers of Jesus had to resist even the very least of the temptations.

Of course, Francis was not the first Christian to espouse radical poverty. Countless monks and nuns had done that for centuries. What was different was how Francis understood this mandate. He did not see the commitment to poverty as a burden. Rather, poverty brought with it a carefree and liberated life. Of course, there were awkward moments, as when Francis, begging for oil for the church of San Damiano, knocked at the door of a house where former friends were partying. He did not want to face them and turned away from the door, but, overcome by his awareness that he had been a coward, he returned. When the door opened, he faced his friends from bygone days, shoddy rags and all, to beg for a gift for the poor.

Francis's spontaneous deeds of mercy—for a leper or for a beggar—led to the bizarre scene in the courtroom of the Assisi bishop, who charged him with taking linens and woolens from his father's warehouse, selling them, and giving the proceeds to the poor. Since "taking" was a polite word for "stealing," his father was understandably furious, and the bishop concerned. Francis meekly replied that his Father in heaven had commanded him to do as he did, and, disregarding the dignity of the courtroom, he stripped himself naked to demonstrate Jesus' command to give all to the poor. Neither the bishop nor the father was impressed. Nor were most of the townspeople present.

However, Francis's disposition resonated among his contemporaries. He had followers, and because they did not want to separate themselves from society and the world, as was the case in many monastic orders, they did not want to be known as "monks." They were "brothers," *fratelli*, friars. They sought to be where the common people were. They were destitute and had to survive on what others provided for them.

When the group of followers reached twelve, Francis became concerned, for he was convinced that things were getting out of hand. The last thing on his mind was to start a movement. He concluded that he and his "brothers" must seek the pope's approval for whatever they sought to do for the church. So Francis and his *fratelli* traveled to Rome, and their encounter with the learned Pope Innocent was not altogether smooth. At issue was not their devotion to the church, which was acknowledged, but their commitment to radical poverty, which could be easily understood as a frontal challenge to prevailing societal values. Innocent gently reminded Francis that the revolutionary stipulations of Jesus' Sermon on the Mount were surely not meant to be applied literally. Francis compliantly agreed, but added that the Holy Father would be the last to say that Christ's rule of poverty was unworkable for every last Christian.

Innocent, much concerned about revitalizing the church, sensed that Francis and his impoverished followers could contribute to this process of renewal—as long as they did not insist that all Christians had to take a vow of poverty. Francis had no intention of demanding that all who were rich had to become poor if they wanted to be serious Christians. He simply declared that he himself had accepted Jesus' word of poverty. Innocent was impressed and authorized Francis and his *fratelli* to form a community, but only for a trial period. Innocent was not about to allow something foolish, and his authorization of a temporary community may well have been a ploy to give Francis the opportunity to fail.

The commitment to radical poverty meant that the *fratelli* would beg for food, but always only for the day. Indeed, they ate the simplest of food, simpler than the austere diet of peasants, and when it tasted delicious, they would sprinkle ashes on it so as to not be carried away by its savor. They wore the worst cast-off peasant garments, and they appeared to others a sad and sorry lot. Intriguingly, the very opposite was the case: the determination to live in complete devotion of love for God and their fellow men and women gave them a striking air of happiness.

After Francis's death a carefully guarded secret became known. His body periodically showed five bloody marks at the sites of Jesus' wounds—hands, feet, chest—the phenomenon that is known as receiving "stigmata." A companion recorded what happened: "Suddenly he saw a vision of a seraph, a six-winged angel on a cross. This angel gave him the gift of the five wounds of Christ" (Bonaventure, *Legenda Minor, de Stigmatibus sacris*, 1-4). The place was at Francis's retreat in La Verna north of Assisi in 1224, where he received both vision and stigmata, making him one in a long line of Catholics who were to share that intense psychosomatic experience.

Francis's community, formally the Order of Friars Minor, was soon augmented by a female order. It had its origins when sixteen-year-old Clare from an Assisi family, overwhelmed by Francis's ideals, asked to be admitted to the Franciscan order. In a way, it was Francis' own story all over again, with a prosperous and prestigious family background, fierce objections of her father, alienation between child and parent. Clare was instrumental in setting up the new order of the "Poor Clares" (in Latin, a bit more exalted *Ordo Sanctae Clarae*), at first modeled more after the Rule of Saint Benedict than of Saint Francis. Later, in 1221, a third Franciscan branch, the Brothers and Sisters of Penance, known as Tertiaries, was established. This branch was meant to be for those who could not take vows of radical poverty and celibacy but still wished to follow Saint Francis's vision of the committed Christian life of service to the poor.

When, only in his mid-forties, Francis died in October 1226, some of his followers were beginning to soften his radical notions. Some members of the order had accepted teaching positions at universities—Francis himself deeply distrusted learning—while others served as advisors to the curia in Rome. The principle of radical poverty was relaxed a bit, when Franciscan monasteries, much akin to the development in other mendicant orders, were allowed to have common property, a turn Francis surely would not have approved.

Perhaps not surprisingly given its radical disposition, the Franciscan Order before long split into two branches: a zealous one, the "Franciscan Spirituals," and a moderate one, the "Conventuals," the latter led by Brother Elias, one of Francis's first companions. Elias was elected "minister general" of the Franciscan Order and began to build a grandiose church in Assisi in Francis's memory. The Spirituals, in turn, were not exactly enamored by the idea of an expensive monument to the apostle of poverty. Internal strife commenced, and Bonaventura (1221–74), a theological star and a respected member of the Franciscans, was elected to the post of minister general in 1256 to resolve the strife. He succeeded in bringing the Spirituals into the Franciscan mainstream. Things got messy once again in the order when some Franciscans appropriated notions of Joachim of Fiore (ca. 1135–1202), that strange and exuberant interpreter of the mysteries of Scripture, and dragged the order into the quagmire of cryptic idiosyncrasies about the Last Days.

But despite these turns, the Franciscan order flourished. The notion of a radical commitment to following Jesus appealed far more widely than one might have expected. And the church at large, as Pope Innocent III had so astutely sensed, was willing to utilize this commitment to have the order of the "little brothers" supply the preachers, confessors, and teachers the church so desperately needed. The order became a safety valve for the church. Franciscans built churches marked by striking simplicity, with wide and large naves to make room for crowds listening to sermons. Franciscan scholars became eloquent expositors of scholastic learning, leaning on Aristotelian thought to convey Christian truth. They responded to the moral issues attending the emerging new economic order in Europe by paying a great deal of attention, for example, to the

notion of the "just price"—what could be ethically charged for a particular item—a question increasingly important as the European economy
began its long and tedious progress from recovery to capitalism. The
Franciscan theologians dominated much of the medieval theological discourse, in particular with their persistent advocacy of Mary's Immaculate
Conception.

The Friars Minor constituted a new type of monastic order, focused on
preaching and on popularizing the faith. Like the Dominicans, the
Franciscans thought globally and created an organizational structure that
was international and produced theological works of the highest quality.

The story of Francis serves to illustrate yet another important aspect of
the Christian story in the (Latin) West: the emergence of religious art.
The iconoclastic controversy in the eastern church had been rather
unnoticed in the Western church, and so artistic portrayals of aspects of
salvation history may be found in Late Antiquity. Around 1280,
Cimabue, the pioneer in the move toward naturalistic painting and the
master of Giotto, began to paint frescoes to adorn the upper basilica of
the Papal Basilica of Saint Francis in Assisi. In a way, one might see the
beginnings of religious art in the West, where the artist had not only the
biblical subject matter to draw on but also the story of the church and its
saints. And so, again and again, the artists chose scenes from the Bible
and stories of the saints. They did so being frequently devoid of theological literacy, though often with uncanny awareness of what was theologically at stake, such as God's finger not touching Adam's in the
Michelangelo fresco in the Sistine Chapel. Religious art served a public
as well as a private function—the decorations in churches, the devotional
paintings in the homes of the affluent or powerful, the illustrations of
lives of saints in codices, attentively copied by monks. One should not
underestimate the theological significance and impact of this art; in a
populace that was largely illiterate and the sermon infrequent, religious
art may well have been the major vehicle of communicating the
Christian message.

THE THEOLOGICAL MATURING OF THE FAITH: SCHOLASTICISM

Medieval theologizing in the Western church was dominated by the intellectual movement known as scholasticism. It reached its culmination in the thirteenth century and had its eminent representative in Thomas Aquinas. Prior to the thirteenth century, theologians had pronounced on many aspects of the faith of the church. It was in the thirteenth century, the so-called High Middle Ages, however, that their expositions of the faith began to be grounded in a cohesive philosophical framework. The European rediscovery of Aristotle proved to be of enormous importance for the medieval theological discourse, since his philosophical categories seemed tailor-made to provide a cogent underlying philosophical rationale for the Christian faith.

Thomas Aquinas, the lodestar of medieval scholasticism, was born in southern Italy, probably in 1225. His well-to-do father planned for him a convenient and none-too-strenuous ecclesiastical career, preferably in the Benedictine Order. Thomas proved to be obstreperous, however, and insisted on joining the Order of Preachers, the Dominicans, whose emphasis on learning and poverty he deeply shared. His father was aghast and, aided by Thomas's older brothers, locked him up in the tower of the family castle until he would come to his senses. The story is that two of his brothers even procured a prostitute to deter him from his foolish (so they were convinced) determination. But even faced with this temptation, Thomas remained unmoved. Eventually the family realized the intensity of his conviction and allowed him again into the world. An extended period of studies followed. Strangely, his fellow students were not overly impressed by him, even calling him "dumb ox," an odd label for someone whose brilliant mind influenced the Catholic Church for centuries to come. Aptly, Thomas's teacher responded, "You call him a dumb ox; I tell you this Dumb Ox shall bellow so loud that his bellowing will fill the world." And so it happened. The self-understanding of the Catholic tradition through the centuries that followed is unthinkable without Thomas. He rightly is a "doctor" of the Catholic Church.

Thomas, like so many brilliant minds, was a workaholic. His magnum opus, the *Summa Theologica*, comprised some four thousand pages in manuscript form, and was left incomplete at that. Biblical commentaries as well as theological treatises flowed from his pen; he wrote often two, even three books at the same time, driving his several secretaries to exhaustion. The *Summa Theologica* occupied him steadfastly for more than eight years. Finally, on December 6, 1273, the feast day of Saint Nicolas—Thomas was then forty-eight years of age—he celebrated Mass and afterward announced, "I can write no more. After what I have seen, everything I wrote seems like straw."

He never added another word to his magnificent body of work.

The basic premise of Thomas's theology was that there were two realms: the "natural" and the "supernatural." The former could be sensed, felt, seen; the latter was beyond human ability to apprehend. Humans cannot understand the supernatural sphere unless God chooses to reveal some of it to humankind. The two spheres are in perfect harmony, however; reason, the human mind, can demonstrate parts of the supernatural, such as the existence of God, but revelation is necessary for full knowledge of the spiritual realm. In a revolutionary turn in Western thinking, Thomas argued that the world of the senses is the only basis for natural knowledge. Accordingly, any attempt to prove the existence of God must focus on the senses. Accordingly, Thomas proceeded to propose no less than five proofs of the existence of God, such as the proof "from motion" (God is the final mover) or "from efficient cause" (God is the ultimate cause). The searching question of the relationship of reason and faith was answered by Thomas with the emphatic assertion that the two were in perfect harmony.

Not all were convinced by this approach. Thomas's great antagonist, the Englishman William of Occam, was born around 1285, roughly two generations later than Thomas. William identified the problems with Thomas's theologizing, and in so doing he began a long line of critics of the Thomist system, which essentially challenged Thomas's high view of the power of human reason. William was unimpressed, for example, by Thomas's five proofs of God's existence and argued that only Scripture is a certain road to acknowledging the existence of a supreme being. And if it were not enough to take on Thomas, William voiced other rather radical notions, such as that a general council of the church had more authority than the pope and that Scripture was the final, infallible source of faith and morals. In reaction to Thomas, William rejected one of his principal notions, that of the reality of so-called "universals." William argued that only individual "things" exist. "Universals," such as "flag," or "chair," or "college" exist only as concepts of the human mind. They are linguistic constructs. When Thomas argued that human goodness directs us to God's goodness, William retorted that goodness, a universal, was a mere concept of the human mind. We can know about God only through revelation.

While Thomas Aquinas, William of Occam, and the other scholastic theologians occupied center stage in the theologizing after the thirteenth century, there were critics and dissenters who felt frustrated by the normative declarations of faith and life, theologians such as the Englishman John Wycliffe (ca. 1320–84). Wycliffe, an Oxford don, was overwhelmed by his conviction that the church was in dire need of reform; it was reform across the board that he had in mind—reform in theology no less than in the opulent practices of the church. Influenced by William of Occam, Wycliffe propounded risky theological notions, such as the Bible as the only source of truth, the availability of the Bible in the vernacular (the first English translation was published around 1380), and questions about the transformation of bread and wine in the Lord's Supper.

At the same time, women's voices were heard in the church, as several outstanding women left their mark on the church, perhaps more significantly so than many male theologians at the time. Julian of Norwich (ca. 1342–ca. 1413) had mystical visions that she interpreted in numerous writings. Catherine of Sienna (1347–80), her contemporary in Italy, rejected her parents' insistence on a "good" marriage, found herself under a kind of house arrest, and experienced visions and raptures that focused on her mystical marriage to Jesus and a life of utmost devotion to those in need. Margery Kempe's (1373–1439) spiritual pilgrimage began with the birth of her first child (she had fourteen children in all), which has led to the suggestion that her spiritual experience may have coincided with a period of postpartum depression. Margery had a profound spiritual apparition of Jesus and while initially illiterate, acquired proficiency to write the first spiritual autobiography by a woman in English.

Two centuries earlier, Hildegard of Bingen (a small town on the Rhine River), born in 1098, had expressed the same devotion but manifested a different spirituality. The tenth child of a noble family, Hildegard had her first visions at age three, joined a convent not that much later, was elected abbess of her convent, and became fluent in Latin, the Bible, and a wide range of theological literature. She engaged in correspondence with popes, bishops, emperors and princesses. In 1141 she experienced visions of uncommon intensity and recorded them and their spiritual meaning in writing, the most profound one, perhaps, a book titled *Scivias* (derived from the biblical exhortation "Know the Way of the Lord"). It was a tome of more than 150,000 words. Understandably, Hildegard's prolific literary activities triggered adverse reactions from theologians who could not fathom that a woman would so boldly enunciate her spiritual ruminations. But Hildegard found an important supporter in Pope Eugene III, who endorsed the authenticity of her visions and permitted her to continue writing.

But that was not all. Hildegard ventured beyond the theological arena and became a prolific writer who composed more than seventy musical pieces, and wrote cookbooks (of sorts) as well as books on medicine (in which she described 290 plants, 153 species of animals, and 25 minerals). For Hildegard it all was wonderfully connected—God, the Holy Spirit, the stars, plants, animals. She also preached, though not from the altar, where women were not allowed, but from lecterns outside churches. In short, she moved—comfortably, at that—into the territory that her time reserved exclusively for men. She overcame the obstacle of lacking any formal education and alerted the church to the words and preaching of a woman—and all this with a papal stamp of approval.

As happened with Francis of Assisi, Hildegard was able to take on new roles because the church and the pope recognized that what she had to offer was meaningful and significant. She pointedly described herself as a prophetess—not someone foretelling the future, however, for that would have been a slippery path, but as a faithful daughter of the church explicating the mysteries of salvation history. In other words, Hildegard was able to impinge on the prerogatives of a male-dominated society and church, without explicitly challenging them.

THE CHURCH IN THE EAST

Spread and Expansion of the Church in the East

In the early centuries, the Eastern church scored striking missionary success among the Goths, who had settled in what is now east-central Europe, as well as among the Slavic tribes in Eastern Europe. The missionary effort was aided by Emperor Constantius II (r. 337–61), who, holding to Arian views, made sure that the proselytizing was for the Arian version of the Christian faith. In the ninth century two brothers, Cyril and Methodius, took their missionary effort as far north as Moravia (now in the Czech Republic), where they came into contact with missionaries from western Europe—and promptly clashed with them. The tensions between the two brothers and the missionaries from the western Latin church were another indication of the growing broader theological and liturgical differences between East and West.

The language of the liturgy triggered conflict. It was in Latin in the West and in the vernacular in the East. That, at any rate, was how the distinction was framed, even though the Eastern church did not exactly use the vernacular either. Cyril used the Southern Slavic dialect of the Thessalonica region for the liturgy and a translation of the Bible. The dialect became known as Old Church Slavonic and has continued to be the liturgical language of the Russian Orthodox Church. For a long time it was considered the language of the educated classes, and it constituted the vehicle for the subsequent Christianization of Russia.

By the end of the tenth century Russia was formally Christian after mass baptisms had been administered in the Dnieper River. In 988 Grand Duke of Kiev Vladimir the Great decided that Russia would be well served if its people were to adhere to one of the three major religions competing for acceptance in Europe and the Middle East—Judaism, Christianity (in both its Catholic and Orthodox manifestations), and Islam. It was said that (according to a document known as the *Primary Chronicle*) Vladimir chose the Byzantine form of Christianity because his ambassadors had told him that the Church of Holy Wisdom (the *Hagia Sophia*) in Constantinople was the most beautiful in the world. Vladimir was impressèd and persuaded—perhaps not the worst rationale ever made on behalf of a religion. As time passed and the Muslim onslaught on the eastern Mediterranean deprived the Eastern church of its historical clientele and strength, the center of Orthodox Christianity increasingly shifted to Russia.

The Rivalry between the Eastern and Western Churches

Since Emperor Constantine's endorsement of the Christian religion, the church had become more prominent, more visible, more esteemed, more powerful. At the same time, it was challenged by subtle and not-so-subtle internal rivalries and differences between its Eastern and its Western branches. As the rivalry between the pope in Rome and the patriarch of Constantinople suggested, the two churches vied for ecclesiastical power and influence, the one in the ancient political capital, the other in the capital of the Byzantine Empire. And politics threw long shadows over this rivalry.

Ever since the end of the fourth century, when Emperor Theodosius I appointed his two sons Arcadius and Honorius as emperors of the eastern and the western parts of the empire (thus ending the unity of the Roman Empire), the center of political power had drifted in the eastern Byzantine direction. This division meant a partition of the church into a Western and an Eastern church. This partition was intensified by the controversy over the primacy of authority (and power) in the church.

Political, theological, and geographic considerations interwove as causes of the increasing alienation of the Eastern and the Western churches. As the centuries passed, the relationship between Rome and Constantinople, never altogether smooth and harmonious, drifted apart. Both emperor and patriarch resided side by side in Constantinople, which meant that ecclesiastical authority was too close to the holder of political power to enjoy full independence. This all the more so, because the Byzantine emperors saw themselves not only as "servants" of God but also as "saviors," consecrated like bishops, entitled to a special role in church affairs. Emperor and patriarch were understood to rule together, in "*symphonia*," in harmony, for the greater good. No wonder the Byzantine emperors felt free to step in heavy-handedly whenever in their judgment the church needed to make a decision. Thus, Emperor Justinian (483–565) decided that the modified Nicene Creed was the only acceptable normative statement of faith of the church, and he saw to it that the Fifth Ecumenical Council of Constantinople (553) definitively resolved the christological controversies so fiercely contended since the late third century.

At the same time, something else increasingly characterized the Eastern church: the conviction that the tradition of the church, as embodied in the decrees and canons of the first seven ecumenical councils, contained the fullness of revelatory truth. These pronouncements of the past entailed a deeper insight into divine truth than any pronouncement since. Claims of new insights, new propositions, new interpretations, were suspect. The so-called church fathers had delineated a cohesive theological whole, and the task of the theologian ever since was simply to reiterate and harmonize what they and the first seven ecumenical councils had propounded. To be sure, in Eastern Orthodoxy, as in all Christian traditions, the Bible was afforded primacy of place as source of religious authority. However, its meaning was mediated by tradition, as enunciated by the church fathers.

One theological issue came to overshadow the relationship between East and West. It had to do with the third person of the Trinity, the Holy Spirit, a topic not exactly occupying a pivotal place in Christian theologizing. Over the years, theologians had either paid no attention to the Holy Spirit at all or had propounded different notions as to what this divine spirit "did" for believers—it comforted, strengthened, sanctified. Clear definitions of the Spirit were lacking. The Council of Nicea had stated that the Spirit was divine in the full sense of the word and related to the Father ("proceeded" from the Father) the same way as did the Son.

There was, however, another view. It was mainly held in the West and argued that the Spirit emanated from both the Father and the Son. Accordingly, it became more and more customary in the West to modify the Nicene Creed by adding the phrase "and from the Son" (in Latin, *filioque*) to the accepted declaration "who proceeds from the Father." This addition was formally endorsed by the Third Council of Toledo in 589. From that time on, the Western churches recited the Nicene Creed with the *filioque* phrase added.

The Eastern church was furious. The Western stance, unilaterally, elicited a fierce protest from the Eastern church, but the West remained rigid. Since Father and Son were *homoousios*, of the same substance, so the West argued, the added phrase represented no substantive theological alteration. The main Eastern complaint was that the *filioque* phrase had been added without consultation, as a way of strengthening opposition to Arianism.

Political issues accompanied the increasing alienation of East and West, what came to be known as Orthodox and Latin Christianity. The crusades, the effort on which part of the religious and political West to free the Holy Land from the Muslims, who had taken Jerusalem in 638, which had not helped relations between the two churches, but in fact had worsened them. When, in 1071, the Byzantine Empire sought to score a decisive military blow on the Seljuk Turks, it suffered a catastrophic defeat. The eastern Emperor Michael VII was forced to seek the support of Pope Gregory VII to stem the Arab tide. The pope turned to the German Emperor Henry IV to help regain the military initiative against the Turks, but pope and emperor were deeply involved in the Investiture Controversy, and the Byzantine emperor's plea for help brought no tangible support. Pope Gregory, however, had been sympathetic to the Byzantine summons, aware that Western intervention in the East could buttress the papal claims of jurisdiction over the Eastern Church.

As had been so often the case in Christian history, a minor issue triggered a major confrontation. Several "western" churches in Constantinople used Latin in their liturgy and unleavened bread in the Eucharist, both contrary to Eastern practice. The patriarch of Constantinople, for whom these Western practices were an abomination, decided to close these churches. A papal legate, Cardinal Humbert, was dispatched by Pope Leo IX to Constantinople in 1054 to reopen these churches. Humbert was one of the leading church reformers and had successfully introduced a new way of electing the popes, but his mission to Constantinople tried the patience of Job. Patriarch Michael Cerularius refused to receive the delegation from Rome, and Humbert waited for months for an audience. Moreover, Cerularius escalated the tensions by referring to Leo as "Brother" rather than as "Father," thus declaring him to be an equal rather than a superior. In exasperation, after the endless wait for an audience, Humbert barged into a Mass celebrated by Michael and hurled a papal verdict of excommunication on the altar. Undismayed, the patriarch responded by excommunicating Humbert.

This confrontation at the altar of the church of Hagia Sophia in Constantinople has been seen as the dramatic event that finalized the division between East and West. Actually, for years to come the Eastern Orthodox and the Roman churches did not consider themselves as being in schism; indeed, Eastern Christians saw the whole episode as a dispute among individuals, pointing out that the excommunication was hurled at the feet of individuals, and not churches. Symbolically, however, the event proved incisive. The disagreement over the *filioque* phrase contributed to the severing of communion between the Eastern and Western churches. But there were also mutual misunderstandings between the two traditions, not to mention the fiery temperaments of the chief protagonists.

Relations between the two churches worsened. In 1274, the Second Council of Lyons, with the Patriarch of Constantinople in attendance, declared that the Holy Spirit proceeded from the Father and the Son, in accord with the *filioque* in the Western (Latin) version of the Nicene Creed. This declaration increased the resentment of Byzantine Christians against the West, especially since relations had not been particularly helped by the crusaders' devastating sack of Constantinople in the Fourth Crusade, when the crusaders directed their hostility against fellow Christians rather than the infidel Turks. The Eastern church did not consider reconciliation desirable. Nonetheless, renewed efforts at reconciliation were undertaken in the fourteenth century, but they suffered from a hopelessly divided papacy in what came to be known as the "Babylonian Captivity" of the church. Obviously, the two churches could not be reunited as long as the Western church was itself divided.

In the early fifteenth century, a delegation from the Eastern church, including Emperor John VIII Palaiologos and the Patriarch of Constantinople, Joseph II, together with twenty-three Metropolitan bishops and a sizable contingent of theologians, participated in the Council of Florence. Once again, religion and politics mixed. Most members of the Eastern delegation were eager to achieve reconciliation with Rome and at the same time to obtain Western military support for the increasingly looming threat of the Ottoman Empire. Reconciliation, of course, was impossible as long as theological disagreement prevailed. After extensive discussions, first in Ferrara and then in Florence, the Byzantine delegation conceded that Western theologians had been influenced by Greek theology when reflecting on the "procession" of the Holy Spirit. Since the Byzantine delegation held that the consensus of the theologians of the early church was the authentic witness to the apostolic faith, it could not accept a modification of the Eastern understanding of the "procession" of the Holy Spirit only from the Father. The emperor, desperate for military support from the West in the face of the Ottoman danger, pressured the Eastern bishops to agree to a document of union. Lengthy deliberations followed, and in the end the Byzantine delegation accepted the *filioque* phrase as being in harmony with Orthodox teaching. For good measure, it also accepted the Western position on the Mass and on papal primacy. Understandably, the document embodying the agreement in 1439 was titled *Laetentur Coeli* ("The Heavens Rejoice"). After centuries, the Western Latin and the Eastern Orthodox churches were formally again in communion with each other. The principle underlying the pronouncement of the Council of Florence was that the adherents of the Christian faith must be one in core beliefs but may be diverse in customs and rites. The disagreement over the *filioque* was understood not to violate that unity.

Alas, if the council fathers at Florence exhibited a spirit of optimism and a sense of accomplishment, the dream of true reconciliation quickly vanished. One of the Orthodox bishops, Markos Eugenikos, Metropolitan of Ephesus, refused to sign the *Laetentur Coeli* agreement on the grounds that Rome was both schismatic and heretical because of its acceptance of the *filioque* and the claim of papal jurisdiction over the entire church. Other Orthodox bishops promptly fell in line, rejecting the agreement and refusing to sign it. As far as they were concerned, the document was an improper imposition of scholastic theology on Orthodox theologizing.

The pledge of military support was honored, however, but the Western armies were unable to prevent the fall of Constantinople to the Turks in 1453. The new Turkish rulers allowed a measure of autonomy to the Orthodox Church in the newly occupied territories, but they were hardly interested in fostering close ties between the Orthodox Church and the West, specifically with Rome, which continued to be a fierce opponent of the Ottoman Empire. The patriarchs of Constantinople became subject to the will of their Muslim overlords; the Eastern church was no longer free.

Theology

Eastern Orthodox Christianity refers to itself as "orthodox," meaning that it sees itself in possession of "right, proper belief." This label not only was meant to draw a line separating the Eastern from the Western church under the jurisdiction of Rome; it also expressed the self-understanding of Eastern Christianity, which saw its theology as based on Scripture as interpreted by the first seven ecumenical councils of the church, particularly those of Nicea and Constantinople—and nothing else. Eastern theology and Eastern theologians accordingly have seen their task as expounding and elucidating the decisions of those councils and the thought of the theologians who influenced them. In decided contrast, the Western theological tradition adopted the notion of a "development" of dogma, the gradual unfolding of biblical and theological truths. It was precisely this understanding of a gradual unfolding of truth that allowed the Roman Catholic Church in the nineteenth and twentieth centuries to promulgate such new dogmas as Mary's Immaculate Conception and her bodily assumption into heaven as being consistent and harmonious with Scripture and previous church teaching. This notion is unthinkable in Orthodox theology, in which no development of dogma is possible. The task of the theologian is to illuminate what has already been recorded and affirmed.

Nonetheless, Orthodox Christianity has not escaped theological controversy. Early on, it became embroiled in the Monophysite controversy, triggered by theologians who argued that Jesus possessed a divine spirit but not a full human nature, making his body a glorified and spiritualized form of human nature. Monophysite theology was appealing because it

Figure 2C
Mary and the infant Jesus. Modern mosaic. Panaghia Kapnikarea, Athens, Greece.

did not need to explain how Jesus' divine nature intermingled with his human nature. Simply put, the Monophysite theologians insisted that only the divine Jesus suffered on the cross—even at his birth he did not assume full human nature. These views were at variance with the pronouncements of the councils of Nicea and Chalcedon, which had affirmed the full humanity and divinity of Jesus. In the seventh century, Patriarch Sergius of Constantinople sought to conciliate these views by suggesting that Jesus had two natures but only one will, a position known as "Monothelitism." Even though it was not altogether clear what that exactly meant, Pope Honorius (d. 638) agreed. Not to be outdone, the Council of Constantinople in 681 condemned Monothelitism and declared Honorius a heretic. Monophysite theology continued to be prominent in the eastern Mediterranean, and its influence only dwindled with the Muslim conquests of places where most of the Monophysite congregations were found. Thanks to the Muslims, Monophysitism ceased being an issue for the church.

A second controversy in the Orthodox Church had to do with the use of images in churches. It is known as the "iconoclastic controversy." The point of departure for this emotionally charged conflagration was the Old Testament mandate against "graven images." The initial Christian attitude toward images seems to have echoed the Jewish prohibition, but by the third century the first pictorial representations of saints and biblical figures began to appear in Christian contexts. As matters turned out, it was a small step from the pictorial representation of heroes of the faith to their veneration in ceremonies and liturgy.

It took until the eighth century for the theological opposition against images to coalesce, and even then a political rather than a theological issue was the immediate cause of the controversy. Eastern monasticism favored the use of images (given the dedication of monks to engage in extended periods of devotion), and the enormous spiritual and political influence of the monastics in the Eastern church meant that those who wished to use icons enjoyed powerful support. However, the emperors, never hesitant to pronounce on theological issues, found that images and their veneration was plain idolatry. The defenders of images insisted that the Council of Chalcedon's definition held that Jesus was "in" both the human and the divine nature, and therefore he was also "in" the image—and it was therefore legitimate to create an image of him. An image represented reality, and "he who reveres an image reveres in it the subject represented" (Council of Nicea, 787).

Accordingly, bishops began to authorize the use of images in churches and in worship, despite a concern that this would lead to idolatry. Then Caliph Yazid II ordered the destruction of all Christian icons in Syria in 722, an understandable move given the Islamic injunction against images. Somehow, Emperor Leo III (r. 717–41) had an iconoclast conversion and, unconvinced of the propriety of icons, moved decisively against them. The veneration of images was declared nothing short of idolatry.

The Western church took note of this pronouncement but chose to ignore it. Indeed, Pope Stephen III (r. 752–57) defended images, as did the eminent Eastern theologian John of Damascus (d. 749), who argued that images were found in the Bible. After all, the incarnation and the Eucharist were physical manifestations of the divine. Icons, he insisted, were books for the unlearned. "I do not worship matter, but the God of matter" (John of Damascus, *In Defense of Icons*).

A council was called to sort out the issue and when the Second Council of Nicea (the seventh and last of the "ecumenical" councils) met in 787, it declared that there was a difference between the adoration of God and the veneration of sacred images, and it encouraged the latter: icons came to occupy an important place in Orthodox worship. They were "windows into heaven" for the faithful. It was not until 843, however, that the veneration of icons was finally restored permanently, after an empress, an emperor, and another empress had weighed in pro and con.

John of Damascus was arguably the over-towering Eastern theologian whose significance went far beyond his role in enabling the introduction of images in the Orthodox churches. In particular, his book *The Fount of Wisdom* summarized the teachings of the Greek theologians on creation, the Trinity, the incarnation, and the Virgin Mary. John's underlying presumption was pivotal to Eastern theology: the key to understanding the Christian faith fully and comprehensively lay in the writings of the "fathers" (the early theologians) of the church, and there was no need to go beyond them. Consequently, Eastern theology received its depth and creativity from the probing exploration of the theology of the first ecumenical councils, which decided a host of theological and church issues. The Council of Ephesus (431), for example, proclaimed the Virgin Mary as the *Theotokos* ("God-bearer"). The Council meeting in Trullo (692), known as the Qunisext Council (meaning "fifth-sixth" because it was to complete the work of the fifth and the sixth councils), addressed matters of ecclesiastical discipline and of the biblical canon, which the previous councils had left unattended. The council also sought to gain some uniformity between Eastern and Western liturgical practices, but since all of the 211 bishops in attendance came from the East, the council rendered the hardly surprising judgment that Eastern liturgical practice was the authentic one. The issues debated had become rather subtle. For example, among the practices of the Latin church condemned by the council were celebrating Mass on weekdays during Lent rather than using what are called the "Pre-Sanctified Liturgies," which were more somber, and thus more appropriate for Lent; fasting on Saturdays throughout the year; omitting the "Alleluia" in the Lenten liturgies; depicting Christ as a lamb; and insisting on celibacy for all priests and deacons.

The list included more than one hundred specific items. Not surprisingly, Pope Sergius I protested the decisions of the council and refused to sign its canons, even though space had been provided on the official copy of the document for his signature. Emperor Justinian II, who had presided over the council, promptly dispatched an armed force to Rome to compel the pope to sign, but without success. Subsequent popes were more amenable. In the ninth century, Pope John VIII declared that "he accepted all those canons" but added the rather cryptic proviso "which did not contradict the true faith, good morals, and the decrees of Rome." The disagreement continued.

THE CRUSADES

November 27, 1096. Pope Urban II, who had come to the southern French town of Clermont to preside over a church council, preached an open-air sermon that day to a crowd assembled outside town. The sermon was occasioned by a communication he had received on his way from Rome to Clermont from the Byzantine emperor Alexius I, who requested assistance against the militant Seljuk Turks. No authentic text of the pope's sermon exists, and it may well be that the accounts available express the sentiment of the scribes rather than the cadences of the pope. But no matter how formulated, the pope's sentences were fiery and eloquent and moving. An accursed race, the pope proclaimed, has invaded the lands of the East. Christians are enslaved, tortured, and killed. The swordsmen practice on them to see whether a neck can be cut into two with one blow. Churches are used as stables, or wrecked, or turned into

Muslim mosques. The Church of the Blessed Virgin Mary is in their hands. Who can avenge if not you come now to the defense of Christ? Forget feuds, fight infidels.

It was a picture of a sordid state of affairs painted by Urban, an emotional tapestry of the sufferings of Christians under Turkish rule in the Holy Land. Something clearly had to be done; fellow Christians had to be liberated from the bondage of persecution and servitude, the sacred sites where the redeemer had walked must be reclaimed, and the yoke of Muslim oppression removed. In calling for a return to the time when Christians could travel and worship freely in the Holy Land, Urban made not only a political point; he also drew on the historical tradition of pilgrimages and their spiritual benefits. Over time, the nature of pilgrimages had undergone a not-so-subtle change in that they also became military expeditions. The objective was to subdue the infidels while securing for Christians the ability to pray at sites where their savior had been. Well before Pope Urban rallied Christendom to recover the burial place of Jesus from the hands of the Muslim infidels, military expeditions had taken place against the Muslims in northern Spain, so the notion of defending the faith with military might lay clearly in the air. Ironically, the Christian notion of the crusade was much akin to the Muslim notion of the jihad: both sought to achieve religious gains through military means. Or, military gains through religious means.

The notion of rallying Christians to a military action was tied to the presumption that all peoples in Christendom were under the aegis of the pope, who could grant lavish spiritual benefits on those responding to his call. Indeed, the spiritual rewards of the crusaders were striking. They were granted special indulgences and temporal privileges, such as exemption from civil jurisdiction as well as inviolability of their lands during their absence from home. They were to be soldiers of a spiritual kingdom, the church, and their wages spiritual benefits and blessings.

Urban's appeal to take up arms in order to defend Christendom would have been unthinkable before Emperor Constantine's conversion to Christianity, for it was then that the cumbersome journey of the Christian faith to an ever more intimate integration into society began. Unlike the situation in the Muslim world, however, church and state were two different entities, and papal goals and aspirations required allies; the increasing ties between the religious and the secular authorities made the pope's call for a crusade a possibility. The first crusade was an alliance of papacy and European nobility; from the second crusade on, however, the popes allied themselves with kings.

Needless to say, there were nonreligious motives in Urban's call to action: a crusade leading to the Christian possession of the Holy Land put the safety of the profitable trade routes between Asia and Europe into Christian hands. The leadership role exercised by the pope in the venture would strengthen the papacy and urge that the common cause against the infidels would lead to the reunion of the Eastern and Western branches of the church—of course, under papal rule.

What took place in the two hundred years or so after Urban's appeal was a sordid tale, characterized by Ralph Waldo Emerson with the comment "a monument of folly and tyranny." And the relations between (Christian) Europe and the Muslim world took a highly problematic turn when Napoleon invaded Egypt in 1798 and European powers claimed possession of virtually all Muslim states—the Middle East, Pakistan, Egypt, Algeria, to name but a few. From the first crusade to the present, the crusading ideal has been immensely powerful in European affairs: it was the just war concept with overtones of moral and religious self-righteousness. On the Muslim side, however, the elastic concept of Jihad, intrinsic to Islam, demonstrated that the notion of the "holy war" has not been a sole Christian principle.

Back in 1096, the cry "God wills it" ("*Deus vult*")—which may well have come from the lips of Pope Urban himself in his sermon—prompted all sorts of men, led by nobility, to gather for the holy crusade. Eventually there were some thirty thousand of them in France, and in loosely organized fashion they began to make their way across Europe, down the Balkan Peninsula, toward the Holy Land. There were noble knights and adventurers, priests and laity, men and women, the deeply devout and the uncannily adventuresome, the old and the young, initially with neither competent leadership nor clear notions of how to get to the Holy Land and what to do there once they had reached it. A cross on their outer garments was evidence of their purpose and allegiance. Arrangements had been made for the crusaders' absences from their previous responsibilities at home, and their wives and children became temporary widows and orphans. No other voluntary mass movement in history has had such formidable appeal as did the first of the crusades.

But long before the first battle took place against the Muslim masters of the Holy Sites, problems surfaced. Some of the crusaders were hardly paragons of Christian virtues, and others, perhaps even spiritually minded, sought to demonstrate their determination to crush the infidels in faraway Palestine by attacking Jewish communities along the Rhine River in Germany; for a long time these communities had lived in tolerable albeit uneasy coexistence with their Christian neighbors. The crusaders' notion was that fighting the "enemies" of the faith could begin with Jews close to home as easily as it could with Muslims far away. At some places, such as Worms, the local bishop sought to intervene when pogroms ensued, but emotions (and envy) carried the day, with terrible pogroms, prompting one Jewish chronicler to bewail "the 1,100 souls killed, including many children and babies who had never sinned."

Eventually the crusaders reached the Holy Land. After several battles and an extensive and successful siege of Antioch, they conquered Jerusalem in July 1099, massacring the defenders together with Muslim and Jewish women and children in the city, an intriguing solidarity of painful suffering but also a quite different turn from what had happened some four hundred years earlier when the Muslims had taken the city and treated its Christian inhabitants with respect and tolerance. The crusaders' cruelty was a rather strange way to represent the Prince of Peace and filled Muslims with understandable horror and anger. The crusaders established a "Kingdom of Jerusalem," though the most obvious choice to become "king" declined the appellation since it should be reserved for Christ. Several other Latin Christian kingdoms were established in the eastern Mediterranean, notably in Antioch.

A second crusade to take back Edessa, another ancient Christian center, and enhance the European presence in the eastern Mediterranean began in 1145, a third in 1188, both with a mixture of success and defeat. In the Third Crusade the famous Richard the Lionheart was the leader, together with Emperor Frederick Barbarossa, so named for his brilliant, short-cropped red beard. Barbarossa had taken his crusaders on a cumbersome journey down the Balkan peninsula instead of by ship from Italy because it had been prophesized that he would die in water. As it turned out, he did die in water, in the Saleph river, not too far from Antioch, where he encamped and went to the river to drink and bathe, without taking off his armor, and was carried away by the currents.

The crusade yielded a truce with the Turks and the guarantee of free access to Jerusalem for Christian pilgrims; Jerusalem, by that time, was back in Muslim hands. The kings of England and France made a public spectacle with their quarrels. The Fourth Crusade, a tragic mixture of miscommunication and distrust, culminated in the siege and sack not of a Muslim stronghold but of Constantinople. Christians were now fighting Christians.

In the thirteenth century, the French king Louis IX spearheaded two crusades (the seventh, 1249–52, and the eighth, 1270) that failed to bring military success but brought Louis' canonization as Catholic saint and an arch in the city named after him on the Mississippi River. All in all, there were no less than nine crusades, including the infamous Children's Crusade in 1212, a sordid venture clouded in a great deal of sad melodrama. A boy, Stephen, challenged children throughout Europe with the biblical exhortation that "a little child will lead them," after the efforts of adults had brought so little success. When the throng of children reached Rome, the pope told them in no uncertain terms they should return home. But to no avail. The children moved on. Many seeming supporters of their undertaking turned out to be slave traders, and the juvenile crusaders who had not perished in the storms of the sea wound up slaves in the Mameluke Empire, never to be heard of again.

By then, the crusading momentum was exhausting itself. Two hundred years after Pope Urban II had first issued his appeal, the last Christian stronghold in the Holy Land, the town of Akko (now Acre), fell to the Ayyubid Muslim dynasty in 1291. The Christian presence in the eastern Mediterranean was a thing of the past. A powerful religious motif had generated the fervor and commitment of the crusaders. It had mingled with crass economic and political concerns, so that it is as little possible to argue that the Christian faith was responsible for this two-hundred-year conflict as it is that the Muslim religion had an inherent hegemonic momentum.

One fateful by-product of the crusades needs to be mentioned again: the outbreak of anti-Semitic pogroms and hostility. A dramatic change in Jewish-Christian relations occurred in connection with the European preoccupation with liberating the Holy Land from the infidels. Ever since Emperor Theodosius had declared the Christian faith to be the only religion that could be publicly practiced in the Roman Empire, Jews had been suppressed both religiously and socially. From the end of the fourth century onward, with Christians now more or less in control, ever increasing restrictions were imposed on Jews and the Jewish religion. In stages, the public exercise of the Jewish religion was prohibited. Christian converts to Judaism had their property confiscated. The Third Council of Toledo (589) prohibited marriages between Jews and Christians and all social contacts between them. The Fourth Council of Toledo (633) declared:

> By the decree of the most glorious prince this sacred council ordered that Jews should not be allowed to have Christian slaves or to buy Christian slaves, or to obtain them by the kindness of any one; for it is not right that the members of Christ should serve the ministers of Anti-Christ. But if henceforward Jews presume to have Christian slaves or handmaidens they shall be taken from their domination and shall go free. (J. D. Mansi, ed., *Sacrorum Conciliorum Nova et Amplissima Collectio* [Paris: H. Welter, 1901], Vol. X).

The Council of Trullo even prohibited Christians from consulting Jewish physicians. The restrictive measures against Jews were many and increasingly suppressive. A turn occurred from theological repudiation to societal restrictions that call for explanation. What had happened? To begin with, the church councils promulgating these anti-Jewish measures expressed the intimate connection that characterized the relationship between society and church. At the Fourth Council of Toledo the king played a pivotal role, which meant that the pronouncements of an ecclesiastical body—a church council—had societal significance. The church spoke; society followed. Or was it the other way around, with the church merely vindicating in its conciliar pronouncements the sentiment and objectives of society? Regardless, Jews and Christians lived in uneasy coexistence, with Jews seeking places to settle in central Europe devoid of the harshness they experienced in places like Spain.

At the time of the First Crusade this relative toleration and uneasy coexistence of all sorts of dissent began to be replaced by outright expressions of hatred and suppression, undoubtedly nurtured by the intense apocalyptic speculation and frenzy triggered by the years 1000 and 1033 (the presumed millennium of Jesus' passion). The fervor accompanying the First Crusade did its share to make Jews the object of suspicion and hatred. Well before the crusaders were anywhere near the Holy Land, and were still tramping southward along the Rhine from northern Germany, they concluded that accursed infidels were right before them—the Jewish communities in Speyer, Worms, Mainz, and Trier—and the crusaders quickly made them the object of their hatred. They were determined to destroy all infidels, whether Muslims or Jews, whether settled along the Rhine River or in the Holy Land. The pleas of King Henry IV remained by and large unheeded, and when it was all over, many Jews had been killed, and scores more had been forcibly baptized.

A new and dreadful chapter had begun, and bloodshed marked the change. Jews ceased to be mere antagonists of theological argumentation. The sword became the means of suppression, just as the Muslim infidels in the Holy Land were to be suppressed, unless they converted. In the Second Crusade Peter of Cluny called for a crusade also against the Jews. In a letter to the French king he wrote: "What good is it to seek out the enemies of the Christian faith in faraway lands and to fight against them, when disreputable and blasphemous Jews, who are far worse than the Saracens, blaspheme Christ and all the Christian sacraments in our very midst." (*Annales Herbipolenses, Monumenta Germaniae Historiae. Scriptores Series.* Xvi).

The First Crusade thus marked a decisive turn in Christian attitudes toward the Jews. It was neither anticipated nor accompanied by a new theological polemic, even as the rallying cry that resulted in much Jewish suffering was not voiced by the church at large, but by individual preachers, whose cadences were of their own making. To be sure, almost everywhere local bishops sought to provide safety and safe havens for the Jews, but that afforded only temporary relief from an increasing culture of violence.

If the First Crusade marked the first important change in the relationship between Jews and their non-Jewish neighbors in Europe, the bubonic plague (or Black Death) in the fourteenth century became a second important turning point, one that again had little to do with theology, but much with a societal catastrophe for which the Jews provided the explanation. First making its appearance in Genoa and Marseilles in 1348 and occurring five more times in the course of the next century, the bubonic plague was a European catastrophe that killed between one-third and one-half of the population. Europe had never experienced anything like it, and the brutal severity of the Plague (whose epidemiology was not understood until 1894 when an anti-serum was developed) begged for an explanation. Medieval medical science was at a loss, other than to talk about "bad" air that had to be avoided, a perspective that actually was fairly close to the mark, since the disease is spread through coughing, causing infectious droplets to move through the air.

At the time, supernatural explanations seemed more persuasive. Many called the Plague a divine scourge for human sinfulness and sought to escape it through excessive works of penance. In the fall of 1348, a throng of flagellants (so designated for their excessive self-flagellation as acts of penitence) moved through Hungary, Austria, northern France, Flanders, and Germany. A revival of a thirteenth-century phenomenon, these peregrinating penitents paralyzed town and countryside with their dramatic displays of penitence.

Others pointed to the Jews as the cause of the calamity, for they had poisoned—so it was alleged—drinking wells to kill Christians. They also murdered Christian children. Thus, Jews were held responsible for the disease and ensuing misery. Panic gripped men and women, and a wave of frantic pogroms spread through the countryside. In Nuremberg more than five hundred Jews were said to have been victims, the surviving members of the community expelled, though the real issue seems to have been that the Jewish part of town had become valuable property, available if the Jewish community was removed. Some church leaders, such as the archbishop of Magdeburg, took a forceful stand against the pogroms and were able to prevent the fiercest outbreaks of violence. But no longer was the region between the Rhine and the Elbe a safe haven in contrast to persistent violence in France, England, or Spain. The seeds of anti-Judaic hostility were beginning to sprout.

From the thirteenth century onward, the place of Jews in German society, as well as in the rest of Europe, was ever more restricted. A comparison of a message of Rudiger Huozmann, bishop of Speyer, on the occasion of the establishment of a Jewish quarter in 1084 and the decrees of the Fourth Lateran Council, meeting in the Lateran in Rome in 1215, shows the change. The bishop's missive granted extensive religious and legal rights to Jews and used sympathetic language. The Lateran Council, on the other hand, promulgated a number of "constitutions," calculated to turn Jews into second-class individuals. Thus, Canon 67 prohibited interest taking while Canon 68 stipulated that Jews should wear recognizable identification marks on their clothing. Tellingly, this stipulation, which also included the prohibition of Jews to leave their houses on Good Friday, was supported with the argument that without such visible differentiation, Christian, Muslim, and Jewish men and women would become romantically involved.

A final cause of the deterioration of Jewish-Christian relations was the charge of blood libel brought against Jews. It started in Norwich, England, in 1144 when a boy named William was found murdered. In a quixotic turn, a convergence of investigative incompetence, ethnic bias, and the desire (for both religious and commercial reasons) to make Norwich a pilgrimage center turned an ordinary murder case into the seedbed for the accusation that the Jewish religion demanded the drinking of the blood of Christian boys. Even though these ritual murder accusations were persistently rejected by the papacy and church officials, they spread to the Continent, where they surfaced periodically and were used to explain the murder of young boys. Tragically, blood libel accusations and indictments continued into the late nineteenth century.

THE CHRISTIAN FAITH IN ASIA

It is not usually realized that during the Middle Ages the Christian faith expanded not only into what we have come to call Europe but also into Asia. The Byzantine Church was only a part—a small part as a matter of fact—of the much larger transmittal of the Christian faith in the East, for the earliest expansion of the Christian religion took place not only westward but also eastward as well, and the gospel of Jesus was proclaimed in Asia Minor and Asia proper.

One of the "heretics" of early Christianity, Nestorius, deserves credit for having pushed the Christian message eastward. He hailed from Syria, was priest in Antioch, and to general acclaim was elected archbishop of Constantinople in 428. A hothead by personality and theologian by vocation, he quickly succeeded in offending everyone in sight, destroying Arian churches, and publicly offending Pulcheria, the emperor's sister. To make matters worse, Nestorius began to develop rather controversial theological views. He had a special distaste for the designation "God Bearer" or "Mother of God" (in Greek, *theotokos*) that was becoming more and more common for Mary; he proposed *Christotokos*, "Christ Bearer," instead. He was charged with believing that the divine and human in Jesus meant two distinct beings (or persons)—in contrast to the opposing view that the two natures, human and divine, were in one person. In later years when he was widely ostracized, Nestorius went to great lengths to defend himself against the charge that he saw Jesus as a split personality, but, on the other hand, he did insist that no union between the human and divine was possible. In such a union, Christ could not truly be equal with God and equal with humans, for he would grow, suffer, and die (which God would not) and would possess divine power, making him unequal to humans.

Nestorius was accused of heresy, and his abrasive personality may well have played an important role. His opponent was Patriarch Cyril of Alexandria, who charged him with separating Jesus' divinity and humanity into two persons in one body. As far as Cyril was concerned, that was tantamount to denying the reality of the incarnation. Cyril was an insightful theologian and the shrewder (and more ruthless) politician of the two. He won out; Nestorius had to go into exile, making the episode yet another illustration for the reality of bitter disagreements among those who proclaimed to be followers of Jesus and of the importance of personalities in controversy.

It was to be crucially important for the larger Christian story that Nestorius had an extensive throng of followers and that "Nestorian Christianity" became the dominant form of the Christian religion in the Middle East. It was a heretical movement, however, as far as the Latin and the Orthodox churches were concerned, since the Council of Chalcedon had ruled in 451 that Jesus had been one person with two natures. Since the imperial authorities in Constantinople considered the Nestorians disturbers of the peace of both church and empire, Nestorian Christians flocked eastward into Persia, where they found a hospitable place to practice their faith. Toward the end of the fifth century the Sassanid rulers of the Persian Empire (which extended from North Africa to India) appointed a Nestorian bishop, more for political than theological reasons; this meant the end of any Nestorian connection with the Byzantine church.

Consequently, Nestorian Christianity expanded into the four corners of the Sassanid Empire—central east Africa, Asia, southwest India, even China. The sources for this dramatic expansion, however, are scarce. In their expansion, Nestorian Christians were aided by another offshoot from the church catholic, the Monophysites (in Greek, "one nature"), whose concern paralleled that of the Nestorians, namely, to keep the human and divine nature of Jesus neatly separated; their solution was to downplay Jesus' human nature. The Monophysite theologian Apollinaris of Laodicea (d. 390) had argued that Jesus passed through Mary as does water through a tube.

Similarly, the Egyptian church turned Monophysite, as did a variant form in Syria. The Ethiopian church, and the Mar Thomas Church in south India, which had been established according to tradition by the Apostle Thomas, were also largely Monophysite. Arab expansionism, coupled with the rise of Islam, not only brought an end to the mighty Sassanid Empire, it also made the Christian communities into barely tolerated entities in societies that were militantly Muslim. While some of these churches—most obviously in Ethiopia, Egypt, India, and Iraq come to mind—have survived to the twenty-first century, centuries-long experience turned them into inward-oriented churches, constantly exposed to discrimination and suppression, that barely survived. The fate of these churches might well offer a hint of what happens when the Christian religion finds itself, unlike in Europe, without pointed governmental support.

When the European exploration of other continents and peoples in the sixteenth century also sought to take the Christian faith abroad, missionaries were surprised to find the small Christian communities at places and regions altogether unexpected. They were strangely different from European churches.

Reflection 3: Jews and Christians

The worsening of Jewish-Christian relations at the time of the First Crusade calls for explanation. Something must have happened to disturb the uneasy truce between the Christian majority and the Jewish minority that had prevailed for several centuries. To be sure, Jews and their communities were chronically oppressed, but there were few outright instances of persecution and violence. Twelfth-century Europe broke with this past and became a persecuting society, abandoning previous patterns of toleration. Outsiders, whether Jews, heretics, lepers, or other marginalized individuals, were no longer afforded the toleration (or lack of attention) they had earlier enjoyed.

The causes for this turn probably were several. For one, the body politic was challenged by dissenting movements, such as the Cathari and the Waldensians, that triggered apprehension, even fear, on the part of the authorities both religious and secular. At the same time the political authorities were engaged in a process of consolidating their authority and power, which meant the suppression of competing claims. In other words, the rise of intolerance and persecution had little to do with the demeanor of the "outsiders" or with popular impulses of intolerance. Heretics, Jews, and lepers owed their fate not to manifestation of popular hatred, but to the decision of those in power to stifle all forms of dissent.

The hostility toward Jews, of course, had a lengthy history in which broader non-Christian and specific Christian attitudes merged. The broader non-Christian attitudes and polemics were the consequence of the fear of the stranger, the "other." That was the case in the late nineteenth century with the rise of racial anti-Semitism, when a wave of westward migration of Russian Jews brought patterns of diverse cultures into play. Jews promptly were not only castigated for moral improprieties but also for their conspiratorial intent to destroy the "Christian" Europe. The infamous forgery titled *The Protocols of the Elders of Zion* is a telling illustration for how this fear found resonance among the general populace in such countries as Austria-Hungary and Germany, and this despite the demographic reality that pre-World War I Germany had a Jewish population of about three percent. How three percent could successfully take over the reins of power is hard to imagine.

The specific Christian attitudes towards Jews, that is, polemics that engaged theological or biblical argumentation, had their origin in the allegation of the Jewish complicity in Jesus' crucifixion and the corollary

Jewish unwillingness to recognize Jesus as the promised Messiah of Israel. And no sooner had Christianity become the sole recognized religion in the Roman Empire than Christian influence led to ever-new measures to curtail the lives of Jews and their communities. Ever-new legal measures, some proposed by the church but ratified by the state, were calculated to preclude any contact between Christians and Jews.

Something else became prominent in Christian reflection as well: Augustine's notion that Jewish homelessness and suffering were to serve as reminders to Christians of the consequence of rejecting God. Christians had to learn the lesson of Jewish suffering. Accordingly, Jews were not to be persecuted, but left alone in their homeless suffering. Augustine's sentiment meshed harmoniously with the earlier declaration of the Apostle Paul that in the End Days the Jewish people will convert to the gospel. This point, widely propounded in the Middle Ages by Bernard of Clairvaux, suggested that theological insight put a damper on the excesses of the moral polemic.

A second theme in attitudes toward Jews stemmed not from religious or theological sources but from the evident unwillingness of mainstream society to accept outsiders, the "other." It was not only in religion that Jews and their communities were declared to be different. Jews kept to themselves (of course, they were forced to do so by the creation of ghettos), spoke a different language, were marked by a different culture, even different attire. No doubt, thus "cultural" anti-Judaism dominated through the centuries, eventually finding a fateful expression in the nineteenth century with the emergence of a supposed scholarly thesis that declared Jews to be inferior human beings by virtue of their "race." And Christian voices seemed always ready to add theological arguments to the cultural polemic.

Theological anti-Judaism grew out of the difference of Jewish and Christian readings of the Hebrew Scriptures, coupled with the Christian assertion that Jesus of Nazareth had been the Messiah promised to Israel, a claim fiercely rejected by Jews. The polemic was theological and hinged on the assessment of the Messianic claims of Jesus. It entailed the Christian claim to understand the Jewish Scriptures better than did Jews. "Cultural" anti-Judaism was different in that it focused on personal and cultural qualities of Jews. At issue was the allegation of distinctive, morally despicable Jewish character traits. Jews were chided not for their interpretation of their own Scriptures; they were indicted for their cultural and personal traits—dishonesty, greed, deceitfulness—but also for attire and food. Peter the Venerable put this sentiment into words that suggest the foremost reason for anti-Jewish hostility. It is well known, Peter wrote, that the Jews

> are able to fill their barns with grain, their cellars with wine, their purses with gold not because of their tilling the soil or practicing the law, or because of honorable and useful labor. Rather, they deprive Christians with sly maneuvers and sell expensive goods which they acquired cheaply from robbers. (*Adversus Judeorum duritiem*, Yvonne Friedman, ed. [Turnhout, Belgium: Brepols, 1985])

Jewish involvement in finance was resented, especially the activities that led to the charge of usury, a topic endlessly debated by medieval theologians. The evidence suggests that those with whom Jewish lenders had financial dealings were not in the forefront of the anti-usury polemic; they understood how the economy had to function. By the same token, the anti-Jewish pogroms tended to be about more than religion; often, economic causes were the real catalyst. The pogroms were a lower-class phenomenon, graphically noted by an observer: "It was their money that killed them. If the Jews had been poor and the rulers had not been indebted to them, they would also not have been burned" (Jakob von Königshofen, *Chronik*).

The political elites sought to keep themselves harmless while the economic elites were out to remove their Jewish competitors. A mass psychosis of common people mixed with the political and economic considerations of the elite. Emperor Charles IV had become involved in discussions about how to acquire valuable Jewish property in Nuremberg well before the pogrom broke out.

The later Middle Ages brought a wave of expulsions of Jews from their places of residence throughout Europe, first from England, then from Spain, later from numerous German territories. The theologians, including Martin Luther in the sixteenth century, had no problem with such severe measures. In the seventeenth century, Jews were readmitted to England, and, later, to most European countries. Enlightenment thought had triggered a fundamental reinterpretation of the traditional understanding of Jesus, removing the most glaring assertions unacceptable to Jews (for example, that Jesus was truly God). While this should have opened the door to greater harmony, the theological tensions between the two religions persisted.

CHAPTER THREE

THE WESTERN CHURCH DIVIDES: THE PROTESTANT REFORMATION

On October 31, 1517, Martin Luther, Professor of Biblical Studies at the University at Wittenberg, Saxony, posted a set of ninety-five theological propositions, or "theses," dealing with the church practice of indulgences. His intention was to have an academic debate among theologians on the topic. Unexpectedly, Luther's theses led to a controversy that eventually resulted in the Reformation movement, and no one was more confounded by that dramatic turn of events than Martin Luther himself, even though in 1517 he had done his best to make sure that his theses would become widely known.

Some twelve years earlier, Luther had abandoned law school, much against his father's will, in order to become an Augustinian friar. Encouraged by his monastic superior, he pursued doctoral studies in theology, which in 1512 led to his doctorate and his appointment as professor at Wittenberg. His life, so it seemed at the time, was bound to be that of an unknown scholar of the Christian faith. The *Ninety-five Theses* made things turn out quite differently.

What happened?

For a long time, it was a scholarly commonplace that at the beginning of the sixteenth century, the church found itself in a deep trouble—ignorant and immoral priests were abundant, while in Rome, the heart of the church, a perverted leadership was more occupied with Italian politics and secular learning than with the spiritual nurture of the faithful. At the same time, so the argument ran, European society showed signs of a systemic crisis, manifest in restiveness among the common people, especially the peasants, and tensions among the ruling elites, problems with the traditional relationship of the church and the body politic. In short, the time was said to have been ripe for a revolutionary upheaval.

More recently, this view, a combination of dubious methodology and anti-Catholic bias, has been replaced by a more judicious perspective, which sees the late medieval church as having been essentially stable. People were loyal to the church, which provided spiritual solace and comfort in days pleasant and days painful. If many of the priests were illiterate, it was not such a big deal, for so were most of the people. And few people actually knew of the involvements of the papacy in Italian politics.

To be sure, some individuals were perturbed by what they perceived to be the lamentable state of the church and society, the political involvements of the church, for example, or the chronic fiscal burdens placed by the church upon the faithful. Big changes were taking place in European society. In the flourishing towns, a literate and self-conscious laity sought ways to express what it meant to be a community, while political authorities sought tighter control of the body politic and resented the legal and fiscal privileges enjoyed by the clergy and church, such as the exemption of the clergy from much of secular jurisdiction and taxation. New forms of economic endeavor were emerging, first in the prosperous and powerful city republics of Italy, such as Florence and Milan, then in such towns as Frankfurt, Amsterdam, and Nuremberg. Moreover, a loose European fraternity of intellectuals, known as "Humanists," propounded a new kind of learning that they found exemplified in classical Antiquity, and not in the thought and method of the scholastics. These Humanists attacked—sometimes bluntly, sometimes satirically—what they considered the stilted scholastic method of thinking and writing in theology and philosophy. While loyal to the church, they understood the Christian faith differently than the scholastic theologians. With only a bit of overstatement one might say that these Humanists would not have terribly grieved if all the scholastic learning of the prior centuries had disappeared into a black hole. They looked to Antiquity, to the theologians of the early church but also to Greek and Roman philosophers for inspiration—and truth. By the early sixteenth century, these Humanists had a distinguished and renowned representative: Erasmus of Rotterdam, an erstwhile monk turned public intellectual, who relentlessly committed himself to editing and publishing the writings of the early Church Fathers, whom he and his fellow Humanist allies believed to be better guides to authentic

Christianity than the scholastic theologians of the previous centuries.

In short, Luther's *Ninety-five Theses* burst upon a church and a society not without problems and not without critical voices calling for change. Moreover, the rich theological and spiritual engagement of the fifteenth century constituted an important legacy for the ensuing sixteenth century. The theological discourse triggered by Luther's theses is unthinkable without recourse to the fifteenth century. However, despite this complex matrix of critique and affirmation, it is equally clear that something crucial was missing: a pervading sense of a deep crisis in church and state. The commotion about the theses came not so much from any radical tenor of his pronouncement (though several theses were in fact quite critical of the papacy) but from the reality that Luther had reached, however inadvertently, into a political and financial hornet's nest. At issue was the proclamation (and sale) of a special "jubilee" indulgence in north Germany. Unbeknownst to Luther, it was an intriguing mixture of religion and high-stakes politics and finance. Indulgences were (and are) a complicated topic of Catholic theology and practice. According to church teaching, indulgences offered the penitent individual the remission of the church-imposed punishment for sins; to receive such remission the individual had to perform a good work, which might mean visiting a pilgrimage shrine or making a gift to the poor or to the church. By the early sixteenth century, popular and even theological misunderstandings had crept into this ecclesiastical practice, leading to the ditty that "as soon as the coin [given to receive an indulgence] in the coffer rings, the soul from purgatory springs," the notion that for a financial contribution one would receive divine forgiveness of sins.

When the special indulgence was proclaimed (and sold) in the vicinity of Wittenberg, Luther discovered to his dismay that the Wittenberg townspeople assumed precisely that: the mere purchase of a letter of indulgence forgave their sins. The particular indulgence that evoked Luther's ire and was to fill the church's coffers was to provide funds for the construction of a new church of Saint Peter in Rome and to reimburse the young Albert of Brandenburg for the fees he had paid the curia in order to be appointed to the ecclesiastically prestigious and politically powerful position of archbishop of Mainz. On paper it was, as the saying goes, a win-win situation—for Albert, who would recoup the steep fees he had paid to secure the archbishopric when in fact he lacked the necessary canonical qualifications for the office; for the curia, which would obtain revenues to build a magnificent new basilica in Rome; and for the faithful purchasers of indulgences, who could rest comfortable in the knowledge of having received forgiveness for their sins.

In those days academic theses were discussed at formal university occasions. Scholars still are not sure how exactly Luther meant to have his *Ninety-five Theses* debated. It seems likely, however, that Luther, less concerned about an academic exercise than about the spiritual welfare of the common people who were foolishly purchasing indulgences, meant to use the threat of a public discussion to badger Archbishop Albert into stopping the sale. Since Luther had sent copies of his theses to a number of friends and colleagues, one can hardly conclude that his sharp statement was meant to be confidential.

Albert undoubtedly panicked over the possibility that a public debate of Luther's theses would bring to light the confidential financial aspects of the indulgences sale. He promptly dispatched a copy of Luther's theses to the Roman curia, requesting that formal proceedings be commenced to ascertain Luther's theological orthodoxy. Thus, a fateful turn occurred, for Albert's move made Luther's pronouncement (according to the academic custom of the time, nothing more than an invitation to probe unresolved theological questions) an affair of state and, before long, the cause of a fierce conflagration among academic theologians and the laity.

THE CONTROVERSY

In the turbulent years that followed Luther's posting of his *Ninety-five Theses*, several different but intertwining trajectories of events characterized the scene. To begin with, there were the official ecclesiastical proceedings against Luther. Archbishop Albert had sent the theses to the curia, and Rome had acted with unanticipated speed. In the summer of 1518, Luther was ordered to appear in Rome to be examined about his theological orthodoxy. The intervention of his territorial ruler, Elector Frederick of Saxony, who sensed that Luther's examination in Rome would not be a fair hearing, caused this examination to take place in Augsburg, where the German diet (parliament) was in session. Luther's examiner was Cardinal Cajetan, one of the most learned members of the curia, who challenged Luther to recant some statements he had made in an effort to explain his *Ninety-five Theses*. Luther refused, and the exchange between the two men led nowhere.

The question in Rome was how to proceed. Pope Leo X opined that this was nothing but a quarrel among monks. (John Tetzel, the chief "commissioner" of the indulgence, was a Dominican, while Luther was an Augustinian.) There seems to have been support among members of the curia in Rome for that sentiment—not to examine Luther's theses and subsequent writings too painstakingly, to make haste slowly, so to speak, and look the other way. But by the early summer of 1520, the hard-liners, led by the Ingolstadt theologian John Eck, had won out, however, and the curia moved to action and a confrontation. In September, Pope Leo X issued the papal bull (decree) *Exsurge domine* ("Arise, O Lord, a wild boar has invaded Thy vineyard"), which condemned Luther for forty-one sentences and phrases culled from his writings. The bull gave him sixty days to recant and another sixty days to report his recantation to Rome. Luther was defiant, and so a second papal bull formally excommunicated him (and all who shared his views) in January 1521. Roughly three years after he had issued an intra-university document, Luther was excommunicated. He was outside the church and eternally damned.

A second trajectory of the events in the wake of the *Ninety-five Theses* had to do with an ever-widening and ever-sharpening theological debate. Initially, prompted by Luther's theses, the topic was indulgences, but that topic quickly gave way to the question of church authority and of its sacramental system. The major milestone in this theological debate was Luther's *Heidelberg Theses*, in which he outlined his understanding of what he called the "theology of the cross." This was Luther's notion that God always acts in a mysterious, hidden way, of which Jesus' crucifixion is the signal illustration. Empirically, that event was the execution of a religious troublemaker; in the eyes of faith, however, it was God's saving deed for humankind. In much the same way, justification by faith alone makes something not visible—faith—the key element.

In June 1519, a debate in Leipzig was to thrash out the theological disagreement between the new Wittenberg theology and traditional views. Luther and his Wittenberg colleague Andreas Carlstadt faced John Eck, the chief spokesperson for the traditionalist cause. On that occasion Luther denied the ultimate authority of the church (and of church councils) in favor of the authority of Scripture, a stance that evoked gasps of dismay from the faithful Catholics and sharpened the gulf between the Wittenberg friar and his church.

A third trajectory had to do with what might be called the popular appropriation of the theological debate: the increasing involvement of individuals other than professional theologians in the controversy. It was made possible by a technological innovation, the invention of the printing press that had been made roughly half a century earlier. The invention of movable type by Johannes Gutenberg had made printing simpler and more economical, and no sooner had the theological controversy over Luther's theses gotten under way than an avalanche of publications began to flood the German countryside, brief pamphlets written in the vernacular and dealing with general topics of Christian life and faith. These pamphlets differed in tone, content, and style from the sophisticated pronouncements from the pens of the professional theologians who wrote, of course, only for their fellow theologians. The pamphlets that made their appearance were an entirely different genre of writings. Luther took the lead in writing a seemingly endless number of such pamphlets, but he was soon joined by a host of other authors. These pamphlets made the case for a greater commitment to the Christian faith, thus relating only indirectly to the issues of the theological debate going on among the professionals. Their topics—with titles like *How to Pray the Lord's Prayer* or *A Proper Way of Dying* or *A Treatise on Marriage*—were far removed (at least on the face of things) from the sophisticated theological subjects of free will or ecclesiastical authority. The homey style—for example, through the use of the dialogue format—meant that they were accessible to the educated laity as well as, of course, to the professional theologians (not all of whom were truly fluent in Latin).

These pamphlets were a new genre of publication, hardly ever more than thirty-two pages in length, often illustrated with woodcuts. They were less expensive and thus easier to acquire than the hefty Latin tomes of the theologians. Luther used this genre to address the basic concern that had prompted his *Ninety-five Theses* in the first place: the common people needed to be informed of, and encouraged in, the true Christian faith. While there was criticism of the church and its clergy in these pamphlets, their overall tone was positive, and they evoked a vision of true Christian spirituality and life.

A final facet of the initial controversy was the ever louder and ever more forceful demand for reform in church and society. In an amazingly short time, a massive consciousness-raising took place in Germany that convinced people that there was, indeed, a deep crisis in church and society. Things were not what they should be. To be sure, there had been calls of this sort before, including the chronic deliberations about the "gravamina," the official German grievances against church financial dealings, for example. But what had been isolated pronouncements now turned into a tide of concern. Prior to the avalanche of pamphlets, the common people had stood in awe of the church and had been loyal to it. Now they were convinced that the church (and society at large) was in stark crisis. No empirical reality had changed in the span of a few years; the popular mind-set, however, had undergone a major transformation. And Martin Luther had been the catalyst.

All this related to Luther's own spiritual transformation. Sometime between 1516 and 1518—scholars continue to debate the date—Luther became overwhelmed by the awareness that what the church taught about salvation (that humans have to marshal their moral prowess and do good, whereupon God will gracefully accept them) was not working for him. He saw himself as deeply sinful, unable to judge himself other than as condemned to eternal damnation. After much spiritual agony he concluded that God freely forgives the repentant sinner. Many years later, in the 1540s, he wrote about this new insight, that it was "as if the gates of paradise had opened up before me." (*Luther's Works* IV, 336). It led him to the conclusion that salvation came not through "good works" but through grace and faith alone.

Luther's conversion—giving him, as it did, a profound religious certainty—must have been a major factor in his unwillingness to surrender to the demand of the church that he revoke certain statements he had made in the controversy. Until 1519, he had not directly attacked a church doctrine. Nonetheless, the church excommunicated him as a heretic, and the fate of heretics was crystal clear: the political authorities would apprehend him and condemn him in a perfunctory trial to death by burning, the punishment reserved for heretics, whose bodies and souls were reduced to ashes.

There was a complication in Luther's case, however, and it had to do with the structure of the Holy Roman Empire of the German Nation. This empire was an intriguing constellation of a large number of territories, some larger, others small, stretching from the Baltic Sea to the North Italian plain, all of which had territorial rulers who jealously sought to consolidate their power, generally at the expense of the emperor, who represented central authority in the Empire. The imperial office was elective, not hereditary, and in order to secure his election the nineteen-year-old Spanish king Charles had to agree to a number of stipulations, all calculated to curtail his authority and power. One of the stipulations was that no German would be sentenced without a proper court hearing.

Those who, for whatever reason, supported Luther promptly argued that he had been condemned without ever having had the opportunity to present his views. A deeply loyal Catholic, Charles could not understand that one would second-guess a verdict by the church, and he was at first quite adamant that the judgment of the church had to be carried out without further ado. But the stipulations of his election agreement forced his hand—the territorial rulers were clearly not willing to let him get away with ignoring a document he had signed—and after much back-room negotiating he consented that Luther be given a hearing. He summoned Luther to the imperial diet, in session in the city of Worms on the Rhine. The papal legate in Germany, Aleander, vigorously protested as well, arguing that the church had rendered its verdict on Luther, and the body politic had to carry out its responsibility. He found it obnoxious that a convicted heretic was to be given another hearing. His demurs, like those of the emperor, were, however, of no avail.

Toward the end of April 1521, Luther made his appearance in Worms before the emperor and the dignitaries of the empire. He defiantly declared that unless he was convinced by Scripture and common sense that he was in error, he would not recant. With this statement he had thrown a gauntlet at the feet of the emperor and the church. Luther was obviously encouraged by the increasing popular support for him—his journey to Worms had been nothing short of triumphal—but his coming to Worms was still an act of courage. After all, slightly more than a century before, another theologian, Jan Hus, had been promised safe conduct when summoned to appear before the church council in the Swabian city of Constance. His safe-conduct was revoked, and he was burned at the stake—the justification being that it was not necessary to honor a promise made to a heretic. In other words, Luther hardly had reason to be calm about appearing in Worms. What saved him was that he had made broad segments of the German people aware of the need for change in church and society. And he had a powerful protector, Elector Frederick of Saxony. At the elector's instigation, Luther, on his return to Wittenberg, was spirited away to a forlorn site, Wartburg castle, made famous in the nineteenth century in Richard Wagner's opera *Tannhäuser*. There Luther was to spend almost a full year in hiding.

Since Luther's appearance before the diet at Worms had achieved nothing, Emperor Charles V in May 1521 signed an edict, subsequently known as the Edict of Worms, that made Luther and his followers legal outlaws. The case of Martin Luther, convicted heretic, had been dealt with by the church and state. And was settled. The controversy was over.

Quickly it became evident, however, that it was not. Luther, despite being in hiding, continued to exert his influence by publishing pamphlets and engaging in a vast correspondence. He also began a most ambitious project: the translation of the Bible into vernacular German. His translation of the New Testament appeared in September 1522—at a price of one and a half guilder, about half a year's wages for a female servant. Despite its price it became a publishing sensation, a best seller. The translation was in keeping with Luther's notion that the Bible alone was the source of Christian truth; therefore, it had to be as widely accessible as possible.

THE CONSEQUENCES

It is incorrect to suggest that before Luther a widespread notion of a crisis in church and society prevailed and he responded to this reality by sounding a call for reform. Quite the contrary, it was the other way around. Luther was the one who created a sense of crisis, convincing his contemporaries of something they had not felt or thought of before. He persuaded his contemporaries that church and society—while outwardly fine—were in fact in despicable condition and needed reform. At the same time, he pointed to the means of alleviating the crisis: the Word of God, which had the power to set everything straight, correct abuses, and invigorate both church hierarchy and the ordinary people. The controversy, which began as a theological dispute and a call to a deepened commitment to the Christian faith, turned into a movement for reform.

Men (and women) rallied under the banner of the "Word" to bring about reform and change. Their call was to make "evangelical preaching," the Word of God, the center of church and society. For the reformers, the Mass signified everything that was wrong with the papal church—unbiblical theology and unbiblical practice. The notion of replicating the sacrifice of Jesus in the Mass was an abomination, the reformers argued, and the prominence given to the Mass in worship meant the neglect of the proclamation of the Word. Whenever a community followed the lead of Luther and other reformers, the call for the discontinuation of the Mass tended to be the first practical step toward rejecting the papal church and introducing reform.

The message that the Word of God, unencumbered by human accretions and additions, would usher in a new society and a reformed church proved to be liberating; it made the reform movement a dynamic phenomenon. But the popular dimension of the early Reformation must not be overestimated. That people flocked to the evangelical preachers advocating reform is beyond doubt, but there is little evidence that they formed a mass movement. In German territories, moreover, the common people had little say in the decision whether to join the cause of the reformers. That decision was made by the rulers, the political authorities, although popular sentiment undoubtedly played a role. In the town of Nuremberg, for example, the city council may have had extensive support from the town citizens when it decided to discontinue the celebration of the Mass and close the monasteries and convents in the city. Reportedly, the two major churches in town had so many come and listen from the balconies to evangelical sermons that there was concern that the balconies might come crashing down. Such popular expressions of support notwithstanding, the decision to discontinue the celebration of the Mass was made in Nuremberg by the city council and not by a vote of the citizens. In the territory of Hesse, on the other hand, Landgrave Philip's subjects had no say in the matter at all. Many territorial rulers and city councils saw the matter as a test case for future relations between the newly elected emperor and the German "estates," as the territories, such as Saxony, Hesse, and Württemberg, and the imperial cities, such as Nuremberg or Frankfurt, were known.

The decision of the Roman Church in January 1521 to excommunicate Luther and his followers, together with the emperor's edict of May 1521, was to be enforced by the political authorities. In other words, the verdict of the church was not merely an ecclesiastical affair; it also was an affair of state. For those on the receiving end, the two verdicts conveyed the seriousness of the situation: in Luther's case, siding publicly with him had become a matter of life or death.

The Edict of Worms called upon the estates to stamp out Luther and his heresies, but it quickly became evident that while some rulers would do so, others would not. Morever, the emperor's departure from Germany for Spain in May 1521 removed an important pillar of support of the Catholic Church and, in the absence of the emperor's stature, the movement for reform gathered momentum.

Even though some riots and public disturbances occurred, in the main the reform movement turned out to be a rather docile affair without much dramatic agitation. This tranquility was abruptly disturbed, however, in the late summer of 1524, when peasants in southwest Germany rioted and took up arms in insurrection. This turn of events stood, part and parcel, in a long tradition of peasant unrest in the later Middle Ages. In the early sixteenth century German society was changing, Luther had convinced his contemporaries that a crisis beset church and society, and the peasants, whose social and economic standing had deteriorated, decided to do something about it. There had been a localized uprising in the second decade of the sixteenth century, quickly crushed by the authorities, but apprehension about an outbreak of a new insurgency hung ominously over the affairs of state, especially the deliberations about Luther at the Diet of Worms.

The demands of the insurgent peasants and townspeople in the summer of 1524, while largely economic in nature, also reflected the broad reform notions that Luther and others had propounded. The peasants' grievances, broadcast in a document called *The Twelve Articles of the Peasants* (*Die grundtlichen und rechten haupt artickel aller baurschafft*), came right out of the reformers' book; the peasants grounded their socio-economic and political demands in the Bible.

The opponents of reform, however, saw things differently. As far as they were concerned, the movement of reform had been the cause of the disruption of law and order. By the spring of 1525, when large regions of southwest and central Germany, as well as parts of Austria, were in the throes of unrest, both reform-minded and adamantly Catholic rulers allied to crush the uprising. In the end, the peasants were no military match for the well-trained mercenaries of the rulers. Beginning with a fatal battle near the village of Frankenhausen in central Germany in May 1525, the peasants suffered one defeat after another. The uprising collapsed, but not before thousands upon thousands of peasants had been slain.

Luther had written several pamphlets dealing with the relationship of the Christian to the sociopolitical order, at first attempting to remain above the fray; eventually, however, he sided with the rulers, and not with the peasants and townspeople who had claimed him as inspiration for their program of societal (and religious) change. The overriding issue for Luther was not so much that the peasants sought to tie socioeconomic demands to the Bible but that they had used force and insurrection to make their case.

For his disowning them, Luther afterward had to face the disillusionment of the peasants and, so it has been argued, the loss of popular support for the movement of reform. Since the peasants had pursued their demands in the context of a violent insurgency in both town and country, Catholic rulers were convinced that the reform movement was not only heretical but also threatened law and order. They blamed the reformers and their message for the destruction and bloodshed, and at the same time they explored the formation of a military alliance for the twin goals of suppressing the Lutheran heresy and preventing future insurgency. The cause of religious reform became ever more intimately tied to politics.

Little by little, however, the reformers' call for the centrality of the Word and the repudiation of everything not conforming to that Word garnered support. Rulers sympathetic with the cause of reform (for whatever reasons) declared that the Edict of Worms could not be enforced without causing public uproar, while Catholic rulers used the uprising as justification for insisting on a full implementation of the Edict of Worms.

Thus, the turbulence that had dominated the German countryside for more than a year hung very much in the air when a diet in Speyer in 1526 once more addressed the question of what should be done with the edict about Luther. Catholic rulers argued fiercely that the peasants' uprising had been caused by Luther's pernicious teachings, while those rulers with a reforming bent held that the enforcement of the edict would trigger a new wave of violence given Luther's widespread popular support. No agreement between these two views seemed possible. Eventually, both sides agreed that for the time being each ruler should be free to decide how to handle the edict. This was a compromise that did not settle anything. Of course, it was not meant to resolve the disagreements; it was to offer some breathing room before the situation could be reassessed. But matters became complicated when the two sides interpreted the agreement differently. Catholics saw it as a stopgap measure until the shockwaves of the peasant uprising died down, while the reform-minded rulers took the agreement as license to ignore the Worms edict altogether and undertake whatever ecclesiastical reform they deemed necessary.

Three years later, in 1529, many of the Catholic rulers angrily realized that the reformers' interpretation of the 1526 recess was not at all what they had had in mind when they had agreed to it. They reiterated that a comprehensive implementation of the Worms edict was a theological and legal necessity. Since Catholic rulers were the majority in the diet, it

Figure 3A
Lucas Cranach the Elder. Martin Luther.
16th century Germany. Germanisches
National Museum, Nuremberg, Germany.

was so decided. The supporters of reform protested against this majority decision, arguing that since the 1526 recess had been passed unanimously, it had to be rescinded unanimously as well. The Catholic majority dissented, and the reform-minded rulers were given the label "protestants," "those who protested." The label has stuck for centuries.

Yet another diet had ended in discord. Emperor Charles, who had been absent from Germany for almost a decade attending to Spanish affairs (he had left immediately after signing the Edict of Worms), realized that the unresolved religious controversy demanded his return. In preparation for a diet to convene in Augsburg, he invited the two parties of the religious controversy to submit statements of faith that could be examined in order to explore if conciliation might be possible. Understandably, the Catholics demurred, stating that theirs was the faith of more than a millennium and was known to all. Three Protestant statements were submitted, one by Huldrych Zwingli, the Zurich reformer (*Fidei Ratio*), one by four south German cities (the *Confessio Tetrapolitana*), and one by Philip Melanchthon, Luther's Wittenberg colleague, on behalf of Electoral Saxony, Hesse, and several other Lutheran towns and territories. Known as the *Confessio Augustana*, or Augsburg Confession, Melanchthon's irenic summary of Lutheran theology went out of its way to underscore the conservative nature of the new Wittenberg theology. It emphasized the areas of agreement between the Catholic Church and the Wittenberg theology and more or less labeled the disagreements between the two as insignificant. This Augsburg Confession was augmented by a second statement, the *Apology* (or "Explanation") of the Augsburg Confession, and the two documents together became the basic theological confession of many Lutheran churches, perhaps less for its delineation of specific points of doctrine than for its general conceptualization, which faithfully expressed the Lutheran understanding of the biblical message.

After prolonged discussions, the emperor and the Catholic party declared themselves not persuaded that the Lutheran document was in harmony with Catholic belief. The recess of the diet gave the Protestants six months to undo the ecclesiastical and liturgical changes they had introduced in their cities and territories; otherwise, they would be compelled to do so by military force.

As it turned out, this threat was easier made than carried out. Another major issue facing the empire made the Catholic threat hollow and limited Catholic options: the army of the Ottoman Turks stood massed at the southeastern border of the empire, poised to attack. The Turks had advanced up the Balkan Peninsula in the late fifteenth century and were not too far east of Vienna, threatening central Europe with military subjugation. The combination of the military threat and the Muslim religion brought apprehension, even fear, to the hearts and minds of people everywhere. The emperor, whose function it was to coordinate the defenses of the empire, needed the financial support of the territorial rulers for raising an army—and the Protestants were quick to realize that they could use the ominous Turkish threat to exact religious concessions from him. Obviously, Charles could hardly threaten the Protestant rulers with military subjection while at the same time soliciting their financial support. Thus, he was unable to put teeth into his anti-Protestant rhetoric. His threat of armed subjection of the Protestants in six months was written as on water.

Charles's dilemma demonstrates how overwhelmed he was with conflicting responsibilities. As king of Spain he had to deal with the long-standing Spanish conflict with France; as German emperor he faced uncooperative territorial rulers; as staunch Catholic he confronted a growing Protestant menace and an uncooperative papacy. When once he, unrecognized, asked a Spanish peasant for his opinion of recent kings, he had to hear that he, Charles, was the worst of the lot, for "he is always gadding about." True enough, Charles juggled too many balls in the air. Despite his commitment to eradicating the Protestant heresy, he never succeeded in giving the German situation his undivided attention. Time after time he persuaded himself that the measures he had proposed would take care of the nagging religious problem; they did not.

When the deadline given by the recess of the diet came, no military suppression of Protestants took place. But something else had happened that was to alter the political and religious landscape of central Europe. No sooner had the diet adjourned than the rulers of the Lutheran territories and cities met to form a defensive military alliance, the League of Schmalkald (named after the town in which the final deliberations of the Lutheran territories and cities were held). The formation of this league made it clear that military action against the Protestants would face military resistance. Luther was initially quite skeptical about defending the gospel with military might, but eventually agreed.

Protestant expansion was thus able to continue throughout the 1530s, making most of north Germany Protestant by the end of the decade. Late that decade, the emperor, who had left Germany after the adjournment of the Augsburg diet, reappeared on the scene. Apparently he had remained convinced that the theological disagreements between Catholics and Protestants were not fundamental and that reconciliation was possible. Accordingly, he initiated a new round of theological conversations with the aim of reaching agreement. By that time, however, the controversy had in fact produced not two parties, Catholics and Protestants, but four: hard-line Catholics and hard-line Protestants, as well as irenic Catholics and irenic Protestants. Understandably, the hard-liners on both sides, convinced that the theological differences were unbridgeable, refused to become involved, so the colloquies sponsored by the emperor were dominated by theologians of conciliatory disposition. Not surprisingly, they had no sanction from the papacy, only the emperor's determination. The Catholic participants failed to receive the support of Pope Paul III, who was chagrined that the emperor, after all a layman, meddled in theological matters in a frantic effort to reach some agreement, when the position of the church had been clear ever since January 1521, when Luther had been excommunicated.

Surprisingly enough, despite the legacy of two decades of acrimonious theological controversy, these irenic theologians found common theological ground, even on the critical topic of justification. However, no sooner had word spread about this agreement than the hard-liners on both sides voiced their disapproval and rendered the agreement ineffective. Luther opined that "it is a patched thing," and the papacy continued to resent the emperor's involvement in theological controversy.

The situation thus remained ambiguous. By the early 1540s the emperor concluded that theological conciliation was impossible and that the heretical Protestants had to be subjected by force. A peace treaty with France assured him that Spain's old enemy would not complicate matters, giving him the opportunity to pay undivided attention to the religious problem in the empire. At the same time, the League of Schmalkald had been weakened by the scandal of the bigamy of Landgrave Philipp of Hesse, the key figure of the League, an illustration par excellence of a male midlife crisis coupled with spiritual sensitivity. Unhappily married, Philipp was repeatedly unfaithful to his wife, a fact that kept him from receiving Holy Communion. Eventually, he became convinced that marrying his mistress (while remaining married to his duly wedded wife) would be the solution to his problem. When approached about the landgrave's problem, the Wittenberg theologians, including Luther, concurred that there was Old Testament precedent for a polygamous marriage. Promptly Philipp was married a second time, secretly of course, and when the sordid matter became public, Philipp pointed to the Wittenberg theologians' advice.

In order to escape the legal punishment for bigamy (which according to a recently adopted law was capital punishment) and receive the emperor's pardon, Philipp reached a secret understanding with the emperor that he would block any further expansion of the League of Schmalkald, even though several cities and territories had asked to join. Without Philipp's veto of new members, the league would have been militarily and strategically more powerful when the conflict did break out.

Charles skillfully put together an anti-Schmalkald coalition, which included even some Protestant territories, such as Albertine Saxony, where the Lutheran ruler, Moritz, schemed to fish in muddy waters, that is, to use neutrality in the conflict in order to obtain the electorship held by Ernestine Saxony, which dignity the Lutheran territory surely would lose in case of military defeat of the Schmalkadians. Using trumped-up charges, Charles declared war on the two leading members of the League of Schmalkald: (Ernestine) Saxony and Hesse in July 1546. The military confrontation had begun.

A few months had passed since Luther's death. Initially, the forces of the Schmalkald League had the upper hand, but a series of strategic military blunders caused by indecisiveness led in the spring of 1547 to a decisive Protestant defeat in battle near Mühlberg on the Elbe River. The emperor was victorious against the Protestant heretics, and a famous portrait painted by Titian shows him, in full armor, on a horse as if leading his troops to victorious battle. Charles was at the pinnacle of his power, and he at once undertook to accomplish his political and religious objectives. A diet at Augsburg in 1547 ordered the Protestant territories and cities to reintroduce Catholic worship, including the Mass. As an "interim" concession, until a general council of the church rendered a decision on the matter, the laity would continue to receive the Communion cup, and clergy who had married could so remain. Politically, the emperor announced a proposed restructuring of the empire calculated to put more power into his hands.

This "interim" agreement triggered fierce opposition on the part of some Lutherans, who insisted that having the Mass and other Catholic practices, such as clerical vestments, forced on them was an abomination that had to be resisted. Others, notably Philipp Melanchthon, on whom the mantle of Protestant theological leadership had fallen upon Luther's death, found that the agreement pertained only to *adiaphora*, "neutral things," leaving the core of the Protestant faith, at least for the time being, intact.

The Augsburg Interim evoked furious papal opposition. The papacy was once more unhappy that the emperor, a political ruler, had taken it on himself to resolve a theological conflict and decide on ecclesiastical practices at the very time that a general council of the church had convened in the north Italian town of Trent to sort out the theological implications of the challenge of the Reformation. The relationship between pope and emperor, never harmonious, reached a new low.

And if this internal Catholic strife was not enough, the emperor himself proved to be his own worst enemy. Giddy with power after the defeat of the League of Schmalkald, Charles began to implement his proposed changes of the structure and governance of the empire. His objective was laudable, since from the very outset of his rule the territorial rulers (and the free cities) had made the execution of uniform imperial policies difficult, even impossible, rendering the emperor largely powerless. Charles was persuaded that the moment had come to restructure administration and governance in the empire. That move in itself would have been welcomed by the German estates, but Charles obviously meant to clip the wings of the territorial rulers, who, whether Catholic or Protestant, were outraged and drew the proverbial line in the sand. The emperor's anti–Schmalkald coalition broke asunder, and from 1549 onward, Charles was politically on the defensive. Moritz of Saxony, now Elector Moritz, became the heart of the anti-emperor conspiracy of territorial rulers. This conspiracy almost succeeded in taking the emperor prisoner, and while that scheme failed, it became evident that the emperor's efforts to change the religious and political landscape in the empire had proved to be fatally unsuccessful.

The diet was to meet again in Augsburg in 1555, and when it was all over, the diet had sounded the death knell of the policies the emperor had so adamantly pursued for a generation. All along he had differed with the papacy on how to deal with the Protestant menace, and in 1555 it was evident that he had failed. No renewed efforts were made to reach theological agreement, even as the church council meeting in Trent in northern Italy was not inclined to explore theological compromises with Protestants. Charles was not present at the deliberations at Augsburg; health problems gave him a plausible excuse not to attend. But the real explanation for his absence surely was that he did not have the fortitude to preside over the bankruptcy of the policies he had pursued for three decades. Augsburg signaled Charles's good intentions and also his blatant failures. What he had ventured to achieve ever since he first heard the name of Martin Luther back in 1520 had turned into a declaration of bankruptcy.

Charles's brother Ferdinand represented him at Augsburg, and the outcome of the deliberations—the "Peace of Augsburg"—stipulated the radical (and unheard-of) notion that religious uniformity throughout the empire was no longer possible. The rulers of territories and cities were free to determine the faith, Catholic or Lutheran, of their subjects. Calvinism, deemed theologically more extremist, was excluded as an option, as was the even more radical Anabaptist movement. Only Lutheranism and Catholicism were legally recognized.

With the Peace of Augsburg, the empire surrendered the ideal of a commonwealth united in a single faith. It heralded something new in European religious history, a kind of religious pluralism, which strengthened the confessional identity of the individual German territories and cities and was put into a famous Latin phrase, *Cuius regio, eius religio*, meaning "He who rules determines the religion." A far cry from contemporary definitions of religious pluralism, it meant that the political officials had the authority to decide which religion they themselves (and their subjects) wanted to profess.

The Peace of Augsburg ended the Reformation in Germany. What the Protestants had hoped and the Catholics had feared—the empire turning

Protestant—had not happened. Instead, the empire allowed full legality for two religions.

THE ISSUES

It is not altogether clear what caused the support for Luther in the early days of the Reformation. Social and political considerations were undoubtedly important for some, while for others it was hostility toward a church hierarchy that was far away and demanded too much financial support. Support for the message of reform was strong enough to bring about significant changes in the communities in which reform was introduced, including the end to the celebration of the Mass and the introduction of "evangelical" Communion and preaching, not to mention the reordering of those social services, such as the support of the poor and sick, of widows and orphans, that the papal church had previously provided.

If the Protestant reformers largely agreed on what was wrong with the Catholic understanding of the gospel, they fiercely disagreed about the details of a truly biblical faith and worship. The Reformation had begun over the issue of indulgences, a topic of minor theological import, but it had expanded to encompass other issues. At the end stood the categorical declaration of both sides that their theological differences were fundamental and unbridgeable. And so the sentiment stood for centuries until the ecumenical impulses of the late twentieth century revised this assessment by asserting that differences in vocabulary, not in theology, accounted for the theological parting of the ways.

When Protestant theology and Protestant churches had become an established reality, three Latin phrases came to denote the theological grounding of the new faith: *sola gratia, sola fide, sola scriptura*, "solely by grace," "solely by faith," and "solely by scripture." These phrases, and the underlying theological affirmations, replaced the traditional Catholic notions of "grace *and* good works" and "scripture *and* tradition." The first two Protestant affirmations pertained to justification, almost from the very beginning of the conflagration the core theological issue, while the third phrase had to do with the question of authority. The emphasis in each case was on the modifier *alone*, and one might argue that the fundamental disagreement between Catholics and Protestants lay (and lies) in that modifier. It was Protestant propaganda to argue that Catholics did not believe in the authority of Scripture; Catholics affirmed Scripture as much as did Protestants but added the proviso that it needed an authoritative interpreter, the traditions of the church.

The reformers' affirmation of the Bible as the sole guide to the Christian faith was widely experienced as a profound liberation, for it offered an understanding of the Christian faith far simpler than that espoused by Catholicism. The medieval reflection on systematic and moral theology was considered all too complex and was rejected. Moreover, the simple Reformation slogans of "grace alone" and "faith alone" removed the myriad of stipulations the medieval church had imposed on the faithful about good works to be done to shorten the time in purgatory. These legalistic stipulations were replaced with the affirmation of Christian freedom, which allowed the Christian to base moral decisions on faith and love of the neighbor.

Given the intensity of the theological controversy that was the Reformation, it should come as no surprise that the sixteenth century saw a vigorous delineation of new confessions of faith and creedal statements. Such had been the case in early Christianity with numerous baptismal confessions and universal creeds, and in the sixteenth century the Reformation triggered a whole barrage of new confessional statements. These new confessions were, however, no longer "ecumenical" in the sense that all Christians were to subscribe to them. Instead, they were the exact opposite, formulations of points of belief to highlight the particular doctrinal orientation of one or the other of the new Protestant churches. Each new Protestant tradition formulated its own confession, all with the signature Protestant emphasis on the central importance of Scripture as the exclusive source of authority and, secondly, the insistence of justification of the sinner by faith alone.

The beginnings of this wave of new confessional statements were made by a group of South German Anabaptists who drafted the *Brotherly Union*, or *Schleitheim Confession*, in 1527. Theirs was an attempt to find a common theological denominator for the diverse Anabaptist groupings that had emerged in South Germany and Switzerland just a couple of years earlier. Three years later Lutheran theologians and their kindred political allies promulgated the *Confessio Augustana*, and that same year Huldrych Zwingli wrote the *Fidei Ratio*, which summarized the faith of the Zurich and Swiss Protestants. Martin Luther drafted the *Schmalkald Articles* in 1537 as the (rather emotional) statement of belief of the members of the League of Schmalkald; and Parliament in England promulgated the Act of Six Articles in 1539 at King Henry VIII's behest, a daring exercise of royal prowess (and self-confidence) that ventured to reintroduce Catholic theology—transubstantiation, clerical celibacy, private Masses—without reintroducing papal authority. Fourteen years later, in 1553, Archbishop Thomas Cranmer was responsible for the *Forty-two Articles* as the theological creed of the new Church of England. When Queen Elizabeth reestablished this church, the *Forty-two Articles* were modified, by deletions and additions, into the *Thirty-nine Articles* that have continued to this day as the normative theological statement of the Anglican Communion.

Further documents followed. Catholics did not want to be left behind and summarized the Catholic faith anew by promulgating the *Professio fidei Tridentinae* ("The Profession of the Tridentine Faith") and made subscription to it mandatory for all priests and teachers of the Catholic Church. The Lutheran churches in Germany, which around mid-century had experienced an uncommonly fierce set of theological controversies over how to interpret Scripture (and Martin Luther), agreed on the *Formula of Concord* (1577), subsequently incorporated into a document with a rather magnificent title, *The Pious Confession of Faith and Doctrine Reiterated by Unanimous Consent of the Electors, Princes, and Estates of the Empire, and of Their Theologians, who Embrace the Augsburg Confession.* Its brief title, by which it is known, is the *Book of Concord* (1580). In the early seventeenth century, the Antitrinitarian churches in Poland adopted the *Racovian Catechism,* for all purposes both a catechism and a statement of faith, while emerging Baptist congregations in England adopted the (Second London) *Baptist Confession of Faith* (1689), which stated as its authority "Scripture Proofs Adopted by the Ministers and Messengers of the General Assembly." In Switzerland Protestants drafted the two *Helvetic Confessions* (of 1536 and 1564). In the Calvinist/Reformed tradition, the 1618 Synod of Dordt adopted the Canons of Dordt, formally titled *The Decision of the Synod of Dordt on the Five Main Points of Doctrine in Dispute in the Netherlands,* which sought not so much to delineate what was understood as the true biblical faith vis-à-vis other churches as to heal a schism within the Reformed Church, much as what the *Formula of Concord* had attempted to do for the Lutherans. The *Belgic Confession* of the same year represented the Reformed faith to the outside world. The Eastern Orthodox *Confession of Dositheus,* of 1672, written by the Patriarch of Jerusalem, repudiated heretical opinions of the Patriarch of Constantinople.

In one important respect the seventeenth-century confessions strikingly differed from their precursors. They departed from the traditional outline of statements of faith, which began with an affirmation of the proper teachings about God. (The Apostles' Creed, for example, begins with the affirmation "I believe in God, the Father Almighty.") In the seventeenth-century confessions, the affirmation of the authority of Scripture was placed at the beginning, in order to demonstrate the grounds on which Protestant theology was delineated. Accordingly, the *Baptist Confession of Faith* began: "The Holy Scripture is the only sufficient, certain, and infallible rule of all saving knowledge, faith, and obedience, although the light of nature, and the works of creation and providence do so far manifest the goodness, wisdom, and power of God, as to leave men inexcusable; yet are they not sufficient to give that knowledge of God and his will which is necessary unto salvation."

THE DIVIDED HOUSE

Alongside the broad theological affirmations of the Reformation, particular emphases emerged as well. Lutherans stressed the distinction between Law and Gospel, the assertion that God confronts humans always with demands (the Law) and with grace (the gospel), while a second hallmark, the "theology of the cross," conveyed that God's true acts in human affairs are mysteriously hidden. At the heart of Calvinist theology was the affirmation of the overpowering majesty of God, with its corollary concept of predestination (the eternal salvation or damnation of all humans predetermined by God). A marked division within Protestant ranks occurred over the interpretation of Jesus' words of institution at his Last Supper ("Take, eat; this is my body..." [Matthew 26:26]), where several divergent views vied for acceptance.

The Reformation, then, was a theologically divided house characterized by a diversity of points of view. Protestantism and Protestant theology were never fully homogenous movements or systems of theological thought. On the contrary, the reform impulse produced several distinct "Protestant" ecclesiastical and theological traditions, each with its particular emphasis. How did this happen?

From the early 1520s onward—the Reformation controversy had hardly gotten under way—it was evident that the momentum for reform was by no means cohesive and uniform. Not all who clamored for change agreed on what, in fact, needed to be reformed. Some focused on social and political concerns. The highly popular pamphleteer Johann Eberlin von Günzburg, for example, published a series of pamphlets in which he outlined his vision of a perfect society, much like what Thomas More had done a bit earlier in more tranquil days in his *Utopia*. Other pamphleteers wrote on other societal issues. Even Luther focused on the reform of society, exemplified in his 1520 tract addressed *to the Christian Nobility of the German Nation*. Other writers focused on the reform of church practices, while yet others demanded a reform of theology.

This chorus of voices introduced a breadth of ideas and a precarious lack of coherence. Before long, however, a sorting-out process began. The reform movement divided, and it did so along several distinct lines. The parameter of ideas of religious and theological renewal became clear, while those who advocated societal and economic changes, such as the German peasants, came to realize that there was no groundswell of support for their vision of a new society.

The advocates of theological reform saw themselves confronted with diverse notions in their ranks. While affirming the basic tenets of the reform movement—salvation was by grace and by faith alone, and Scripture alone was the authority in the church—they also propagated particular understandings of other topics of the faith. Little by little, different nuances of theological emphasis emerged. As long as the antagonist was the Catholic Church, these different nuances simply expressed the richness of the theological reform movement and had no practical consequences. It become complicated, however, when one new vision of the gospel stood in explicit disagreement with other visions of the gospel. In several instances—one thinks of Huldrych Zwingli in Zurich and of John Calvin in Geneva—this led to the establishment of new, discrete churches.

The first to break ranks of the theological uniformity of reformers was Thomas Müntzer, an erstwhile Catholic priest, who had come under the sway of Luther's message of reform and became its ardent, at times aggressive, advocate. Then doubts about Luther's theology set in, and when in 1523 he settled down as pastor in the small Saxon town of Allstedt, not far from Wittenberg, he publicly questioned Luther's understanding of the gospel. Armed with a heavy measure of self-confidence, but also with a keen theological mind, Müntzer took to the pen and assaulted Luther for preaching a false gospel by making the faith too easy. The true disciples of Jesus, Müntzer insisted, must suffer, both spiritually and physically.

Luther did not take kindly to Müntzer's criticism and had him expelled from Allstedt.

A similar sentiment was voiced by Luther's senior colleague at Wittenberg, Andreas Carlstadt, who resigned his professorship because academic titles, he announced, were against the principles of Jesus. He insisted on being called "Brother Andreas" rather than "Professor Carlstadt," and he argued that parish clergy were more needed than professors of theology. He left Wittenberg, got married, and became pastor in the small town of Orlamünde, where he sought to put his ideas of biblical reform into practice. Carlstadt's open disagreement with Luther echoed that of Müntzer, as did his fate; he too, at Luther's insistence, was expelled from Orlamünde and Saxony.

Despite their trenchant theological criticism of Luther's vision of reform, neither Müntzer nor Carlstadt succeeded in bringing about an actual movement reflecting their understanding of the gospel. They were considered radical and found no support from governmental authorities. Indeed, the opposite was the case: the authorities suppressed them. Luther's repudiation was understandable: he saw their theologies basically as a threat to the cohesiveness of the reform movement. Above all, these two dissenters (and their followers) challenged his fundamental assertion of the clarity of the biblical message. The bedrock of Luther's affirmation that Scripture alone was the source of authority was that all who read the Bible the way it should be read would find themselves in agreement with one another. Quickly it became evident, however, that not all reformers found the same gospel in the Bible.

THE ANABAPTIST DISSENT

Such lack of agreement also occurred in Zurich, Switzerland. Zwingli, the leading priest in the city, had experienced an "evangelical" conversion, and in 1523 city council and citizenry formally endorsed his understanding of the gospel. Although early on, Zwingli was largely in theological agreement with Luther, despite his Humanist orientation, he also faced dissension within his own ranks—much like what Luther had experienced with Müntzer and Carlstadt. A group of followers had problems both with his theology and his "making haste slowly" strategy of ecclesiastical reform. They wanted reform to be undertaken aggressively, led by Scripture and not pragmatic expedience. They parted company with Zwingli, whom they chided for being too slow in the implementation of change. Later the members of this group were labeled "Anabaptists," meaning "re-baptizers," on account of their advocacy that only those individuals should be baptized who had made a mature confession of faith. Like most ecclesiastical labels pinned on by antagonists, the term "Anabaptist" was a label not altogether fair, because the Anabaptists argued that baptism in infancy was not a true baptism. But the distorting label stuck.

The question of infant baptism had been on the table since 1520, when Luther wrote that faith was the essential element in a sacrament, a statement bound to create theological uneasiness about the practice of baptizing infants, who could hardly be said to have faith. Luther dismissed the concerns, writing rather loftily that he had always known that Satan would attack the faithful over this issue. He was to exhibit sovereign self-confidence, arguing that there was scriptural support for baptizing infants, that if faith is understood not as a human "work" but as a divine gift, then infants may be recipients of this divine gift as well as adults. Moreover, a practice that had prevailed for fifteen hundred years could not be wrong. In Zurich the topic created a fatal division, for some of Zwingli's supporters concluded that the church must only consist of those who truly repented of their sins, made a public confession of their faith, and had been baptized as a symbol of their Christian profession.

Matters came to a head in January 1525, when this group of Zwingli supporters, deeply frustrated, met in the kitchen of a peasant house in the village of Zollikon, near Zurich, and their leader, using a wooden ladle, baptized those present. In a way, they did what Luther, compelled by his understanding of Scripture, had done when at Worms he defied the authorities of church and state. As matters turned out, Luther got away with his defiance (though at the time he hardly could have known he would). The Anabaptists, in Zurich and elsewhere, did not, because the authorities felt threatened by public dissent, which raised the specter of a religiously divided community. In Zurich no less than everywhere else in the sixteenth century, the fundamental assumption was that the civic and religious communities were but different sides of the same coin. A community could flourish only if all subscribed to the same faith. Religious diversity threatened this cohesiveness. Perhaps the Zurich dissenters assumed that in the end all—or most—of the Zurich citizenry would follow their lead, and that the clash with Zwingli was mainly over the timing of reform. The Anabaptists may well have wanted to force Zwingli's hand to effect speedy religious reform in the city. We can only speculate. But the ways parted. Moreover, they parted not only in Zurich, but in other places in south Germany, where questions about baptism and the nature of the church led to the affirmation of adult rather than infant baptism—not altogether surprising, given the restless pursuit of the true gospel during those years.

With the dissenters unwilling to fall in line, the civic authorities changed their intolerance into persecution. The small Anabaptist conventicles that were springing up all over Switzerland, south Germany, and Austria became the victims of fierce and vicious persecution. They in turn articulated a vision of the faith that made the true followers of Jesus into a minority, maligned, oppressed, persecuted. Thus, the story of Anabaptism turned into a story of persecution and martyrdom; more Anabaptists were put to death in the sixteenth century than were adherents of all other religious groupings combined. In response, the Anabaptists developed what has been called a "theology of martyrdom," which declared suffering to be inescapable for the true disciples of Jesus. Citing the New Testament, they declared that the disciple was not above the master. Despite the policy of fierce persecution, the Anabaptist conventicles survived.

At the same time, the Anabaptists took Jesus' moral teachings, particularly those of the Sermon on the Mount, with literal seriousness. This included a commitment to nonviolence, concretely expressed in the Anabaptists' refusal to serve in either government or the military. This Anabaptist aloofness from society caused deep-seated suspicion—similar to the suspicion that Christians had evoked in the first centuries of the faith—and undoubtedly played a role in their relentless oppression by governmental authorities. Anabaptism became an underground movement, insignificant in size, but appealing to its committed followers.

The view of the authorities, both secular and ecclesiastical, was simple. The Anabaptists propounded theological notions that the church had long rejected; they were also social revolutionaries in disguise. In the early 1530s, a bizarre happening in the northwest German town of Münster seemed to justify the worst fears of the civic authorities. Münster, like most German cities, had experienced the turbulence of reform in the 1520s and had, in fact, under the leadership of reform-minded preachers followed the pattern of a gradual turn to the evangelical message. Elections to the Münster city council in the spring of 1533 brought political support for the charismatic minister, Bernhard

Rothmann, who proclaimed the message of the Reformation, garnering support among the townspeople and also, importantly, among the members of the city council, who may well have seen their support as a political scheme to limit the power of the bishop of Münster in civic affairs.

Münster turned Protestant and followed the broader pattern of the quest for reform in the 1520s and 1530s. Wherever a charismatic clergyman preached the message of reform, he understandably included his own theological emphases, whether it was in Nuremberg, Strassburg, Zurich, or Münster. In Rothmann's case, however, things took an unusual turn, for it meant an increasing acceptance of the Anabaptist view of baptism. Rothmann sought to introduce believer's baptism in Münster, a rather precarious theological agenda, for a 1529 law had made rebaptism a crime punishable by death. When new elections to the city council brought an Anabaptist majority on the city council in 1533, the good people of Münster were given the choice of either being baptized or leaving town. Many chose to leave.

By making adult baptism the religious norm in the town, an entire community had violated imperial law. Quickly, an alliance of territorial rulers formed, with Catholics and Protestants in splendid harmony, to put an end to this spectacle. Münster had embraced a teaching that both Catholics and Protestants considered heresy; in so doing it had also rejected its proper ruler, the Münster bishop. A siege of the town began by the alliance of rulers. At the same time, a massive in-migration of persecuted Anabaptists from all over north Germany and Holland began and swelled the ranks of the city, all convinced that the victory of the true gospel in Münster heralded that the end-times had begun. Before long the mantle of leadership passed from Rothmann to Jan Matthijs and Jan van Leyden, two migrants from Holland. The two picked up on the new message that these were the last days before Christ's return for the Last Judgment. The establishment of the authentic Christian faith in Münster, the new "kingdom of Jerusalem" with Jan van Leyden as king, was an unmistakable sign of the imminent end.

Initially, the siege was unsuccessful, but increasing economic hardship triggered dramatic changes in the city. Polygamy and communism were introduced as biblical mandates, much to the horror of contemporaries, who now had tangible proof positive of the moral and theological perversion of Anabaptism. The catalyst for these changes, however, probably was the desperate state of affairs in the besieged city, where women vastly outnumbered men and the siege caused severe shortages,

especially of food. Single women had few legal rights, and the introduction of polygamy suggested itself not only as returning to the practice of the patriarchs in the Old Testament but also as giving legal status
to women.

In 1535, treason (committed by a teenager who years later wrote an
altogether biased account of events in Münster) enabled the besieging
forces to enter and conquer the city. A slaughter of those who had survived the fighting, mainly women and children, ended the debacle.
Anabaptists elsewhere in northern Germany and Holland were deeply
disturbed by the events in Münster. Initially, they had followed the developments with a mixture of awe and joy: the restoration of the true gospel
in a community was taken to herald the Second Coming of Jesus. Then,
uneasiness had set in about the Münsterite recourse to arms, not to mention the practice of
polygamy. Ultimately, most
Anabaptists concluded that
Münster had been a dire
aberration.

A former Catholic priest
from Holland by the name
of Menno Simons played
the major role in restoring
theological self-confidence
and organizational cohe-
siveness to the Anabaptists
in north Germany and
Holland, confused over the
failure of the New Jerusalem
in Münster to usher in the
Second Coming. Menno
maintained that the principles of nonresistance, that
is, nonparticipation in war,
and suffering—physical at
the hands of enemies of the
true gospel and spiritual
because of human sinful-
ness—were still the core of
Anabaptist belief. Traveling

Figure 3B
Anonymous. John Calvin. 16th century French.
Museum Boijmans van Beunigen, Rotterdam,
The Netherlands.

and writing incessantly, always underground, always hunted by the authorities as a heretic, he restated the fundamentals of the Anabaptist vision.

The Anabaptist conventicles in the north consolidated theologically under Menno's aegis, and before long were known as "Mennonite," the informal label for Anabaptists from the seventeenth century onward, especially for those who decided, in order to escape persecution, to emigrate to North America. In Europe, as subsequently in North America, Mennonites remained a minority, though in the Netherlands an important one. They came to be known as "Doopsgezinde" ("baptism minded"), who—once the persecution subsided—rose surprisingly to economic prominence.

THE REFORMER OF GENEVA: JOHN CALVIN

The vision of the Christian faith growing out of the theology and churchmanship of the Frenchman John Calvin is truly of world historical significance. Born in Noyon, northern France, in 1509, Jean Cauvin (or, in the Latinized version, Ioannes Calvin) was still a child when the indulgences controversy erupted in 1517 and hardly a teenager when Luther was excommunicated in 1521 and the first theological battles of the Reformation were fought. As theologian and reformer, Calvin benefited immensely from what had taken place in religion and society the two decades before he appeared on the scene.

A conversion experience in the early 1530s made him a committed Protestant. After a wave of persecution of Protestants had caused him to flee France for the safety of Basel, an amnesty announced by King Francis I led to a temporary return to his hometown in 1536 to settle estate issues. On his return travel to Strassburg, where he was to make his home, he made what proved to be a fateful detour in order to avoid areas of military conflict between France and Spain. The detour took him to the town of Geneva, prominent on the southwestern tip of Switzerland.

He planned to stay overnight and then continue on his journey. Geneva had turned Protestant a little while earlier, and when Guillaume Farel, the senior pastor in the city, learned of Calvin's presence, he sought him out at his inn and prevailed on him to stay in Geneva and assist in the work of turning the town Protestant. Farel knew Calvin as the auther of an impressive catechism-like summary of the Protestant faith titled

Institutes of the Christian Religion, which had been published a few months earlier. After rejecting Farel's plea several times, Calvin eventually agreed to stay.

So began Calvin's serendipitous presence in the city that was to become his home and destiny. A conflict with the Genevan city council over the kind of bread to be used in the Communion service led to his (and Farel's) expulsion from city in 1538, and, with a two-year delay, he continued his journey to Strassburg, the town he had meant to reach back in 1536. In this vibrant Protestant place, he became pastor of a congregation of French refugees, worked on an expanded version of his *Institutes*, and got married.

Three years later, in 1541, the Genevan city council solicited his return to Geneva, this time not as Farel's subordinate but as head of the Genevan church. Again, Calvin was reluctant, but eventually he accepted the invitation, not without having laid down a far-reaching condition, the promulgation of a new church order (we would say "bylaws") for the Genevan church. Geneva became his home, though he became a citizen only some twenty years later. Geneva gave Calvin the opportunity to combine his work as a theologian with practical churchmanship, for he was as much committed to turning Geneva into a godly community as he was to delineating, with ever more clarity and insight, the meaning of the Christian faith. Along the way, he participated in the theological debates between the old church and the new and labored to turn his native France into a Protestant country.

John Calvin had burst upon the theological scene at a rather young age: he was in his midtwenties when he published his *Institutes*, the book that proved to be the single most important theological work from the pen of a reformer in the sixteenth century. Most of the book summarized Protestant commonplaces, but they were delineated with striking clarity and systematic cohesiveness. At the same time, the *Institutes* conveyed their author's own theological emphases, not always shared by other reformers. The *Institutes* argued, for example, that the New Testament contained explicit notions of local congregational governance. Luther, by contrast, found the New Testament less than clear in this regard, which made him somewhat unconcerned about particular congregational offices and structures. Indeed, as a short-term solution, Luther was even willing to designate political rulers as the "emergency bishops" of their territories. Calvin, on the other hand, insisted that the New Testament expressly stipulated four congregational offices—pastors, teachers, elders, and deacons—each with specified roles and responsibilities. Pastors preached and administered the sacraments, teachers expounded Scripture, elders (in Latin, "presbyters") had overall responsibility for the life of the congregation, while deacons cared for the physical needs of its members. Calvin determinedly set out to organize the Genevan church—and indeed all congregations he influenced—in accord with this model.

Calvin emphasized church discipline, again in contrast to Martin Luther, who affirmed it in theory but did not implement the structures to make the exercise practical except through a periodic scrutiny of local congregations by "visiting" committees of theologians and government officials. Calvin found the structural tool for church discipline in the institution of the "consistory," a body comprising (in Geneva) an equal number of clergy (pastors) and laypersons. The Genevan consistory met weekly, and its charge was to monitor the faith and lives of the people, a concern that became typical of Calvinist congregations everywhere, whether in France, Hungary, or Scotland. The penalties imposed by the consistory ranged from excommunication and public penance to simple admonitions.

Calvin differed from other theologians, both Catholic and Protestant, on the interpretation of Jesus' words of institution at the Last Supper. The interpretation of the words "This is my body" and "This cup that is poured out for you is the new covenant in my blood" (Luke 22:20) had caused the fierce theological disagreement between Carlstadt, Luther, Zwingli, Johann Oecolampadius, Martin Bucer, and others in the late-1520s. Both Catholic and Lutheran theologians interpreted the words as indicating a real presence of body and blood in bread and wine, the two traditions differing only in whether a philosophical construct was necessary to explain the happening. Zwingli interpreted the words as describing a spiritual presence of Christ in the elements of bread and wine, while Carlstadt and the Anabaptists insisted that the words should be understood symbolically—bread and wine during the Last Supper symbolized the body and blood of Jesus that were to be given.

John Calvin's starting point was not so much the words of institution as it was a christological argument. Since Jesus is seated "at the right hand of the Father," according to the ancient creeds, his body could not literally be *in* bread and wine. Nonetheless, Calvin argued that receiving the bread and the wine was more than a symbolic act. In receiving these elements of Communion, the believer communed spiritually with the heavenly Christ.

Calvin's thought included other emphases, including his theology of predestination. Calvin conceded that the notion that God from all eternity destined some humans to eternal bliss while condemning others to eternal damnation was a "horrible doctrine," but he nonetheless declared it to be firmly grounded in Scripture (like Luther), and he forcefully advocated it for both the redeemed and the eternally lost (unlike Luther).

Interestingly, Calvin introduced the exposition of this doctrine in his *Institutes* by pointing to an empirical reality: the saving message of Jesus was not proclaimed equally among all people—and yet it was considered pivotal for eternal salvation. Calvin called this a "great and difficult question" and concluded, on the basis of scriptural passages, that the explanation was that God had determined to whom the "covenant of life" was to be preached and to whom not. We call predestination, Calvin wrote in the *Institutes*, "the eternal decree of God by which he determined with himself whatever he wished to happen with regard to every person." Divine omnipotence and salvation solely by grace went hand in hand. Calvin tied the notion of predestination to the question of salvation, God's amazing grace, and so it was good and proper to talk about it.

The clarity and simplicity of Calvin's understanding of the Christian faith were widely found compelling and attractive, and they help explain the appeal of Calvinism throughout Europe, especially in Scotland, which formally turned Protestant in 1560. But even more important, Calvin's notions of the organization of local congregations afforded laypersons (as "elders" or "presbyters") the opportunity to be active leaders in running the affairs of the congregation. Calvinism, in other words, presented itself as the religion of the new type of individual in Europe: the self-confident layman, the lower nobility, the gentry. In Calvinist congregations, the laypersons had the opportunity to play an enormously important role. And since Calvinism in many places—France, the Low Countries, England—was struggling to receive formal recognition by the authorities, its ethos helped form a personality type that was fiercely independent, even stubborn, but deeply convinced that God had laid down prescriptions for both the religious and the political and economic realm.

But there were also shadow sides to the story of John Calvin and Geneva, and our account will not be complete without acknowledgment that to oppose or question Calvin was done at one's own peril. Not for nothing was Calvin in the eyes of some an ecclesiastical tyrant, and it should not surprise that, at least according to legend, dogs were named after the reformer. The event that for some epitomized the adverse side of

Calvin took place on October 27, 1553. On that day a Spanish physician and lay theologian by the name of Michael Servetus was burned at the stake just outside Geneva's city walls. Servetus had challenged the ancient doctrine of the Trinity—as well as Calvin's ecclesiastical leadership in Geneva—and the punishment for blasphemy was death. Servetus had been a melodramatic enfant terrible among the reforming theologians of the early Reformation, moving from place to place, pestering other reformers with his ideas, writing books that ostensibly claimed to be orthodox but were not, a foible unfortunately understood too late by those given to superficial reading.

What prompted Servetus to travel to Geneva, the home of his nemesis, Calvin, is not altogether clear, but once there he was promptly arrested, brought to trial on charges of blasphemy, and sentenced to die. Calvin announced that Servetus's rejection of the Christology promulgated at the Council of Nicea had put the very honor of God at stake, and he found both support for and opposition to his manner of dealing with theological dissent.

Events were soon to show that others in that turbulent age shared Servetus's uneasiness about the Nicene dogma. Among them were two Italian relatives, Laelius Socinus (d. 1562) and his nephew Faustus Socinus (d. 1604). Laelius, who had found refuge in Zurich, carefully camouflaged his radical theological ideas about traditional doctrine and thus lived unmolested. As he saw it, the entire edifice of Christian theology was based on an erroneous interpretation of Scripture. Save for a commentary on the Gospel of John (titled *Brevis Explicatio*, of 1561) Laelius pondered his thoughts without ever committing them to print and sharing them with the world at large. On his death, however, his nephew Faustus obtained the lode of his uncle's unpublished papers, which converted him to a radically untraditional understanding of the Christian faith. Its truths had to be reasonable and open to rational delineation. Faustus reserved particular scorn for the traditional teaching of the atonement and put the argument into a book titled *De Jesu Christo Salvatore* (1578). Realizing that Switzerland was hardly a hospitable climate for someone with his views, he found his way to Poland, where a more tolerant religious atmosphere prevailed. He connected with others of like views and was instrumental in the establishment of a new church that took the name the Minor Reformed Church (the "major" Reformed Church being the Calvinist church) and embraced most prominently a rejection of traditional Trinitarian theology. The affirmation of notions that had been first formulated by Arius in the late third century became the hallmark of the Minor Reformed Church. It fought hard for acceptance and flourished for a while. Early in the seventeenth century, however, a resurgent Catholicism began again to dominate religion in Poland and most of the Antitrinitarians, now also called "Socinians," found it best to migrate westward to Holland, the one place in Europe where a measure of religious freedom prevailed. Not until two centuries later could unorthodox views concerning the Trinity be voiced without risk of life or limb.

THE CATHOLIC CHURCH IN THE SIXTEENTH CENTURY

The story of the Catholic Church in the sixteenth century was dramatically overshadowed by the vitality and creativity of the Protestant Reformation. Not surprisingly, therefore, Catholic history in the sixteenth century was referred to as the "Counter–Reformation," suggesting that Catholic history was a string of anti-Protestant "counter" moves to deal with the damage wrought by the Reformation. Understandably, Catholics did not take too well to such an understanding of the period, but it took some time to acknowledge that the sixteenth-century Catholic story was rich and complex in its own right, if for no other reason than that the Catholic Church demonstrated an impressive ability to marshal resources to rebound from the wounds inflicted by the Protestant reform. With the realization that Catholicism in the sixteenth century was more than anti-Protestantism came a new term, "Catholic Reform," coined to denote that Catholic life in the sixteenth century was nurtured by sources other than the Protestant challenge. But that term, too, had the liability of being all too reminiscent of the Protestant vocabulary of "reform," viewing Catholicism once again though a Protestant lens. The two terms "Counter–Reformation" and "Catholic Reform" have also been used conjointly, though the best label is by all odds a purely chronological one employed here—"Catholicism in the sixteenth century," since a parallel term, "Catholicism in Early Modern Europe," suffers from the same chronological mushiness as does that term "early modern" applied to the story of Christianity in general.

There can be little doubt that in the early sixteenth century, the Catholic Church was as vital, as rich in its mission to the faithful (and not so faithful) as it had been earlier. To be sure, as we have already observed, there were weaknesses. The higher clergy tended to be preoccupied with issues of political and fiscal power, while the parish clergy were often an ignorant and incompetent lot. In the main, however, the church met the spiritual needs of the people. The notion of a Catholic Church in deep throes of perversion and worldliness in the early sixteenth century is biased Protestant fiction that cast a dark shadow over the Roman church so as to make Protestantism appear in even greater splendor.

The leadership of the Roman church was oblivious, however, to the implications of change taking place in Europe: if the church had understood these developments, it might also have understood that the case of a single individual, the Wittenberg professor Martin Luther, was bound to become embroiled in larger considerations, which provided, at least in part, its momentum from them.

It has been suggested that the hallmark of church and society in Europe in the opening years of the sixteenth century was a ubiquitous anticlericalism, expressed in a strident denunciation of the lower clergy, especially the priests, as being incompetent and failing to provide for the spiritual nurture of the faithful. To be sure, there was some noisy criticism of this sort, but overall the evidence does not allow us so to define the atmosphere before Luther's *Ninety-five Theses*. The church was thus caught unawares of the conflagration, surely the most painful episode in the history of the Catholic tradition alongside the more subtle process of alienation from the Eastern church. But the real failure of the church was not so much that it underestimated the times as that it underestimated the prowess of the Wittenberg professor.

Once Luther's *Ninety-five Theses* had triggered an intense controversy, in part because of Luther's swift excommunication, which promptly turned Luther into a kind of folk hero and even martyr of sorts, the curia thwarted all efforts to resolve the controversy through a church council, either of the universal church or of the German church, which was loudly advocated in Germany. In other words, the chronicler must report that the papacy might well have proceeded quite differently, could have "made haste slowly" with respect to Luther rather than excommunicate him. That was not to be; the church acted swiftly and categorically.

On the face of things, the Catholic Church had a loyal supporter, Emperor Charles V, elected in 1519 at the youthful age of nineteen. Charles was a faithful son of the Roman church, but as it turned out, his support was idiosyncratic. He had his own ideas about how to resolve the controversy, but, more important, he had other problems to contend with, notably the restlessness in his Spanish domains and Spain's chronic enmity with France. Charles turned into a tragic, if pathetic, figure, even though on the morning after Luther's appearance before the diet in Worms he boldly declared that he was prepared to stake his possessions and his life on the eradication of the Lutheran heresy. He never was called upon to do this, but symbolically he lost both his life and his possessions.

The problem was that he had no sooner uttered these words than he left Germany, not to return for a decade. In the first two decades of the Reformation controversy, Charles spent barely three years in Germany dealing with the Luther problem, always under the impression, erroneous as it promptly turned out, that his decisions would end the controversy. Moreover, he showed himself naively optimistic in assuming that his intermittent involvement would settle the matter—at Worms in 1521 or in Augsburg in 1530, for example—when it did nothing of the sort. At his return to Germany in 1530 to preside over the diet at Augsburg, he acted as theological arbiter of the controversy, making the church and the papacy ill at ease about his involvement in a matter that had been settled by Luther's excommunication. After all, heresy was the church's business.

Of course, the Roman church had other faithful political supporters throughout Europe, but each came, no matter how devoted, with liabilities. Take King Henry VIII, who ventured to render his support by writing the *Assertio Septem Sacramentorum* ("Defense of the Seven Sacraments"), a repudiation of Luther's understanding of the sacraments as delineated in *The Babylonian Captivity of the Church*. But then came his marital problems and his fickle theological stance, and Henry found himself blatantly outside Catholic ranks. King Francis I of France was another loyal supporter of Rome, but enforcing orthodoxy in the land was hardly his game.

The Roman church did not state the full theological case against the Protestant challenge until a council convened in the town of Trent, northern Italy, in 1546. Only then were the proper Catholic positions in the controversial theological issues delineated and affirmed. In three periods of sessions that lasted intermittently until 1563, the council reaffirmed all traditional Catholic assumptions and doctrines. The council fathers were only prepared to make compromises in intra-Catholic disagreements—such as the relationship of tradition and Scripture—but they adamantly refrained from finding a middle ground with Protestant thought.

Importantly, Trent endorsed a large number of practical reform measures for the church—from seminary education and the requirement that bishops reside in their dioceses to the censorship of religious publications (the infamous *Index Librorum Prohibitorum*, or *List of Prohibited Books*). These Tridentine decisions and pronouncements molded Catholicism until the Second Vatican Council in the middle of the twentieth century. More than anything else, Trent symbolized Catholic theological and ecclesiastical self-confidence. At the same time it also revealed the historical tensions between the papacy and councils over final authority in the church, for no sooner had Giovanni Pietro Cardinal Carafa been elected Pope Paul IV in 1555 than this rigid and unbending individual not only announced plans to shut down the Trent council but also implemented a long string of harsh "puritanical" initiatives, such as beginning to compile the *Index*, mentioned above, ordering fig leaves painted on the bodies of Michelangelo's frescoes in the Sistine Chapel, ending the artist's papal pension (Michelangelo ignored the papal directive about the fig leaves), putting the Jewish community in Rome into a ghetto, and forcing Jews to wear distinctive signs on their clothing.

By all odds, the foremost manifestation of Catholic vitality in the sixteenth century—largely unrelated to the Protestant Reformation—was the founding of several monastic orders, such as the Theatines and the Discalced Carmelites, the vitality of the monastic orders always being an indicator of vitality in the church at large. These new orders, together with the revitalized existing monastic orders, molded new forms of Catholic piety and thought. Best known, and deserving priority of importance, is the Society of Jesus, better known as the Jesuits, who came to epitomize Catholic commitment and spirituality in the sixteenth century and beyond.

The Society of Jesus came into being through the initiative of the Spaniard Ignatius of Loyola, an erstwhile army officer whose serious injury in one of the numerous military clashes between Spain and France forced him to abandon his promising military career. A lengthy period of painful convalescence prompted his decision to dedicate his life to the church, particularly the Virgin Mary, and labor in the Holy Land to convert the infidels. Against formidable odds but with an iron-willed determination, Ignatius succeeded in reaching the Holy Land, begging his way from the western to the eastern Mediterranean. However, his exuberance irritated the token Christian guardians of the Holy Sites, who became concerned that his zeal might upset the Muslim overlords, and they made it clear to him that he was not wanted.

Anything but discouraged, Ignatius dutifully returned home to Spain, realizing that his intentions, while honorable, had been too ambitious. After all, he had not had a single lesson in theology, and he did not even know Latin, the language of the church. He began a rigid routine of schooling, first in grammar school, then at the university in Paris. This phase of his life ended in 1534, when he and six "companions," who had come to share his vision of devoted service to the church, pledged themselves to Ignatius's vision—to go to the Holy Land to evangelize the infidels. If that were to be impossible, they would journey to Rome and put themselves at the disposal of the pope to serve the church in whatever capacity he would assign them.

As it turned out, Ignatius and his companions got only as far as Venice. Hostilities in the eastern Mediterranean made travel to the Holy Land impossible. And so the seven companions turned to Rome, on their way performing works of Christian mercy. In Rome, they gained curious attention with their devotion, especially when, upon being asked who they were, answered, "we are the companions of Jesus." In 1540, Pope Paul III formally authorized their new community, called the Society of Jesus (*Societas Jesu*), boldly so, because no monastic community had dared to invoke the name of Jesus in their appellation.

The pope, not sure how this new community would develop, wisely restricted the maximum number of members to sixty, but this restriction was soon removed as the Jesuits became the expression of Catholic fidelity and purpose. If the Catholic Church successfully countered the Protestant onslaught in the late sixteenth century and at the same time experienced a stunning resurgence of spirituality in its ranks, much of the credit must go to the Jesuits. Before long Jesuits could be found everywhere, frequently in positions of importance—directing zealous missionaries across the oceans and serving as distinguished faculty at universities training the young, thoughtful advisors to crowned heads.

The audacity of including the name of Jesus in their name was paralleled by several other unusual ways by which the Jesuits understood their communal life and rule. The Jesuit rule became the vehicle that made the Jesuits a successful elite force in the Catholic Church. Strictly speaking, the Jesuits are not a monastic order, since they are not commanded to follow a regimen of multiple periods of prayer, worship, and work each day;

instead, they are free to fashion their daily routine so as to best serve the church. Only once a year for a period of four weeks are Jesuits obliged to perform a set of devotional exercises that Ignatius began to design in the early 1520s in a manual called *Spiritual Exercises*. Nor were the Jesuits marked by a distinctive habit, as were the Franciscans and the Dominicans, for example, choosing instead to wear ordinary attire rather than a unique habit, picturesque and symbolic, as was the norm for members of the monastic orders, both male and female. Ignatius's experience as a military officer influenced much that found its way into the *Rule of the Society*, and it was his genius to have sensed that his secular experience as a soldier could be meaningfully translated into the principles of an organization committed to serving the church. The Rule of the Society stipulated different classes or categories of members, for example, which ingeniously allowed the society to place the best-qualified members in the most appropriate places. To be sure, other monastic orders had ventured the same, but the Jesuits demonstrably pursued an elitist path.

A woman and fellow Spaniard rivaled Ignatius in contributing lastingly to the Catholic Church in early modern Europe and beyond: Teresa Sánchez de Cepeda y Ahumada, known as Teresa of Avila (1515–82), skillful organizer and administrator, thoughtful author of devotional books, Catholic saint, indeed, "doctor of the church." Even as a young girl, Teresa had shown deep religious sensitivity (she persuaded her younger brother to accompany her on a mission to convert the Muslims; the two did not get beyond the Avila city gates, however, and earned a spanking from their distraught father). As a teenager, Teresa's focus on a truly committed spirituality remained undiminished and permeated her life. Much against her father's will, she entered a convent of the Carmelite Order in Avila and before long emerged, despite serious chronic illnesses, as a charismatic spiritual and administrative leader in her order, demonstrating once again how Catholic monasticism gave women in convents the opportunity to assume leadership roles that society at large (and the church) disallowed.

Convinced that the Carmelite Order no longer expressed the original intent of its founders, Teresa energetically pursued reform in the order, mainly by insisting on the strict observation of its original Rule. With the help of relatives (and to the dismay of neighbors), Teresa surreptitiously purchased a house in Avila that became a convent of the "Discalced Carmelites"—the "sandals-wearing Carmelites"—who sought to separate themselves radically from the world by keeping contact with those

Figure 3C
Gian Lorenzo Bernini (1598–1680). Ecstasy of St. Theresa. S. Maria della Vittoria, Rome, Italy.

outside the convent to a minimum.

By the time of her death in 1582, Teresa had established some sixteen Carmelite convents, frequently working and collaborating with a spiritual kinsman, Juan de Yepes, known as John of the Cross. What connected the two was not only their mutual commitment to monastic reform but also an intensely mystical understanding of the Christian faith. Alongside their organizational involvement in the Carmelite order, both Teresa and John wrote numerous spiritual treatises. Teresa's *Interior Castle*, for example, was a comprehensive exposition of "interior prayer." Both Teresa and John were declared to be saints of the Catholic Church, and alongside John, Teresa holds the designation—rare for a woman—of being a "doctor of the church," which means that her exposition of forms of spirituality are deemed to be instructive for the entire Catholic Church.

When the century turned, the canons and decrees of the Council of Trent were being implemented, Jesuits were active in faraway places around the globe, and Teresa's Discalced Carmelites helped usher in a resurgence of Catholic spirituality in Spain and beyond. In short, the Roman church had overcome the losses and humiliation caused by the

Protestant Reformation. The church had clarified its teachings and regained its vigor and dynamism.

THE REFORM IN EUROPE

In one way or another, all European countries got caught up in the turbulence of the Reformation, either as sites of fierce theological battles or heavy-handed political interference. Of course, some were more affected than others, and in the end Europe was a religiously divided house. The exclusive dominance of the Catholic Church had been challenged and was a thing of the past; new Protestant churches filled the vacuum. Among the Protestants, the formal Lutheran presence was most pervasive. The Scandinavian countries (Denmark, Norway, Sweden, and Finland) turned Lutheran, as did most of the north German territories and cities. The vitality of Calvinism was extensive among the people, though its strength did not always find expression in its acceptance as the formal religion of a town or principality. Calvinism was successful, that is, it obtained governmental endorsement, in Switzerland and Scotland, while the Netherlands, Hungary, France, and Poland proved to be battlefields of the old church and the Calvinist faith. Only the southern tier of European countries (mainly Portugal, Spain, and Italy) remained more or less untouched by the massive religious turbulence.

That virtually all of Europe became embroiled in the Reformation controversy is noteworthy, since it suggests that a common denominator may well have caused the ubiquitous emergence of reform sentiment. And indeed, people throughout Europe applied the new vision of the gospel not only to religion, but to social, economic, and political issues as well. At the same time, the quest for religious and theological reform was marked by the intimate involvement of the political authorities—so much so, as a matter of fact, that it was the voice of the ruler that determined whether or not a country formally remained Catholic or turned Protestant. The Reformation in England serves as a splendid case in point, but the same holds true for the course of events in Scandinavia, particularly in Sweden, for without King Gustavus Vasa's determination to sever the ties of the Swedish church with Rome the country would have remained Catholic. Germany followed a similar path, especially when the Peace of Augsburg vested the territorial rulers explicitly with the authority to determine the religion of their subjects—a decision that explains why in the opening years of the twenty-first century, most people in Bavaria are Catholic, while most in Saxony are Lutheran.

Scholars have disagreed whether the reform movements in European countries—such as France, the Low Countries, or England—were influenced by Luther and events in Germany or whether they were autonomous movements that just happened to take place simultaneously with the Reformation turbulence in Germany. Understandably, German historians have tended to argue for a pervading German influence, while scholars outside Germany have been slow to acknowledge the priority of German events.

There is evidence that reform sentiment did exist throughout Europe well before anyone inside (not to mention outside) Germany had ever heard the name of Martin Luther. Also, many of the supposedly new ideas bandied about by Luther and the other reformers had in some way or other been advanced well before the sixteenth century. By the third decade of the sixteenth century, advocates of reform and of the centrality of the gospel had become more frequent throughout Europe. They were voices in the wind, represented by the sentiment of intellectuals and theologians, Lefevre d'Etaples (1455–1536) in France, for example, or John Colet (1467–1519) in England. Or Desiderius Erasmus of Rotterdam (1466–1536), the Christian Humanist who despised medieval theologizing and worked for a revival of the importance of the theologians of Antiquity. Social critiques and proposals for religious reform became a matter of widespread societal consciousness, increasingly propounded in confrontation with the Roman church. Even if this describes the situation in several European countries, and thus seems to justify the notion of independent origins, there should be little doubt that the dynamic for reform throughout Europe benefited from the awareness of what was taking place in Germany. The dynamic of the course of events in European countries was different precisely because of this awareness. None other than Huldrych Zwingli offered an apt commentary on how to understand both his own transformation into a reformer and the nature of events in Europe. Martin Luther, he observed, "propelled me to eagerness." The same could be said about the throng of reformers-to-be—and even Catholics—throughout Europe. Events in Germany propelled them to an eager commitment to change in church and society. Surely, King Henry VIII in England was well aware in the early 1530s that, in view of what was going on in Germany, it was possible to confront the papal church successfully.

KINGS, QUEENS, AND BISHOPS: REFORMATION IN ENGLAND

England is here an excellent case in point. When the indulgences controversy broke out in Germany, there were voices in England discontent with the religious and ecclesiastical status quo. Such discontent was found among the remnants of the medieval Lollard movement (the followers of John Wycliffe) and among the disciples of Erasmus of Rotterdam. A convocation sermon by John Colet in 1512 and the prosecution at the same time of Richard Hunne, a London merchant tailor, on dubious charges of heresy, suggest that there were incidents of religious restlessness in England well before events in Germany catapulted into European consciousness and reached England. Yet at the same time, one can hardly speak of a pervasive sense of a religious "crisis" in England or a widespread loss of confidence in the role of the church as mediator of eternal life—that is, not until King Henry VIII became burdened in his conscience, as he claimed, by the absence of a male heir and called the legitimacy of his marriage to Katherine of Aragon into question.

When the Reformation controversy erupted on the Continent, England had a staunchly Catholic monarch. The boisterous and self-confident Henry VIII seemed to ensure that no matter what happened elsewhere, England would remain committed to the old religion. In 1521, Henry even wrote a theological treatise (or had it written for him by Thomas More) against Luther's treatise *On the Babylonian Captivity of the Church*, defending the traditional sacramental teachings of the Catholic Church. This earned the king the papal honor of being a "Defender of the Faith," a title still used by English monarchs today, even though the faith they are defending nowadays has long ceased to be Roman Catholicism.

This harmony between pope and king was not to last, however, for by the late 1520s serious tensions had arisen between the two. They had little to do (at least on the face of things) with the great theological issues of the day and everything to do with the king's petition to the pope that he annul Henry's marriage with Katherine of Aragon or, more precisely, that he withdraw the papal dispensation that had allowed Henry and Katherine to be married in the first place. Though Katherine and Henry had been married for almost twenty years and were widely seen, for example by Erasmus, as a model of Christian matrimony, their marriage was complicated from the start. Katherine had come to England as the bride of Henry's older brother Arthur. When Arthur died unexpectedly and

Henry became the successor to the English throne, a papal dispensation allowed Henry and Katherine to be married, even though marriage to one's brother's widow was against canon law. The couple was not exactly well matched either. Katherine, a serious type who always wore black, wished to live quietly in religious devotion, while Henry, a jovial extrovert, was given to restlessness. In those days, however, dynastic marriages were not assumed to have been made in heaven.

Nonetheless, the two were meant to live happily ever after. Things became troublesome when Katherine failed to bear a son. The king claimed to be deeply distraught by this reality, musing if Katherine and he were under a divine curse for having married. That he had fallen hopelessly in love with Anne Boleyn, a young and vivacious lady-in-waiting at court, complicated things. Nowadays, we would surmise that the king was going through a male midlife crisis.

Henry petitioned the pope to nullify the dispensation—a move that would enable him to marry Anne Boleyn—but what Henry expected to be a routine request was not so routine at all, and he promptly ran into difficulties. For one, Henry's petition called on Pope Clement VII to acknowledge publicly that his predecessor had made an error by allowing the marriage. Moreover, Henry's request reached Rome at about the time when the soldiers of Emperor Charles V were sacking the city, making the pope virtually a prisoner. Under such circumstances, Clement could hardly be expected to render a judgment against Katherine, who determinedly insisted that she and Henry were duly married; after all, Katherine was the emperor's aunt.

To complicate things even more, Clement VII was not temperamentally given to making complex decisions, so he delayed his response to Henry's petition—a strategy that worked until the king's patience came to an end. Henry prevailed on Parliament to pass a bill depriving the papacy of all revenue from the English church, a plain attempt at blackmail; the king presumed that this parliamentary maneuver would put the heat on the pope. It is to Clement's credit that he was not badgered by Henry's wooden scheme.

Having failed at blackmail, Henry turned to Parliament in 1532 to have passed several measures that progressively, one by one, severed the ties between the English church and Rome. Thomas More—the great Humanist, author of the book *Utopia*, and devout Catholic loyalist—resigned from the office of chancellor, a gesture indicating the radicality of the parliamentary maneuvers. The legislation culminated in the Act of

Supremacy of 1534, which declared the king to be "the supreme head of the church in England." Though this novel designation went out of its way to indicate that it did not allow the king to adjudicate theological matters, indirectly it did, of course, and understandably loyal English Catholics found the act outrageous. But Henry had reached his goal, for as supreme head of the church he could order an English ecclesiastical court to render the definitive verdict on his marriage. And so it happened—with predictable results. Once more, Henry became Europe's most eligible bachelor, though his infatuation with and speedy marriage to Anne Boleyn clipped this eligibility. Religiously, the ties of the English church with Rome were irreparably severed.

While it is tempting to view the ensuing religious changes in England as the consequence of governmental authority determining the course of ecclesiastical affairs, reality was more complicated. Increasingly, English men and women were enthralled by the new vision of the Christian faith propounded by churchmen and theologians with a reforming bent, by the Bible available in the vernacular (in this case, the English language), by Christian freedom, and the other clarion calls as had been sounded by the reformers on the Continent. By the early 1530s, it was obvious that the Continental reformers and their supportive political allies had gotten away with their defiance of Rome, suggesting that the same could hold true in England. Protestant gatherings increased.

Theologically, not much changed in the land, especially since Henry had no intention of allowing the supremacy to lead to the acceptance of Protestantism. And he was brutal when it came to suppressing criticism and dissent. One John Haile was sentenced to death because he characterized the king's marriage to Anne Boleyn as "more foul and stinking as a sow." Henry sought to pursue an ecclesiastical policy that was theologically Catholic while allowing for enough Protestant sentiment to keep official religion in a state of indeterminate flux, a tightrope-balancing act. He found a willing helpmate in Thomas Cranmer, a Cambridge don, whom he designated archbishop of Canterbury.

The first major theological statement of the new English church came in 1539, when at Henry's behest Parliament enacted the Act of Six Articles, a document remarkably Catholic that affirmed the doctrine of transubstantiation and prohibited clerical marriage. The latter was bad news for the clergy who had followed the Reformation call for an end to clerical celibacy, particularly Archbishop Cranmer, who had married a niece of the Nuremberg reformer Osiander's wife. He concluded that she had best return to her native Germany. The Act of Six Articles stipulated severe penalties for violations, but these were, as matters turned out, hardly ever applied. It was as if the king meant to keep both sides of the great religious dispute off balance. As one caustic observer noted, England was the country where Protestant heretics and adamant Catholics were burned on the same day.

Sanctioned by Thomas Cranmer, Henry married Anne Boleyn, but soon sent her to the executioner's block for alleged adultery, and married a third time. Jane Seymour bore the son he had long desired, the future King Edward VI. Toward the end of his reign Henry formed a council of regency for his minor son, and shrewdly saw to it that neither religious reformers nor conservatives held a majority on that council.

But as matters developed following Henry's death in 1547, the reformers on the council took over, and the country embarked on a decidedly Protestant course. The force behind the Protestant agitation was Cranmer, whose hand (and theology) lay heavily on a Protestant statement of faith—the *Forty-two Articles* of 1553—and, more important, on a new order of worship, the *Book of Common Prayer*, first issued in 1549 and revised and reissued in 1552. This prayer book has had a lasting influence on the liturgical and devotional language of English-speaking Christianity. It gave England a Protestant form of worship.

The youthful king Edward VI's reign and life were short, and in 1553 his half-sister Mary succeeded him to the English throne. As Katherine of Aragon's daughter, Mary had been shamed as a bastard by her father, and like her mother she had found solace in the Catholic religion. Understandably, her goal was to reestablish the Catholic faith in the land, and she did so with grim determination. Parliament submissively rescinded all religious legislation passed since 1528, which took the country back to the time when Henry and Katherine still appeared to be happily married. Mary paralleled the reintroduction of Catholicism with a policy of persecution of prominent Protestants. Thomas Cranmer, the most illustrious victim, was burned at the stake in Oxford as a heretic and a political insurrectionist: he had actively worked to prevent Mary's succession. Once again, politics and religion flowed together like hues in a watercolor. At issue was not only the theological heresy called Protestantism but also the political question of whether Mary was the legitimate incumbent on the English throne, a matter in which the leading noble families of the realm had a stake—and on which they took sides. Cranmer backed the losing side, understandable given Mary's obvious Catholic disposition. At his trial he recanted in two statements his involvement in reform, but when it became clear to him that his fate was sealed, he recanted his recantations with the declaration that since his hand had sinned by writing the statements of recantation, it should be the first exposed to the fire. Martyrs tend to be given to famous last words.

Mary's reign turned out to be as short-lived as Edward's. After five brief years on the throne she died in 1558, and the brevity of her rule had not afforded her the sustained influence that might have graced her ecclesiastical efforts with success, especially since the monarch who followed, Elizabeth I, was bound to favor Protestantism. Elizabeth, daughter of Henry VIII's second wife, Anne Boleyn, was a bastard in the eyes of the Catholic Church and of all Catholics. Astutely, her decision about religion, the so-called settlement of religion, promulgated by Parliament at her behest early in 1559, took a mediating stance between adamant Protestantism and traditional Catholicism. The settlement reintroduced the Protestant religion as it had prevailed during the early years of the rule of Edward VI. This created a measure of theological ambivalence, particularly with respect to the interpretation of the Lord's Supper, which had become the touchstone of theological identity among the Protestant reformers. Elizabeth's version of the prayer book juxtaposed the words from the first and second editions of the *Book of Common Prayer* as they were spoken by the priest when distributing the bread and wine: "The body of Christ given for you" and "Take this in remembrance that Christ died for you." The former clearly affirmed a "real" presence, while the latter left bread and wine as nothing more than a symbol. Theologically, the new version enjoined by the prayer book left things quite mushy.

Political considerations influenced Elizabeth's decision to favor a moderate form of Protestantism: she did not want to invoke the wrath of Catholic Spain by making England radically Protestant. After all, the Spanish ruler, King Philip II, had been married to Queen Mary and appeared altogether willing to be a suitor to the new queen as well. Elizabeth declined, as she was to do with several other suitors in later years. Spain remained a formidable political menace to England, but hardly influenced English religion as Elizabeth had promulgated it in 1559.

The major problem plaguing established English religion until the end of Elizabeth's rule (and beyond) was the presence of two factions that fiercely opposed the settlement of 1559—adamant Catholics and adamant Protestants, both deeply unhappy. The resolute Catholics grieved because the official religion of the land enjoined what they considered heresy, while the staunch Protestants were furious because the official religion retained too much of what they called "popery" in worship and belief. Of these two groups of dissidents, the former remained underground, since being Catholic was tantamount to high treason. English Catholics received their spiritual guidance from priests who were unwilling to adapt to the Elizabethan religion, and from a new type of aggressive young priests coming from the Continent, who crossed the English Channel in clandestine cloak-and-dagger fashion, pursued and haunted by the authorities, constantly in fear for their lives. Many were apprehended and some put to death for high treason.

The adamant Protestants, on the other hand, were very much in the public eye for loudly voicing their opposition to the official religion of the land. Early on, their rejection of the 1559 settlement focused on the clergy's use of vestments. The ensuing conflagration came to be known as the "vestments controversy." It primarily concerned the clergy (though, of course, the people in a congregation could see whether their priest officiated in vestments). The retention of vestments seemed to be a most glaring artifact of the retention of Catholic superstition in worship. Critics deemed it pure popery.

THE PURITAN DISSENT

The proponents of more comprehensive ecclesiastical change in England than Queen Elizabeth's settlement stubbornly clamored for a "pure" Christianity; before long they were known as "Puritans." The history of Christianity knows of many of such "puritans" through the centuries, a timeless set of individuals, earnest Christians—such as Tertullian in early Christianity—who were committed to a pure spirituality and despaired of the laxity of life and doctrine of their fellow Christians and their leaders. A timeless element, however, is not to be understood to be the same as a mass movement. Prior to sixteenth-century England, the number of such "puritans" was always modest, the intensity and vehemence of their pronouncements notwithstanding.

In late sixteenth-century England, the demand for "purity" initially focused on doctrine and liturgy, not on pious living, with which the label "Puritan" has subsequently come to be associated. That happened later. The early "dissenters," or "non-conformists," wanted none of what they called the "hocus pocus" of the Mass. They rejected kneeling when receiving the sacrament of bread and wine; they found no biblical warrant for the office of bishop as it was understood by the Anglican Church. Nor did they want to have clergy attired in vestments reminiscent of Rome. Making the sign of the cross was an act of superstition.

Cambridge and its university were the hotbed of such sentiment; its initial leader was the professor of theology Thomas Cartwright (1535–1603), whose extended stays in Geneva, Heidelberg, and Antwerp had acquainted him with the Calvinist version of the gospel and made him Calvinism's ardent partisan. In 1572 two stalwart Puritans, John Field and Thomas Wilcox, published (anonymously, of course) an *Admonition to Parliament*, in which they asked that a presbyterian form of church government, without bishops, be introduced in England. They, too, were unsuccessful, and both had occasion to ponder their convictions in jail for a year.

Despite their dogged persistence, the Puritans failed in their attempt to alter the 1559 settlement, increasingly posing the question for them whether they should remain in the official church or form their own, separatist congregations. Not surprisingly two responses were formulated, and by the turn of the century the Puritan movement had become divided between "separatists" and "non-separatists." Some of the resolute separatist Puritans chose to migrate to the town of Leyden in the Netherlands, where religious freedom prevailed, but when after a dozen years they still did not feel completely at home in the Dutch town, they decided to head for that mysterious place North America, making famous their small and leaky vessel, the *Mayflower*, and the vicissitudes of establishing Plymouth Colony.

Whether separatist or non-separatist, Puritans put their stamp on seventeenth-century English religious and political history. Their opposition to the formal religion of the land had the psychological effect of creating a personality unwilling to accept the status quo, a revolutionary-in-waiting, so to speak—precisely the sentiment that was to cause such political turmoil in the first half of the seventeenth century. Moreover, Calvin's notion that the New Testament clearly indicated how a local congregation should be governed, with lay "elders" ("presbyters") playing the pivotal role, also nurtured the religious self-confidence of lay people.

SUCCESS AND FAILURE IN FRANCE

Whatever the possible antecedents of reform, by the early 1520s Lutheran publications and ideas had reached France. They were extensively disseminated, and before long outspoken partisans of reform made their case in public. At an academic ceremony at the University of Paris in November 1533, Nicolas Cop, the newly elected rector of the university, delivered what amounted to a "Protestant" speech, a summary of the Christian faith with its words taken straight out of Luther's and Erasmus's books. The speech caused uproar, both pro and con, clearly an indication that public sentiment and personal religious conviction were beginning to divide the country. Some yearned for new ways to express the Christian faith, while others were furious over the pernicious spread of heresy. Things got worse when a little later a second event shook the country. Protestants distributed handbills throughout Paris denouncing the Mass as the abomination of abominations—even leaving one handbill at the door to the king's bedroom.

The king, Francis I, was incensed (if for no other reason than that the Protestant heretics had gotten close to his bedroom), and he quickly made it plain that he would not tolerate the propagation of Reformation ideas in his realm. Suppression and persecution of Protestant sentiment became the order of the day. Nonetheless, the next two decades brought increasing Protestant agitation coupled with the governmental efforts to stamp out the movement. Many ardent Protestants—John Calvin among them—preferred to leave their native land and go into exile abroad. Calvin, landing in Geneva by accident, turned that town into a training ground for missionaries and pastors to France, and Geneva became a refuge for persecuted French Protestants. His dream was that his native land be ruled by the same gospel to which he himself subscribed.

No matter how extensive the network of Protestant congregations throughout France, mainly in the south of the country, Francis I did not waver in his Catholic loyalty and in his policy of suppressing Protestant sentiment. He even remained passive when some twenty-two villages were burned as alleged hotbeds of Protestant agitation in 1545 and more than four thousand inhabitants were brutally put to death.

But despite their vigor, the Protestants remained a minority. In France, as elsewhere in Europe, much hinged on the Protestants' ability to receive political support or to tie their cause to a political issue. Initially they had neither the one nor the other. There was no political or legal cause to which French Protestants might have attached themselves, as had been the case in England, for example, with Henry VIII's "great matter." And unlike Henry VIII, Francis I and his successor kings had all the prerogatives in church affairs they wanted, giving them no reason to support the movement of reform merely to gain greater authority over the church.

Then, in 1559, events changed all that. For one, after some seventy years of intermittent warfare, the two great European Catholic powers, France and Spain, concluded a peace treaty at Câteau-Cambrésis, which ended the two countries' incessant fighting. Since this chronic warfare had diverted the kings' attention from domestic issues, this was bad news for Protestants. At that point the affairs of state took an unexpected turn. In celebration of the treaty, Francis I's successor, Henry II, participated in a jousting tournament. The tip of a lance went through his face mask, penetrated his eye, and ended in his brain. Henry's excruciating pain and death after several days meant the death sentence for his unsuccessful court physician and, more importantly, threw the country into a constitutional crisis. Henry's son and presumptive heir, Francis II, was a child, and there was strong sentiment among the powerful noble families in the land that a council of regency should rule until the youth attained majority. The machinations of the ambitious and crafty queen mother, Catherine de' Medici, and of the influential Guise family led to Catherine's assuming the regency for her son, a move that was adamantly opposed by the powerful Bourbon family, represented by the King of Navarre, the region north of the Pyrenees.

None of this would have had much impact on the course of the Protestant movement in France had it not been for the fact that these two important families, the Guise and the Bourbons, had different religious allegiances. While the Guise family was adamantly Catholic, even claiming a cardinal in its ranks, the Bourbons were Protestant. The constitutional conflict over the minor king's regency thus smoothly turned into a religious conflict, especially when the Huguenots, as the French Protestants were called, allied themselves in 1560 with the Bourbon family in the so-called "Conspiracy of Amboise," a scheme to abduct the young king and assume power in France.

The increasingly self-confident Protestants began to seize Catholic churches for their worship (by then, there were some one thousand Protestant congregations in the land). Amid increasing tensions, a theological colloquy was held in Poissy in 1561 to discern if reconciliation between Protestants and Catholics was possible, a rather naive undertaking, considering all that had been discussed (and disagreed on) since 1517. Indeed, the two sides at the colloquy eventually agreed to disagree, but the Huguenots were given the right to public worship outside towns. But tempers were high. Only a few weeks after the colloquy a group of Huguenot men, women, and children were found worshiping in a barn by a group of Catholic mercenaries, a bloody skirmish resulted, and when it was all over more than one hundred men, women, and children had been killed. To be sure, the Protestants had no right to worship at that location, but the bloodshed was a tragic indication of how intensely emotional the religious situation in France had become.

In 1562, increasing tensions led to the outbreak of civil war, the first of the several so-called French Wars of Religion—actually wars of both religion and politics—that lasted intermittently until the end of the century. The first war, in which neither side was able to score a decisive victory, was followed by a second outbreak of hostilities in 1567 and yet a third conflict one year later. While fierce and bloody, as civil strife always tends to be, none of these confrontations gave clear victory to either side. Importantly, however, the Protestants' quest to have their religion recognized as the formal faith of the land had ceased being religious in nature: the goal was to be achieved by military force.

The intense tensions and emotions, not to mention hostility, reached a horrible climax in 1572. Numerous Protestant nobles had come to Paris to celebrate the wedding of Henry of Navarre to a sister of the king. The Guise family used this gathering on Saint Bartholomew's Day as a welcome opportunity to eliminate the Protestant elite—and indeed it succeeded: more than two thousand were killed in Paris and more than twenty thousand throughout France, if contemporary statistics can be trusted. The pope celebrated a Mass of Thanksgiving. The most prominent victim was Admiral Coligny, the leader of the political Protestant faction and elder statesman of France. Henry of Navarre assumed the leadership of the Protestant party, and the anger caused by the Saint Bartholomew's Massacre kept the strife going. In 1576, hostilities broke out again, but again they brought no resolution to the controversy.

The death of King Henry III in 1589 led to the succession of Henry of Navarre. A Protestant had succeeded to the French throne, and the French Protestants undoubtedly offered prayers of thanksgiving for this turn of events, since they saw their fondest hopes and aspirations realized. A Protestant king would rule over a Protestant country, they thought. But their joy turned out to be short-lived and premature. Henry, now King

Henry IV, uttering the famous words "Paris is well worth a Mass," converted to Catholicism. He astutely understood that the country had remained overwhelmingly Catholic and that ruling as a Protestant (or making Protestantism the formal religion of the land) would endlessly prolong the conflict.

Seeking a resolution, Henry issued the Edict of Nantes in 1598, which provided formal toleration for French Protestants, who also received several military concessions, such as the possession of several fortified strongholds, which signified that they were still a military power. The edict was, of course, a striking turn of events and significantly enhanced the Protestant presence, but it also showed that the quest to turn France into a Protestant country had failed. For more than a century, French Catholics and French Huguenots lived side by side until Louis XIV rescinded the Edict of Nantes and insisted that the Huguenots accept the Catholic religion. Some did, though most preferred to emigrate—some to North America, most to Prussia—rather than change their religious beliefs.

THE AGE OF CONFESSIONALISM

As the sixteenth century came to an end, the religious landscape of Europe was dramatically different from what it had been when that century began. New Protestant churches had been established, each insisting—so as to sustain the rationale for its existence—that it alone proclaimed the authentic gospel of Jesus. This argument required that each church have a theology backing its views and positions, forcing the generation after the Reformation to formulate these theologies.

The Protestant churches, in most places established and legally secure, expressed their self-consciousness with an increasing emphasis on proper doctrine. That was understandable because, after all, theology had been a major cause of the conflagration and division in the first place. Before too long, Protestant theologians and churchmen, whether Lutheran or Calvinist or Anglican, vied with one another in expounding the Christian faith again in the manner of medieval scholasticism, with a heavy reliance on Aristotle and the use of the Latin language rather than the vernacular—a rather striking contrast from the way the first reformers had done theology. The new approach produced massive theological tomes, including Richard Hooker's eight-volume *Of the Laws of Ecclesiastical Polity* in England.

A long series of "confessions of faith" produced by Protestant churches toward the end of the sixteenth century and in the early part of the seventeenth century sought to clarify the defining features of the various churches. Distinct confessional identities emerged as, in the course of the seventeenth century, the Protestant churches acquired those characteristics by which they have become known. Lutherans became Lutherans; Calvinists became Calvinists; Mennonites became Mennonites. And not only did they attain their confessional identity, they also sought to bring the ethos of their theological confessions to bear on all aspects of society. This process, known as "confessionalization," has been understood by scholars as a comprehensive process that helped create modern European society and religion, for it affected not only theology and religion, but law, science, the arts, and literature as well.

Given the competing theological claims of the new churches, both Lutheranism and Calvinism (the largest new Protestant traditions) faced the searching question of the authority for their doctrinal affirmations. For Catholic theologians it was fairly simple, since they were able to point to the declarations of the Council of Trent about the authority of both Scripture and tradition. Protestants insisted that Scripture alone was the ground of Christian teaching, *sola scriptura* being one of the key slogans of the Reformation. This Protestant assertion led to the question of why Scripture was the source of authority. The answer was, of course, because it was divinely inspired, but that answer only raised the new question of how exactly this divine inspiration of Scripture was to be understood. Eventually, Protestant theologians asserted that every word of the original text of Scripture was divinely inspired, a notion that was meant to assure a firm ground for Protestant theologizing. It was, however, a new way of looking at Scripture, for previously theologians had left unanswered the question of how exactly the Bible was revelatory truth. Martin Luther, for example, called the Letter of James "an epistle of straw"; now it was considered to be verbally inspired. The larger difficulty arose from the fact that the notion of a "verbal inspiration" of Scripture was formulated at precisely the time when European society embraced new notions of critical analyses of ancient texts. Seventeenth-century Protestant theology has the label "orthodoxy" because it strove to offer the "pure teaching" of the Christian faith.

On the Catholic side a parallel development took place, for the Catholic Church experienced a dramatic and vibrant surge as well. The Council of Trent had not only laid down practical guidelines for the invigoration of the church but also spelled out proper Catholic doctrine. If prior to the outbreak of the Reformation controversy certain theological topics had not been formally defined by the Catholic Church—indulgences, for example—Trent proceeded to remove ambivalence and uncertainty and clearly define Catholic teachings (a few points of continued mushiness notwithstanding). With the "Counter-Reformation," the Catholic Church succeeded in recatholizing areas in south Germany and Austria that had been Protestant, even as in France Catholic vitality and resilience triumphed over the Huguenots with the Edict of Nantes. In England, the succession of King Charles I in the early seventeenth century raised the prospects of the recatholization of Anglican England and Calvinist Scotland.

The seventeenth century became the "golden age" of the Society of Jesus, which labored ubiquitously beyond Catholic lands, such as Poland, Sweden, England, even Saxony! Jesuits also played a crucial theological role, reconceptualizing Catholic moral theology, for example, with the concept of focusing on "cases" to apply principles of moral theology, an approach that became known as "casuistry." Jesuits were also a significant cultural force. They wrote plays and dramas that expressed a distinct Catholic ethos; they even sought to codify the Bavarian dialect as the normative German language, a well-meant effort that failed miserably. Jesuit influence extended beyond the waters of the Atlantic into the New World—in particular in the area of present-day Paraguay, where Jesuits established the so-called "reductions," the Christianization of the native peoples without forcing them to give up their traditional culture, while at the same time protecting them against the increasing threat of slave traders. This impressive Catholic resilience found expression in the colorful vibrancy of Baroque painting and the richness of the massive building of churches in the Baroque style.

Such theologizing and everyday living took place in the context of the Thirty Years' War (1618–48), which brought unheard of calamity, destruction, and misery to the German countryside. According to estimates, one-third of the German population of fifteen million perished in the course of the generational conflict. For thirty years—the lifetime of an entire generation—hostilities began, ended, and began again. The sites of the battles shifted—from Bohemia and south Germany to central and north Germany. The belligerents changed as well, for initially the war was an intra-German conflict, but soon France and eventually Sweden entered the fray. And since Protestants always seemed to line up on one side and Catholics on the other, and those in charge chronically invoked their religious commitment as the rationale for waging a bloody war, the notion quickly emerged that this was a war of religion. However, the Thirty Years' War (in fact, a motley of no less than thirteen distinct wars and ten peace treaties) was far more complicated: political rivalries between emperor and the German territories; rivalries among countries with access to the Atlantic; and rivalries between Spain and the Netherlands and between Spain and France for European hegemony. Religion was used to camouflage secular interests and pursuits. Assuredly, Cardinal Richelieu of France and King Gustavus II Adolf of Sweden were primarily concerned to enhance the power and influence of their countries. The story of the Christian faith during the Age of Confessionalism is thus the story of the faith in the setting of great societal vicissitudes.

The conflagration began in 1617, when the Habsburg Archduke Ferdinand II was crowned king of Bohemia. Ferdinand, an arch-Catholic, promptly proceeded to curtail the freedom of Protestant worship that had been granted to the Bohemian nobility. Ferdinand also made it clear that he would not honor the traditional political privileges of the nobility and systematically removed Protestant nobility from royal offices. Tensions increased between the archduke and the nobility until, in May 1618, a bizarre incident took place in Prague. It is known as the "Defenestration of Prague," when two of Ferdinand's officials were unceremoniously thrown out a window of the imperial Hradschin palace. Fortunately, the two gentlemen fell on soft ground and suffered no injuries (except, one suspects, some laundry bills), but this humiliating event led to Ferdinand's aggressive countermoves and eventually to the outbreak of open hostilities between king and nobility in Bohemia. The battlefields of the ensuing war were in Germany, and the conflict of opposing foreign rulers and armies brought immense suffering and devastation over German lands.

Were the Thirty Years' War, and the developments in England after the death of Queen Elizabeth I, essentially religious or political conflicts? Clearly religion was a factor, though it can hardly be said to have been the dominating force in these conflagrations. This military confrontation was yet another instance of the intertwining of religion and politics.

Reflection 4: Studying the Faith of the People

The Reformation of the sixteenth century serves as a useful point of departure for reflections on the role of the common people in the story of the Christian faith. Indeed, the Reformation has often been seen as an illustration par excellence of a popular movement in the history of Christianity.

The importance of the topic is obvious. Surely, narratives of Christian history should not only be accounts and ruminations on the great ideas of the Christian faith, on the power struggles between those representing the church and those representing the body politic, on the elites of the church, the theologians, bishops, and popes. The narratives of Christian history should also be about the men and women in the pews, the common people, the ordinary believers, who through the centuries made up the majority of the adherents committed to the faith, and yet their voices, their deeds, have tended to get lost in the shuffle. This lack of visibility has not just been a matter of gender either; ordinary men have been just as absent from the narrative as have been women, though decisions about the faith and their theological rationale were made by the male elites, secular and ecclesiastical. The common people were expected to fall in line.

Men and women were "followers," whose loyalty made it possible to build churches, to create works of religious art, to support priests. They stood under the pulpits to hear the sermons, they brought their infants to be baptized, they participated in the sacred meal of bread and wine, and they then went out to put what they heard into their daily lives—or to continue as before. Sometimes they took to the streets to demonstrate on behalf of their religious conviction; sometimes they interrupted sermons; sometimes they were called upon to vouchsafe their faith with the ultimate sacrifice, their lives.

These men and women in the pews were the church, perhaps not theologically but practically. Without them the church would not have existed the way we have come to know it. In the history of the Christian story, however, they are often nameless, and historical oblivion has fallen on them. While it is tempting to wax eloquently about the common people and the church, in fact, we know embarrassingly little.

From the historian's perspective, the voices of the people have tended to be mute and their actions invisible. To be sure, there were important exceptions—for example, when new monastic communities came into being or dissidents voiced concern over a particular church teaching. Francis of Assisi or John Wycliffe or Teresa of Avila and their followers are cases in point; their voices and actions were heard and can be seen in the historical record. The Anabaptists of the sixteenth century are a good illustration, for the endless governmental interrogations of ordinary women and men, suspected to be part of the Anabaptist movement, do throw telling light on their religious literacy and their convictions. The records of these interrogations offer a glimpse of the faith of some common people caught up in the turbulence of the Reformation. They show men and women marked by deep convictions about the "simple" teachings of Scripture—that Jesus taught to turn the other cheek, that one had to forfeit one's possessions to be a follower of Jesus—but woefully ill equipped to counter the theological sophistication of their interrogators, who bombarded them with other Scripture verses countering those they had cited.

The question arises, What is the point of focusing on the place of common men and women in the church? Surely not to learn of amazing divergences of belief, even though this might make things quite dramatic, such as the sentiment of the Italian miller who asserted that "in my opinion, all was chaos... and out of that bulk a mass formed—just as cheese is made out of milk—and worms appeared in it"—for which heretical notion he was burned at the stake. To pursue popular religion must not be a quest for the bizarre. Rather, the assumption must be that the common people echoed in their way the formal teachings of the churches. The focus then becomes the degree to which the men and women in the pews understood, appropriated, and accepted the assertions of the theologians and the teachings of the church. They obviously had opinions, convictions, and biases about the official faith, they participated (or failed to participate) in the rites and other activities of the churches, even if it meant simply that the particulars of a theological controversy were beyond their understanding and interest. In Protestant churches, pastors sought to edify, instruct, counsel, and cajole their congregations from their pulpits, Sunday after Sunday, week after week, year after year. Many, though by no means all, heard and became involved. Yet it is difficult to reconstruct what was preached, with the exception of a relatively small number of published sermons and sermon books, unless we assume the sentences from the sermon books were heard from countless pulpits in countless sermons all over the land. Plagiarism was widely accepted. Moreover, whatever might be reconstructed of the proclamation of the faith says nothing about the reception

of this proclamation. There are exceptions, of course, and recent scholarship has explored those with great benefit.

Other more formal aspects of popular religiosity can be more meaningfully established. We can reconstruct general patterns of church attendance, reception of Communion, and (later on) baptisms of newborn
infants—and use them as evidence of involvement and personal piety.
For the more distant past this is made possible through the availability of
church visitation records, which allow some rough statistical conclusions,
though one must be always mindful that people attended church not only
for the lofty purpose of enhancing and enriching their faith.

To talk about "popular" Christianity means making a distinction
between laity with formal education, with the ability to read, and laity
who were illiterate. Given the almost universal illiteracy in Europe until
the early nineteenth century, when compulsory schooling became the
norm, most people, dependent on an oral culture, could not be active participants in the theological and ecclesiastical debates. In other words, not
all laity were equal. The elites in a community were likely to be powerful
voices also in church affairs. The investiture controversy ended with a
victory for the papacy and the church, but it was a Pyrrhic victory, for the
political elites rebounded and relentlessly pursued their goal of control
over the church. Henry VIII in England torpedoed the theological conversations with the Schmalkald League, and in German lands the
Lutheran ruler served at once as "summepiscopus," as head of the church.

Add to this the absence of widespread book production until
Gutenberg's invention of movable type in the fifteenth century, and it
becomes obvious that the majority of Christians simply could not appropriate the Christian truths. In fact, the lower clergy were hardly better
equipped, especially since until the late sixteenth century formal education for the priesthood was nonexistent: priests merely needed to know a
modicum of Latin to find their way through the Latin of the Missal.
When in the mid-sixteenth century the clergy of the Diocese of Lincoln
were examined about their knowledge of the Ten Commandments, the
Apostles' Creed, and the Lord's Prayer, the results were disastrous. Most
men of the cloth were appalling in their ignorance. One well-meaning
priest opined that the Lord's Prayer was so called because it was issued "by
our lord, the king."

It stands to reason that the common people, no matter in what epoch
of the history of the church, were exposed to influences and forces other
than those coming from the pulpits of their churches, making their

Christian beliefs then as well as since an amalgam of diverse influences. Indeed, as the Donatists in early Christianity or the Puritans in seventeenth-century England suggest, theological dissent could also have a formidable social agenda, in which the place of religious belief was subsidiary to economic and political issues.

A final consideration: The reflection on the role of the common people in the life of faith takes us squarely back to the church, for popular belief and personal piety had a symbiotic relationship with the formal pronouncements of the church about faith and life. Thus, the church canonized saintly women and men, while the common people found these saints to be role models for mundane no less than for spiritual help. Thus, the church pronounced that in the Mass the consecrated bread and wine were the true body and blood of Christ, and some common folk took this to mean that the consecrated host was a miracle to be used in romance or bodily pain as well. Thus, theologians wrote words of comfort for those suffering spiritual pain—Thomas à Kempis's *Imitation of Christ* or the German Theology or John Bunyan's *Pilgrim's Progress* come to mind—and the common people made these books into best sellers. Often more so than Scripture, these devotional books were the ground of the people's faith. By the same token, the church made sure that its proclamation was not solely a series of intellectual pronouncements with finely honed interpretations of the faith. The proclamation was also to appeal to the senses of the faithful: in the stained glass windows of churches, the smoke of incense at the altar, the mystery of inaudible words spoken by the priest in the Mass. In short, the church's proclamation of the drama of salvation, paraphrased in the theologians' language, pictorialized in works of art, and formed in stone in shrines of worship, was given meaning by the common people in myriad ways.

We are left, in the end, with an ambiguous picture of the common people and the Christian faith. There can be no leaders if there are no followers. But just as in studying World War II, the memoirs of Dwight Eisenhower provide valuable insight into the larger scheme of things as compared to those of a French resistance fighter, yet both are illuminating and stones of a larger mosaic. So it is with telling the story of the Christian church. Inevitably, we are taken back to those who were the catalysts of momentous change, the heroes of the faith.

CHAPTER FOUR

THE NEW CHALLENGE: MODERNITY

T he Christian churches entered the seventeenth century with vigor and self-confidence—rather surprising, in view of the fierce disagreements and controversies of the Reformation era. The Protestant Reformation had caused a fateful division of the Christian religion in the West into no fewer than six branches, but all of them—the Catholic Church and the five new Protestant churches (Lutheran, Calvinist/Reformed, Anabaptist, Anglican, and Antitrinitarian/ Unitarian)—had quickly consolidated their theologies and polities. At the turn of the century a precarious religious peace in France had given the Protestants a measure of formal recognition. In England the Puritan opposition to the settlement of religion persisted but the Church of England had found eloquent apologists, such as Richard Hooker (1554–1600), whose magisterial *Laws of Ecclesiastical Polity* set the general direction of the Church of England for a long time to come. The first four volumes of this monumental undertaking were published in 1594, the fifth volume three years later, and the final three volumes posthumously. The books eloquently argued a via media, a middle way, for the Church of England, between Roman Catholicism and Calvinist Protestantism.

In German lands the better part of the seventeenth century was dominated by the cataclysmic event of the Thirty Years' War, with its seemingly endless invasion of foreign armies, changing alliances, never-ending warfare, unimaginable devastation, horrible suffering, and devastating loss of lives. The Christian faith was put to the test in those terrible years, and Christians found themselves in great agony as they searched for meaning and solace.

And across the channel in England turbulence and suffering reigned as well. If on the Continent the Thirty Years' War was about religion and politics, the same applied to the course of events in England. Religious dissent turned into political opposition. Oliver Cromwell exhorted his followers to trust in God and keep their powder dry, John Milton published political tracts, and the Levelers, that alliance of agitators and pamphleteers, demanded equality of all people.

Afterward, the face of religion in England was not to be the same. Whatever hope the Puritans had with the succession of James I in 1603 did not materialize, for not much in matters of religion changed in the land—other than the king's sponsorship of a new English translation of the Bible, which has memorialized his name ever since. His *Book of Sports*, a document that enjoined a rather liberal notion of how to keep the Sabbath, was an anathema to all stalwart Puritans. But once more, the Puritans were powerless to stem the tide of the official religion. The Church of England stood firm. The succession of Charles I in 1625 brought a so-called high churchman to the British throne—someone whose Anglicanism was influenced more by Catholicism than by Protestantism, hardly endearing him to the Puritan party in the Church of England. To make matters worse, the new king was married to a French Catholic, Henriette Marie. For the Puritans that, too, spelled trouble.

Little concerned about the theology of the *Thirty-nine Articles* and the liturgy of the *Book of Common Prayer*, Charles ordered the use of traditional clerical vestments in the worship service. Clerical vestments had been the touchy subject that had coalesced the initial Puritan objection to the settlement of religion. The king's order provoked widespread suspicion of his motives and brought about resolute opposition—and for good reason, as those who had dealings with him quickly realized. Charles was unwilling to work with Parliament, where a coalition of ardent Puritans and unhappy gentry was forming. Charles's autocratic style added to the restiveness. Not surprisingly, the king's political and religious enemies multiplied, and before long he was detested by just about everyone who counted in the realm.

Moreover, by the second decade of the seventeenth century the more radical opponents of the Elizabethan settlement, the "dissenters," realized that the settlement was not going to be changed and concluded that the Church of England was beyond redemption. They proceeded to separate themselves from that church by holding meetings and worship services of their own, using neither the *Book of Common Prayer* nor the ministrations of Church of England clergy. The "separatist" movement in England was born, presenting the more adamant Puritans with the unpleasant choice of either defying the law of the land and "separating" from the church, or leaving the country. As every American schoolchild knows, the *Mayflower* Pilgrims chose the latter.

Things came to a head in 1637, when Charles sought to introduce the *Book of Common Prayer* in Calvinist-Reformed Scotland. A vehement reaction ensued, once more born of both religious and political resentment. Eventually things reached a fever pitch, and a Scottish army moved south to invade England. To finance the army needed to repel the Scottish invasion, Charles was forced to turn to Parliament, which he had blatantly ignored and despised ever since his succession to the throne. A period of uneasy compromises between king and Parliament followed, until in 1642 tensions led to the outbreak of outright civil conflict. Royalists (known as "Cavaliers" for their attention to outer appearance) and Puritans (called "Roundheads" for their closely cropped hair) confronted each other. The military showdown was inconclusive until the parliamentary army received a brilliant leader in Oliver Cromwell (1599–1658), a member of the gentry who could claim no military training or expertise. Still, his New Model Army scored a decisive victory. After all, the Army had taken up "Armes in the cause of God and his people" (*The Soldier's Catechism*, London, 1644).

The conflict was as much political as it was religious. Apart from the Puritan objections to the Church of England, opposition had coalesced among the gentry in Parliament against the increasingly absolutist tendencies of the monarchs—first James I, then Charles I. As this political opposition formed, the unhappy gentry found comrades-in-arms in the Puritans who were displeased with the state of religious affairs in England. Those who opposed the king on political grounds made common cause with those who opposed him on religious grounds. If your enemy is also my enemy, we are allies—the phrase captures well the strange alliance between gentry and Puritans.

The rest of the story is quickly told. The king was removed from his throne, brought to trial, found guilty, and executed—a first regicide prompting a wave of consternation throughout Europe. A "protectorate" was established under Cromwell's aegis, but after his death the monarchy was quickly restored. The ongoing political and religious turbulence led to the official promulgation of religious freedom, including the readmission of Jews to England. In this atmosphere of openness (a truly radical turn), new religious groups sprung up like spring flowers, ranging from relatively staid ones, such as the Congregationalists and the Baptists, to radical ones, such as the Fifth Monarchy Men, the Muggletonians, the Ranters, and the Seekers.

Somewhere in the middle of this spectrum (though more radical than their subsequent characteristics might suggest) were the Quakers. Formally the Society of Friends, the Quakers were the institutional embodiment of the ministry of George Fox, the most charismatic religious figure in seventeenth-century Christianity. Fox rehabilitated the role of the Holy Spirit in Christian life and thought, even as he also introduced a whole new Christian vocabulary—Sunday, for example, became "First Day," the gatherings of Friends were "meetings."

The new Baptist churches, in turn, were united in their affirmation of the centrality of believer's or adult baptism, but were less unified when it came to some of the other big theological issues, such as eternal election and predestination. Eventually, Baptists came to be of two sorts—the "Particular" Baptists, who affirmed predestination, and the "General" Baptists, who espoused the notion of Dutch theologian Jacob Arminius, a towering figure of moderate seventeenth-century Calvinism, that humans were free to accept or reject the offer of divine grace.

The path to salvation was narrow in mid-seventeenth-century England, for once the Puritans had gained control of the Commonwealth, they made sure that their values were implemented, and they concluded, as did their fellows in New England, that freedom of religion was too precious to be given to their opponents. Theaters and taverns were shut down, the celebration of Christmas and Easter outlawed. Personal demeanor was monitored as well; one ordinance, for example, prohibited public swearing. The rich decorations of the exteriors and interiors of many churches—paintings of biblical scenes and sculptures of biblical personages—were removed, because the Bible, so it was held, contained explicit prohibitions of "graven images." Church buildings, as well as individual believers, were to be "pure."

When the "Lord Protector," Oliver Cromwell, died in 1658, the English people had come to resent the moral straitjacket imposed by the Protectorate. The succession of Charles II—a closet Catholic who on his deathbed converted to Rome—in 1660 brought the collapse of the Puritan experiment and the restoration of the monarchy as well as that of theaters and taverns (and perhaps swearing as well). One wonders which of these changes were most desired by the people in England. Be that as it may, Parliament rescinded the sum total of the religious legislation of the Protectorate, and even the dead were not secure in their eternal sleep: Oliver Cromwell's remains were disinterred and hanged. Ever since, England has been a monarchy unperturbed by traumatic revolutions.

THE NEW SCIENCE

In the setting of this turbulent convergence of religion and politics in England, the Christian faith experienced another new and dramatic challenge. At first subtle, then radical—and quite apart from theological reflection—this challenge increasingly cast its long shadow over the traditional Christian self-understanding. The sum of these changes is known as the Scientific Revolution. Beginning in the early seventeenth century,

Figure 4A
Nikolaus Copernicus holding a compass and armillary sphere.
Sculpture 1830, Warsaw, Poland.

an ever greater myriad of scientific discoveries brought about a change of perspective that fundamentally altered the way Europeans understood the natural world and themselves. Natural science began its increasingly impressive journey to ever new discoveries and ever new insights in mathematics, physics, and astronomy. The impact on society—and before long on the Christian faith—was profound and far-reaching.

It may be said to have all begun with the voyages of Columbus and Magellan across the seas, which confirmed that the earth was not flat, and it continued with Nicolas Copernicus's 1543 book *On The Revolutions of the Heavenly Bodies*, which suggested that the astronomers and physicists had it all wrong about the relationship of the earth and the planets. The ancient Ptolemaic system, which posited a flat earth with the sun and stars rotating dome-like over it, had become excessively complicated as new observations of the firmament had to be integrated into this picture. Copernicus offered the "hypothesis," as he called it, that in fact it was the other way around—the earth was not the center of the universe; rather, the earth rotated around the sun, as did the other planets.

Roughly a century after Copernicus's book, which puzzled theologians and angered fellow astronomers, a piece of glass, polished into a lens by Protestant artisans in Holland and made into a telescope, vindicated Copernicus's hypothesis and brought about a revolution in astronomy. The Italian Galileo Galilei used the telescope to confirm Copernicus's hypothesis, and even though he put his scientific discovery into the literary form of a dialogue to obscure his own views, a Catholic inquisitorial court took notice. Galileo was forced to declare that he had no verifiable facts to support the "heliocentric" theory. The Catholic Church, represented by six cardinals, condemned Galileo's notions as "absurd, philosophically false, and formally heretical, expressly contrary to Holy Scriptures" (Giorgio de Santillana, *The Crime of Galileo*, 306).

Galileo, seventy years of age at the time and virtually blind, dutifully renounced his views, but reportedly uttered under his breath the words, referring to the earth, "it does move." Publicly he declared that he was undecided "between the two opinions, but once the church had condemned the opinion of Copernicus, my uncertainty ended." This was a masterpiece of evasion, and his punishment was rather benign: he was ordered to recite the Seven Penitential Psalms once a week for three years. The year was 1633, and Galileo's book would not be removed from the *Index of Prohibited Books* for two hundred years.

Religion and the new science appeared to be on a collision course. For more than a millennium, the theologians and the church understood the Bible as expressing and confirming the Ptolemaic worldview. After all, Joshua had ordered the sun to stand still (and not the earth), demonstrating that the sun moved over a static earth. More than that, by adopting the Ptolemaic model, the Christian religion found in the heavens the confirmation of a biblical truth: the planet earth was the center of the universe, just as medieval maps had pointedly put Jerusalem and the Holy Land at the center of the flat earth.

Galileo had made a case for a new understanding of the universe, but in so doing he challenged not so much an explicit church teaching or dogma but the way the church and its self-understanding were embedded in tradition. Before long, other scientists appeared on the scene and made new discoveries. And as discovery was added to discovery, the days of splendid harmony between the Bible and natural science were over.

This relationship between the old religion and the new science was all the more dramatic because the new breed of scientists moved exuberantly from insight to insight, from discovery to discovery. In so doing, they challenged the mind-set that had dominated European thinking for centuries and had defined the relationship between tradition and innovation, between the "old" and the "new." Traditionally, the old had been revered and the new despised. Men of science were as conservative as men of theology. Then came the scientific discoveries, and they changed everything: the new became exciting, while the old was considered questionable and outdated. Tellingly, Descartes referred to his philosophy as the "new" philosophy, and he did so proudly. A seemingly insatiable quest to investigate, explore, understand, and measure characterized the seventeenth century, and in the process old truths were found wanting. Little by little the implicit challenges to the traditional understanding of the Christian faith became obvious.

What made this development all the more poignant was that none of the new scientists, from Nicolaus Copernicus to Isaac Newton, from Galileo Galilei to Francis Bacon, to name but a few, saw their scientific pursuits as a challenge to the truths of the Christian faith. Quite the contrary. They meant to be devout Christian believers. Isaac Newton, for example, thought of himself more as a theologian (with Arian inclinations, to be sure) than a mathematician. The task of the scientist, he said, was to rethink the profound thoughts of God, the creator of the universe.

Despite the personal piety of the new scientists, their work implicitly challenged traditional religious affirmations, including the understanding of God. Previously, the faithful had thought of God in altogether human ways—the way the first chapters of the book of Genesis described God, walking in the Garden of Eden in the cool breeze of the evening, not knowing where to find Adam and Eve, in short, as portrayed in Michelangelo's frescoes in the Sistine Chapel in Rome, a grandfatherly type, with gray hair and beard, floating in a cloud, arm outstretched, his finger not quite touching that of Adam. Of course, the theologians knew that God was not really male, had neither human form nor face, but even they spoke of him in human terms and had no problem allowing the artists to give him a physical image.

Accordingly, the iconography of God was simple. There were biblical words of caution, such as the verse "no one has ever seen God" (John 1:18) or the psalmist's pronouncement that God was at once everywhere, but these acknowledgments seemed relevant only for the theologians. Popular piety was marked by a deeply anthropomorphic view, with important theological consequences. Understanding God in human terms offered immediacy and intimacy in the believer's relationship. If God was visualized as "Father," one could pray to this fatherly God the same way children spoke to their fathers—pleading, asking, thanking, cajoling. The faithful thus had reason to expect that God would respond to their pleas very much the way a father responded to the pleas of his children. And even as fathers could be made to change their minds, so could God when approached in prayer. That God would change his mind or punish disobedience was understandable as well. Miracles, whether recorded in the Bible or recorded in the history of the church or experienced in one's own life, posed no problems in that context: they were answers to prayerful requests made to God, just as Jesus had told his followers to do. Emphasizing the biblical God in human terms allowed Christians to make the biblical stories come alive—the story of Noah, for example, or God sending the flood after having regretted creating the human race, or of Abraham and God's demand to sacrifice his son.

The Scientific Revolution subtly challenged this tradition. Scientists discovered that natural happenings were measurable and could be verified and replicated by experiments. Indeed, the realization that natural phenomena happen with lawful regularity may well have been the most profound insight of the new science. The scientists who discovered (and then used) these laws were overawed by what they perceived as the mathematical regularity of the entire universe, for them the work of God. They were convinced, as Isaac Newton observed, that by pursuing their scientific work they were uncovering God's true grandeur and wisdom.

In the process, however, something got lost: the traditional understanding of God was rejected as childish, immature, unworthy of God's magnificence. A God who changed his mind in response to prayer or changed the laws he had ordained with miracles was an unworthy God. The new vision was of a God who did not have to search for Adam and Eve in the cool of the garden, did not get angry, did not repent, and did not change his mind. A passage such as Exodus 32:14, "And the LORD changed his mind about the disaster that he planned to bring on his people" was found to be offensive. God set laws for the universe he created, and they were good laws, even as God was benevolently good.

There was a second religious consequence of the Scientific Revolution. Scholars did not confine their explorations to natural phenomena, such as the motion of the stars or the laws of gravity. Their questioning minds pursued everything, and that included the traditional understanding of the past, the stories that had been revered and embraced as part of tradition for millennia. Some Renaissance thinkers in Italy had anticipated this new kind of questioning. In the fifteenth century, Lorenzo Valla examined the long-accepted claim that on his deathbed Emperor Constantine had "donated" his domains to the papacy, a gift that made the popes superior to all secular rulers, including the emperors. Valla demonstrated that this "Donation of Constantine" was a medieval forgery. His discovery was revolutionary in its own right, but even more so was the probing mind-set that questioned traditional truths.

By the seventeenth century, traditional theology was increasingly in a quandary. On the Catholic side, the church held its theologians in line by affirming theological orthodoxy concerning the relationship of faith and science. It exercised—with the tools provided by the Inquisition and the *Index of Prohibited Books*—tight control over scientists in Catholic lands by strict censorship of publications. This strategy assured enforced uniformity but stymied scientific exploration; Catholic lands produced few scientists and discoveries. In Protestant lands, on the other hand, the new science was allowed to flourish more or less freely, thereby in many ways challenged traditional notions and truths. But no outright clash or confrontation occurred, for the new science entered into a rapprochement with the Christian faith, a precarious one, to be sure, but one that postponed outright conflict between science and religion until the nineteenth century and Charles Darwin's theory of evolution.

But a price had to be paid for this uneasy coexistence. First in England, then elsewhere in Europe, theologians began to accept the findings of science and delineate a vision of the Christian faith that was to be in harmony with the new discoveries of science. It was, however, a fundamentally new vision that insisted that there was no conflict with the Christian faith, properly understood. Only a false and perverted understanding of the faith, so some argued, had led to conflict and tensions.

The issue joined in the understanding of the Bible, for the relentless scientific pursuit caused questions to be raised about the accuracy of its narratives. The Bible, the "book of books," vessel of divine revelation, that had guided Europeans for centuries not only in matters of religion but also of geography, politics, and history, began to be critically examined. For centuries the Bible had been seen as speaking explicitly to natural phenomena—it described people who had risen from the dead, a sun that rotated around the earth but could be made to stand still, a human being who had been swallowed by a whale and survived.

The new science put chinks into that armor. Scholars found that the delivered Hebrew text of the Old Testament was problematic in its clarity since the vowel marks of the language were a later addition to the text. Accordingly, they could not have been part of the original revelatory words, though they had been accepted as such. Other passages of the Bible were challenged as well, for example, the notion that Moses was the author of a book that described his own death. Clearly, many scriptural accounts of natural phenomena did not seem to lend themselves to validation in a laboratory. In this dilemma some theologians argued that some biblical stories ran counter to the insights of science because they had been erroneously interpreted. And so a painstaking examination of the biblical narratives began. Rather than dismissing the Christian religion as misguided or, worse yet, as a fraud, this new breed of theologians insisted that by challenging traditional understandings of the Bible the new science served as a catalyst that restored authentic Christianity, after centuries of misunderstanding and distortion by priestly greed.

Two particular concerns came to the fore: the concept of a divine revelation and the facticity of biblical miracles. Theologians and philosophers raised the question whether the claim of revelatory truth in the Bible could be sustained. They asked whether the notion of a divine revelation did in fact complicate the proper understanding of God. Why would God reveal his truth only to a particular people at a particular time? Was that not a perspective unworthy of God, for it divided humankind into two classes, those who received and those who did not receive revelatory truth? The new theologians replaced the traditional notion of revelation with the concept of "natural religion," that is, of a religion whose precepts were not revealed by special dispensation but were knowable by all humans.

The case for this universal natural religion was famously made early in the seventeenth century by Herbert of Cherbury in his book *De Veritate* ("Concerning Truth") of 1624. Herbert identified several religious "common notions" universally held by humans. These included the existence of a Supreme Being, the existence of a moral code of right and wrong, the obligation to venerate this Supreme Being, and a Final Judgment of all humankind. These "common notions," Herbert argued, were the sum of true and authentic religion; no divine revelation was necessary.

Later, other authors jumped into the fray to restate the case for Christianity, now dramatically reinterpreted. The initial locale for much of this new kind of theological reflection was England, and the authors were the likes of Thomas Woolston, Anthony Collins, John Toland, Matthew Tindal, William Whiston, Conyers Middleton, and Thomas Chubb. Quite a few of them were bright men, though not all had formal theological training, and their writings often reveal shallowness of argument. Nonetheless, they all wrote with stunning self-assurance. Their argument was simple: traditional Christianity was no longer tenable; indeed, it distorted the simple "natural" religion proclaimed by Jesus.

Collectively, these thinkers are known as "Christian Deists," and they dominated English Christianity during the first part of the eighteenth century and Protestant Europe about half a century later. They approached their task of elucidating true Christianity not so much as devoted supporters of the faith but as increasingly fierce critics who employed the new methods of science to reestablish the meaning of the original Christian faith. John Toland's *Christianity Not Mysterious* of 1696 argued that the priestly caste, for personal profit, had turned Jesus' simple religion into something akin to a mystery cult. By order of the Irish Parliament the book was burned in 1697. A generation later, the title of Matthew Tindal's *Christianity as Old as the Creation* expressed the same conclusion, now offered in radicalized form. The true Christian faith was identical with the religion of nature, known to all people of all times. In Tindal's scheme of things, the notion of a particular divine revelation was beside the point. Thomas Chubb declared, in his *The True Gospel of Jesus Christ Asserted*, that the purpose of Jesus was to be a teacher whose moral principles must be followed in order to attain eternal salvation.

The polemic against miracles touched on a crucial hallmark of the traditional understanding of the Christian faith. Miracles had been cited since the days of the early church as proof of the truth and authenticity of the Christian message. The Christian Deists asked why would God, the author of the laws of nature, deign to violate them? What purpose did the miracles in the Bible serve? Even if Jesus did raise Lazarus from the dead, the miracle offered him only a brief respite, for in the end Lazarus, too, suffered the death suffered by all humans. The Christian Deist Thomas Woolston, a Cambridge don until he lost his fellowship because of his "disorderly mind," published a series of "discourses" on the miracles in the Gospels, in which he subjected the biblical accounts of miracles to the same scrutiny that scholars of his time had learned to apply to all documentary claims of the past. Even though he wrote no less than half a dozen of these discourses, his conclusion about biblical miracles is not altogether clear: were they embellished accounts of actual happenings or plain fiction? Plainly, however, Woolston had little patience with the traditional reading of supernatural events in the Bible and rejected it. As matters turned out, he paid dearly for his radical notions. When his final "discourse" examined the evidence for the bodily resurrection of Jesus, and concluded there was none, the British authorities concluded in turn that enough was enough. Woolston was brought to trial for blasphemy, found guilty, and sentenced to jail. Since he would not give assurance about his future behavior, he was kept in jail, where he died.

Of course, there was no dearth of defenders of traditional Christianity. Not quite as numerous as the flood of Deist writers, the anti-Deist authors, such as Samuel Clark and Joseph Butler (together with John Wesley), eloquently defended time-honored Christian notions. In particular, Bishop Joseph Butler's work, *The Analogy of Religion, Natural and Revealed, to the Constitution and Course of Nature* (1736), exerted enormous influence and appeared to clinch the case for traditional revelatory religion, for it argued that the difficulties attending the acceptance of supernatural religion also attend the acceptance of a religion of nature. Deists, in other words, have the same problem as those who affirmed revelatory religion. Nor was John Wesley, the spearhead of the evangelical revival in England in the second half of the eighteenth century, slow to attack the new theologians and their thought. Freethinkers, he observed, are hardly deep thinkers—a rather salient judgment, because that was, of course, precisely what the Deists claimed to be.

Before long, the Deist understanding of the Christian faith found its way across the English Channel to the Continent, where it assumed different forms in different countries. In France, Deist agitation took a decidedly anti-Catholic Church turn. The criticism of the Catholic Church, both past and present, was radical, famously expressed in Voltaire's battle cry "écrasez l'infâme" ("crush the infamy") and in his strident quip that humankind would not be truly liberated until the last priest had been strangled with the entrails of the last bishop. Such confrontational language was hardly calculated to endear the still-conservative common people to the new currents of the Enlightenment.

The intriguing reality was that awareness of the Deist controversy in England reached Germany first through anti-Deist publications. These informed theologians and churchmen in Germany of what was going on in England. Deist writings found their way to German lands slowly, perhaps because rigid censorship made the publication of new or dissenting theological views difficult. Soon, however, theologians in Germany began to explore the issues that had agitated the discussion in England. Christian Wolff (1679–1754), professor in Halle, sought to synthesize the new notions of natural religion and traditional revelatory religion. Then, in 1777, the publication of a modest section of a voluminous manuscript of more than a thousand pages triggered a major and emotional controversy over the Deist understanding of the faith. The author of the manuscript, a systematic summary of what the English Deists had parlayed for some time, was Hermann Samuel Reimarus, professor of Oriental languages in Hamburg. Reimarus had published in 1755 a widely read volume of moderate Deist orientation, titled *Abhandlungen von den vornehmsten Wahrheiten der natürlichen Religion* ("Discourses on the Noblest Truths of Natural Religion"), but his real energies were devoted to a far more ambitious and radical manuscript, the *Apologie oder Schutzschrift für die vernünftigen Verehrer Gottes* ("Apology or Defense of the Thoughtful Worshipers of God"), a radical rejection of the Bible as the revelatory source for Christian teachings. The manuscript was heavy medicine. The Bible, so Reimarus argued, abounded in factual errors, contradicted human experience, reason, and morality, and was, all in all, a despicable story of human folly, deceit, enthusiasm, selfishness, and crime. This was radical Christian Deism, indeed. No wonder that fear of

221

censorship and retaliation prompted Reimarus, a respected and esteemed citizen of his community, to guard his manuscript from the printer's ink.

Eventually, however, after his death, the manuscript found its way into the hands of the playwright Gotthold Ephraim Lessing, librarian at the ducal library at Wolfenbüttel, near Braunschweig. Sympathetic with the notions of Reimarus, he decided to publish parts of the manuscript. Knowing full well the identity of the author, Lessing nonetheless stated that he had come across the manuscript in the archives of the Wolfenbüttel library quite by accident and gave the publication the title *Fragments from the Pen of an Anonymous Author*. But the bland title did not disguise the radicalism of the content. The publication of the *Fragments* triggered a fierce controversy. To be sure, the *Fragments* hardly said anything the English Deists, notably Chubb and Woolston, had not already said many times, but the publication marked the dramatic entrance of Deist ideas into German intellectual life. From then on Enlightenment notions of Christianity all but dominated the German theological scene.

The face of European Christianity was changing, perhaps even more radically than it had in the Reformation of the sixteenth century. Old affirmations and assertions were losing their sway, and this time the broad challenge had not come from inside the church but from outside. It had come from society, from science, and before long the Christian faith and science found themselves in an uneasy coexistence. A new form of the Christian religion, known as "liberal Christianity," made its entrance. Importantly, the new liberal impulses (despite challenging traditional Christianity) did not lead to the formation of new churches; they remained a movement of ideas rather than becoming a social movement. Nonetheless, they have accompanied the story of existing churches to the present.

RELIGIONS OF THE HEART

German Pietism

Well before the Deist movement began its sweep through Europe, a reform movement of a different sort had emerged in German Lutheranism in the late seventeenth century, soon affecting Reformed Protestantism and even the Catholic Church as well. Its concern was not so much the rationalism of the new type of Christianity making the rounds nor, for that matter, a rigid and arid theologizing. Rather, the new reformers were pained by a church with too many lukewarm Christians, an intellectualized understanding of the faith, and a bureaucratic clergy. Reform was the need of the hour.

True enough, in church pulpits and university lecterns seventeenth-century German Lutheranism was preoccupied with lofty theological issues, and some of its leading theologians saw Calvinism as a far greater theological threat than Catholicism, and this all the more so since some Lutherans had obliquely introduced Calvinist notions into Lutheran theology. Doctrinal correctness and, thereby, an insistence on clear confessional theological identity, dominated German Lutheranism. Intense theological controversies were the norm, so much so, in fact, that in the middle of the seventeenth century the Prussian elector required the clergy of his territory to take a formal oath not to use the pulpit for confessional polemics.

At the same time, there was also a vibrant tradition that did not understand the Christian faith principally as a set of intellectual propositions but emphasized personal piety and the devotional life. This tradition, while not prominent, was present in all churches at the time—Catholic and Anglican no less than Lutheran and Reformed. It was aided by dismay over endless theological bickering. The emphasis on theological sophistication seemed to lose an important aspect of the Christian faith—the mandate for Christian living.

These spiritual and devotional yearnings found expression in the Lutheran pastor Johann Arndt, who had personally experienced the theological feuds between Lutherans and Reformed when, upon refusing to remove images from his church, he was dismissed from his pastorate. Of a decidedly mystical bent, Arndt's *Bücher vom wahren Christentum* (*Books on True Christianity*) became immensely popular and were republished numerous times throughout the seventeenth century. By the end of the seventeenth century Arndt's popularity had surpassed that of Martin Luther.

Arndt was born in 1555, studied medicine, then theology. He fell under the spell of Thomas à Kempis's famous *Imitation of Christ* and of the *German Theology*, the devotional guide written by a Bavarian bishop at the turn of the sixteenth century and subsequently published by none other than Martin Luther. Arndt appropriated this medieval Catholic devotional piety, gave it a Protestant twist, and forged a "Protestant" spirituality that replaced the Catholic emphasis on Mary and the saints with a centered focus on Jesus as the model for Christian living. In his *Books on True Christianity*, Arndt wrote that "true Christianity consists of proving a living, active faith through genuine godliness."

Arndt was anything but a lone voice. Other authors included Arndt's comrade-in-arms Jakob Böhme (1575–1624), also a Lutheran and a mystic of purest waters, who gorged in visions and spiritual revelations. A prolific author, Böhme published an endless string of mystical tracts, all with a Lutheran veneer, but based on the assumption of the human ability to apprehend God directly, without revelation. Other writers were Valentin Weigel (1533–88) and Paul Felgenhauer (1593–1677), the latter a prolific purveyor of bizarre notions about the End Times, which he declared to be imminent.

The same concern for personal piety was found elsewhere in Europe. In England devotional books were widely read and exerted massive influence. These included *A Declaration of the True Manner of Knowing Christ Crucified* (1596) by William Perkins (1558–1602), a Puritan clergy in Cambridge. John Tillotson (1630–94), archbishop of Canterbury, wrote *The Wisdom of Being Religious*, while Richard Baxter (1615–91) was the author of *A Call to the Unconverted to Turn and Live* and also *The Saints' Everlasting Rest*, the former credited with the conversion of thousands to the faith. William Law's *A Serious Call to a Devout and Holy Life*, published somewhat later (in 1728), became the most famous devotional book in the English language, republished, and republished ever since. In France, François de Sales (1567–1622) wrote his *Introduction à la vie dévote* (*Introduction to the Committed Life*) for those who had no intention of becoming monastics but wished to be fully committed Christians. François insisted that the true spiritual life was open to all, finding expression in the love of God and neighbor.

In light of this dual concern for pure doctrine and the centrality of the devotional life, it will not surprise that the time was also the great period of sacred music. It was an immensely rich and productive time, especially on the Continent, where theologians and nontheologians wrote ever more hymns—one of them, Benjamin Schmolck, no less than 1,300. The prominent theme was the affirmation of Luther's understanding of the gospel and the trust in God's goodness despite the agony and pain brought by the horrific Thirty Years' War.

Paul Gerhardt's life (1607–76) spanned all of this terrible time. Little is known about his life. He studied theology at Wittenberg and received his first parish in 1651, when he was forty-four years of age, a biographical turn that demands explanation. Six years later he was appointed to the prestigious Saint Nikolai church in Berlin, where he promptly ran into trouble for refusing to sign the obligatory statement, issued by Elector Fredrick William I, that forbade partisan theological polemics in the pulpit. Even though influential friends succeeded in obtaining a special exemption, Gerhardt remained adamant—and was promptly dismissed from office. In 1668 he received an appointment in Lübben in the Spreewald near Berlin. His wife and he had five children; all save one died within months of their births. That, together with his unfortunate experience in Berlin as well as the suffering observed in the Thirty Years' War may well explain the subdued tenor that pervades some of his pronouncements, for example, the verse from Genesis 47 that he had put onto a plaque in the church in Lübben: "My years have been few and difficult" (v. 9).

But this appraisal, realistic as it strikes the reader, is overshadowed by the joyous affirmations he put into his hymns. Of the more than 130 hymns he wrote, here is one stanza from "Nun ruhen alle Wälder":

> The sun's bright light now closes,
> Each house and barn reposes,
> Night covers fields and woods.
> Let us, as dark is falling,
> On God, our creator calling,
> To offer praise to him, for all the good. (author's translation)

All of these streams of concern for lived practical Christianity came together in a book by Philip Jakob Spener (1635–1705), a Lutheran pastor in Frankfurt. He was approached in 1670 by a Frankfurt printer to write a preface for yet another edition of Arndt's *Books on True Christianity*. The invitation gave Spener the opportunity to pour his notions about the current state of "true Christianity" onto paper. As he pondered the matter, his preface grew longer and longer, eventually warranting publication as a separate book. It appeared in 1675 and had the title *Pia Desideria* (*Pious Wishes*). The preface had turned into an extensive inventory of Spener's ideas for how to revitalize the church. To avoid being misunderstood by orthodox Lutheran theologians—who promptly chided him anyhow for being unfaithful to the Lutheran tradition—Spener went out of his way to assure his readers that Lutheran theology needed no reform; it was a reform of Lutheran practice that was sorely needed. To the end of his life, despite chronic recriminations about his alleged lack of faithfulness to Lutheran theology, Spener declared himself a loyal heir of that tradition.

Spener's book put forward concrete proposals for church reform: (1) sermons should focus on Christian living, not expound theological niceties, (2) seminary courses of study should pay more attention to the spiritual formation of the students, (3) the spiritual nurture of the laity should receive greater attention, (4) the laity should be more involved in the activities of the church and have the opportunity to participate in weekly prayer meetings and Bible studies (which Spener called "collegia pietatis," or "gatherings for piety"), and (5) committed Christian living should mean moderation in food, drink, attire, and lifestyle. In short, Spener proposed a vision for the clergy, whom he identified as the crucial part of any church reform, and also for the laity, by providing for more appropriately trained pastors, who would receive a more relevant theological education and consequently would preach sermons that emphasized moral exhortation rather than intellectual subtleties. The central concern was to create a culture of regular Bible study for the laity.

Spener's book quickly made the rounds in Protestant Germany. Expectedly, the response from the ecclesiastical and theological establishment was negative. Spener's proposals were repudiated especially by those whom he had implicitly challenged (and, perhaps, threatened)— the theologians at the universities and the church leaders. The opposition was particularly intense among the theologians at the University of Wittenberg, who accused Spener of perverting Luther's theology. Spener's practical initiatives in Frankfurt also created tensions—some of the leading citizens, for example, active in Spener's collegia, stopped attending the Sunday services of the established church and refused to receive Communion from pastors they considered unworthy. Not surprisingly, Spener felt it prudent to accept an invitation to move to Dresden, although before long his bluntness created a problem there as well: from the pulpit he criticized the lifestyle of one of the Saxon princes, hardly the way to be popular with the ruling elite. No wonder then that he was pushed from his position, though an invitation to move to Berlin offered a convenient way out.

In Berlin, Spener's ideas of a practical reform of the Lutheran church came to full bloom—and for a good reason. Prussia was a Lutheran territory, but the ruling Brandenburg dynasty had been Calvinist/Reformed since the second decade of the seventeenth century, when Elector Johann Sigismund converted to Calvinism. Brandenburg-Prussia was thus ruled by electors whose faith differed from that of their subjects, a difficult situation made worse by the ongoing fierce theological antagonism between Lutherans and Calvinists. Understandably, the Prussian electors were interested in minimizing theological polemics and squabbles in their realm, and Spener's message of emphasizing piety over doctrine meshed neatly with their concerns. Spener's agenda seemed tailor-made for the Prussian ruling house. Minimizing confessional polemics would also take the wind out of the sails of the powerful Prussian nobility, which was not only staunchly Lutheran but also resented the autocratic tendencies of the Prussian rulers.

Enter a near-contemporary of Spener: August Hermann Francke (1663–1727), professor of Greek and Oriental languages at the University of Leipzig, whose experience of a conversion, a "new birth," had made him an ardent Pietist. Francke was deeply perturbed by a new kind of spiritual dilemma, modern in its connotation: how could the truth of the Christian faith affirmed in the face of the truth claims of other religions? His conversion gave him certainty about the superiority of Christian truth for its ability to change lives, thus directing him to Spener's understanding of the Christian faith as a commitment to pious living. Spener and Francke became spiritual soul mates and comrades-in-arms, though their theological views were not in full harmony. Francke had organized a Bible study group, called *collegium philobiblicum*, at the university in Leipzig, much akin to Spener's Frankfurt *collegia pietatis*. And as had been the case in Frankfurt, these lay gatherings both prompted support and created tensions, particularly among students. Francke was expelled from the university and the city, but Spener's intervention secured him a professorship at the University of Halle and a pastorate in the nearby village of Glaucha.

In his new setting Francke found time to systematize the theological basis for the "Pietist" impulses that had come from Spener and also to demonstrate his exceptional organizational talents, which allowed him to translate Pietist principles into successful practice. Theologically, Francke simplified Spener's notions of the proper Christian faith and life, which helped make Pietism the most important movement in eighteenth-century German Protestantism. A distinctive Pietist theology was formed. It emphasized the centrality of conversion and the "new birth," and made the two central to the Christian faith. Francke argued that conversion began with true repentance accompanied by a radical break with one's old life. God gave the gift of faith, and a new sanctified life began.

Christians must experience a genuine spiritual rebirth that will lead to a "lasting new condition." This experience will direct them to true repentance and a penitential struggle, called *Busskampf*. Francke found the biblical basis for this notion in Psalm 51, where David is the perfect example of what it means to be genuinely repentant. Francke insisted that those who experience a new birth will alter their lives and reject the values of the secular world.

Francke had not had much experience in practical churchmanship when he arrived in the village of Glaucha, but he threw himself into his new task with commitment and determination. He soon was made aware of the deep problems besetting the village and its people. The decrease in salt production, which had been the economic mainstay of the village, had left most men chronically unemployed. But even more appalling, as far as Francke was concerned, was the condition of the village children, who were economically destitute and religiously ignorant. The clergy in Glaucha had not been particularly impressive either: Francke's predecessor had been removed from office because he had propositioned a woman in the confessional.

From the outset, Francke insisted on the importance of church discipline for those whose walk of life was blemished. Taverns had to be closed during worship hours, for example, and strict regulations spelled out what activities could and could not be done on Sundays. Aware of the deplorable condition of the children, especially orphan children, in Glaucha, Francke worked to provide schooling for them. He was convinced that thorough schooling was the prerequisite for proper Christian living and faith in adulthood. A gift from the Prussian ruler provided the fiscal resources for a school and in 1698 began construction of an orphanage in Halle. By offering older pupils free room and board in return for tutoring younger pupils, Francke was able to keep expenses to a minimum. The high standards of the school soon became the envy of the nobility in the region, who were intent to have their sons enrolled there. That had not exactly been Francke's intention, but he agreed, and, shrewd entrepreneur that he was, used the additional tuition income to cover other expenses of his increasingly widespread set of activities.

The ruling house of Prussia continued to be exceptionally generous with subsidies and privileges for Francke's practical efforts. Over time, Francke launched a host of initiatives in Halle that collectively came to be known as the *Franckesche Stiftungen* ("Francke Foundations"): a print shop, a bookstore, and a pharmacy. Since some of Francke's activities were in direct competition with already-established businesses in Halle—for example, the pharmacy—chronic tension prevailed between the town and the Foundations. In 1708, Francke launched a newspaper, the *Hallesche Zeitung*, the first of its kind in Germany. Initially printed three times a week, it continued for two and a half centuries until 1995, when the economic vicissitudes of German unification brought about its demise.

The institutions of the Francke *Stiftungen* were instrumental in spreading the Pietist understanding of the Christian faith. Pietist notions were carried far beyond Halle and Prussia, especially since Francke and his successors came to emphasize that the ancient missionary mandate of the Christian faith was still valid. In 1706, the Pietist Bartholomäus Ziegenbalg embarked on a missionary venture to East India, becoming the first of a long line of Pietist missionaries throughout the world.

Francke's ventures took place in the setting of an intense controversy in the Lutheran (and Reformed) churches over the theological appropriateness of the Pietist emphasis on conversion and Christian living. Pastor stood against pastor, church against church, university against university. To be called a "Pietist" was for some to be ranked among the worst of scoundrels, the epitome of perversion and of faithlessness to the legacy of Martin Luther. Nonetheless, the Pietist vision of the gospel proved to be immensely meaningful and captured the imagination of individuals and churches. Somehow Spener, Francke, and many others had touched a nerve. In Silesia, seemingly a perpetual battlefield of the great European powers, even children were affected by the emotions and insights of Pietism. A children's prayer movement took place there, where hundreds of children and adolescents day after day spent hours in prayer and hymn singing, and all efforts of the embarrassed authorities to disperse them proved to be of no avail.

A third eminent advocate of the religion of the heart was the committed, complicated, religious Nikolaus Ludwig, Count of Zinzendorf. Born in Dresden in 1700 into a wealthy landed family, Zinzendorf represented what might be called the third generation of German Pietism. He also was, by all odds, a most important theologian of the movement, who creatively appropriated the theological notions of both Spener and Francke and molded them into a cohesive understanding of the Christian faith. Perhaps he was also the most complicated figure—deeply emotional, easily upset, inconsistent and erratic, authoritarian, and humble.

Zinzendorf's upbringing was intensely religious. "From my childhood days," he wrote, "I dearly loved the precious savior and had deep bonds with him." He developed a kind of mystical affection for Jesus as his brother, and at the tender age of four he wrote letters to Jesus, leaving them on the windowsill of his room to be miraculously taken to their destination. Yet alongside an extraordinary religiosity and love for Jesus, there was a proud, stubborn, self-centered youngster. At the age of ten, Zinzendorf was sent to Francke's school in Halle in part to free him from these traits. A report card from that time described him as gifted but haughty.

His religiosity prompted him to seek out other students who shared his affection for Jesus, and in the seven years he spent as a pupil at Halle he established (and led!) no less than seven religious societies. In 1716, he matriculated at the University of Wittenberg, the citadel of Lutheran Orthodoxy, sent there to escape what his guardians considered the excessive Pietist influence in Halle. As matters turned out, his exposure to orthodox theology only confirmed his Pietist leanings. Formally pursuing the study of law, he showed little interest in his course of study and spent most of his time with matters religious.

Three years later, in the spring of 1719, he interrupted his studies for an expansive (and undoubtedly expensive) cultural tour of Europe, as was common in those days for the sons of the upper classes. Holland, France, Switzerland, and south Germany were stations along the way, and it was in Düsseldorf that he saw a painting of the crucified Jesus by Domenico Feti, a devout Catholic Baroque painter, who had added the caption to his canvas "All this I have done for you, what have you done for me?" Zinzendorf's encounter with the painting has been seen as bringing about his conversion, probably a simplification of his religious journey, but as was common among the Pietists, he wanted to be able to pinpoint accurately the time of his "new birth," and he found the encounter with the painting of the suffering Jesus a deeply moving experience; in a way, it was indeed the turning point of his life.

On his return home Zinzendorf visited a Franconian noble family and promptly fell in love with the youngest daughter, Theodora. When Zinzendorf formally proposed to her, Theodora responded that if God would change her attitude toward him, she would not resist. The response was assuredly on the cryptic side, worthy of the Delphic oracle, though most interpreters will be of the opinion that Theodora's convoluted sentence was meant to let her impatient suitor know that she presently held no affection for him. But Nikolaus took Theodora's enigmatic response as consent, wrote his last will and testament, making his bride-to-be his sole heir. He then returned south to Franconia to bring the matter to a blissful conclusion.

On the way Zinzendorf stayed with a friend, and their talk turned to Theodora. Nikolaus quickly realized that his friend, too, aspired to marry Theodora, and he was so taken by his friend's affection for her that "in this conversation God directed his heart to a resolution not easily fulfilled, that the person so intensely beloved by him, should be turned to his friend if he so desired" (Friedhelm Ackva, *Geschichte des Pietismus*, vol. 2). One wonders, of course, about Theodora's role in all this, but the chronicler can record that Zinzendorf overcame his romantic disappointment quickly, for less than two years later he was happily married—to Erdmuthe Dorothea, the sister of the friend to whom he had so graciously yielded his first love. The marriage—on the face of things not particularly germane to church history—is noteworthy, nonetheless, not only because it reveals something of young Zinzendorf's personality and temperament, but also because it was a union characterized by deep spiritual companionship. Zinzendorf's subsequent achievements are unthinkable without her.

On the conclusion of his legal studies Zinzendorf was appointed to a position at the Saxon court in Dresden, but soon his dislike of the world of law became evident. Lengthy absences from his office followed. Zinzendorf himself was utterly candid about his professional negligence and made it clear that his foremost commitment was to live for Jesus. What this meant concretely, however, remained unclear until in 1722 he found his calling. He purchased a large estate in eastern Saxony, and a short time later, four Protestant families from Moravia and Bohemia (today the Czech Republic) who had fled their native land to escape the vicissitudes of the Catholic Counter–Reformation were given permission by the manager of Zindendorf's estate to settle there. These four families stood in the tradition of the Bohemian Brethren, and they found Zinzendorf's welcome a change from the persecution they had experienced at home.

A year later more refugee families arrived from Moravia and Bohemia as word spread of Zinzendorf's hospitality. Within half a decade, the number of refugees on Zinzendorf's estate had reached two hundred. Alongside the Moravians, there also were Lutherans, Reformed, even radical Pietists, all attracted for one reason or another by the atmosphere of toleration and commitment to Jesus. These arrivals provided needed labor for the estate; they also afforded him the opportunity to create a truly Christian community, which he called "Herrnhut," ("Under the Lord's Protection"). Since some of the Moravian refugees were anything but docile—after all, for their faith's sake they had faced oppression in their native land and embarked on a trek into an unknown future—tensions between Zinzendorf and the community often marked the day, the Moravians not hesitating to call Zinzendorf the "Beast of the Apocalypse." But they remained committed to Zinzendorf's vision of the Christian faith.

In 1727, Zinzendorf outlined the organizational structure of the Herrnhut community, and in August of that year the community celebrated the Lord's Supper and became a cohesive entity, with clear notions of belief, organization, discipline, and evangelism. Zinzendorf resigned his governmental position in Dresden and in 1737 was consecrated bishop by the Herrnhut community, a rather incisive act, since German Protestantism, Lutheran or Reformed, had not used the episcopal title. Zinzendorf began extensive travels as an ambassador of sorts of Herrnhut—to the West Indies in 1738, to London three years later—but the center of his life was the community he had created. Since it had no resources of its own, and possibly also lacked the expertise needed for the well-functioning of a complex entity, there were constant financial problems, remedied by Zinzendorf, who accordingly teetered at the verge of bankruptcy.

Nikolaus Zinzendorf died in May 1760. He never shared Francke's categorical determination to remain in the Lutheran Church, no matter what; rather, he believed the renewal of the Lutheran Church would be found in new entities that pursued novel organizational and ecclesiastical structures. In North America, the Moravian communities of Bethlehem (Pennsylvania) and Salem (North Carolina) expressed his ecclesiastical ideal. The experiment in Christian communal living evolved into an ecclesiastical structure of its own, and by the time the eighteenth century ended, a new branch of Protestantism, the Moravian Church, officially the Unitas Fratrum ("Unity of the Brethren"), had come into being.

Pietist sentiment dominated German Protestantism (and beyond) for the better part of two generations, but the notion of Christianity as a religion of the heart and of pious living, combined with a conservative theology, exerted enormous influence in the nineteenth and twentieth centuries. From the halcyon days of German Pietism onward,

Protestantism in Germany (and in Europe) was not only divided into a Lutheran and a Reformed/Calvinist tradition, it was also divided between those who embraced the new Enlightenment interpretation of the faith and those who were committed to the religion of conversion and of the heart.

The Wesleyan Revival in England

The Pietist movement in Germany was well on its way in 1703 when John Wesley was born to the Reverend Samuel Wesley and his wife, Susanna. The couple had nineteen children, and two of them—John Wesley (1703–91), along with his brother Charles (1707–88)—came to personify the movement that dominated so much of eighteenth-century English religious history and in its own way resonated with the impulses of Continental Pietism. Both John and Charles studied theology at Oxford, where John was ordained to the Anglican priesthood in 1729. From all accounts, he was a diligent and highly organized student (the latter trait undoubtedly inherited from his mother), who showed immense intellectual curiosity and brilliance. When Charles came to Oxford, he organized a "club" of students who met regularly to study, read religious books, and exhort one another to regular reception of Communion. The members fasted until three o'clock in the afternoon twice a week, studied the Greek New Testament and the devotional giants, such as Johann Arndt, Jakob Böhme, and William Law, and received Communion once a week, a pattern their Anglican contemporaries considered wildly excessive.

John was away from Oxford when his brother organized this venture, but upon his return he joined the group and soon became its intellectual leader. The "club" was a modest venture, never more than twenty or so students, but it gained the attention of fellow students, who labeled it the "Holy Club" and its members "the Methodists"—a slur, to be sure, referring to their "methodical" approach to their studies and commitment to the Christian faith. In later years, John Wesley saw the beginnings of the Methodist movement in the Holy Club.

In 1735, John's and Charles's religious commitment took them to North America. Their destination was the colony of Georgia, which had been established two years earlier by James Oglethorpe as a humanitarian domicile for "subjects" (debtors and criminals) as well as "foreigners" (persecuted Protestants) with the utopian goal of "no rum, no slaves, and

Figure 4B
John Wesley, 1969. Reynolds Square, Savannah, Georgia. The monument consists of a
stepped rectangular granite pedestal, which supports the bronze statue.

no large estates." On shipboard, the two brothers encountered a group of German immigrants, Moravians from the tutelage of Count Zinzendorf. When the ship encountered a tropical storm that threatened to bring death for all, John observed the amazing calm and fearlessness of the Moravians. He saw how their faith provided them with comfort that his own religion failed to provide.

John and Charles had made the hazardous journey across the Atlantic under the auspices of the newly established Society for the Propagation of the Gospel in Foreign Parts, and their intention was to evangelize Native American peoples. As it happened, they worked mainly among European immigrants—and that not without tension and problems, caused by their rigidity about what constituted a proper Christian walk of life. John gathered a group of men and women who met regularly, as had been the pattern of the Holy Club in Oxford; he later referred to this as the second beginning of Methodism. While this venture was fairly successful, there were other problems. John Wesley fell in love with a young woman who, much to his dismay, rejected his advances. When the woman got married, John refused to give her Communion, a rather intriguing exercise of church discipline. John's explanation failed to persuade the ecclesiastical authorities, and he was given to understand that he best return to England posthaste, prompting John to start a hurried journey home at night across swampland.

Early in 1738 John was back in England and soon thereafter had the experience that changed his life. On the evening of May 4, he attended a meeting of a Moravian religious society on Aldersgate Street. He heard a reading from Martin Luther's commentary on the Letter to the Romans and "about a quarter before nine, while Luther was describing the change which God works in the heart through faith in Christ, I felt my heart strangely warmed. I felt that I did trust in Christ, Christ alone, for salvation" (*The Journal of The Rev. John Wesley*, 1:475–76). In a way, Wesley had replicated Martin Luther's spiritual experience, which Luther had described as understanding the meaning of the word of the Apostle Paul. For Luther, the experience had been as if "the gates of paradise had opened up," while Wesley spoke of feeling his heart "strangely warmed." Both realized that salvation was by faith alone. In recalling the happening and giving it a central place in his spiritual journey, John Wesley echoed the Pietist notion of pinpointing the exact time and place of one's conversion.

John Wesley's conversion centered his life and gave it purpose, at the end of which stood a new Protestant tradition. It was by no means a foregone conclusion, of course, that John's spiritual experience would translate into a new movement. The immediate consequence of his conversion was a visit to Herrnhut, the home of the Moravian immigrants whom he had encountered on the boat to North America and of the gathering on Aldersgate. Upon his return, John undertook an extensive preaching tour, which quickly led to outright as well as latent opposition. The Church of England was not prepared for a clergy with John Wesley's passion. The problem was not doctrinal, for John faithfully accepted the teachings of the Anglican Church. At issue was the insistence on a committed Christian life and the concern for the lower classes of English society, whom the church had come to neglect. The church sought to rein in Wesley's preaching.

Then came John Wesley's fateful encounter with George Whitefield, who had been a member of the Oxford Holy Club. Born in 1714, Whitefield left school at age fifteen to work in the inn run by his widowed mother, convinced that formal education was not for him. Despite this disclaimer, he did eventually matriculate at Oxford, an outstanding accomplishment for someone of his social background. There in 1735 he experienced a conversion of which he later observed: "I know the place.... Whenever I go to Oxford, I cannot help running to the spot where Jesus Christ first revealed himself to me, and gave me the new birth" (George Whitefield, *Sermons on Important Subjects*, 755). Ordained a priest in the Church of England one year later, he began a preaching ministry that over the span of three decades would have him deliver eighteen thousand sermons and cross the Atlantic to North America no less than thirteen times.

Whitefield persuaded John Wesley to take his preaching outdoors after the Anglican establishment had labeled him a rabble-rouser and more and more Anglican parishes refused to allow him to preach from their pulpits. Anglican Church law stipulated that the permission of the rector had to be secured in order to be allowed to preach in a parish. Announcing that "the world is my parish," a slogan that was to become a Methodist hallmark, John Wesley preached in the open air without the permission of local rectors. As word about him and his preaching spread—he clearly was a stunning preacher—the crowds got larger and larger. England had not seen anything like it.

John Wesley found his listeners and followers among the lower and middle classes of English society, and his personal qualities meshed with his public proclamation of the gospel of commitment and godly living. He was methodical. He was a superb organizer. He was open to suggestions and ideas from others. When the question arose of how to nurture those attending his sermons after he moved on to the next community—a challenge for all itinerant preachers through the centuries—he fell back on the model of the Oxford Holy Club and organized local "societies" composed of those who took seriously the call to a committed Christian life. It proved to be a successful venture.

At the time of John Wesley's death in 1791, these "Methodist societies" in England had more than seventy thousand members. Becoming a member was not easy, however. Those who desired to join a local society had to go through a probationary period; only afterward did they become full-fledged members. Moreover, all members were subjected to a close monitoring of their faith and lives. "Tickets" were issued to those in good standing, and those tickets allowed their holders to participate in Holy Communion. The stipulations for the members of a Methodist Class Meeting were

> By doing no harm, by avoiding evil of every kind, especially that which is most generally practiced, such as: The taking of the name of God in vain; the profaning the day of the Lord, either by doing ordinary work therein or by buying or selling; drunkenness: buying or selling spirituous liquors, or drinking them, unless in cases of extreme necessity; slaveholding; buying or selling slaves; fighting, quarreling, brawling, brother going to law with brother; returning evil for evil, or railing for railing; . . . uncharitable or unprofitable conversation; particularly speaking evil of magistrates or of ministers; doing to others as we would not they should do unto us; doing what we know is not for the glory of God, as the "putting on of gold and costly apparel"; the taking such diversions as cannot be used in the name of the Lord Jesus; the singing those songs, or reading those books, which do not tend to the knowledge or love of God; softness and needless self-indulgence; laying up treasure upon earth; borrowing without a probability of paying; or taking up goods without a probability of paying for them. (*The Works of John Wesley* 9:70)

John Wesley's organizational talent found expression in innovative approaches to practical churchmanship, such as convening the clergy in an area (some of whom were "lay preachers," that is, preachers who had

not been ordained but were licensed to preach) for a "quarterly conference" every three months for consultation and edification. Wesley introduced the position of "superintendent" to oversee the Methodist societies
in a given "district," a responsibility exercised in the Anglican Church by
the bishop.

The separation of the Methodist societies from the Church of England
took place slowly and subtly. It was an intriguing turn, in light of the fact
that the German Pietist movement, the broad Continental parallel to the
English Methodist revivals, remained in the established Lutheran or
Reformed churches, a handful of radical separatists notwithstanding.
John Wesley saw himself as a loyal son of the Church of England and had
no substantive theological disagreements with it. Indeed, he encouraged
the members of the Methodist Societies to receive Communion in
Church of England services. Nonetheless, a growing alienation occurred,
especially in North America after the independence of the colonies; in
1784 The Methodist Episcopal Church became a separate church body.
Wesley commissioned Thomas Coke as "superintendent" of the
Methodist movement in the United States. Coke commissioned Francis
Asbury to the same position, which for both men quickly evolved into
the office of "bishop." Because the Anglican Church did not recognize
Wesley's authority to take this action, historians regard this event as the
decisive moment in Methodism's evolution into an independent church.
Asbury became the primary architect of the new church in the fledgling
American republic.

While the Methodist societies were a small, albeit important, part of
the late eighteenth-century English religious scene, in North America
the Methodist societies became the large Methodist Church. This dramatic increase had to do with the core of the Methodist engagement—to
take the gospel message to the common people. Methodist preachers
proved themselves adroit in relating their message to the conditions and
circumstances of the people in the newly formed United States.

The Wesleyan revival was undoubtedly the major factor in preventing
Deist sentiment from capturing the imagination of the masses of the common people in England. Moreover, the preaching of the gospel by the various stripes of religious dissenters—Quakers, Congregationalists, Baptists,
and Methodists—also has played a role in mollifying societal issues in
England, thus sparing the country the radical social and political
upheavals that occurred in revolutionary France. On the Continent,
those alienated from society and autocratic rulers found little solace in

religion, for the only church they knew, Catholic or Protestant, was intimately aligned with the holders of political power. In England, the diversity of dissenters' assemblies offered a religious alternative to the status quo; given this diversity, it was hardly possible to make blanket denunciations of the Christian faith as handmaiden of the political establishment.

THE TURBULENT NINETEENTH CENTURY

When the French king Louis XVI convened the Estates-General, a kind of representative body of the country, in Paris on May 5, 1789, his purpose was to obtain support for the alleviation of an acute governmental fiscal crisis. It did not appear to be a world-shaking matter. By all accounts, the atmosphere in Paris on that day was jovial, carnival-like, and few people realized the dramatic changes that were about to take place, changes that would forever alter the face of France and, indeed, of Europe. By implication, the events in France, and their repercussions throughout Europe, also ushered in a new chapter in the story of the Christian faith.

The old societal order was demolished, and the birth pangs of a new order were felt. The upheaval that began that day had deep roots, and they went beyond the immediate fiscal crisis of the king's government. The "philosophes," the polemical intellectuals of the Enlightenment, had proclaimed new ideas about the individual, about society, about a democratic republic as the best form of government. They had been increasingly critical of prevailing customs, traditions, laws, even religion, and they propounded new notions of freedom. The convening of the Estates-General set in motion a string of events that in July brought about the assault on the Bastille, in August the passage of the Declaration of the Rights of Man, in 1792 the proclamation of a republic, and the following year the execution of the king. A ruthless period of persecution of representatives of the old order—the "reign of terror"—followed until an army officer, Napoleon Bonaparte by name, both normalized affairs in France and waged an expansionist policy throughout Europe.

For a generation and beyond the shockwaves of this revolution were felt throughout Europe, affecting all aspects of society. The shockwaves were also felt, directly as well as indirectly, in the Christian religion. An event, political on its face, began a new chapter in the history of

Christianity. Traditional structures of the faith were challenged, in a strange way making the French Revolution an important (and convenient) point of demarcation for the beginnings of modern Christianity.

For some, the new ideas and the turbulence of events signaled the end of the Christian religion. A plethora of Cassandra calls bewailed the state of the Christian faith and announced its imminent demise. Such calls were not at all new, however. When in the seventeenth century Thomas Fuller was writing his *Church History of Britain*, an "ingenious gentleman" urged him to hurry with his project "lest the Church of England be ended before the history thereof." In 1798, the General Assembly of the Presbyterian Church in the newly independent United States noted that there was "a general dereliction of religious principles and practice among our fellow citizens, a visible and prevailing impiety and contempt for the laws and institutions of religion, and an abounding infidelity, which in many instances tend to atheism itself" (*Minutes of the General Assembly of the Presbyterian Church in the United States of America 1789*). In a way, the concern was much to the point, for educated individuals increasingly stayed aloof from the life of the churches. As matters turned out, a process called "secularization" had begun that progressively diminished the role of religion in society.

Both the Protestant and the Catholic churches entered the nineteenth century in intimate relationship with political events. In France the Christian religion was disestablished in the wake of the Revolution; and in Europe, churches were restructured, as dictated by Napoleon who, unimpressed by the splendor of the papacy, had focused on its real power by asking the famous question of how many divisions of soldiers were under the pope's command. Napoleon's decisive defeat in 1815 by a coalition of European powers was accompanied by a conservative backlash against the politics and philosophy of the Enlightenment, of which the events of the French Revolution were taken to be fatal expressions. In varying ways, efforts were made to restore the European state system and religion to what they had been before the French Revolution, that is, an enlightened but absolutist rule of kings and state churches.

The revolutionary regime in France had left no doubt about its hostility of the Christian faith, which was declared to be intellectually reprehensible and politically tainted through its close alliances with absolutist regimes. The new holders of power in France had shut down churches and converted them into "temples of reason." They had forced the Catholic clergy to become puppets of the state through a law titled "Civil

Constitution of the Clergy," which showed that the new regime, just like the old, was determined to control religion. It was as if the clock had been turned back in France for more than a millennium and a half, for once again Christians and their religion were on the defensive, suppressed, persecuted.

Elsewhere in Europe, however, the churches had continued to enjoy the privilege of being "state churches," which meant that the state supported, politically and financially, one church as the only state-approved religion of the realm; other churches continued to find themselves either outrightly illegal or variously restricted. Nonetheless, in a variety of subtle ways these ties between the churches and the political powers were loosening.

For a while, Christianity continued to exude self-confidence, surprisingly so, given the dramatic developments in the political realm. Its unity long gone, the Christian religion consisted of a coterie of competing churches, each claiming to be the sole possessor of biblical truth. The relationship of Christian thought and science continued uneasily. The Protestant churches were divided into conservative and liberal factions, while the more disciplined Catholic Church espoused a consistent conservative line. In Protestantism both factions were content to remain in the existing churches rather than establish new organizations—the conservatives because they saw the church as their church, the liberals because they hoped that the church would take up their cause.

The anti-Enlightenment sentiment that gathered momentum around the turn of the century found its intellectual expression in the Romantic Movement, which became a powerful phenomenon throughout Europe in the first three decades of the nineteenth century. Romanticism, whether in literature, philosophy, the arts, or in theology, was a quintessentially conservative movement, oriented toward the past. It glorified the Middle Ages, especially its Gothic churches; found a place for the importance of feeling in human experience; and emphasized traditional values and beliefs. For the Protestant churches this meant a revival of traditional religion and a massive repudiation of Enlightenment ideals. At the same time, in a subtle way, long-established ecclesiastical differences resurfaced.

The German theologian Friedrich Daniel Ernst Schleiermacher personified the new trend in theology, for he sought to reconcile traditional Christianity with Enlightenment thinking. By all accounts the foremost Protestant theologian at the beginning of modernity, and perhaps since,

Schleiermacher has influenced the course of theological reflection to the present day. Born in 1768, he was a deeply religious youth, despite his intellectual problems with traditional Christian doctrines, such as the atonement. His father, a Prussian army chaplain influenced by Moravian Pietists, felt no empathy for his son's religious problems and sent him to a Pietist boarding school to embrace a conservative theology and fervent commitment to a godly walk of life. The opposite happened; young Friedrich was taken by the writings of Immanuel Kant, the German Enlightenment philosopher, whose writings were forbidden as unwholesome at the school. Kant gave primacy of place to reason, its possibilities as well as its limitations, and not to revelation.

Schleiermacher studied theology and became a hospital chaplain in Berlin. In that intellectually and culturally thriving city his remarkable erudition (not to mention his personal charm) quickly gained attention, and he quickly became a part of Berlin high society. He discovered, however, that there was little interest in religion among that society. In reaction he published in 1799 a modest book that was to bring him unexpectedly wide fame—and notoriety. Titled *Über die Religion: Reden an die Gebildeten unter ihren Verächtern* (*Talks on Religion Addressed to Its Learned Despisers*), the book addressed the widespread rejection of Christianity by the educated elite. Schleiermacher's goal was to make the Christian religion again a viable and winsome option for all classes of society, especially those with education and social standing. Religion, as Schleiermacher presented it, was to be more than a tranquilizer for the uncouth or a consolation for the ill. It was the noblest intellectual manifestation of humankind. Christianity was not so much a body of doctrine or a system of moral precepts as it was a profound feeling or awareness. It was, in Schleiermacher's famous phrase, the "feeling of absolute dependence," a feeling of conscious dependence, on God. This notion was not exactly traditional theology, yet it was also different from the utterly rationalistic sentiment of Enlightenment Deism.

Schleiermacher systematized his understanding of the faith in his major contribution, which appeared in 1821 under the title *Der Christliche Glaube* (*The Christian Faith*). The book established its author's sway over the theological discourse of the nineteenth century and beyond. Many influences shaped Schleiermacher's thought: Pietism, with its emphasis on a religion "of the heart"; the Enlightenment, with its emphasis on critical thought; the Napoleonic era, with its political turbulence; the Western philosophical tradition—such as Plato, Spinoza,

Leibniz, Kant. In line with his notion that faith was the feeling of absolute dependence on a higher power, called God, Schleiermacher argued that Jesus had been the one human being with a deeper God consciousness than any other human had experienced, before him or since. In that sense he might even be labeled "divine."

Conservative theologians bluntly rejected this vision of Jesus, and they were not exactly pleased with Schleiermacher's avoidance of the question of the accuracy (or inaccuracy) of the supernatural record in the Bible. In that sense, he was neither liberal nor conservative, a steadfast supporter of neither the old nor the new. He radically reformulated the basic affirmations of the Christian faith, and most theologians in the nineteenth century followed his course.

Schleiermacher was a child of the Romantic Movement with its premise that humans were defined not only by thought and will but also, and mainly, by feeling and emotion. The universe was a work of art, vibrant, explosive, and emotional—not a cold mechanism. Given that premise, Schleiermacher had little patience with understandings of Christianity that focused on dogma and doctrine. Human experience was the pivotal point of departure for all religions. More important than pitting theological argument against theological argument was the pursuit of the awareness that humans possessed an inner dimension. This is the "feeling of absolute dependence," which understands God as the linchpin of all that is—a feeling at the center of all religions, even as all religions have particular revelatory insights. The Christian religion has its distinguishing core in the redemption brought by Jesus, not through his teaching or his miracles or the fulfillment of prophecy (the hallmarks of traditional apologetics) but through his God-consciousness, which he imparted to others, thereby redeeming them. Dependence made possible the union with God. In the context of sin and forgiveness, alienation and reconciliation, the Christian religion mediates reconciliation through its focus on Jesus.

Schleiermacher's appeal lay in his ability to speak to the experience and life of ordinary people. Nonetheless, no matter how pervasive his influence, the theological landscape of the nineteenth century was diverse. The liberal insistence on a new reading of Scripture was strong and continued to attract followers, even though in its extreme form the Christian faith degenerated into an assortment of trifles, making, for example, the Christmas story into an exhortation to show hospitality to strangers and an exposition of proper barn-cleaning methods.

Enlightenment thought had turned the Christian faith into a how-to manual and Jesus into a moral teacher.

While the early decades of the nineteenth century were conservative, by the middle of the century a new and vigorous wave of liberal theological thinking challenged the conservatives. Three theological approaches came to exist side by side: liberalism, conservatism, and a mediating approach that sought to acknowledge the positive aspects of the other two perspectives.

Analogously, there were pointed differences about how the supernatural stories and accounts in the Bible were to be understood. The "supernatural" approach argued that everything in the historical books of the Bible was factual, for it related supernatural facts. In turn, the "natural" method insisted that the Gospels and the historical books of the Old Testament were true because they narrated natural, rational happenings that had been misinterpreted as supernatural events. The story of Jesus feeding the five thousand was interpreted either as the account of a supernatural miracle or as the natural story of Jesus' listeners, who were willing to share what they had brought as a result of Jesus' preaching so that in the end everybody was fed. The natural/supernatural stalemate of interpretation ended when, in 1835, David Friedrich Strauss, a young theologian at the verge of beginning his academic career, published a life of Jesus "critically examined." The book was mainly a survey of previous interpretations of the life of Jesus, but it highlighted the unresolved conflict between the two interpretations and argued that the Gospels and the other historical accounts in the Bible were neither the record of actual supernatural facts nor records of actual natural happenings. Instead, they were "myths," and as such, deep, abiding truths. The point was not so much whether the events had actually happened, naturally or supernaturally, but that they expressed an eternal truth. Strauss disputed neither the historicity of Jesus nor the residue of factual happenings in the Gospels, but asserted that these were few and they were unimportant. Strauss's key concept was myth, by which he meant a divine truth unrelated to a historical event. Thus, there was "mythical" truth in the story of Jesus' resurrection even though historically it never occurred.

Strauss's book evoked fierce opposition not only because he denied the supernatural in the Gospels (and by implication in the entire Bible) but also because he offered a radically new understanding of how to interpret the historical record of Jesus. His conservative critics were furious; they found particularly irritating the ironic eloquence that characterized

Strauss's book. Thus, the chapter on the nature of Jesus' miracles was titled "Tales of Fish and the Sea"—a phrase hardly calculated to mollify traditionalists.

Strauss paved the way for the publication, in 1841, of a work by Bruno Bauer, a Tübingen colleague, with the title *Kritik der evangelischen Geschichte der Synoptiker* (*Critique of the Gospel Accounts of the Synoptics*). This book was heavy medicine for all those who continued to affirm the traditional understanding of the New Testament writings, for it argued that both the Gospels and the letters of the Apostle Paul were pseudonymous products of the second century (with only five of the letters ascribed to Paul being genuine). The four Gospels were theological treatises without meaningful historical content. Even the Gospel of Mark, the source of the Gospels of Luke and Matthew, was a product of theological reflection and not a record of historical events. The figure of Jesus, as related in the four Gospels, was a creation of faith: Christianity had its origin in Rome and Alexandria as a second-century synthesis of Stoic ethics and Jewish messianic hopes.

Several other Tübingen theologians shared this radical perspective of the origins of Christianity. The central figure was Ferdinand Christian Baur, who argued that the fundamental divergence between the apostles Peter and Paul, and the concomitant split in earliest Christianity, challenged the notion of a harmonious development of the Christian faith beginning with Jesus' disciples. Even more unsettling, however, was the insistence of the "Tübingen School" that theology had to be a scientific enterprise, employing the tools and methods of scientific research—whatever the outcome. This approach, which came to be known as the "history of religions" approach, was to be enormously influential in the second half of the century with such theologians as Albrecht Ritschl and Adolf von Harnack in Germany, F. D. Maurice in England, and Walter Rauschenbusch in North America.

The outsider and loner to all this was Søren Kierkegaard (1813–55), a highly sensitive soul and keenly insightful theologian. A childhood in a contorted family left its emotional marks on him, but the redeeming element was that his parental affluence allowed him to live the life of a private scholar, obviously the envy of many. Søren died at the precise time his inheritance ran out. A romantic relationship with Regine Olson was broken off by him because he saw himself unfit for the kind of domestic life that came with marriage. Early on, he had written prolifically, on a variety of topics, both philosophical and theological; after 1851 the floodgates of his assessment of the Danish Lutheran state church broke loose. In a series of pamphlets (*The Moment*) he fiercely and mercilessly attacked that church and its clergy for its bureaucracy, and for its theological liberalism, which declared the incarnation was unnecessary and the crucifixion an embarrassment. His language was extreme—he called the Lutheran pastors "liars," "hypocrites," "destroyers of Christianity"— and his argument radical. In a way, his was the timeless attack of those overwhelmed by the challenge to take the mandates of Jesus with literal seriousness. Kierkegaard clearly found the Danish church sorely wanting. In his journal he asked how we could call ourselves "Christians according to the New Testament, when the ideals of the New Testament have gone out of life?" (Søren Kierkegaard, *Journals*, 446).

Not surprisingly, Kierkegaard was by and large ignored by his contemporaries, and it was not until the aftermath of World War I and its unspeakable horror and devastation that his notions began to be appreciated—for example, his focus on "existence" as over against "living," the former a profound engagement, the latter a mere coasting, as well as his insistence on the continued viability of the traditional faith. Kierkegaard understandably was seen as one of the spiritual mentors of twentieth-century Protestant Neo-orthodoxy.

Schleiermacher, Strauss, Kierkegaard—three theologians out of hundreds, but telling examples of the development of the diverse Christian self-understanding in the course of the nineteenth century. The thought and the church loyalty of the people in the pews, especially in rural areas, are another story, and it would appear that throughout the nineteenth century those remained largely unaffected by new (and radical) theological currents. The greatest defection from the Christian religion in terms of such aspects as baptism, church attendance and reception of Communion, the best yardsticks available for measuring ecclesiastical loyalty, appears to have been among the educated middle class and, later in the nineteenth century, among the working class. In a way, speaking about the loyalty of church folk of the nineteenth century is none too different from that in earlier centuries, when the number of those actively involved in church affairs was quite modest. An endless string of governmental and ecclesiastical pronouncements, exhortations, mandates, and visitation records offer ample evidence for the chronic badgering of the common people to be more faithful in church attendance and more serious about Christian living.

The striking change related to the new intellectual climate in Europe. The Enlightenment had brought a plethora of attacks on traditional Christian teaching, but theologians had responded to this challenge with bold reinterpretations of traditional Christian theology, a task first undertaken, at times arrogantly, at times subtly, by the Christian Deists in England in the early eighteenth century.

By the same token, however, the broader intellectual climate of the nineteenth century was dominated by worldviews hostile to religion in general and Christianity in particular. Philosophers such as Karl Marx, Ludwig Feuerbach, Arthur Schopenhauer, Ernst Haeckel, and Friedrich Nietzsche come to mind, all of whom insisted to the educated classes of European society that religion was outmoded and intellectually disreputable. In particular, a single book, Charles Darwin's *On the Origin of Species*, seemed to capture the imagination of all those who found the modern scientific worldview a more persuasive explanation of the enigmas of human existence than traditional religion. Darwin's book renewed the conflict between religion and science that had begun in the seventeenth century but had been dormant, certainly in England, ever since the publication of Joseph Butler's *The Analogy of Religion* in 1736.

The word *secularization* has been used to denote the eminent characteristic of the nineteenth century. Caution is called for, however, for the concept of secularization focuses not only on such data as church attendance or reception of the sacraments or even intellectual discourse, though those were troublesome spots in nineteenth-century religion. Rather, secularization also argues that the churches' traditional role in society, in education, concern for the poor, and so on, eroded throughout the century. Responsibilities that had been carried out by the churches were "secularized" and assumed by the body politic. This process took two forms in Europe, with Sweden and France providing divergent yet interesting paradigms. In Sweden, the process occurred subtly, with the (Lutheran) church frequently leading the way in advocating changes in traditional church functions, with the result that Swedish society became more "secular." In Catholic France the process of secularization was different in that the state sought an outright confrontation with the church, so that the diminished public role was forced on the church.

In sum, the story of the Christian faith in the nineteenth century was, on one level, not too different from the story of earlier centuries—groping for a new, meaningful understanding of the faith; the exercises of spirituality; the commitment of the rank and file. Yet one must conclude that at the end of the century a broad perspective would find that the faith had weakened.

ROMAN CATHOLICISM ENTERS MODERNITY

The story of modern Catholicism began with a fierce clash of the Catholic Church with the ideals of the French Revolution, but well before that conflagration there were tensions between the Roman church and the advocates of the Enlightenment. Political pressure prompted Pope Clement XIV in 1773 to dissolve the Society of Jesus, which by that time had come to be widely seen as the embodiment of authoritarianism and intolerance, the promulgator of bygone and outdated values. As it turned out, Jesuits remained very much active, particularly in Protestant lands and in Russia, where they enjoyed intriguing toleration. The abolition of the Society was short-lived, moreover, for in 1814 it was reauthorized by Pope Pius VII.

In France, the Revolution brought the passage of statutes that rescinded the traditional privileges of the church and the clergy, such as the right to the tithe or freedom from taxation and from trial in secular courts. When the French government teetered on the brink of bankruptcy in 1789, it confiscated church property—a move that failed to solve the fiscal problem, since rampant inflation reduced the value of the paper money the government had issued as collateral for the church lands. In August 1789, the revolutionary government dissolved the monastic orders, and one year later the French national assembly promulgated the Civil Constitution of the Clergy, which made the point that the church was autonomous only with respect to theology but was under governmental jurisdiction in all other respects. There had been a sixteenth-century English precedent in the 1534 Submission of the Clergy and even though that document seemed to exempt theological issues from Henry VIII's prerogative, in fact it did not. The same must be said about the Civil Constitution, which also stipulated that bishops and clergy were to be elected by popular plebiscite, not appointed by the pope, a notion that harkened back to the medieval investiture struggle between popes and kings—a struggle the kings had lost.

The stipulation that the clergy subscribe to the "Constitution" brought a confrontation between the Roman church and French state, between priests who subscribed (the "jurors") and those who did not (the "non-jurors"); it raised questions about the place of the church in society. After some politically motivated delay, Pope Pius VI declared the "Constitution" unacceptable, and the tensions between the National Assembly and the church intensified. During the Reign of Terror (1793–94), several hundred Catholic priests were put to death, and several thousand more emigrated. When Napoleon Bonaparte came to power, the tensions eased somewhat, since Napoleon saw the Catholic Church as a useful tool for his imperial aspirations. He concluded a concordat of conciliation with the Vatican in 1801, signifying a turn to rapprochement.

Two intertwining features increasingly characterized the Catholic Church in the nineteenth century. One was a conservative backlash against all manifestations of "modernity," inside the church and out, an orientation that lasted until the middle of the twentieth century. The other was the emergence, in 1820, of the so-called "ultramontanist" sentiment. The term itself meant "beyond the mountains" and expressed the notion that religious and moral authority lay "beyond the mountains" (that is, beyond the Alps from a French, Swiss, Austrian, or German geographic perspective) in Rome. While the term came into widespread usage in the second half of the century, its first use earlier in the century during the Romantic period suggested a yearning for authority and hierarchically ordered structures in church and in society. A widely influential literary expression of this sentiment was Joseph de Maistre's *Du Pape* ("Concerning the Pope") of 1819, which argued that there was no Christianity without the Catholic Church, no Catholic Church without the pope, and no pope without absolute authority. The argument had been anticipated in a 1799 publication (*Il trionfo della santa sede*) by the future Pope Gregory XVI. There were other indications that the Catholic Church was unwilling to embrace the tenets of the Enlightenment. In 1832, the papal encyclical *Mirari vos* declared the demand for freedom of conscience an "absurd and erroneous notion, in short, a delusion."

These conservative tendencies grew stronger during the rule of the most prominent pope of the nineteenth century: Pius IX, who has the distinction of being the only pope with a main street of an American town named after him—Pio Nono Avenue in Macon, Georgia, a surprising recognition of papal mystique in a southern American town (though the street was named after a parochial school with the same name). Born Giovanni Maria Mastai-Ferretti, Pius succeeded to the Throne of Saint

Peter in 1846 and at first (so the story goes) appeared to be fairly liberal. Pius wanted to use the developments and accomplishments of the modern age for the glory of God. He was responsible, for example, for introducing gaslights in the streets in Rome, hardly a theological feat, but surely an indicator of openness to the new.

Despite Pius IX's eminence, which led to his beatification in the year 2000, he has been a highly controversial figure—an individual of charming personality and deep piety, of pastoral concerns and warmth, but also a moody, manipulative, and unpredictable man. It is perhaps not beside the point that it was Pope John Paul II, who personified the notion of a categorical "no" to the theological and ecclesiastical change wanted by the modern elements in the Catholic Church in the second half of the twentieth century, who pushed the beatification of his nineteenth-century predecessor.

Pius's pontificate was marked by two pivotal events. The first came within eight years of his election to the papacy with the promulgation of the dogma of Mary's Immaculate Conception, the affirmation that Mary, the mother of Jesus, had been conceived without original sin. This theological topic had a long history and was highly controversial in the Middle Ages, when it triggered an intense controversy between the Dominican and the Franciscan orders. The Franciscans supported the notion of Mary's Immaculate Conception, whereas the Dominicans argued that the work of Jesus had removed original sin from humankind, and a special focus on Mary was neither necessary nor theologically appropriate. Bernard of Clairvaux, Thomas Aquinas, and many others were pointedly against the teaching, which had its most renowned proponent in Duns Scotus. The theological intent of the notion was simple enough—to enhance Mary's place in the drama of salvation history and, at the same time, safeguard the sinlessness of Jesus.

In the context of the conservative tenor of the Romantic Movement in the early nineteenth century, the discussion of the Immaculate Conception revived. An important step occurred when a papal theological commission rendered the judgment that the consensus of the church at a particular time was sufficient for the promulgation of doctrine, a notion that flowed harmoniously from the Catholic understanding of the nature of the church and the concept of the evolution of dogma. Pope Pius's bull *Ineffabilis Deus* of 1854 affirmed the commission's judgment by concluding that the pope had the authority to define dogma, apart from a formal concurrence of the church at large, if a consensus existed on the issue in the church.

Soon after his elevation to the papal throne, Pius IX had put the query to some twenty eminent theologians of the Catholic Church if a dogmatic definition of Mary's Immaculate Conception would be in order. Three years later, in 1849, he solicited the opinion of the bishops of the church, which revealed overwhelming support for such a dogma. There were some dissenting voices, mainly from German theologians, but their sentiment notwithstanding, Pius proclaimed the dogma of Mary's Immaculate Conception on December 8, 1854. Tellingly, the new dogma was promulgated during a time when an unusually large number of Marian apparitions occurred, most famously to a young French girl by the name of Marie-Bernarde Soubirous (1844–79), later canonized as Saint Bernadette, who had a vision of Mary in the small southern French town of Lourdes in 1858.

Ten years later, in 1864, Pius IX issued the encyclical *Quanta Cura*, which included an infamous appendix, the *Syllabus of Errors*. The encyclical offered a comprehensive tally of the evils of modernity, while the "Syllabus" summarized some eighty previously identified modern "errors." It included a detailed list of what Roman Catholics were to believe about church, state, society, and modernity. The document amounted to an aggressive declaration of war against the ideals of the Enlightenment, the French Revolution, and modernity, and it castigated such modern ideals as freedom of the press, freedom of religion, and popular democracy. Some religious condemnations, such as the censure of those who denied the existence of God, were in keeping with long-standing and even fundamental doctrines of the church.

The catalyst for the encyclical had been two theological conferences, one in Munich, Germany, and the other in Malines, Belgium, at which rather radical propositions were propounded as viable options for Catholics, such as academic freedom, modern historical scholarship, and even political liberalism. This agitation surfaced in the Catholic Church at precisely the moment when political liberalism, as manifested in the newly united Kingdom of Italy, threatened the existence of the Papal States, the large area of central Italy under papal political control. In reaction, and at least in part in order to retain control over the Papal States, political conservatism, with its notions of absolutism and a hierarchically ordered society, became the proper Catholic position on how a society should be governed.

While Pope Pius IX did consult the bishops of the church about the possibility of a dogma of Mary's Immaculate Conception and received their overwhelming support, he himself promulgated the formal pronouncement, an indication that papal authority was a driving and dominant force behind the new dogma. This papal centrality reached its climax in the second major event of Pius IX's pontificate, the promulgation by the First Vatican Council (1870) of the dogma of papal infallibility. This council was the first since Trent in the sixteenth century. General councils of the church had a long and important history: the Council of Constance healed the papal schism, while the Council of Trent set the theological and practical agenda for Catholicism for four centuries. Nonetheless, popes and councils had anything but smooth relations through the centuries. Indeed, their relationship over the issue of final authority in the church was a chronic tug-of-war.

Pius IX had evidently begun to entertain the notion of convening a council as early as 1864. He solicited the views of twenty-one cardinals about the advisability of convening a council. Only two cardinals responded that a council was a bad idea; the others were positive, though some voiced reservations as to its political prudence. The cardinals offered a variety of suggestions for the agenda, such as revision of canon law, a renewed focus on missions to the heathen, and the improvement of seminary education. Only two cardinals cited the clarification of the meaning of papal infallibility. The following year, thirty-four bishops received a confidential papal communication, in which he conveyed his intention to convene a council and asked for suggestions for its agenda. Again, a variety of suggestions was made; again, only a minority (eight of thirty-four bishops) mentioned papal infallibility.

Two years passed. Then, on June 29, 1867, the day the Catholic Church celebrated the eighteenth centennial of the martyrdom of the Apostles Peter and Paul, Pius IX publicly announced the convening of a general council of the church to meet in the Vatican in Rome. Its purpose was "to bring necessary and salutary remedies to the many evils which oppress the church." No specific date was set for the opening of the council, but one year later, in 1868, the pope set the feast day of Mary's Immaculate Conception, December 8, 1869, as the first day of the council. Committees were appointed to deal with specific issues; rules and procedures were drawn up, the latter with the help of the eminent scholar of church councils, Karl Joseph von Hefele, who then was in the midst of writing what turned into a nine-volume history of the general councils of the church. Hefele turned out to be a problem, however, since he turned into a fierce opponent of the infallibility dogma. Since the council was also to deal with the divisions in the Christian religion, Pius in September 1868 invited the "heretics" and "schismatics" to return "to Christ's only sheepfold." Understandably, they declined—the patriarch of Constantinople was even unwilling to accept the pope's letter, though it was magnificently bound in red leather, with his name imprinted in gold. The patriarch observed that he had already read of the invitation in a Roman newspaper; moreover, he said, the council's principles were inconsistent with the teaching of the Gospels and of the ecumenical councils.

An editorial in the Jesuit newspaper *Civiltà Cattolica* in February 1869 was taken to reveal inside information about the real objective of the proposed council. All loyal Catholics, so the piece noted, had a heartfelt desire for the council to promulgate the dogma of papal infallibility, formalize the condemnations of the *Syllabus* as dogma, and promulgate the dogma of Mary's bodily assumption into heaven. The article, which was said to be "from our correspondent in Paris," prompted consternation and led to a backlash; opposition against the council taking up these topics quickly galvanized.

The promulgation of the dogma of papal infallibility (whatever its theological rationale) was a defiant challenge to the reigning political mood in Europe. The opposition to the proposed dogma, which included the American bishop Edward Fitzgerald from Arkansas, focused on the controversial nature of the topic in the history of the church but was not strong enough to influence the course of events. In a famous exchange, Cardinal Guidi of Bologna told the pope that the notion of papal infallibility was against tradition, whereupon Pius allegedly replied, "tradition am I."

In a vote on July 18, 1870, the council fathers approved the *Constitutio de ecclesia*, which stipulated the universal episcopacy of the pope (his primacy over the bishops of the church) and declared that the pope was infallible in religious judgment. Several stipulations sharpened the meaning of the new dogma: papal pronouncements were infallible only if the pope spoke "ex cathedra," that is, in the exercise of his teaching office, on matters of faith and morals. The pronouncement must be obligatory for the entire church, and new dogmas could not be promulgated unless there existed a church tradition. Obviously, the dogma of papal infallibility was not to mean that any and all statements from a pope were infallible.

The new dogma was eventually affirmed by most of the opposition, including Bishop Joseph von Hefele, who acknowledged that the dogma, while historically untenable, did represent the current thinking of the church. Only in German-speaking lands—Germany, Switzerland, Austria—did the opposition galvanize into institutional form. A congress in Munich established the "Old Catholic Church," which affirmed the traditional faith against the "new" church established by the Vatican Council. This new "old" church failed, however, to make a major impact on the Catholic Church.

The promulgation of the dogma intensified the tensions between the Roman church and various European governments, particularly those of France and Germany. In Germany, numerous restrictions were placed on the Catholic Church and its traditional practices (for example, new law stipulated that only civil weddings were legal, and church weddings had to follow after civil weddings, the result being that, ever since, Catholic and Lutheran couples have been married twice). The confrontation between church and state became known as the *Kulturkampf* ("Culture War"), and even though the German chancellor Otto von Bismarck had vowed that he would never "go to Canossa," evoking the memory of the confrontation of Gregory VII and Henry IV in 1077, he did come to realize that he had overreached and had to withdraw some of the more radical anti-Catholic measures. In France, however, the tensions led to the full separation of church and state in 1905.

The story of the Catholic Church in the nineteenth century thus offers two divergent perspectives. On the one hand, evidence abounds of Catholic vitality and self-confidence, expressed in the founding of a number of new monastic orders, such as the Congregation of Holy Cross, which established the University of Notre Dame. The promulgation of two new dogmas by the Catholic Church surely should also be seen as a sign of vitality, especially since the dogma of Mary's Immaculate Conception ushered in a widespread preoccupation with Mary in Catholic theology. All these trends may be said to have found summary sentiment in the papal encyclical *Aeternis patris* (1879), which named Thomas Aquinas as the normative theologian of the Catholic Church; his thought was declared to offer the church the tools for explicating the authentic faith against all errors.

If these impulses testified to the liveliness of the Catholic Church in the nineteenth century, they also demonstrated that their dynamic was derived from medieval ideals and were forged in pointed opposition to modernity.

This continuing battle against all forms of modernity led to the formal imposition of the "antimodernist oath" and to the "modernist" controversy in the Catholic Church in the early twentieth century. In 1907, Pope Pius X issued the encyclical *Pascendi Dominici gregis*, which condemned any reinterpretation of the dogmas of the church and the use of critical methods of biblical studies. Pius also issued a new catalog of modern errors, titled *Lamentabili sane exitu*; it identified no less than sixty-five "modernist" erroneous understandings of Scripture and Catholic doctrine. The document put an end to critical Catholic scriptural and historical studies.

In 1910, a papal pronouncement, a so-called *Motu Proprio* from Pius X, titled *Sacrorum antistitum*, made an antimodernist oath mandatory for all priests and Catholic teachers. Until its revision in 1967, its original version was part of canon law. Priests and teachers had to swear fidelity to church teaching with regard to no less than sixty-five topics.

> I sincerely hold that the doctrine of faith was handed down to us from the apostles through the orthodox Fathers in exactly the same meaning and always in the same purport. Therefore, I entirely reject the heretical misrepresentation that dogmas evolve and change from one meaning to another different from the one which the Church held previously. I also condemn every error according to which, in place of the divine deposit which has been given to the spouse of Christ to be carefully guarded by her, there is put a philosophical figment or product of a human conscience that has gradually been developed by human effort and will continue to develop indefinitely.

The conservative stance of the Roman church was a matter of record.

THE MODERN MISSIONARY IMPULSE

If the emergence of a new worldview that left little room for the traditional Christian faith was one major development in modernity, the globalization of the Christian religion was the other. For more than a millennium and a half, the Christian church was foremost a European phenomenon, with small Christian communities in such places as East Africa, India, and China. The missionary impulse that had been such a forceful element in the first centuries of Christianity had waned by the High Middle Ages. The "known world" had been Christianized, so the argument ran, Jesus' missionary command had been fulfilled, and no further evangelistic effort was needed. The rise of Islam, moreover, not only meant the end of vital and important Christian centers in the Middle East, it also made evangelization in Muslim countries impossible and ruled out any proselytizing in areas beyond their spheres of influence. Ever since then, the overwhelming majority of those who called themselves Christians have lived in Europe. The Christian story became a European story—and later a North American story.

This story centering on Europe led to the neglect of the various Christian communities outside Europe, such as those in Ethiopia, where Christianity had arrived early (according to some with the apostles, according to others around the year 330), but became geographically separated from "European" Christianity with the rise of Islam. Today the Ethiopian Orthodox Tewahedo Church has over forty million members, which is slightly less than the number of Protestants in the United States. There are Christian communities in India that trace their beginnings to the Apostle Thomas, not to mention the spread of Nestorian Christianity into Asia and even China, well before Jesuit missionaries ever appeared in those lands in the middle of the sixteenth century.

The preoccupation with the story of European Christianity has meant that notions of Christian theology, art, and music—indeed, all artifacts of Christian material culture—have tended to be European and did not really change much when the missionary effort began anew in the eighteenth century. The expansion of Christianity beyond Europe followed the geographic and chronological pattern of the European exploration of new continents and the quest for colonies. The European (and later the American) missionary was part of a complex convergence of factors: the religious zeal to spread the message of Jesus was tied to the European intent to expand trade, the scientific interest to understand as much of the globe as possible, and the economic strategy of obtaining cheap labor through the forced migration of Africans to the Americas. In the end, European languages, institutions, technologies, and production, accompanied by political and military force, spread around the globe.

The Christian missionary effort began with Spanish and Portuguese Catholic missionaries who followed the conquistadores, first southward along the western coast of Africa and then across the Indian Ocean, to China and Japan, and also across the Atlantic to the Americas. And when European political and economic hegemony over other cultures and places expanded in the late eighteenth century, so did the missionary effort. At the outset, the missionaries were to provide spiritual comfort for their fellow Europeans, but soon the issue of evangelizing the native peoples came to the fore, for some altogether inappropriately, since the native peoples were alleged not to have souls and, thus, could not embrace the Christian faith. Others, however, declared the noble humanity of the native peoples, treated them as equals, and sought to convert them.

In 1537, Pope Paul III was asked to serve as arbiter between these competing views. His bull *Sublimis Deus* affirmed the humanity of the native peoples in the Americas. They possessed souls, just like Europeans: "We are aware through what we have been told that those Indians, as true human beings, have not only the capacity for the Christian faith, but the willingness to flock to it," Paul III wrote. "They are to have, to hold, to enjoy both liberty and dominion, freely, lawfully....They must not be enslaved." Bartholomé de las Casas, arguably the most vigorous defender of the dignity of the native peoples in the Americas, found it disgraceful, as he wrote in his *Defense of the Indians* of 1550, "that the gospel and the forgiveness of sins should be proclaimed with arms and bombardments," and then asked the rhetorical question, "What do joyful tidings have to do with wounds, massacres, conflagrations, the destruction of cities, and the common evils of war?" By the middle of the sixteenth century, Franciscan friars were actively proselytizing in Central and South America, though not without problems and challenges. When de las Casas was named bishop of Chiapas in Guatemala in 1544 and declared that anyone refusing to release Indian slaves would be denied absolution, many clergy refused to obey. And a great deal of the missionary story in the Americas of the sixteenth century turned into a most woeful tale.

Of course, there was truly spiritual motivation among those who sought to convert and baptize indigenous people. To have them accept the Christian religion would allow them to escape eternal damnation and receive eternal life. Such religious motivation was paralleled, however, and often overshadowed, by enforced mass conversions, brutality, and enslavement. Francisco Pizarro, the bizarre conqueror of Peru and exterminator of the Incas, said quite pointedly, when reminded of his religious responsibilities, that he had not come across the Atlantic for religious reasons; he had come for gold.

In short, when, in the sixteenth century, Europeans began to explore continents and peoples previously unknown to them, the ancient missionary impulse resurfaced, at first haphazardly and in a political context in Central and South America, but before long around the globe. A while later, a renewed impulse came in the middle of the eighteenth century in connection with the evangelical revival in England and Pietism in Germany. Importantly, most of the modern missionary impulse of the eighteenth century did not come from official church bodies but from private societies that were founded throughout Europe and North America. European expansion into the four corners of the globe raised the consciousness of European Christians, particularly those along the western perimeter of the Continent, that there were peoples unaware of the Christian message. The proclamation of the gospel to foreign parts became a central focus for many Christians, and missionaries set out across the seas to the places where Europeans had established a political and military presence.

In 1732, the Moravian Brethren sent two missionaries to the Island of Saint Thomas in the Caribbean, and the same year three missionaries went to Greenland. By 1776, the Moravians had commissioned no less than 226 missionaries, of whom 49 were engaged in missionary work abroad, a number that by the end of the century had swelled to 138. These Moravian missionaries discovered that the proclamation of the gospel was not simple, in that it had to take place in a complicated political context. South Africa, for example, governed by the Dutch East India Company, had a strong Dutch Reformed Church presence, so that missionary effort seemed to be unnecessary. However, the Dutch Reformed Church was not concerned about the evangelization of the indigenous peoples; it represented the status quo. No sooner had Moravian missionaries arrived on the scene than tensions with the Dutch Reformed Church (and the Dutch "landowners") became a chronic part of the story. Those who wielded power in South Africa feared that exposure to the Christian religion as preached by the Moravian missionaries would prompt disobedience and restlessness on the part of the native peoples.

In Africa, the Christian missionaries appeared in tandem with the representatives of European imperialism and faced the competition of a zealous Islam, which, especially in northern and eastern Africa, was frequently more successful than the Christian effort. Until the middle of the nineteenth century, the unexplored interior of the African continent appeared accessible only to the most adventuresome of the European explorers, but before long most of Africa had a network of mission outposts—Catholic, Anglican, and Lutheran. Some of the missionaries, such as David Livingston, conjure up the best of the European as explorer who at times took unpopular positions, for example, against the enslavement of the native peoples.

In Asia, Christianity was a presence well before all of Europe had been Christianized, a reality frequently ignored or forgotten. When European missionaries appeared in East Asia, the major political force was the British East India Company, established in England in the eighteenth century and effectively ruling India until the company's dissolution in 1874. Understandably, the company was not particularly disposed to include spiritual nurture or missionary activities among its business priorities. Europe was present in Asia economically but not religiously.

Serious missionary efforts in Asia were launched toward the end of the eighteenth century, and the first missionary success occurred in 1800, when William Carey (1761–1834), a missionary sponsored by the (English) Baptist Missionary Society, who had been laboring in India for almost a decade, baptized the first two converts. Carey, the "father of modern missions," illustrates the powerful sway of the missionary impulse in the early nineteenth century. Apprenticed and trained as a shoemaker, he was baptized in a Baptist congregation in 1783 and, completely self-taught, became a schoolteacher and minister. Convinced of the obligation to spread the faith, he wrote what became the groundbreaking missionary manifesto, *An Enquiry into the Obligations of Christians to Use Means for the Conversion of the Heathens* (1792). The following year he sailed to India, accompanied by his wife (and children) who had at first bitterly opposed her husband's venture. Carey was to spend the rest of his life in India, teaching, preaching, and translating the Bible into Indian languages. The first years were a time of stark discouragement, for there were years without a single convert. There were serious financial hardships as well, together with the burden of a wife whose mind steadily deteriorated. Success in the evangelistic effort was slow. After a century of missionary effort, there were fewer than a million Protestant Christians in populous India.

A major missionary foray took place in China, where Catholic missionaries had arrived in the sixteenth century without, however, being able to establish a permanent Christian community. In the nineteenth century, the so-called "Opium Wars" (1839–42 and 1856–60) led both to European influence and missionary presence, even though—as evidenced by the infamous Boxer Rebellion of 1900—China was not at all disposed to open itself to Western ways, quite in contrast, for example, to Japan, where the adoption of Western ways became virtually a national priority.

Japanese medical students, for example, studied in Germany, and until the end of World War II, records in Japanese hospitals tended to be kept in German.

Most of the missionary societies that undertook to proclaim the gospel across the seas were theologically conservative, and there had been organized an ever increasing number of them—seven major missionary societies were founded in England, five in the United States, and eight in Germany. These societies were private initiatives, pursued by men and women convinced of the pivotal mandate to take the gospel across the seas. William Carey facilitated the founding of the Particular Baptist Missionary Society in 1792, while the London Missionary Society was established in 1795. In Germany, the initial commitment to foreign missions came from the Zinzendorf Moravians and from Francke's work at Halle (1705). Slightly more than a century later, in 1824, a missionary society with the lengthy name Society for the Advancement of Protestant Missions among the Heathen (*Gesellschaft zur Beförderung der Evangelischen Missionen unter den Heiden*) was established, though missionary commitment must have been greater than fiscal resources, for the first missionaries did not head for South Africa until ten years later, in 1834.

Understandably, this multiplicity of organizational effort caused a goodly duplication, which was complicated even more when official church bodies decided to make the cause of foreign mission their own as well. Eventually, this situation of implicit competition and duplication of effort became a major impetus for the World Missionary Conference, held in Edinburgh in 1910. Its goal was to effect better cooperation among those who were committed to evangelizing the world.

The missionary effort occurred in the context of the waves of European imperialism. Christian missionaries followed the European military conquest and the gunboat, and the Christian faith was preached as a European phenomenon, a mixture of European culture and the Christian faith. Convinced of the superiority of both, missionaries tended to imply the inferiority of the indigenous cultures of the native peoples.

The new churches established were European outposts, bringing with them not only the gospel as Europeans had understood it but also European culture. This convergence of missionary commitment and political power only ended after World War II, when native individuals assumed the leadership of indigenous Christian communities.

There were missionary ventures, of course, well before the rise of European imperialism in the middle of the nineteenth century, even as the men (and soon following them, the women) who crossed the oceans to preach the gospel were not merely stooges for those who exercised political power. It is often hard to tell what motivated them to leave their familiar surroundings, friends, and family, to travel far to an unknown country, but surely the best explanation for the convergence of political power and religious zeal is to surmise that deeply devoted men and women had been alerted by the imperialist impulse to become missionaries for the gospel.

Often the missionaries were unlearned in theology and actually artisans by trade (they had to make a livelihood in their new environment), and their simple background had intriguing ramifications: the indigenous peoples were not only to be exposed to Christian sermons and catechetical instruction, they were also taught to write and read (two abilities deemed necessary to understand the Christian faith). In the process of teaching these skills, the missionaries also taught aspects of European culture.

Converts to Christianity found themselves embracing not only a religion but also a culture. Sometimes they were not afforded the option of remaining with their traditional faith. Just like the religious dissenters in Europe, native peoples, especially in early modern South America, discovered that the Europeans gave them the option of becoming Christians or facing persecution, enslavement, or even death—so much so, as a matter of fact, that Pope John Paul II apologized on the occasion of his visit to South America in 1992 that "mistakes had been made in the evangelization of native tribes." In the seventeenth century the traffic in slaves had increased dramatically as adventurers, called Mamelucos, carried off into slavery (or murdered) tens of thousands of Indians in the regions of present-day Brazil and Paraguay, royal ordinances and ecclesiastical pronouncements notwithstanding.

Protestant church leaders realized the competition and misspent energy among the missionary societies and boards, each pursuing its own priorities and its own approach. Coordination of effort would make the missionary enterprise more efficient and at the same time do away with, however modestly, the seemingly endless divisions within Christianity. The Edinburgh conference had in fact suggested that the cooperation of churches in the mission fields might also be pursued at home: the effort to globalize the Christian religion exerted enormous influence on the emergence of what is known as the ecumenical movement—the move-ment toward cooperation and unity—in the twentieth century.

The ecumenical movement was born. Its leaders, foremost the Swedish Lutheran archbishop Nathan Söderblom, found the division of the Christian faith into an endless number of churches and traditions an offense against the very heart of the gospel. The ecumenical movement was determined, both practically and theologically, to explore common ground among the Christian traditions. The determination to form a coordinating body of Christian churches around the globe first took the form of ecumenical conferences under the heading of "Life and Work" and "Faith and Order" and eventually came to fruition in Amsterdam in 1948, when a large number of churches formed a new entity called the World Council of Churches. Today, that Council has more than 350 large- and small-member churches from around the globe. However, the single largest Christian church, the Roman Catholic Church, is not a member, since it is not prepared to acknowledge other Christian tradi-tions as "churches." Nonetheless, it has actively participated in numerous ecumenical dialogues and conversations. In turn, the Catholic Church and the Eastern Orthodox churches reached agreement that the excom-munications of the year 1054 were not intended to set the members of the two churches apart, but in fact pertained only to the two key figures in the clash between Rome and Constantinople.

Independent of the work of the World Council of Churches, but heav-ily influenced by its ethos, regional bodies have been formed—in the United States there is the National Council of the Churches of Christ and in Germany the Evangelische Kirche in Deutschland, an association of twenty-two regional Lutheran, Reformed, and United churches. Symbolizing the ongoing split between conservative and liberal churches, the National Association of Evangelicals represents more than forty con-servative denominations in the United States.

Churches have engaged in theological conversations with other churches, resulting in discovering more commonalities in theology and polity than centuries of bitter division and antagonisms might have sug-gested. For example, on the topic of the Lord's Supper, major theological understanding among Anglican, Lutheran, and Reformed theology has been achieved through meetings at Leuenberg (Switzerland) and Porvoo (Finland). Actual organizational mergers of churches, however, have been virtually nonexistent. They have mainly occurred among historically related churches that for one reason or another had separated—such as the American Lutheran Church and the Lutheran Church in America.

Christian missionary activity has yielded results that defy easy generalization. The successes of the great "missionary century" occurred in places, such as Africa, where the missionary appeared in company with the forces of European imperialism. The result was remarkable conversions to the Christian faith. In the past half-century, significant alterations have occurred. In South Korea, a massive wave of conversions has taken place, making it arguably one of the liveliest places of Christian presence in the twenty-first century. The same may be said about Central America, where Pentecostal evangelism and missionary work have led to large-scale conversions. Indeed, the missionary impulse on the whole has created dynamic and flourishing churches outside Europe and North America at a time when the hold of the Christian faith on people in those traditional places appears to be waning. At the beginning of the twenty-first century, more Christians lived south of the equator than in the traditionally Christian Europe and North America. It has been suggested that within the next generation, the Christian religion will have disappeared in the Northern Hemisphere, becoming a phenomenon exclusive to the Southern.

CHRISTIANITY IN THE TWENTIETH CENTURY

The two prominent features of twentieth-century Christianity were its encounter—for the first time in more than a millennium and a half—with organized and systematic suppression by political authorities and the increasing number of non-European Christians. At the end of the twentieth century, more Christians had suffered for their faith than at any other time in the two-thousand-year history of the religion.

The encounter with totalitarianism took the Christian religion back, so to speak, to the first centuries of the faith, when its sojourn was marked by governmental hostility and persecution. In the twentieth century, the Christian religion was severely challenged by the political authorities in the Soviet Union, Italy, Mexico, and Germany. In each of these countries, Christians were unprepared for the challenge.

A prelude took place at the time of the French Revolution, and it proved to be a foreboding of things to come. The premonition became a stark reality with the Bolshevik Revolution in 1917, which changed church-state relations in Russia even more dramatically than had been the case roughly a century earlier in France. The new Soviet government suppressed the Russian Orthodox Church, which had been a strong supporter of the tsarist regime and thereby had enjoyed broad fiscal and political privileges in addition to being one of the largest landowners in Russia. It is not easy to sort out whether Bolshevik hostility was directed primarily against the church that had supported an oppressive monarchy or against Christianity as religion—undoubtedly it was against both.

No sooner was the new communist regime in control than it began to implement a policy of suppression and persecution of the Orthodox Church. The Soviets declared atheism the creed of the land and persecuted those loyal to the Orthodox Church as "counter-revolutionaries," a label portending imprisonment, exile to Siberia, and even death. In January 1918 the separation of church and state was decreed officially, and at the same time all ecclesiastical property, including churches, monasteries, and land holdings as well as liturgical items, was declared to be state property, even though church buildings could be used for divine services. Parochial schools were closed. Bolshevik policy favored a radical separation of church and state, the confiscation of church property, and the curtailment of public church activities. A government order requiring that gold, silver, and other precious metals be confiscated by the state caused a severe crisis in 1922, for the decree included the confiscation of the silver and gold frames of icons—a sacrilegious act in the eyes of Russian Orthodox Christians. Leaders of the church protested, and in the ensuing confrontation some twenty-eight Russian Orthodox bishops lost their lives, while thousands of priests and laypersons active in the church were tried as "counter-revolutionaries." It is surely one of the ironies of modern history that the driving spirit behind this policy was a former seminary student in Georgia, albeit not a distinguished one, whose mother had prayed that her son might become a bishop, Ioseb Besarionis dze Jughashvili, who later took the name Stalin.

A formal declaration of loyalty to the state by Metropolitan Sergius in 1927 hardly changed things, except that the Orthodox churches outside the Soviet Union took this declaration as proof that the Russian church had lost its freedom and severed their ties with it. While the Soviet state focused its attack on the Orthodox Church because of its close relationship with the tsarist regime, Roman Catholics as well as Muslims also found themselves at the receiving end of Soviet oppression. It was not only Christianity that was considered, in the words of Karl Marx, to be the "opiate of the people." In 1929 legislation was drafted that severely prohibited religious activities and attacked religion. The previous year Stalin had criticized the fifteenth congress of the Communist Party for not having succeeded in diminishing religion in the Soviet Union.

In the 1930s the situation improved somewhat: overt governmental suppression subsided, but massive atheistic propaganda continued throughout the Soviet Union. The Orthodox Church had a difficult time adjusting to the new reality, as, for example when Orthodox churches were turned into "museums of atheism." This uneasy situation continued until the German invasion of the Soviet Union in June 1941. The Soviet regime, desperate for support in the war effort, decreed the official toleration of religion in 1943. A period of uneasy truce began that lasted until the collapse of the Soviet Union in the 1980s.

Germany was a second site of confrontation between the Christian religion and political totalitarianism, though in comparison with the Soviet Union, the German situation proved to be far subtler. Once again, religious and nonreligious factors intertwined. Ever since the early nineteenth century, Protestantism in Germany had been essentially composed of autonomous Lutheran regional synods and regional "evangelical" synods, established when the Prussian king Friedrich Wilhelm III maneuvered a merger of Lutheran and Calvinist (Reformed) churches. While some regional Lutheran churches refused to participate in this merger, those that did took the name "Protestant" or "Evangelical" church, but were formally known as the synods "of the Prussian Union." German Protestantism in the nineteenth and twentieth centuries, therefore, essentially comprised two (and only two) large church bodies: the territorial Lutheran churches that had resisted the king's merger efforts and the territorial "Protestant" or "Evangelical" or "Prussian Union" churches that had agreed. Within both of these two churches, the individual regional synods were completely autonomous.

When the Nazis rose to power in Germany in January 1933, large segments of the Evangelical and Lutheran churches, both pastors and laity, assumed the Nazi movement to be a conservative movement that would bring law and order, discipline, love of country—as well as the restoration of the status the churches had enjoyed until the establishment of the Weimar Republic and the curtailment of the seemingly blatant secularism and decay of morality, which allegedly characterized postwar Germany. Most of the Protestant clergy were politically conservative, yearned for the restoration of the monarchy, and despised the democratic government (and the alleged antireligious ethos) of the Weimar Republic. Many of them harbored anti-Semitic notions. Otto Dibelius, superintendent (bishop) of the Berlin Protestant Church in the 1920s, later a stalwart leader of the Confessing Church, who appeared on the cover of *Time* magazine because of his staunch anti-communism views during the Cold War, observed in 1933, "I have always seen myself as an anti-Semite, despite the bad reputation which that word has assumed. One can hardly deny that Jews played a leading role in all the negative manifestations of modernity" (Ernst Klee, *Das Personenlexikon zum Dritten Reich. Wer war was vor und nach 1945*, 107).

At the same time, theological liberalism continued to cast a long shadow over the Evangelical and Lutheran churches. In a strange twist, some churchmen found it possible to merge their liberalism with the social and economic zeitgeist and arrive at a version of the Christian faith that highlighted a German, or "Germanic" identity. Christianity was seen as a German religion for the German people. This meant, of course, considerable unease about the Jewish roots of the traditional faith. This was personified, before the turn of the century, by Houston Chamberlain, son-in-law of Richard Wagner and English Germanophile, and his book *Foundations of the Nineteenth Century*, which offered an altogether unscholarly mishmash of a radical liberal interpretation of the Christian religion and a racial ideology that argued that Jesus had been the illegitimate son of a Roman soldier, thus an Aryan. A true "Germanic" Christianity would need to be purged of all Jewish elements, including the Old Testament.

This radical interpretation appealed to a small fringe group of Protestant church members who eventually called themselves "*Deutsche Christen*" ("Germanic Christians"). Hitler, who was himself nominally Catholic, had frequently insisted that Nazi ideology had no problems with "positive Christianity," an irritatingly vague term by which he undoubtedly meant an understanding of the Christian faith in harmony with Nazi ideology. The anti-Semitic program of the German Christians clearly meshed with that of the Nazi Party, and was undoubtedly influenced by it.

Until Hitler's rise to power in January 1933, these "German Christians" had no impact at all on the churches. Understandably, the new Nazi regime changed that dramatically, since the churches represented the kind of Christianity that was to Nazi liking, and they clearly

266

Figure 4C
Emblem of the Nazi-related *Deutsche Christen* ("Germanic Christians") in
Germany after 1933.

benefited from such informal government support. The fringe group all of
a sudden became the majority in synodical elections. Before long, this
new position of power emboldened the Germanic Christians to impose
their theological and administrative notions on the German Protestant
churches.

Theologically, the German Christians' program had the goal of "liberating" Christianity from its Jewish "entanglements," a goal that struck at
the very heart of the traditional understanding of the faith. A story making the rounds at the time recounted how an anti-Semitic pastor of the
German Christian ilk began his sermon with the pronouncement that "if
a Jew is present in this House of God he should get up and leave." No one
got up and not a word was spoken. But then the figure on the crucifix
above the pulpit detached itself from the cross and slowly disappeared.
Jesus, after all, was a Jew.

Administratively, the Germanic Christians advocated a centralized
German Protestant church, much like the Nazis were introducing politically in Germany. The four-hundred-year tradition of autonomous territorial churches was to be abandoned in favor of a single entity,
characterized by a hierarchical administrative structure and a single

presiding bishop (*Reichsbischof*). The regional synod assemblies were deprived of any power and authority in governance.

This dual agenda of de-Judaizing Christianity and streamlining the administrative structure of German Protestantism, both matters that cor-responded neatly to Nazi ideology, found favor with the Hitler govern-ment, which in various ways supported the efforts of the Germanic Christians. While the number of those acknowledging themselves to be Germanic Christians swelled dramatically after January 1933, stalwart Protestants realized that a fringe theology had been turned into the nor-mative faith of the church and began to organize an opposition. A "church struggle" (*Kirchenkampf*) erupted between the advocates of bibli-cally oriented and traditionally structured Protestantism and the Nazi government–supported, liberal Germanic Christians. Those who opposed the radical changes pursued by the Germanic Christians were known as "confessing Christians," their loose organization the "Confessing Church."

The opposition of the traditionalists in the Lutheran and Evangelical churches first took the form of the spontaneous creation of a *Pfarrernotbund* ("Clergy Emergency League"), an association of clergy who opposed the ultraliberal theological stance of the Germanic Christians and their administrative objective. The leaders met in the west German town of Barmen in May 1934 and adopted a document—known as the Barmen Declaration—that sounded a theologically conser-vative note (its main author was the "father" of Neo-Orthodox theology, Karl Barth) and affirmed the Jewish roots of Christianity. The declaration rejected the notion, central to the beliefs of the Germanic Christians, that divine revelation was found in places other than in the Bible—such as in history, in a people, or in a race. This rejection countered the asser-tion of the Germanic Christians and their Nazi allies that the *Volk* (German for "people") was carrier of God's will. The Barmen Declaration, with its categorical insistence on God's sole revelation in Scripture (and not in an ideology or a political movement), led to a split between Lutheran and Evangelical theologians, since Lutheran theology allowed for God's involvement in creation by positing the so-called "orders of creation"—the institutions of the state, the family, where divine principles are also at work, of course with the addition that it was in Scripture that God's will in Jesus was most dramatically revealed.

After World War II and the end of the Nazi regime, the term "church struggle" became a synonym for the opposition of the German Protestant churches to the Nazi regime. That understanding, however, broadens the meaning of the term "opposition." To be sure, there were clashes of Protestant church members and church leaders with the Nazi regime. When one of the first laws passed by the Nazi government removed all Jews and "politically unreliable" individuals from the German civil service (the law had the intriguing title "Law Pertaining to the Restoration of a Professional Government Civil Service"), key figures in the German Christian movement demanded that the Protestant churches enact the same policy and dismiss all clergy who were Jewish converts to Christianity. That was, needless to say, an anathema for all who embraced the traditional Christian affirmation that baptism removed all distinctions of class, race, and gender. For those in the "Confessing Church," this mandate was a fundamental issue and utter heresy, even though the actual number of Jewish converts to Christianity who were pastors was not more than a dozen. Mainly, however, the opposition against the totalitarian Nazi state focused on matters that directly affected the churches, such as religious publishing houses, church youth groups, and so forth. The boycott of Jewish businesses in May 1933 was not opposed by Lutheran or Evangelical Christians, nor was the promulgation of the Nazi racial laws in 1935. Moreover, since the Nazi government backpedaled on the matter of establishing a single Evangelical Church in Germany and decided to stay out of ecclesiastical politics, a main point of contention between the government and the churches became moot.

There were instances where pastors and laypeople were subjected to physical abuse, dismissal from office, and even arrest. Christian commitment also turned individuals into outright opponents of the Nazi state for political reasons; the theologians and church leaders Martin Niemöller and Dietrich Bonhoeffer are often cited as cases in point. Niemöller, a decorated German submarine captain in World War I, had been an early supporter (and even member) of the Nazi Party but had become disillusioned even before the Nazi rise to power. From his pulpit in suburban Berlin, he voiced ardent criticism of Nazi policy, and in 1934 he was one of the major movers behind the Barmen Declaration. When, in a meeting of Protestant church leaders with Hitler, he got into an argument with the German Fuehrer, the dictator's wrath fell on him, and he was forbidden to preach. Eventually, he was arrested by the Gestapo and sent to a concentration camp, from which he was liberated by Allied troops in 1945 to become a major figure in postwar German Protestantism.

Dietrich Bonhoeffer, a brilliant theologian of the new generation, was an early and outspoken opponent of the Germanic Christians. Born in 1906, Bonhoeffer decided on a career in theology (somewhat to the surprise of his parents) and at the universities of Berlin and Göttingen imbibed the impulses both of fading liberal Christianity and of the exciting new theological current of Karl Barth's Neo-Orthodoxy. After stays in New York, Barcelona, and London, he became an important figure in the Confessing Church and for a while headed a seminary run by the Confessing Church until it was closed by the Gestapo in 1938. In an ironic turn, his stays abroad and his contacts with foreign church leaders secured him a position in the German counterintelligence during the war. He joined an anti-Nazi resistance group that sought, in July 1944, to assassinate Hitler. Bonhoeffer was arrested a year earlier, when the Gestapo discovered his involvement in helping Jews escape to Switzerland. He was kept in prison without even the kind of show trial rampant in totalitarian regimes, wrote moving letters from prison about how to deal with adversity and what it meant to be a Christian in the twentieth century, when the old certainties (including those of God) had disappeared. He spoke of the ideal of a "religionless Christianity," a much-discussed phrase by which he undoubtedly meant a Christian religion without all the privileges and trappings of a state church. Bonhoeffer did not survive the Nazi regime. Barely three short weeks before the end of the war in Germany, on April 9, 1945, he was hanged without ever having been brought to trial.

Niemöller and Bonhoeffer were exceptional figures, sad to say, in their opposition to the Nazi regime apart from its early attempts to incorporate German Protestantism into the Nazi movement. For most Protestants in Germany, allegiance to the ordained governmental authority of Hitler and the Nazi regime overruled all other factors—an understandable attitude, perhaps, if one considers the smoothness of the Nazi propaganda machine, which called for the restoration of the traditional virtues of hard work, love of country, and concern for others, and which portrayed the war as a struggle for the survival of Christian civilization. This Protestant and Lutheran submissiveness to the Nazi regime found poignant expression in July 1944, when, after the failed assassination attempt on Hitler, several Protestant bishops sent Hitler a telegram attributing his survival to divine providence.

The story of the Catholic Church in Nazi Germany was different in some crucial respects. For one, Catholic doctrine was clear enough on the issues so controversial in German Protestantism so that the theological movement of the Germanic Christians was unthinkable in the Catholic orbit. Similarly, the administrative structure of the Catholic Church was a categorical given. Tensions between the Nazi regime and the Catholic Church arose over the dogged Nazi effort to curtail and even end the public engagement of the Catholic Church—the Catholic youth organizations, workers associations, newspapers, and so on. All the same, Hitler wanted to avoid an outright confrontation with the Catholic Church and agreed to sign a concordat ("agreement") with the Vatican in September 1933. The document was characterized by a virtually wholesale acquiescence of the Nazi government to Catholic demands. It affirmed most of the traditional privileges of the Catholic Church in Germany, making it difficult for Catholics to oppose the government. It affirmed, for example, Catholic religious instruction in public schools, required Catholic religion teachers to secure the approval of the diocesan bishop, and confirmed the legitimacy of Catholic voluntary organizations and Catholic practices, such as public Corpus Christi processions. The concordat gave the Nazi regime an aura of religious respectability, especially among those conservative German Catholics whose political orientation had prompted them to oppose the Nazi Party.

The Roman Catholic Church in Germany was spared from having to deal with a parallel movement to the Germanic Christians, even as the Nazi government seemed initially to honor the provisions of the 1933 concordat and rationalized instances of suppression as "unfortunate but understandable excesses." An uneasy coexistence prevailed between the Catholic Church and the Nazi state, though the Nazi government's disapproval of the Catholic Church was blatantly obvious. In 1937, Pope Pius XI, aware of developments in Germany relating foremost to Catholics but also Jews, issued the encyclical *Mit brennender Sorge* ("With Burning Concern"), in which he castigated (though in somewhat veiled language) the Nazi regime for its policies:

> Whoever exalts race, or the people, or the State, or a particular form of State, or the depositories of power, or any other fundamental value of the human community—however necessary and honorable be their function in worldly things—whoever raises these notions above their acceptable value and divinizes them to an idolatrous level, distorts and perverts an order planned and created by God; he is far from the true faith in God and from the concept of life which that faith upholds.

Outspoken members of the Catholic hierarchy and simple parish priests criticized policies of the Nazi regime. Bishop (later cardinal) Clemens August von Galen of Münster chastised the Nazi government for subtly restricting the freedom of the Catholic Church and condemned the euthanasia of mentally disabled patients in hospitals. Galen minced no words when he told his listeners in the Münster cathedral:

> I am reliably informed that lists are also being drawn up in the mental hospitals of the province of Westphalia of those patients who are to be transferred as so-called "unproductive citizens" shortly to be killed. The first transport left Marienthal, an institution near Münster, during this past week. German men and women, paragraph 211 of the German Penal Code is still valid. It states: "Anyone deliberately murdering another person will receive the death penalty for murder if the killing is premeditated." Those patients who are to be killed are transported to a distant hospital presumably to protect those who deliberately kill those poor people, including members of our families, from legal consequences. Some illness or disease is then stated as the cause of death. Since the corpse was cremated straight away, the relatives and the police are unable to establish whether the illness really occurred. I have been informed that the Interior Ministry and the office of the German Medical Association, do not deny that a large number of mentally ill people in Germany have been deliberately put to death and that more will be put to death in the future. (www.catholictradition.org/Life/galen-sermon.htm)

While Bishop Galen himself suffered no adverse consequences at the hands of the Nazi regime for his sermon (perhaps as bishop he was too important a church dignitary for the Nazis to confront), three parish priests who distributed copies of his sermon were arrested and executed.

The relationship between the Catholic Church and the totalitarian fascist government of Il Duce Benito Mussolini in Fascist Italy was more peaceable. Mussolini had no intention of engaging in a quarrel with the pope in the homeland of the Catholic Church, and he consequently left the church more or less alone. When Italian Jews were rounded up to be sent to the concentration camps, the church's reaction was ambivalent. Latent anti-Semitic sentiment stood side by side with courageous support of Jewish people. The role of Pope Pius XII in these mass deportations has been highly controversial, with the persistent charge made that he did not speak up enough to prevent the deportation and extermination of Jews.

Neither Fascist Italy nor Nazi Germany suppressed the Christian churches outright. The traditional privileges of the churches were curtailed, while the demand for total allegiance to the state triggered conflicts for men and women bound by their Christian conscience to oppose the actions of the totalitarian regimes. It was a totally new situation that made the state no longer a protector but an enemy of the church. The obligation of loyalty toward any state, as expressed in Romans 13, proved to be a hindrance of action as well.

When the German Third Reich collapsed in defeat and the enormity of Nazi atrocities became evident, church leaders and theologians embarked on a period of reflection. In particular, the role of the Protestant and Lutheran churches during the twelve years of Nazi rule posed a challenge to Lutheran theology, whose doctrine of the two "realms" seemed to justify the acceptance of the autonomy of the political order. Within months of the end of World War II, German Protestant church leaders signed what came to be known as the Stuttgart Declaration of Guilt, in which they acknowledged their guilt for having been silent during the Nazi dictatorship when they should have spoken out. The Declaration proved to be controversial—an indication that not all German Protestants saw things that way.

Twentieth-century Catholicism is most noteworthy for the roster of three striking popes. Pope Pius XII has been a controversial figure for his failure to speak out on behalf of Italian and Roman Jews deported to camps in Poland, though the canonization process presently under way indicates the high esteem in which he is held in the Catholic Church. The foremost event of his pontificate was the declaration of the dogma of Mary's bodily assumption into heaven which, like the dogma of Mary's Immaculate Conception promulgated a century earlier, was a teaching that had been contested through the centuries but evidently had reached a consensus by the middle of the twentieth century.

Two later popes, John XXIII and John Paul II, were determined (in different ways, to be sure) to bring the Catholic Church into the twentieth century, thereby dramatically influencing the direction of the church. John XXIII, who because of his age had been elected as a kind of caretaker pope in 1958 (he was born in 1881), startled everyone with the dynamic energy with which he infused the Catholic Church with a program of "modernization." The Second Vatican Council, which he convened in October 1962, was his tool. While the reforms enacted by the council energized the church in some ways, developments since the council indicate that they failed to resolve serious issues—for example, the drastic decline of the number of men and women choosing the religious life and the equally dramatic decline of those in Europe and North America choosing a priestly vocation. Also, the aftermath of the council accentuated the split between conservatives and liberals in the church.

The Second Vatican Council brought together almost three thousand council fathers, bishops, and heads of monastic orders. While the First Vatican Council had been almost exclusively a European (if not Italian) affair, the Second Vatican Council demonstrated that the Catholic Church was a global church. When John XXIII died in 1963, his successor, Pope Paul VI (r. 1963–78), continued the council and reiterated the four major goals of the gathering: to define the nature of the church and the role of the bishops in it; to renew the church; to restore unity among Christians, including confessing guilt for any Catholic contribution to the separation; and to enter into dialogue with the contemporary world. The council issued statements on religious freedom; the liturgy, including the use of the vernacular in the Mass; and, importantly, on non-Christian religions, titled "Nostra Aetate," which stated that Jews of the time of Christ and today were no more responsible for the death of Christ than were Christians:

> True, the Jewish authorities and those who followed their lead pressed for the death of Christ; still, what happened in His passion cannot be charged against all the Jews, without distinction, then alive, nor against the Jews of today. Although the Church is the new people of God, Jews should not be presented as rejected or accursed by God, as if this followed from the Holy Scriptures. All should see to it, then, that in catechetical work or in the preaching of the word of God they do not teach anything that does not conform to the truth of the gospel and the spirit of Christ. Furthermore, in her rejection of every persecution against any individual, the Church, mindful of the patrimony she shares with the Jews and moved not by political reasons but by the gospel's spiritual love, rejects hatred, persecutions, manifestations of anti-Semitism, directed against Jews at any time and by anyone. (Pope Paul VI, *Declaration on the relation of the church to non-Christian religions. Nostra Aetate*, 1965, www.vatican.va)

For all the positive consequences of the council, there can be also no doubt that in a broader sense the council also triggered considerable tensions in the Catholic Church. Foremost, perhaps, were the changes in the liturgy, which changed from Latin to the vernacular. Pope Paul VI sought

to stem mistaken notions about contraception by ignoring a papal commission and issuing on his authority the encyclical *Humanae vitae*
("Concerning Human Life"), which categorically prohibited artificial
birth control. The evidence shows that Catholic couples were hardly
swayed by the papal pronouncements, since large segments of the church
were influenced by liberal notions derived from the Second Vatican
Council and secularized society.

Pope John Paul II (r. 1978–2005) was the first non-Italian pope since
the tragic Adrian VI in the early sixteenth century, who tried so hard to
resolve the Reformation controversy, yet was given a year as pope before
he died. John Paul's charismatic and folksy personality combined with a
deeply conservative orientation. He was constantly in the public lime-
light for his incessant travels around the globe to fashion a common bond
among Catholics everywhere. He attempted to cement the cohesiveness
of the global Catholic Church while at the same time affirming conservative theological positions on the issues plaguing Christian churches in
the second half of the twentieth century: the ordination of women, abortion, homosexuality. John Paul and his church said a categorical no to all
attempts to change the traditional practices and teachings. Undoubtedly,
John Paul's experiences in communist Poland, his native land, influenced
his thinking, for the Polish Catholic Church had been unyielding in its
opposition to the communist regime and emerged from that conflict
lively and dynamic. It remains to be seen whether John Paul II's pontificate will be a cause of lasting, unifying direction for the Catholic Church.

In the second half of the twentieth century, the Catholic Church saw
the rise of a theological movement, first in South America, that virtually
dominated Catholic theologizing and may well have been a belated
response to the encounter of the churches with political dictatorship and
totalitarianism in Europe as well as the role of the churches in the period
of European imperialism. It also reflected the effort to relate the Catholic
Church to the social and political challenges of the twentieth century.
The movement, known as "liberation theology," became a significant
force in Central and South America, and soon was embraced by
Protestant theologians as well. Liberation theologians argued that the
gospel liberates humans both religiously and politically. The pivotal publication came from the pen of Gustavo Gutiérrez, a Peruvian theologian
and Dominican monk, and had the title *A Theology of Liberation: History,
Politics, Salvation* (1971). It focused on the phenomenon of poverty in the
modern world and called for voluntary Christian poverty as an act of

solidarity with the poor. According to Gutiérrez, authentic Christian "freedom," or "liberation," must include not only religion but also politics and society. Religiously, a theology of liberation frees humans from selfishness and sin and leads to the restoration of the broken relationship with God. At the same time, Christians and the church are called upon to work for the elimination of the causes of poverty and injustice in society. Then all those oppressed by "those things that limit their capacity to develop themselves freely and in dignity" will be emancipated. In delineating such a theology of liberation, Gutiérrez focused on those aspects of the Gospels that describe Jesus' concern for the marginalized of society, the despised poor, the helpless widows and orphans, whom Jesus pointedly included in his proclamation of the coming Kingdom.

The richness of efforts to relate the Christian faith meaningfully to the early twenty-first century leads to two additional observations. First, much of the theological diversity subsumed under the heading of liberation theology has remained confined to academic circles and to discussions among theologians. While sympathy for one or the other of the current theological perspectives is undoubtedly found among the men and women in the pews, it is difficult to see any of these strands—with the possible exception of liberation theology and its concern with social justice—having generated the kind of pervasive popular support that would turn theological ideas into a social movement.

Second, behind the diverse forms of new theologies continues to lurk the fundamental division that has plagued the Christian faith in the Western world since the eighteenth century: the division between conservative and liberal theologizing, between those for whom the supernatural narratives in the Bible represent portrayals of actual events and those who see these narratives mythically. The Christian self-understanding at present does not lack attempts to overcome this division, but none has so far been successful in capturing the minds and souls of the people in the pews. Though the history of Christianity encompasses numerous instances in which new visions have suddenly emerged and become influential in the church, none would seem to be on the present horizon.

Reflection 5: Women in Christianity

Recounting the story of several outstanding women in the medieval church and beyond raises the question of the role and place of women in Christian history. The story of women's role in Christianity is a complicated one, in which cultural stereotypes mingled with biblical interpretation, with male bias undoubtedly an additional element. However, no matter what the explanation, traditional accounts of Christian history had little to say about women, other than noting the roles played by female saints. The story told was that of eminent (and humble) men, with a few women (Catholic saints) added for good measure. In the Catholic tradition, of course, the Virgin Mary has had an enormously important function.

In the earliest Christian assemblies women appear to have played important roles as theologians and even as leaders in local congregations. Early Christian writings, including those that found their way into the canon of the New Testament, convey that women exercised public functions in local Christian gatherings. Both the book of Acts and the Epistles of the New Testament refer to women, though their precise roles in the gatherings are not clear. The argument has been made that the "apostle" Junia, named in Romans 16:7, was a woman. On the other hand, the Apostle Paul bluntly declares in 1 Timothy 2:11-14 that women are not to exercise any leadership function in the church, even as he also announces that women are to be silent in the congregations—if nothing else surely a declaration of opposition to prevailing practice. Whatever the role of women in apostolic and postapostolic assemblies, as the church began to form permanent structures women were excluded from positions of leadership they undoubtedly had earlier enjoyed. The emerging priestly office was categorically understood as an exclusively male prerogative, derived from Jesus' selection of twelve male apostles who were seen as paradigmatic of an exclusively male priesthood. The Catholic Church has maintained this notion to the present, despite an avalanche of challenges by those, within and outside the Catholic Church, who insisted that women be eligible for ordination as priests. The response has been the reiteration of the traditional teaching of the Catholic Church.

Nonetheless, women have had avenues of significance in the Catholic tradition. The female monastic orders provided women with the opportunity to exercise intellectual and administrative talents. Nuns taught the young in schools and cared for the sick in hospitals. They engaged in theological and devotional pursuits, and administered the affairs of their monastic communities. They did so in the convent, a woman's "world." Convents tended to guard their autonomy jealously, and resented outside influence, whether from civic authorities or the local bishop. The reason nuns were so committed to cloistered convents may well have been that this was the way to avoid interference by the bishop. While this exciting pursuit of things intellectual and spiritual had closely observed parameters, it was important and an essential part of Catholic life through the centuries.

The Protestant Reformation repudiation of monasticism also affected the place of women in the church. The reformers rejected the notion underlying the monastic profession that the religious life was a path of spiritual perfection for the exemplary few. They argued that there was no such optional path of spiritual perfection; all believers had the same mandates and commandments. All human endeavors served, in fact, a spiritual purpose, making the change of a baby's diaper as spiritual a chore as time spent in devotional exercises. The Protestant notion of "vocation" meant that all secular endeavors were divinely ordained "vocations," callings from God. This turning the profane into the sacred meant, however, the rejection of those spiritual and administrative venues that had been open to women in the Catholic Church. In the world of Protestantism, woman's place was relegated, almost exclusively for all women, to the home, to tend to the three "*k's*" of "*Kinder, Küche, Kirche*"—children, kitchen, church. Not surprisingly, many nuns in the early Reformation refused to leave their convents.

However, the Protestant Reformation also brought another turn that was as radical theologically as it was moot practically: Martin Luther's pronouncement of the "priesthood of all believers." This notion, first enunciated in his 1520 "Open Letter to the Christian Nobility" declared that all the faithful, male and female, were "priests." All the faithful were able to exercise the ministerial office. Arguably this principle could hardly exclude women. Accordingly, Luther found a way to argue that the theological principle had a practical limitation. Women's inability to project their voices loudly in a church to preach, Luther argued, was a practical hindrance to female pastors. So nothing changed in the traditional pattern, as in Protestant countries women practically could not play a public role in religion.

If in the mainstream Protestant churches nothing changed, much changed in the Protestant fringe. In Anabaptism women took on leadership roles in local congregations. Margaret Fell (1614–1702), the "mother of Quakerism," helped found the Society of Friends, the Quakers. Selina Hastings, Countess of Huntingdon (1707–91), called the "patriarchess of the Methodists," was a major figure in early Methodism, though her role was mainly that of a facilitator rather than that of a public figure. In 1880 Anna Howard Shaw was ordained in a predecessor church of The United Methodist Church. In short, in Protestantism there is clear evidence of a tradition of a public role of women in congregations, even though this role was most prominent in marginal groups and not in mainstream traditions.

The Catholic Church continued to provide spiritually minded women an outlet of leadership, theological and otherwise, in the monastic life. As female religious orders proliferated in early modern Europe, female convents offered women spheres of autonomous theological and administrative endeavor. Convents were self-contained both administratively (an "abbess" was the head of a convent, an elected lifetime office). Teresa of Avila is a splendid illustration—she was formally recognized by the Catholic Church as a "doctor of the church"—for the continuing importance of women in the Catholic Church.

In both Protestantism and Catholicism, the nineteenth and early twentieth centuries opened a new arena of women's endeavors in leadership roles. The formidable missionary effort undertaken by European and North American Christians gave women, both single and married, a new venue for leadership. Single women especially responded to the call to the mission field in large numbers. They served as teachers and nurses, working alongside male missionaries and growing into leadership positions. At home, voluntary societies sprung up that supported the efforts abroad, and those in North America were run by women, who coordinated, encouraged, and witnessed to the challenge of proclaiming the gospel in foreign lands, thereby underscoring the pivotal role played by women. Well before society began to be agitated by the women's movement and even well before the Protestant churches had sorted their sentiment with respect to the viability of ordained women clergy, there was agitation that women, given their work in the mission field, should be ordained so that their work could be adequately expressed at home and abroad. The women's circles and associations were ahead of their time. In several Protestant denominations, such ordinations were authorized well before women themselves began to agitate for ordination, while in others, such as the Quakers, the ordination of women was hardly problematic.

CHAPTER FIVE

CHRISTIANITY IN THE AMERICAS

THE COLONIAL PERIOD

Christianity found its way to the continent Europeans called "the Americas" when explorers, adventurers, and mercenaries—as well as priests and monks—began to sail the Atlantic westward in the wake of Christopher Columbus. These ventures were, of course, part of the western European expansionist phenomenon of the late fifteenth century, when a Portuguese vessel rounded the Cape of Good Hope into the Indian Ocean in 1488 and Columbus set out for India in 1492.

After Christopher Columbus had returned from his first voyage across the Atlantic, the traditional rivalry between Spain and Portugal raised the question of how these two powers should divide the "spoils" to be obtained from lands beyond the Atlantic Ocean and peoples previously unknown. In a gesture that underscored the pope's continuing role in European affairs, the rulers of these two countries turned to Pope Alexander VI to act as arbiter. Alexander complied with his bull *Inter caetera* of 1493 by granting the kings of Spain "the regions and lands found in the west ocean sea by the navigations of the Spanish." The pope had drawn a line from the North Pole to the South Pole "370 Leagues west of the Cape Verde Islands." And he assigned the lands to the west of that line to Spain, and the lands to the east to Portugal; eventually this line of demarcation meant that one part of the South American continent spoke Portuguese, and the other Spanish.

Tellingly, calling on the pope to arbitrate the political power struggle between Portugal and Spain meant that the Portuguese, the Spaniards, and the pope took it for granted that these lands and peoples were available to be assigned, a notion that in the late twentieth century evoked dire protests. The Portuguese king Manuel arrogantly called himself the lord of "navigation and commerce of Ethiopia, Arabia, Persia, and India," assuredly a rather bold declaration, unbeknownst, of course, to the peoples in the countries mentioned.

In addition to being a key player in European power politics, the pope's concern was the propagation of the Christian religion:

> Among other works well pleasing to the Divine Majesty and cherished of our heart, this assuredly ranks highest, that in our times especially the Catholic faith and the Christian religion be exalted and be everywhere increased and spread, that the health of souls be cared for and that barbarous nations be overthrown and brought to the faith itself. (*Quellen zur Gechichte des Völkerrechts*, Vol. 2, 1493–1515, 103–8)

While Catholic missionaries and political authorities, both Spanish and Portuguese, initially placed little emphasis on having the church carry out the same functions as in Europe, such as preaching and education, by 1551 universities had been established in both Mexico City and Lima, Peru, making these two among the oldest universities in the Western world.

If, in keeping with Pope Alexander VI's bull, Spain and Portugal transmitted Christianity to Central and South America, French explorers, settlers, and missionaries pursued the region that is now Canada. The first important French settlement in the "new world" was Quebec City, established in 1608. In contrast to some of the English settlers of about the same time, notably those of Plymouth Rock and the *Mayflower*, who left their native land for a life and a society envisioned to be radically different from their own, the French settlers came to Canada generously supported by the French government, whose objective it was to make the North American continent a French possession. Indeed, France made considerable headway, claiming Canada and Louisiana, as well as the northern half of what is now New England. And wherever the banner of the French crown was hoisted, Catholic missionaries quickly followed. Samuel de Champlain and Robert de LaSalle explored parts of the continent with political conviction and missionary fervor. But despite the initial success in claiming American possessions, France lost out in the end. After the European Seven Years' War ended in 1763, France surrendered its North American possessions, and the dominance of Catholicism in

North America diminished. To this day, however, the province of Quebec stands as a symbol for the continued French influence and Catholic presence in Canada.

The European explorers who went ashore in Central and South America were anything but a homogeneous lot, and religion was assuredly not foremost on their mind; they were after more tangible benefits. But before long religion did become important. Priests and monks began to accompany the European conquistadores on the vessels that sailed across the Atlantic, and while their charge was to look after the spiritual needs of their fellow European adventurers, before long they made an effort to convert the native peoples to Christianity. That was controversial, for an intense discussion was taking place among theologians and church leaders about whether the native peoples of the Americas actually possessed souls and were, therefore, proper targets of their missionary efforts. There were "Indophone" and "Indophile" missionaries.

To this day, the "missions" in the southwest United States offer vivid testimony to the early spread of Catholicism from Mexico northward.

Figure 5A
Cathedral of Mary's Assumption into Heaven (Catedral Metropolitana de la Asunción de Marí)

This Catholic preponderance is easily explained. Until the end of the seventeenth century, Spain and Portugal were the dominant European empires, and their strategic location on the Atlantic Ocean allowed them easy access to the territories in the Americas from their central American base. By the end of the sixteenth century, Christian congregations had been established in the area that was later to become New Mexico and Texas. The creation of an ecclesiastical administrative structure to support these congregations followed quickly. Bishoprics and archbishoprics were created in Santo Domingo in 1511, Santiago de Cuba in 1522, and in Mexico City in 1530. The cornerstone for the cathedral in Lima was laid by Francisco Pizarro in 1535. And no sooner had the Society of Jesus been formally approved by the pope than Jesuit missionaries found their way to areas of present-day Mexico, Peru, Chile, and Paraguay.

In short, a lively Christian presence was found in the New World well before the *Mayflower* landed at Plymouth Rock early in the seventeenth century.

THE PROTESTANTS ARRIVE

On a Friday morning in March 1622 Native Americans attacked the English who had come ashore in 1607 to establish a settlement along the James River in Virginia. The attack was a telling illustration of the tensions between the American native peoples and the European settlers. Among the English who had arrived in Virginia to settle had been an Anglican priest, Robert Hunt, whose successor, Alexander Whitaker (who converted Pocahontas), was persuaded that his calling was to preach the gospel to both the English and the Indians. The attack of 1622 changed that; the native peoples from then on were left alone. The Christian faith—the religion of the *Book of Common Prayer*—was meant for the English settlers only.

There had been two previous English efforts to settle along the east coast of the North American continent. In 1584, a generation before the attack on Jamestown, Walter Raleigh had explored the coast of "Virginia" (which included North Carolina) and established a settlement at Roanoke Island, close to the Outer Banks. His glowing report home led other would-be settlers to long to move across the Atlantic to join the colony, but when English vessels returned to the colony in 1590, they could not find it; the colony and all of its inhabitants had vanished, thus shrouding that first English settlement in the New World in a veil of mystery that has never been lifted. Seventeen years later, in 1607, the new settlement on the James River was established, and soon a church was built, representing not only one of the first permanent structures of the settlement but also the first official Anglican ecclesiastical edifice in the Americas. It was a congregation in full harmony with the official Church of England.

But soon another group of English settlers arrived on North American soil who detested the *Book of Common Prayer*. This group of individuals— Protestant Separatist dissenters—saw the vast spaces of the North American continent as the refuge and the Promised Land they longed for. They wanted to live their faith unmolested by king or government, but the lands controlled by Catholics to the south of the North American continent were hardly welcoming to radicals. The Protestant English had to consider places farther north. A few hundred miles to the north, quite a different group of English settlers had stepped onto land in 1620. Some 102 men, women, and children had crowded into a small vessel, the *Mayflower*, about one hundred feet in length. They were Separatists, men and women who adamantly rejected the Elizabethan settlement of religion and refused to worship in the services of the Church of England. At first they had fled to Holland to exercise their faith there freely, but after a decade of difficult adjustment to the Dutch, they heard tales of North America and decided to start a new life across the Atlantic Ocean. As it turned out, a navigational error, coupled with bad weather, made them miss the mouth of the Hudson River, their intended destination, and their vessel made landfall inside the hook tip of Cape Cod. What was later to be called Massachusetts became their home.

Before long, other settlers followed, and the North American continent became the destination for a diversity of immigrants—loyal members of the Church of England, and separatist dissenters from that church; Church of England loyalists and German Lutherans; Scotch Calvinists and Dutch Mennonites—and by the early seventeenth century the men and women who sought freedom of religion and expression no less than a good life included not only Anglicans but also Baptists, Quakers, Presbyterians, Mennonites, with a few Catholics added for good measure. They all put up with the dangerous (and expensive) voyage across the Atlantic, enduring the painful experience of bidding farewell to family, relatives, and friends, and saw their venture not merely in economic or political terms. They referred to the lands that they would till with words taken from the Bible. Across the Atlantic Ocean they would worship God as he was to be worshiped and create a godly community. Glowingly, John Winthrop spoke of the "city upon a hill," the "New Jerusalem." While their lives were harsh and in constant danger of Indian raids, not to mention the cruel vicissitudes of nature, it never occurred to them to question that they were at the right place at the right time. It was their destiny to have been sent by divine providence on this "errand into the wilderness," even though they seem not to have lost their hope eventually to be able to return to England. And as the centuries passed, this deeply rooted commitment never disappeared, that the settling of the North American continent was blessed by divine providence as none other had been blessed. In the nineteenth century it was the watchword of "manifest destiny," a secular phrase, but one rooted in the language of Scripture.

The voyagers on the *Mayflower* were Separatist Puritans who found the ecclesiastical policies of King Charles I and Archbishop William Laud detestable and who wanted to get away from constant surveillance and suppression. They yearned for religious freedom, but once the harsh winter experiences in the New World had been overcome, the attacks of the Native Americans were repelled, and a steady stream of new immigrants was arriving, the Puritans fell into the same trap as many others had before (and after): they found religious freedom too precious to waste it on those who disagreed with them, for the structures they established for their communities and the social discipline they exercised were restrictive and welcoming only for those who shared their faith. The Baptist Roger Williams had to remind his fellow Puritans, in his book *The Bloody Tenent of Persecution, for Cause of Conscience*, published in 1644, of the importance of religious liberty and the separation of church and state.

In the course of the eighteenth century, ever more immigrants arrived and the land along the eastern seaboard was large enough to provide room for a diverse mixture of settlers: stalwart Puritan dissenters and loyal Anglicans, devout Christians and ruthless adventurers. Catholics settled in Maryland, while Virginia and South Carolina attracted loyal sons and daughters of the Anglican Church, which continued, for all intents and purposes, as the established church. Toward the end of the eighteenth century, distinguished Anglicans in Virginia included George Washington, James Madison, John Marshall, Patrick Henry, Thomas Jefferson, and Alexander Hamilton. This illustrious roster has prompted some to insist that these Virginia gentlemen were committed Christians who envisioned the new United States as a deeply Christian country. The notion has evoked controversy, since others have argued that the founding documents of the young country hardly may be said to be explicit about a commitment to biblical religion.

The issue, with its explicit connection to twenty-first-century views, hinges on the definition of Christianity. One can hardly argue that the Founding Fathers were committed partisans of traditional Christianity. They were not. Clearly, most of them did consider themselves Christian, even as they wanted the new republic to be Christian. But theirs was the religion of the Christian Deists, Christianity of a new kind, neatly exemplified by Thomas Jefferson's edition of the New Testament, in which he simply excised all those verses and passages that did not support his "modern" understanding of Jesus. The Founding Fathers affirmed the moral and social role of religion in society (of course, everybody did in the late eighteenth century) but they did not look kindly on the established Church of England and its traditional tenets. The number of those who held membership in one of the Christian churches in the colonies in the eighteenth century was fairly modest. Yet while they do not seem to have been the majority, the European background of the immigrants made a basic commitment to the Christian faith a natural matter.

In sum, religiously the colonies were an intriguing mix of orthodox and heterodox, of traditional and nontraditional, of elite and popular. The lines between these tempers were porous. Moreover, whether liberal or conservative, they considered themselves Christian and were prepared to allow for what they considered a "Christian" body politic.

This picture changed a bit once the thirteen colonies attained their independence from England. The constitutional assembly in Philadelphia did not want any kind of "state" religion on the European model in the newly formed United States, though it was prepared to look the other way when it came to European-type state church arrangements in the thirteen states that had united. Several states required church membership as religious litmus test for political office.

One obvious consequence of the Declaration of Independence was that two churches in the colonies could hardly continue as part of their mother churches in England. During the American Revolution, North American Anglicans did not particularly benefit from their ties to the Church of England. And the same held true for the new Methodist societies, offshoots, so to speak, of the Wesleyan revival. Both the Anglican Church and the Methodist movement found it necessary to sever their organizational ties with their English mother churches and develop new structures to express their independence from England. Accordingly, the Protestant Episcopal Church was organized as an autonomous entity in the United States in 1789. It maintained the liturgy of the *Book of Common Prayer* (though understandably without the intercessory prayers for the English king) and introduced a more democratic form of church governance, somewhat modeled after the governance of the United States. The problem was that, the political developments aside, the Anglican Church in the colonies had lost vitality because of its close connection to the upper class and its failure to embrace the new evangelical spirit that made the pseudo-Anglican Methodist societies so successful. The separation from England was easier for the Methodists, who were well on their way to establishing themselves as a separate ecclesiastical body from the Anglican Church when Thomas Coke and Francis Asbury arrived in 1784 to become the new Methodist Episcopal Church's de facto bishops, symbolizing the severed ties with the Church of England.

Of the Protestant churches in the original thirteen colonies, the Congregationalists were politically most influential. Theologically descended from the Separatist Puritans of the early seventeenth century, they had provided effective spiritual nurture and political guidance to the New England colonists. Both the Salem witchcraft trials and their aftermath of remorse and grief conveyed the depth of the Puritan mind-set, as did the rather frequent official calls for "days of fasting" by the community. The outstanding religious figure in eighteenth-century New England was Jonathan Edwards, who came to personify the phenomenal revival, the first "Great Awakening," in New England in 1734. Edwards, a faculty member at Yale College, argued along the lines of Saint Augustine that the churchly sphere in society was more important than the secular sphere and that the church was bigger than the body politic. That, of course, was hardly an expression of a separation of church and state.

With the independence of the republic and the steady westward expansion of the newly established United States—the population in North America increased from roughly four million in 1790 to thirty-one million in 1860—Protestantism took on new and distinctive characteristics. One was the emphasis on personal conversion, frequently brought about by a phenomenon largely unknown in Europe: the revivals. The German Pietists and the English Methodists were insisting that true Christians had to have a conversion experience that could be pinpointed as to time and place. This theological assertion became the basis for periodic revival meetings, where those in attendance were challenged to experience a conversion. A sequence of noted revivalist preachers, including Timothy Dwight, president of Yale College, led countless revivals that swept from town to town, region to region.

These revivals, conducted by itinerant ministers, gave particularly the Methodists and the Baptists—minorities in England—a great deal of vitality in the young country, and they also explain the steady increase in membership of these churches in the course of the nineteenth century. Moreover, a creative innovation, the Methodist circuit rider, with seemingly endless miles on horseback to reach one sparse settlement after the other, was able to provide for the religious needs of frontier communities that otherwise would have been without clergy and worship. It was a brilliant idea to introduce an itinerant ministry, a clergy responsible for several smaller churches, "charges," by riding on horseback from one to the next, conducting services in each. They were found everywhere along the frontier, as one envious Presbyterian observed "In several days I traveled from settlement to settlement . . . but into every hovel I entered, I learned that the Methodist missionary had been there before me." The traditional notion of having a resident minister in every community, as universally was the case in Europe, was not practically viable as the nation expanded westward, with the geographic distances to be covered, the proliferation of settlements, and the small number of clergy.

Some churches continued their traditional European pattern, the Lutheran immigrants, for example, who stuck rigidly to the liturgy, hymns, and ministry they had brought with them from the old countries. They, too, depended on ordained clergy, who simply could not be provided. Since these mainly Scandinavian and German immigrant communities fiercely sought to retain the culture of the home country, a language barrier precluded expansion beyond the smallish circles of ethnically cohesive immigrant communities. As recently as the middle of the twentieth century ethnic Lutheran congregations in the United States made proficiency in preaching in Swedish the foremost criterion for extending a call.

NEW CHURCHES

The absence of a dominant state church made it possible in North America for new churches to come into being and organize more readily and easily than had been the case in Europe. Not surprisingly, a stunningly large number (in comparison with Europe) of new Protestant denominations were established. One of the most significant was the Seventh-day Adventist Church, which had its beginning with William Miller (1782–1849), a farmer who became a Baptist preacher, then a Deist, and eventually the charismatic leader of a new Christian tradition. Like many others before and after him, Miller's study of the Bible prompted him to become deeply enthralled by the numbers found in Scripture, and he became convinced that the Bible contained a clear (but hidden) date for the second coming of Jesus. His views, which he proclaimed with self-confidence and assurance, resonated among others, especially when he received a striking opportunity of communication with his contemporaries: a Vermont newspaper, perhaps out of a need to fill the pages in a community where little else was happening, provided him with the outlet of a regular column.

In 1834, Miller published a synopsis of his teachings in a slender pamphlet of sixty-four pages titled *Evidence from Scripture and History of the Second Coming of Christ, about the Year 1843: Exhibited in a Course of Lectures.* The message of the pamphlet was simple: Jesus would return presently: "My principles in brief, are that Jesus Christ will come again to this earth, cleanse, purify, and take possession of the same, with all the saints, sometime between March 1843 and March 1844." Miller was aided in his zeal by writing a veritable flood of pamphlets and books, all of which focused on the End Times and Jesus' return. His message resonated; the number of his followers increased, according to some estimates reaching more than one hundred thousand.

It turned out that the appointed day of the Lord's return was a day like any other; Jesus had not returned. Miller redid his calculations and set a new date, which also passed uneventfully. When he died in 1849, still convinced that the Second Coming was imminent, many of his followers deserted the cause. Those who did not eventually coalesced into a new Christian tradition that was organized in 1863 by a remarkable woman, Ellen G. White, and others. It took the name Seventh-day Adventist Church, which, alongside its theological affirmations, such as keeping the

Sabbath on Saturday rather than Sunday as the day of rest and worship, made physical health a major tenet, expressed in strict vegetarianism.

An earlier, also quintessentially American denomination was the "United Society of Believers in Christ's Second Appearance." Again, the focus was on Christ's second coming. The leader was "Mother" Ann Lee, an erstwhile cook and washerwoman who concluded, after having given birth to four children, all of whom died in infancy, that sexual intercourse was sinful. This was a not altogether novel teaching; Saint Augustine had wrestled with it, as did the Catholic Church with its judgment that celibacy was the commitment to a more spiritual life. Ann Lee concluded, quite consistently, that salvation required sexual abstinence. She joined a group of Quakers, and together they made their way to upstate New York, where they put their principles into practice. Since they also held that possession of the divine spirit led to uncontrollable shaking, which allowed sins to be shaken off, their critics first called them shaking Quakers, then Shakers, and that label stuck.

Though Mother Ann Lee died early, her followers eventually encompassed a number of "colonies" (communities) and several thousand members. These Shaker communities took on distinct characteristics, including an emphasis on simplicity, cleanliness, and usefulness. Their members held no private property and hoped to perpetuate their communities (a challenge, given their commitment to celibacy) through the adoption of orphans. The Shakers vigorously opposed slavery and refused to fight in the military. They created furniture and utensils—even houses—of striking simplicity and beauty.

The most striking American contribution to the panoply of Christian traditions was Mormonism, or, as it officially is known, the Church of Jesus Christ of Latter-day Saints. Theirs was a dramatic story of claimed divine revelation, hardship, persecution, and persistence. It is a story intimately tied to the founder, Joseph Smith Jr.; to the intolerance of their neighbors; and to the vicissitudes of the frontier. In our own day, Mormons are known for their missionary effort, expressed in the image of two young men, properly attired in white shirt and tie, going from door to door as evangelists for their faith. There is by no means unanimity if, in fact, Mormons should be considered part of the Christian tradition, since they accept, alongside the Bible, an additional source of divine revelation.

Born in 1805 into a farming family, Joseph Smith was a religiously oriented youngster; he later recorded that prior to his fifteenth birthday, he prayed that God would direct him to the true church. The divine response, which came in a vision, apprised him that none of the existing churches taught the true biblical religion. Even the early church had quickly forsaken the authentic biblical message, but—so Smith's vision informed him—God would bring about, in his own time, the true reform of Christianity. Smith had additional visions, and in September 1823, the apparition of an angel by the name of Moroni confided the existence of a new divine revelation recorded on golden plates hidden underneath a nearby rock.

Four years later, the apparition was repeated and instructed Joseph to take the plates and translate them into English. Joseph's autobiographical account noted how, after retrieving the plates, he began the tedious work of translation. Sitting behind a curtain in a room, he translated sentence after sentence, while on the other side several scribes recorded his translation. The angel Moroni instructed Smith to show the golden plates to several individuals, who later testified—their statement is found in the editions of The Book of Mormon—that indeed they had seen them.

When the work of translation was completed, it had become a book of almost six hundred pages, and it was called the Book of Mormon. It challenged its readers with a fascinating account of the migration of the lost tribe of Israelites to America. There, these Israelites were visited by Jesus, who shared with them the word of salvation. The great warrior Mormon, having died in the fifth century, reappeared in angelic form, wrote the story on golden plates, and hid them on the hillside near Palmyra in upstate New York, where a millennium and a half later they were retrieved by Joseph Smith.

Not at all surprisingly, the Book of Mormon proved to be highly controversial. Skeptics pointed out that no outsider had ever seen the golden plates, while those favorably disposed answered that only a miracle could have yielded such a striking book from the pen of someone who had had no formal education. Smith's followers believed that the book contained a new revelation, while opponents declared it to be a work of exquisite religious imagination or even outright fraud.

All the while, Smith acquired supporters and followers, prompting him to organize a church, which he called the Church of Jesus Christ. The growth of the movement brought opposition because other Christians, provocatively labeled "Gentiles" by Smith and his followers, objected to the notion that there was a book equal to the Bible. When the opposition of locals to this "bizarre" fellowship became formidable, the group moved to Ohio, where Smith received additional revelations from the angel Moroni, the son of Mormon, providing theological instruction, importantly declaring the practice of polygamy to be biblical.

Soon, intolerance and harassment by the surrounding community triggered a second exodus, this time to northwestern Missouri. But things were hardly better there, not only because of the suspicion of the old-timers but also because of the provocative behavior of the "Mormon" group. Within a year, Smith and most of his followers felt it prudent to move eastward again to Illinois, this time to a village on the Mississippi River. By the early 1840s, the Mormon community had grown to ten thousand. It prospered economically. Joseph Smith rounded out its theology, introducing, among other innovations, the practice of baptizing the dead of at least four generations and putting the earlier justification of polygamy into practice.

The size and prosperity of the Mormon community, together with the chronic frictions with its "Gentile" neighbors, prompted Smith to form a Mormon militia, declare himself King of the Kingdom of God, and announce his candidacy for president of the United States. In June 1844, he and his brother Hyrum Smith were jailed in Carthage, Illinois, on trumped-up charges. When a "Gentile" crowd learned about the arrest, they broke into the jailhouse and lynched both Joseph and Hyrum.

The leaderless community found Joseph Smith's successor in Brigham Young, a former Methodist who had unhappily left that church. Though he lacked Joseph Smith's charismatic personality, Young possessed the qualities the Mormon community needed at this juncture. He was a skillful administrator who concluded that the future of the community would best be served if away from already settled areas. In the winter of 1846, he accordingly took the throng of Mormons on a long trek westward without having a clear notion of the goal and destination. After months of immense hardship, the group crossed the Rocky Mountains and reached the Great Salt Lake basin. Upon seeing it, Young declared, "This is the place," the trek ended, and the Mormon settlement began. In 1852, the Mormons officially embraced the teaching of polygamy (Brigham Young had no less than nineteen wives), but a short ten years later the U.S. Congress prohibited the practice. The Utah Territory became a Mormon outpost, and when in 1892 it petitioned to join the United States, the Church of Jesus Christ of Latter-Day Saints had to abandon the practice of polygamy and relinquish its claims of a theocracy in Utah. The territory joined the Union, endorsing female suffrage, the second state to do so, an intriguing illustration of the gender complexity of a polygamous culture.

In the past century, the Church of Jesus Christ of Latter-Day Saints, employed a systematic approach to evangelism by calling on its youthful members to engage in missionary work—there were more than fifty thousand of them in 2009 with more than two hundred thousand recorded conversions to the Mormon Church. The exclusion of black men from the universal priesthood was lifted in 1978, while the doctrine of the baptism of the dead stimulated a vast interest in genealogy. With more than thirteen million members worldwide, the Church of Jesus Christ of Latter-Day Saints has become not only one of America's largest denominations but also a global church.

Another late nineteenth-century American religious movement also attained global status: the Watchtower Society, or, as the organization is better known, the Jehovah's Witnesses. Once again, a new Christian tradition was born of the religious experience of an individual, in this case the experience of one Charles Taze Russell. Born in 1852, Russell founded the magazine *Zion's Watch Tower and Herald of Christ's Presence* in 1879, and in 1881, at age thirty-two, he was a cofounder of the Zion's Watch Tower Tract Society, based on beliefs he had come to embrace in the course of his biblical studies, which, because of his charismatic appeal, attracted supporters. Russell rejected many of the traditional Christian teachings, including that of the Trinity; he did not believe that Jesus was fully divine as affirmed by mainstream Christianity in the Nicene Creed.

Importantly, Russell's view of the Bible prompted him to focus on the second coming of Jesus, who, he argued, had spiritually returned to earth in 1874 and would return visible to all in 1878. The failure of Jesus to return on this date did little, however, to lessen the impact of Russell's preaching and writing. He organized the Zion's Watchtower Tract Society, which, as the name suggested, printed and distributed tracts, theological books, Bibles, and later even motion pictures. Referring to God as "Jehovah" and to themselves as "Jehovah's Witnesses" (since 1931), the members of this denomination still place the imminent return of Jesus at the center of their teachings, while at the same time seeking to uphold high moral standards. As in the Church of Jesus Christ of Latter-Day Saints, smoking tobacco and drinking alcohol are not allowed. Convinced of the fundamental enmity of secular governments to the God

Jehovah, the Witnesses have refused to serve in the military, a stance that at times has exposed them to severe persecution, particularly in Nazi Germany.

To this day, the *Watchtower* magazine, published monthly, directs the spiritual nurture and theological edification of the members of the Watchtower Society. It continues to be offered by Jehovah's Witnesses standing in front of department stores or (when permitted) train stations and airports, distributing copies of the magazine.

The importance of these new "American" manifestations of the Christian faith and denominations notwithstanding, mainstream Protestantism in North America was characterized at the end of the nineteenth century by the fierce controversy between liberals and conservatives. Their skirmish came to be known as "the Fundamentalist controversy," the consequences of which continue to characterize American Protestantism. The term "Fundamentalism" itself, and its widespread usage, derived from the publishing activities of Lyman Stewart, a wealthy Presbyterian layman, who, in 1910, sponsored the publication of pamphlets on the "fundamentals" of the historic Christian faith. The twelve pamphlets were titled *The Fundamentals: A Testimony to the Truth* and eventually included some ninety essays on key traditional teachings of Scripture, written by sixty-four authors.

Critical biblical scholarship, whose origins lay in English Deism and the German Enlightenment, had made its way to North America in the middle of the nineteenth century, mainly by way of American scholars who had gone to Germany to study theology and frequently returned as ardent believers in the historical-critical method of reading the Bible. A conservative reaction set in, in which theologians like Charles Hodge of Princeton Theological Seminary and James Orr defended the traditional reading of the Bible as revelation of supernatural truth. The turn of the twentieth century arrived with American Protestantism deeply and dramatically divided. The fault line ran through the denominations, which soon had a liberal and a conservative wing. Fundamentalism quickly revealed a Puritan streak with its disavowal of certain forms of entertainment, such as the ever more popular motion pictures coming from Hollywood, or the opposition to Charles Darwin's theory of evolution, culminating in the famous Scopes trial in 1925.

THE REVIVALS

American Fundamentalism proclaimed the gospel in a novel way: the revival. There had been antecedents, such as the Wesleyan revival in eighteenth-century England, or the first Great Awakening in New England at about the same time, but in the course of the nineteenth century revivals began to become ever more popular and ever more crucial in American Protestantism. Its vehicles were both new methods and charismatic individuals. The camp meeting—a combination of a weekend retreat and Bible study—proved particularly popular. It created its own culture, with camp meeting hymns and testimonies. The message preached was a detailed enumeration of all the evils and sins of society, the evocation of a golden past, when Scripture and the Christian faith were taken seriously, and a called to be converted. The preachers were eloquent and melodramatic.

Figure 5B
Camp Meeting. J. Maze Burbank (fl. 1839–58), American.

Take the shoe salesman by the name of Dwight L. Moody. Huge, barrel-chested, with a bushy beard, and weighing well over 250 pounds, Moody cut an imposing figure. He had moved to Chicago in 1856 with the intention of securing a fortune and then retiring. From all accounts he was a persuasive salesman who, before too long, became a Sunday school teacher for children from the Chicago slums. Over time, he took on additional teaching and preaching responsibilities so that a contemporary remarked, "I never saw such high pressure; he made me think of these breathing steamboats on the Mississippi that must go fast or bust." There followed trips to England, where Moody chose Ira Sankey to be his song leader and deepened his commitment to evangelism. Moody and Sankey withstood the criticism of their message and their methods, which many considered too showy and too melodramatic. When they returned to North America, their fame had spread in conservative evangelical circles and beyond. Their first revival took place in Brooklyn, where five thousand people came to every service. Then Moody and Sankey moved on to Philadelphia, then to New York City, and endlessly to every major American city. By the time Dwight Moody ended his evangelistic activities, his preaching had reportedly converted one million individuals. Of course, religious statistics are notoriously problematic, but there can be little doubt that those touched by his preaching became conduits for the infusion of new ideas and approaches into the local churches. In style, word, and music, Moody and Sankey changed the face of much of North American Protestantism.

Moody made evangelistic crusades a mainstay of Protestant Christianity. His accomplishment was to make the evangelistic sermon a standard part of American Protestantism. He was never ordained and showed little patience with the theological subtleties so important to the learned. His theology was conservative, even though he painstakingly avoided speaking publicly about the vexing issue of evolution that had emerged as a controversial issue among Protestants. The Bible was studied and preached simply to encourage individuals to "accept Jesus as savior." At the same time, Moody's helper Ira Sankey popularized a new hymnody—the gospel hymn. It was characterized by tunes that were part of the musical mainstream of the second half of the nineteenth century. Its lyrics were highly subjective, with a preponderance of accounts of the individual's spiritual pilgrimage. A long string of writers composed the words—Fanny Crosby (1820–1915), blind from infancy, wrote more than eight thousand hymns that expressed the joy of being Christian, including the widely popular "Blessed Assurance," "Jesus, keep me near the Cross," and "Rescue the Perishing." The revival movement was a singing faith that, much like the Protestant Reformation, helped shape the piety and deeds of thousands.

Moody also left a striking legacy of institutions. He received enormous royalties from the sale of the gospel song hymnals, and he put these moneys into such institutions as the Moody Bible Institute in Chicago, founded for the training of future preachers of the gospel. The institute soon added an ambitious publication activity and produced evangelical motion pictures, mainly documentaries, at a time when evangelical Christians in North America viewed Hollywood and its films as the epitome of evil. In East Northfield, Massachusetts, Dwight Moody established a Christian boarding school for girls, in Mount Hermon a school for boys. When Moody died in 1899, he had inspired and trained a vast array of fellow evangelists and revival preachers. They echoed Moody's approach and explored for themselves new ways of proclaiming the gospel. The revival tent became a standard feature, especially in the rural South and Midwest, as did the sawdust, used to keep the ground over which the tent was pitched reasonably dry. The benches were hard, and the orations of many preachers rather bizarre, so that outsiders derided the sawdust trail (leading to the preacher's platform for those who experienced a conversion), and the "Holy Rollers," with their high emotions characterizing a revival meeting.

The towering figure among these revival preachers following Dwight Moody was William "Billy" Sunday. A professional baseball player for the Chicago White Sox, Sunday had a conversion, prompting his decision to become an evangelist. If Moody had emphasized God's love in his sermons, accentuating the positive, Billy Sunday was a preacher of God's judgment. He railed against all the evils he could identify—alcohol, gambling, prostitution, communism, Roman Catholicism, and, most especially, the devil. Sunday's was the religion of human sin and an angry God. And to top it all off, Sunday was a showman par excellence. He would get down on the floor, challenging the devil to come and fight him right then and there. When the devil did not appear, Billy Sunday raised his hands in the fashion of successful prizefighters. He won, of course, this spiritual fight, and sinners were scared into conversion.

PROTESTANTISM AND THE SOCIAL ORDER

A different revivalist form of Protestantism had its origins in England, where two Methodists, William and Catherine Booth, husband and wife, dissatisfied with their own church's inability to minister to the lower classes of English society, founded a religious revival movement modeled after the British army. William himself came from humble circumstances and had a deep passion for the outcasts of society. He moved to the slums of London to minister to the poorest of the poor, first calling his venture Christian Mission and subsequently Salvation Army. Its members wore uniforms not unlike those of the British military, the movement featured bands like in the military, and its members held ranks modeled after the ranks of the British army. William Booth was the commanding general. His book *In Darkest England and the Way Out* (1890) sounded a clarion call for comprehensive social and economic reform in England. His wife, Catherine Booth, served as his true helpmate and partner, focusing especially on the conversion of women.

Booth's Salvation Army, which enjoyed a dramatic spread in both Great Britain and the United Sates, demonstrated the close connection, even among conservatives, between the proclamation of the gospel and the amelioration of social and economic hardship caused by the industrial revolution. In the United States this took the form of what was soon called the "Social Gospel," the notion that the Christian gospel had not only religious but also social relevance. All of life was to conform to the teachings of Jesus. Of course, the Christian faith has always sought to be attentive to material as well as spiritual needs. The American "Social Gospel," however, sought to make them equal, and its main proponents were liberals. In North America several distinguished individuals propounded the message of the Social Gospel, Washington Gladden (1836–1918), for example, a pastor in Columbus, Ohio, where he served on the city council. Or Walter Rauschenbusch (1861–1918), pastor in New York City, then professor at the Rochester Theological Seminary. He argued that the church had truly failed its promise to deal with soul and body.

"Will some Gibbon of Mongol race sit by the shore of the Pacific in the year A.D. 3000 and write on the 'Decline and Fall of the Christian Empire'? If so, he will probably describe the nineteenth and twentieth centuries as the golden age when outwardly life flourished as never before, but when that decay, which resulted in the gradual collapse of the twenty-first and twenty-second centuries, was already far advanced. Or will the twentieth century mark for the future historian the real adolescence of humanity, the great emancipation from barbarism and from the paralysis of injustice, and the beginning of a progress in the intellectual, social, and moral life of mankind to which all past history has no parallel? It will depend almost wholly on the moral forces which the Christian nations can bring to the fighting line against wrong, and the fighting energy of those moral forces will again depend on the degree to which they are inspired by religious faith and enthusiasm. It is either a revival of social religion or the deluge" (Rauschenbusch, *Christianity and the Social Crisis*, 286).

Rauschenbusch argued that the gospel had the power to change society, not simply individuals, and usher in the Kingdom of God, where harmony and justice would prevail. Salvation meant the commitment of men and women to live according to the teachings of Jesus. Rauschenbusch had something to say about all of society—about the professions, about local and state governments. There was an uncommon exuberance and optimism in Rauschenbusch and those who shared his understanding of the gospel. Now that the way had been shown, the goal would soon be reached. The church had been made aware of its responsibility for justice in the social and political order.

THE CONSERVATIVE REACTION

Conservatives were uneasy about the Social Gospel. They saw it as minimizing the reality of sin in human affairs, and found it to express an inopportune optimism that defied the teaching of the Scriptures. Indeed, conservatives found much to reject in liberal Christianity: Darwin's influence, historical criticism of Scripture, the Social Gospel. A Bible conference held in upstate New York in 1895 threw down the conservative gauntlet. It declared that there were five nonnegotiable truths of the Christian faith: the virgin birth of Jesus, Christ's atoning and substitutianary death on the cross, Jesus' bodily resurrection, the bodily return of Jesus to earth, and the inerrancy of Scripture. A movement coalesced that came to be known as "Fundamentalism." The term was taken from a set of publications called *The Fundamentals*, one of whose purposes was to lay out the five Christian beliefs the authors saw as fundamental to the faith. The movement was large in scale and dynamic in leadership, and a string of eloquent preachers found new and dynamic ways to preach the traditional gospel, as did countless books, magazines, Bible conferences, and lay organizations, such as the Gideons, devoted to the distribution of Bibles, or the Young Men's (and Young Women's) Christian Associations. All stressed a traditional reading of the Bible.

The combination of charismatic leaders and new approaches to proclaim the traditional message does not suffice, however, to explain the impact of the conservative movement on American church life. Its success must also be related to the tensions and turbulence in American society during the closing decades of the nineteenth century and opening decades of the twentieth. While continuing to welcome the European poor and dispossessed to its shores, the young country experienced serious social and economic dislocation: increasing urbanization; new types of immigrants, such as Catholics and Jews; changing social mores, especially after World War I; the famous Scopes trial of 1925 and its impact on the teaching of evolution in public schools; the stock market crash of 1929; and the unsettling pronouncements of philosophers and theologians against traditional Christianity. All these made for a threatening societal atmosphere for conservative Protestants, who increasingly tended to remove themselves from the larger American society and liberal Christianity.

During the years after World War II the revivals of a young charismatic Baptist preacher by the name of Billy Graham made American Christianity at large aware of the continuing vitality of conservative Protestantism. Graham's highly and splendidly organized "crusades" filled major sports arenas in metropolitan areas with tens of thousands of attendees, many of whom professed faith in Christ as the result of his preaching. Graham's sermons skillfully combined the proclamation of the "old-fashioned gospel" and an anti-communist rhetoric that fit smoothly with the broader American mind-set of the Cold War. Though a golf partner of several presidents and frequently invited to the White House, Graham ostensibly refrained from engaging in political issues, for example, the civil rights struggle. A dramatic change occurred in the 1980s, when evangelical preachers such as Pat Robertson and Jerry Falwell entered the political arena by rallying conservative Protestants behind conservative political causes. This was the beginning of the "silent majority" movement, which made abortion a major issue and touchstone for proper Christian views of society.

THE CATHOLIC STORY

At the end of the nineteenth century the religious configuration of the United States was dramatically different from what it had been a hundred years earlier. Most significant was the increase in the number of Catholics in North America. Only two percent of the United States population had described itself as Catholic at the end of the eighteenth century, but by the end of the nineteenth century that figure had risen to almost twenty percent. A series of crop failures in Ireland in the 1840s had caused a mass exodus of Irish Catholics to the United States. Their increasingly strong presence allowed Irish Catholics, mainly settled in Boston, to dominate American Catholicism for a century, particularly the clergy and the higher church offices.

But Irish Catholics were not the only significant Catholic population in the United States. In the 1850s, German Catholics began arriving in large numbers, settling in Chicago, Milwaukee, and St. Louis, where they worked on farms and labored as shopkeepers and craftsmen. In all three places they also quickly distinguished themselves as beer brewers, a skill they had brought with them from the old country. A new wave of Catholic immigrants, this time from Poland, arrived after the middle of the nineteenth century, and in the end more than two million Polish Catholics immigrated to the United States. They were joined by an equally large number of Italian Catholics. Each of these streams of Catholic immigrants held to a particular understanding of what it meant to be Catholic, resisting in various ways what they perceived as the heavy influence of the Irish in the Catholic Church in North America.

AFRICAN AMERICAN CHRISTIANITY

Still another group of people came to North America, though not at all voluntarily, as did the European immigrants. They came as slaves. By the time of the Civil War, some four million Africans had been forcefully brought to North America, virtually all of them as slaves, and virtually all of them to live in the American South. When African slaves first reached the North American shores, probably in 1619, most knew nothing about Christianity or had only the vaguest inkling of it. Not much changed for decades, particularly since slaveholders had little interest in allowing their slaves to be exposed to the Christian religion, which can be, as Marx observed, opium for the people, but can also be profoundly revolutionary (as was the conviction of Saint Francis). This revolutionary character of the Christian faith with respect to social issues was little in evidence in eighteenth-century North America, however, where the pulpits preached that slavery was found in the Bible and entailed no divine disapproval.

Things changed after the American Revolution, when Baptists and Methodists became more numerous and practiced the Christian religion with considerably less stately formality than was the case in Anglican services. Slaves began to worship with their masters in their masters' churches, hearing the same sermons and gathering by the side of their masters to receive the bread and wine of Communion. They were slaves with all the legal and human indignities that status entailed, anything but social equals, but they were exposed to the Christian religion.

Figure 5C
River Baptism. ca. 1911, Nebraska.

As slaves learned about the religion of their masters, they found that, even though whites propounded a Christian rationale for slavery, the Christian faith could also provide meaning and comfort for them. The biblical stories they heard did more than offer consolation. While the slaves heard a great many sermons on the topic of obedience to the masters and even on the biblical justification of slavery, they also heard the story of bondage and liberation from Egypt's pharaoh, of Jesus' words about the blessedness of the poor, and of the Apostle Paul's exhortation that in Christ there are neither slaves nor free (Gal. 3:28).

Against great odds, some slaves succeeded in forming African American congregations, but these were promptly suppressed and dissolved by the authorities: in a society fearful of slave rebellions, any inkling of independence expressed by slaves seemed threatening. It was in the northern states that independent African American churches were first formally established—notably the African Methodist Episcopal Church in 1816, known to this day as the AME Church.

The emancipation of the slaves in the wake of the Civil War meant that the clandestine gatherings of African American slaves and their participation in white churches gave way to the formation of black churches. The remainder of the nineteenth century saw the rise of independent African American denominations, such as the Colored Episcopal Methodist Church and the National Baptist Convention. These and other predominantly African American churches, together with denominationally unaligned congregations, have persisted into the twenty-first century. Most African American Christians continue to worship in predominantly black churches. Deeply conservative in theological matters, yet profoundly liberal in social issues, the African American churches developed a distinctive style of preaching and worship, some of which, such as the Spiritual, were widely appropriated by white churches. Some of the most thoughtful and eloquent preachers in the late twentieth century were African American.

Reflection 6: Christianity as a Global Phenomenon

For centuries the Christian religion was almost entirely a European phenomenon, which eventually extended to North America and to other continents. Accordingly, narratives of the history of Christianity have centered on Europe and North America. This Eurocentrism, as it is called, has in recent years come under attack and criticism. The awareness, in the late twentieth century, that presently the most dynamic Christian communities are not found in Europe or North America but in the so-called "third" or "developing world" has prompted a reappraisal and awareness that pointed out that the history of the Christian faith, in the course of the nineteenth century, has been far more global than the traditional perspective suggested. Not surprisingly, new kinds of histories of Christianity have been published in recent years, and they see the stories of the faith in Europe and North America as only parts of a larger and global whole. As a result, nowadays "global" histories of the Christian faith are "in." Of course, even the traditional historical accounts of the Christian faith have not been unaware of the non-European developments and expansions. One cannot write about Nestorius and his followers, for example, without mentioning the remarkable spread of his movement into Asia.

The Christian faith has undergone major geographic shifts before. Until the seventh century and the rise of Islam, the geographic center of the Christian religion was the eastern Mediterranean (and beyond). Indeed, it might be argued that it lay in present-day Iraq, that is, in Asia; the northern shoreline of Africa was more solidly Christian than Europe north of the Alps. By the end of the third century, some twenty bishoprics existed in the Tigris-Euphrates valley. Christian assemblies were found along the southern shores of the Black Sea. Rome, the capital of the Roman Empire, was geographically and even theologically on the fringe, evidenced by the relative absence of meaningful Western involvement in the great christological and Trinitarian debates of the fourth century.

The dramatic geographic shift began in the seventh century. Hardly thirty years after the formal beginning of the Muslim era in 622, Muslim Arabs had occupied Palestine, Syria, Mesopotamia, Persia, and virtually all of Egypt. In 698 they conquered Carthage after a fierce battle, and a little more than a decade later most of Spain was in Arab hands. To be sure, these were political forays, but they were accompanied by the spread of Islam and the gradual disappearance of Christian churches and communities. The Christian faith might have ended right then and there, had it not been for its northward missionary expansion into central and northern Europe at about the same time. As the faith lost its dominant mainstays in the Middle East, it gained new ones in central and northern Europe.

Most of this vital Christian presence in the eastern Mediterranean has not been etched in Christian memory, making Europe seemingly the only site of Christian life, and Christianity and Europe virtual synonyms. When Europeans began to cross the Atlantic Ocean to what they soon called "the Americas," priests and monks crossed the ocean with them. Their assignment was to serve as spiritual guides for the European explorers. Soon, however, the paramount task was evangelizing the indigenous peoples. It was not always successful, nor were the methods of evangelism always proper. Reflecting on the coming of Christianity to places and peoples theretofore untouched and unaware of the Christian message tells us how this "Europeanized" faith was appropriated by different peoples and cultures. The awareness of the global history of the Christian faith must ask the question of meaning. What insights and lessons can be derived from envisioning the history of Christianity as truly global?

On one level, of course, such an approach will truly encompass the entire Christian story. It will see the Mar Thomas Church in India not as a quaint collection of congregations but as a vibrant part of the larger Christian journey. Yet the fact of the matter is that unless a nearly two-thousand-year history becomes a suffocating array of facts and happenings, choices must be made between what is deemed important and what not, what was consequential, and what was not. It then becomes quickly evident that not all of the history of the Christian faith is equally relevant for the twenty-first-century observer in all places. Relevant are those ideas, structures, and individuals that have influenced the present. Thus, the question should be asked, what in this rich and overwhelming Christian past explains the contemporary Christian situation in Sweden, or North America, or South Korea? Clearly, Lutherans will be enriched by the study of their tradition, Calvinists by theirs, Catholics by theirs. Being familiar with the history of Christianity in Africa or with the survival of Orthodox Christians in Ethiopia will prove to be greatly enriching for all those who stand in those respective traditions; for Coptic Christians in Egypt the story of their contacts with their brethren and sisters in Ethiopia will be more important than the story of Martin Luther or John Calvin. Being familiar with theologizing in the nineteenth and twentieth centuries will make a difference in understanding the Christian faith in Europe and North America in the twenty-first century.

For students in Europe and North America, the story of the faith on those two continents, therefore, needs to be in the center, because it is that history that serves to explain the faith in the present. Our discourse about the Christian faith is determined by the historical legacy of those two continents. The same applies to the Christian self-understanding in other places and continents. For Christians in India, the key to their appropriation of the faith is not so much what happened in faraway Europe or North America, but rather the story of the proclamation of the faith in their own land. This is deeply meaningful on its own terms, and the historian will find it a remarkable parallel to the European and North American story: the impact of the surrounding culture on the faith.

BY WAY OF AN
EPILOGUE

APPENDIX A: THEOLOGICAL CURRENTS IN THE EARLY TWENTY-FIRST CENTURY

In the first years of the twenty-first century Protestant theology is characterized by a plethora of approaches and methodologies, with no widely accepted, dominating "school" of theology. Diversity reigns. Also, much theological reflection, certainly in North America, comes not from church theologians teaching in denominational seminaries but from theologians who think and write about the Christian faith as individual scholars rather than as church leaders, just as the English Deists did in the eighteenth century.

In a way, these diverse approaches have a common denominator in the impulses of liberation theology, which has argued that the traditional Christian self-understanding distorts authentic Christianity and that those strains of Scripture must be recovered that call for social justice variously defined. For example, the proponents of Black Theology have argued that the church must recover the Jesus who identified with the poor and those who suffered, as they have a privileged place in the kingdom of God. Black Theology is liberation theology geared to the experience of descendants of African slaves.

Feminist Theology has its point of departure in the insistence on a historic oppression of women in patriarchal society and calls for affording a central place for the biblical message of liberation for women. Womanist Theology seeks to address the experience of black women, particularly poor black women. While Black liberation theology was male-oriented and did not speak to issues relevant for black women, Womanist Theology attempted the affirmation of black women, particularly black feminists, with a wide-ranging methodological approach that fused a variety of sources, including African American fiction.

Eco-theology, to cite a final example of the current theological pluralism, seeks to bring biblical insights to bear on burning questions of the environment by calling attention to the intimate connection between religion and nature. Much like Black Theology and Womanist Theology, Eco-theology can be both specifically Christian and generically human.

Most of the contemporary theological emphases are "liberation" theologies in the broad sense of that word. They reflect on the meaning of the Christian faith for society—for humans marginalized for reasons of race or gender or class; children in dire poverty; the elderly without adequate medical care. Liberation theology argues that the Bible is fundamentally concerned not only with the liberation of the soul, but also of the body.

At the same time, conservative theology—in North America generally referred to as "evangelical"—is demonstrating considerable vigor. While one may doubt the accuracy of opinion surveys that suggest that a major portion of the North American population affirms "conservative" Christian theological notions—such as the bodily resurrection of Jesus—the North American evangelical community clearly continues to exhibit impressive strength. The evangelical version of the Christian faith has a surprisingly strong presence on the airwaves and television screens, while evangelical colleges and universities flourish and evangelical Christianity is taken to exert considerable influence on the political life of the nation.

None of these approaches to understanding Christianity in the early twenty-first century has succeeded, however, in capturing the minds and hearts of all Christians. The deep divide between a liberal and a conservative interpretation of the Christian faith is arguably the eminent hallmark of North American Christianity at present.

APPENDIX B: RECURRENT THEMES IN THE HISTORY OF CHRISTIANITY

Certain themes seem to recur over and over again in the history of the Christian faith. A recent book even suggested that the theme of reform has forcefully come to the fore in Christian history every five hundred years. Such a neat chronology must be suspect, of course, but there is no doubt that recurrent themes exist. These include the themes of creeds and confessions, reform and renewal, faith versus morals, faith and culture, and the Christian life. These themes not only characterize the Christian story through the centuries; they also have determined its inner dynamic.

Take the theme of creeds and confessions. In the early church, the affirmation of what was believed about Jesus of Nazareth took the form of concise propositional statements, called creeds, confessed by the faithful, generally prior to their baptism. Since then numerous creeds and confessions have been formulated by Christians around the globe, and in the twenty-first century, creeds, old and new, continue to be evoked. Indeed, in many services of worship the Apostles' or Nicene creeds are faithfully recited by the congregants Sunday after Sunday. This striking continuity suggests the centrality of affirming propositional truths about the faith for Christians and, at the same time, the timelessness of what was promulgated more than two millennia ago.

Since creeds are shorthand ciphers for complicated theological affirmations, this is not surprising. But what does this recitation mean? Is it a rote recitation of theological mumbo jumbo? Do the faithful in the pews understand what they recite? Do they affirm it? Since creeds were formulated when certain theological issues were controversial, it would follow that in the opening years of the twenty-first century new creeds and confessions would address the pertinent issues of the day. That has not been the case, however, except for evangelical denominations that have focused on the inerrancy and verbal inspiration of the Bible. In some North American Protestant traditions the notion of a confession, that is, a set of propositional truths binding for all members, appears to have been largely abandoned. Indeed, sociological research suggests that the younger generation in particular is staying aloof from doctrinal commitments. More than one-quarter of American adults leave the faith in which they were reared to practice another religion—or no religion at all. Did the language of creeds and confessions of faith prompt this change?

Almost one-half of adults have switched religious affiliation, moved from being affiliated with a particular faith to being unaffiliated with any religion, or dropped any connection to a specific religious tradition altogether. Again, was this prompted by the necessity of affirming a creed, which they could not do?

The theme of reform has similarly emerged repeatedly through the centuries as a burning concern of many loyal to the church. The word *reform* itself has almost become a cliché, easily and universally voiced in many traditions. It received most prominent expression, of course, in the Reformation—John Calvin even wrote a treatise on "the necessity of reforming the church." What needs to be reformed can include a rich palette of concerns in theological understanding or in personal piety. Centuries ago, the Reformed theologian Gisbert Voetius (d. 1676) coined the phrase *"ecclesia semper reformanda"* ("the church is always in need of reform"), and this phrase became the hallmark of the Second Vatican Council in the 1960s, which reformed the Roman Catholic Church—in the opinion of some, too much so. This means, of course, that the Christian faith exists in imperfect form, prompting insightful theologians and ardent believers to issue calls for reform. In the late fifteenth century, the call included the additional phrase "in head and members" (*in caput et membris*) to indicate that reform was necessary both among the common people and among the highest dignitaries and practices of the church.

The relationship of the Christian faith to culture has proved to be a vexing problem virtually from the very beginning. As we saw, it was one of the characteristics of the emerging Christian communities—leading to stark suspicion—that their members stayed aloof from the practices and values of Roman society. As a rule, Christians did not join the Roman army, nor did they serve in governmental offices. When circuses provided entertainment for the masses, Christians stayed at home.

The turn to the sole legal religion in the Roman Empire brought a dramatic change, as the Christian faith entered a symbiotic relationship with society. Over the centuries, several distinctive patterns of the relationship between the Christian faith and society emerged. The most prominent one—characteristic of the Middle Ages and of Catholicism as well as Calvin and Calvinism—has sought to infuse Christian principles into society. Specific illustrations of the societal consequences of this understanding are the phenomenon of Prohibition in the United States or the opposition of evangelical and Catholic Christians to *Roe v. Wade*.

A second pattern, diametrically opposed to this vision, asserts a radical distinction between the "world" and the values of Jesus. The principles and values of the "world" are taken to be irreconcilably removed from those of the Gospels. Thus, Tertullian inveighed against the practices of Roman society and all worldly pleasures. In the sixteenth century the Anabaptists sought to separate themselves from the "world" by refusing military service or service in governmental offices, and insisted on a believer's separation from an unbelieving spouse.

A third pattern was personified in none other than Martin Luther, who understood both the radicalism of Jesus' message and the necessity of societal structures—for example, governmental authority as a divinely ordered means to assure law and order in a society. For Luther and the Lutheran tradition both the principles of society and of the Sermon on the Mount had to be kept together in dialectic relationship.

A final theme in Christian history has been the pursuit of the principles of the perfect godly life. Various writers of the New Testament undertook to address the issue and the string of suggestions and proposals continued until the twenty-first century. In the Catholic tradition the rich panoply of monastic orders has sought to offer guidance as well as opportunity, for each order delineated an approach to be emulated, though in every last instance the monastic ideal hovered around the two poles of "*ora et labora*" ("pray and work"), of devoting selfless time to the life of the spirit while at the same time seeking to ameliorate suffering of whatever sort in society. Protestants have argued that such godly pursuit should take place in one's ordinary life, as artisan, or farmer, or wife. At the same time, the Calvinist tradition from its beginning in Geneva placed great weight on the exercise of church discipline, the affirmation of certain moral standards as inescapably normative for Christians. On this point, too, change has occurred, for the term "church discipline," in earlier generations so pivotal for the public role of the church in society, has largely disappeared from the Christian vocabulary. That is intriguing, for otherwise the generalization is surely appropriate that in modernity the Christian religion has retained the vocabulary of tradition but offered a new content.

APPENDIX C: ON THE GAP BETWEEN IDEALS AND PRACTICE

No survey of the history of the Christian faith should ignore the uncomfortable reality that through the centuries a dark side of the Christian religion was very much present alongside intellectual splendor, personal commitment, and selfless moral action. Some of what was said, and done, allegedly rooted in the Bible, was assuredly a strange interpretation of the teachings of Jesus of Nazareth. No serious student of Christian history will be able to deny that alongside the positive splendor found in the Christian story through the centuries, there was also a negative side—a side of hatred rather than love, of suffering rather than happiness, of quarrel rather than peace, of intolerance rather than acceptance. The list is lengthy—the lamentable treatment of Jews, the use of fire and sword in dealing with dissenting groups and conventicles, the incarceration and death of dissenters, the ruthlessness of the Inquisition, the forced "conversions" of native peoples in South America, the condoning of slavery, and the iciness of the polemic against other theologians or churchmen. The list is regrettably long.

To be sure, the church did not carry the sword, nor did it light the torch that was put to the pile. But it offered the ideological support for such actions, and the reasons for doing so were diverse—to consolidate its power and to stymie dissent above all, so it would seem, because the men and women of bygone days were programmed to place religious purity above everything else. Why did the theological controversy over the nature(s) of Christ trigger such physical violence? Why was it necessary to engage in a crusade against the medieval Cathari? How was it that Michael Servetus was burned outside Geneva for having reiterated the Arian understanding of the divinity of Jesus? Or why were Christians in eighteenth-century Russia put to death for crossing themselves incorrectly? Of course, there often was more than just religion involved in these incidents, with religion affording a convenient (and lofty) justification. And even though most of these engagements are a thing of the past, they throw a long, dark shadow over the Christian story.

Many theories have been advanced to elucidate this dark side of the Christian faith, for example, that it is the very characteristic of monotheism to be intolerant or that this dark side is merely the story of excesses and aberrations, not of the true faith. Often the reality has been an embarrassing gap between the lofty rhetoric of the theologians and the actual reality "on the ground." It seems fair to say that most folks in the pews show little if any interest in the theological issues that are the lifeblood of theologians. There is striking discontinuity so that the story of the laity in the church through the centuries (if we had ample sources to write it) would undoubtedly read quite differently from what is written about the church in general.

Moreover, reading theological treatises often suggests that their authors live in a different universe, where pettiness, envy, haughtiness, and greediness toward church members seem to be irrelevant or drowned in a rich and winsome exposition of an idealized faith.

Perhaps the explanation is to be found in the fundamental reality that humans always wish their thought and action to be understood as expressing high and lofty ideals. This disposition has two potential ramifications. It may lead to the usurpation of religious and moral values for courses of action that are, in fact, blatant egotism or an exercise of raw power. It may also mean the sincere invocation of ideals when engaging in acts otherwise considered immoral or despicable.

An illustration for the former would be the European Thirty Years' War. It is known as a "war of religion" so as to suggest that this conflict was primarily over religion. But such was not the case; the war was a signal illustration of European power politics. In turn, King Henry VIII claimed to be overwhelmed by his violation of the divine command not to wed your brother's widow, when in fact more egotistical considerations were operative. One should not blame religion for every instance in which religion is invoked.

The second ramification is far weightier. The concept of the "just war" might serve as a telling illustration, for it essentially asserts that it is moral to kill for a "just" cause. At issue is the notion of moral (and religious) values and principles that make it permissible to engage in behavior and action otherwise considered immoral. That way of thinking lies at the core of the institution of the Inquisition (the honor of God must be defended) or of Christian anti-Semitism (Jews must be expelled, wear distinctive clothing, and so on, to make sure that Christians are not affected by innocent contact with Jews).

Either way of thinking represents a burdensome legacy for the Christian faith, which is not mollified by the reality that to be fearful of the "other" appears to be a human, and not a peculiarly Christian, foible.

APPENDIX D: THE CHURCH MOVES INTO THE FUTURE

The story of the Christian faith continues. In the early years of the twenty-first century, Christians throughout the world continue to gather for worship, edification, and fellowship as they have for almost two millennia. New believers are baptized, old believers receive the bread and wine of the sacred Christian meal, and still others receive the final rites of the church. At the same time, the Christian faith is increasingly confronting two rivals: a pointed secularism in what used to be the Christian homelands and the emergence of Islam as a dynamic rival religion.

What are the prospects for the Christian religion? The answer does not come easy, since any reflection on the future is most precarious, especially when historians engage in the exercise, insinuating that the future will be déjà vu all over again, as the cliché has it. Still, assessments of the state of the Christian faith in the early years of the twenty-first century appear to be marked by a sense of uncertainty, even gloom. In a way, this is nothing new. In the two thousand years of the faith, there has never been a dearth of gloomy assessments of the present and of dire prognoses of the future. In recent times, such gazing into the crystal ball seems to have escalated, and a variety of discouraging pronouncements has been made. These tend to be buttressed by statistics and surveys about, for example, church membership, church attendance, or belief in basic Christian doctrines. These data suggest a decline of church involvement and, both in Europe and in North America, a desertion from the faith. Europe, in particular, is uniformly cited as a worst-case scenario of secularization. The major Protestant denominations in North America have experienced membership losses of ten percent in the past fifteen years or so; if the current trends were to continue, it would be a simple mathematical exercise to find when these denominations will have a membership of one.

The difficulty in using statistical data to document the state of the vibrancy of Christianity lies in the absence of viable historical baselines to which the current situation can be related. Compared to the time when each infant born in European lands was routinely baptized into the Christian faith, making for a "Christian Europe" or a "Christian society," the present state of affairs leaves something to be desired. A slender majority of infants is baptized these days, and churches, especially in Europe, are notoriously empty on Sunday mornings. "Christian" Europe is a thing of the past. In North America, where formal membership statistics show moderate (but real) declines, the situation is more difficult to interpret. It is not clear, for example, if the rise of memberships in conservative, evangelical denominations is due to the greater attractiveness of their beliefs or to the demographics of younger families, which appear to be more heavily represented in evangelical churches. Despite the seeming importance of what is called the "Christian Right," there is little doubt that overall the Christian influence on the body politic—perhaps the legacy of New England Puritanism—has declined.

Nonetheless, no matter how discouraging some developments, it would be folly to ignore signs of Christian vitality in Europe and North America as well as in the rest of the world. Creative and thoughtful initiatives and experiments, for example, with small groups or house churches, can be found. Opinion surveys point to astonishingly high concurrences among American adults of traditional theological doctrines, such as the divinity of Jesus. One may see Christianity in the early twenty-first century as an impressive movement, especially if the purview extends beyond Europe and North America to the rest of the globe. It is, in terms of membership, the largest of the world religions, though it would not seem exactly clear what to make of that impressive statistic. Comparing the reality of hundreds of Muslim men kneeling for prayer in a mosque with that of a few elderly worshipers in churches in Europe offers little confidence in the vitality of the Christian faith.

Still, the present state of Christianity ought to be interpreted with a bit of caution, for the state of affairs would appear to be none too different from that of centuries past. Even in the supposedly stellar days of the Christian faith, the Middle Ages or the age of the Reformation, churches and cathedrals were rarely overcrowded, as most people had a rather loose relationship with the church. This is not to say that they were agnostics in disguise or disagreed with church teachings; they simply had other priorities.

This situation poses the question of whether we are experiencing a decline of the Christian religion in Europe and North America, or the emergence of new models and configurations of the Christian faith. Are we in the beginning of a dramatic geographic shift of the faith to new regions and places? The vibrant centers of the Christian faith in the early twenty-first century appear to be outside Europe and North America—in South Korea, Central America, and Africa. In Korea such vibrancy is expressed in the practice among Christians of daily morning prayer held at 4:30 a.m. If in Seoul you dare get up early, you will easily see many people rushing to church for this prayer.

Geographic shifts of centers of the Christian religion have happened before. Prior to the rise of Islam, the dynamic centers of the Christian religion were in North Africa, the eastern Mediterranean, and beyond, including present-day Turkey and Iraq. Today, only memories and ruins of once-impressive Christian edifices remain, say, of the Cappadocian Fathers. Were such a shift from north to south to occur in the course of the twenty-first century, it would not only be a geographic move, it would also herald a theological reorientation. The current controversy in the Anglican Communion between the churches in North America and Africa over the issue of homosexuality suggests a theological divergence between the Christianity of the global north and global south.

One implication of this possible, even likely, global realignment will be that decisions and declarations that have been meaningful for European and North American Christians, such as the issues of church-state relationship or the history of Pietism, are not likely to generate the same engagement for non-European and non-American Christians, who live in societies and cultures marked by different values, histories, and presuppositions. The geographic realignment will open new avenues of theologizing and encourage new ways of narrating the Christian story. So it has been throughout the long centuries of the faith.

The current ethical and theological controversies in most mainline Protestant churches in Europe and North America suggest yet another observation. One can hardly characterize the changes in Christian self-understanding that have occurred during the last century as having come from the studies of theologians and church leaders. Rather, developments in society, such as the increase of divorce and remarriage or new societal roles for women, were the catalysts that prompted fresh biblical and theological reflection. This involved the reinterpretation of the traditional consensus, accompanied by fierce controversies over whether such reinterpretation was warranted. Interestingly, the Catholic response to developments in modern thought and society was the exact opposite of the Protestant responses of accommodation. The Catholic Church (or, at least, its official leadership) has pursued a policy of confrontation with modernity. Theological pronouncements such as the promulgation of the dogmas of papal infallibility and Mary's Immaculate Conception had a political context, for they drew a line in the sand against all forms of liberal thought. In short, changes or proposed alterations in the Christian self-understanding came about because of changes in the value system of Western societies, leaving churches and theologians to choose between adapting to these changes or being left behind. Certain issues—such as the place of women in the church or the understanding of human sexuality—were societal issues before they became theological issues. Change, therefore, was understood by some as the surrender to secular values. The categorical "no" of conservatives to changes of traditional patterns and affirmations finds here its explanation.

What, then, are the challenges facing the Christian faith in the early years of a new century? One challenge clearly pertains to the ecumenical movement. Those who early in the twentieth century raised the banner of church unity were convinced that the days of arguments over subtle points of Christian doctrine had to be a thing of the past and that the division of Christianity into a seemingly endless array of churches and denominations was disgraceful. Today, a century after these concerns were first forcefully voiced, one must conclude that despite a striking richness of successful ecumenical dialogues, the movement has not succeeded in overcoming the structural divisions of the Christian religion, which organizationally remains as divided as ever. In that sense, the ecumenical movement must be pronounced a failure, despite such active ecumenical bodies as the World Council of Churches and despite the host of ecumenical dialogues between different churches, such as between Lutherans and Episcopalians or Catholics.

These dialogues have followed a similar pattern. After extended discussion in joint committees a statement is issued to the effect that agreement was reached on specific theological issues that divided the churches involved in the dialogue during the Reformation or after. Some of these agreements were hailed as positive achievements, while others—such as the agreement between Catholics and Lutherans on justification—evoked pointed protest. One might hazard the observation that these ecumenical agreements have been successful because they dealt with issues that have ceased to be the topics of intense and emotional disagreements that they once were. The ecumenical impulse was not able to address what might be considered the far more divisive fault line that runs straight through the mainline denominations, namely the split between those for whom the Bible contains supernatural truths and facts and those for whom it does not.

A few notable exceptions notwithstanding, mergers of churches have not proved to be possible. To be sure, North American denominations whose differences were mainly those of ethnic or geographic backgrounds found ways to come together. The several mergers of essentially ethnic Lutheran synods, whose differences were that they had come into being through different groups of Lutheran immigrants—from Sweden, Finland, Austria-Hungary, and Germany—substantiated the thesis of "social" origins of denominations in this country. Similarly, the Evangelical and Reformed Church, itself a result of the merger of the Reformed Church and the Evangelical Synod of North America in the 1930s, merged with the Congregational Christian Churches in 1957 to form the United Church of Christ.

A second set of mergers grew out of the legacy of slavery and the Civil War. Beginning in the 1840s several Protestant denominations, notably Baptists, Methodists, and Presbyterians, split into northern and southern components, such as the Southern Baptist Convention or the American Baptist Churches. Several of these geographically defined denominations reunited in the course of the twentieth century. In 1939, The Methodist Protestant Church, The Methodist Episcopal Church, and The Methodist Episcopal Church, South, agreed to unite under the name "The Methodist Church," and twenty-nine years later, in 1968, this Methodist Church formed a new church body, The United Methodist Church, after merging with The Evangelical United Brethren Church.

Jesus' prayer for unity among his disciples notwithstanding, his follow-ers were a divided lot from the very outset. The events recorded in the book of Acts are a story of disagreements even in the earliest Christian gatherings, while the letters of the Apostle Paul include a hefty amount of dismay and impatience over divisions and disagreements as well. The divisions have continued through the centuries. They have taken the form of endless battles over what was labeled orthodoxy and heresy. The development of absolute central authority in the Roman Catholic Church in the office of the Roman pontiff was prompted by the need to have a clear voice of authority in the church in the face of disagreement. Yet it would be a simplification to suggest that, therefore, the Roman Catholic Church has been bereft of internal strife. The popes would pro-nounce on critical issues—readmission of the lapsed, declericalization of apostates, Christology—and go unheeded. Internal strife generally ended with the passing of time, but not immediately after a papal dictum. Such turns as the dissolution and then reestablishment of the Society of Jesus in the eighteenth century, or, more recently, the recalcitrant conservatives under the French Archbishop Marcel Lefebvre opposing the decisions of the Second Vatican Council underscore this.

Through the centuries the Christian religion has shown an amazing ability to adjust to its surrounding culture—or, to state it more precisely, the story of the faith is also the story of Christian adaptation. This convergence has tended to prompt internal strife, with one faction embracing new norms and values, and the other faction rejecting them. Historically, Augustine's delineation of a Christian "just war" theory is a good case in point, for it was developed in contradistinction to the then-prevailing notion that Christians must abstain from the use of force but very much in harmony with the new societal role of the Christian faith in the Roman Empire. In the sixteenth century an increasingly self-confident and self-assured laity clamored for a meaningful role in society and the church, influencing Protestant notions of lay participation in church governance; things also worked the other way. The increasing self-confidence of the laity, say, in early modern England, prompted the reformers to embrace the kind of clericalism that they themselves had in principle dismissed.

In the nineteenth century, theologians such as Friedrich Schleiermacher or Albrecht Ritschl appropriated the intellectual currents of their day to offer interpretations of the faith. And in the twentieth and twenty-first centuries, changes in the traditional understanding of such issues as remarriage, sexuality, and abortion are best understood as the result of a dialogue between the Christian faith and surrounding culture. In past and present the outcome of such dialogues failed to be universally accepted and led to intense controversy, strife, and division. This internal strife within the churches or among theologians has been as intense as the strife between the Christian faith and its surrounding culture. By the same token, however, the remarkable adaptability of the Christian faith to new circumstances also explains its ongoing vigor.

Despite a variety of new exciting initiatives to make the Christian faith theologically meaningful and persuasive in Europe and North America, no magic wand has been discovered to alter the broader place of the faith on these two continents. In the opening years of the twenty-first century, there is no dominant school of theology that might command the allegiance of wide segments of Christians, as had been the case in mid-twentieth century, when Neo-Orthodoxy dominated the theological scene. The various expressions of liberation theology have emphasized certain aspects of the faith and attracted supporters without, however, gaining universal (or even widespread) support. Again, this is not too different from the way things have been in the past. Times of excitement and exhilaration have alternated with times of lethargy and paralysis. Somehow, the seeds for the former were sown in the latter. Hope overshadowed despair.

In one respect, one might argue, a radical change has occurred in the cogency of the faith: the ultimate questions the Christian faith has sought to answer for two millennia are no longer matters of deep concern. In premodern days people lived with chronic poverty, dire famine, and ubiquitous illness and early death. Their search for the meaning of these painful companions of their life journey took them to the Christian answer and explanation. The modern world has done away with ubiquitous infant mortality and removed famine from the First World vocabulary. The passenger on a Caribbean cruise ship has a different outlook on life than the mother standing at the graveside of yet another infant, and one might conclude from this reality that the number of those who wish for answers to death, and injustice, and suffering (all of which are very much around in the twenty-first century) will be small, and the Christian faith in Europe and North America will be small as well.

To be sure, throughout Christian history there have always been the naysayers, inside as well as outside the community of faith, trumpeting their conviction of the imminent demise of the faith. They have always proven to be wrong. The message of the Christian faith has had profound meaning for men and women. It has influenced lives. It has opened the doors to ridicule, oppression, even death. It has set, as Jesus himself anticipated, child against parents and parents against child. Millions have lived and died comforted by its precepts. At its best, it has meant unheard-of concern for the weak and helpless at the margins of society, though at its worst, intolerance and bloodshed.

Is it too much to hope that it will continue at its best?

APPENDIX E: THE HOUSES OF GOD: CHRISTIANITY AND MATERIAL CULTURE

One of the many consequences of Emperor Constantine's decision to make Christianity a legal religion in the Roman Empire was that the Christian religion went public. Christians appeared confidently in the public square, and before long numerous Christian impulses permeated Roman society. A "Christian" society came into being. It existed for more than a millennium, as all aspects of European society were "baptized" with Christian meaning. This was particularly true in the realm of the arts, where liturgical needs met aesthetic considerations. The story of European (and North American) Christianity thus incorporates myriad artistic commentaries, reflections, and reiterations of the faith in such artistic endeavors as painting, music, and architecture. Even in an increasingly secularized Europe, the artistic dimension of the faith is both a meaningful historical legacy and a continuing artistic inspiration.

To be sure, the preponderance of Christian motifs in music, art, and architecture through the centuries can be seen not so much as the expression of the long and powerful sway of the Christian message in the realm of the arts as it is a simple story of economic sponsorship. For centuries the church and its representatives were the foremost arts patrons: churches were built and decorated, artistic representations of the sacred story displayed, pious memories enshrined, and the mystery of the divine service rendered in sound. Artists in need to earn a comfortable livelihood (or simply to survive) took on assignments to create works of visual art with religious themes or to compose liturgical music. To acknowledge this down-to-earth reality, however, does not lessen the impact of the artistic portrayal of the Christian story for almost two millennia. European and North American art is unthinkable without Christian motifs. Nor are the skyscapes of towns and villages, large and small.

Architecture

Church buildings are foremost architectural spaces, and they reflect the technical expertise and the aesthetic values of the time of construction. Neither tastes nor artistic values nor technology are timeless: they change generationally, and so it is no wonder that architectural styles have undergone change upon change as the centuries have passed.

Of course, churches are more than mere space, for they serve the deeply spiritual purpose of giving the Christian community a place for the worship of God. For many Christians, particularly those in the Catholic and Orthodox traditions, to be in a church means to be in a sacred space in the presence of God. Thus, church buildings have profound spiritual meaning, a fact in bygone days superbly illustrated by the desire to have ones final resting place in a church, as close to the altar as possible (a desire generally fulfilled for the high and mighty rather than the poor and lowly). Also, in days gone by churches functioned, in times of crisis, as sanctuaries—as safe havens that armed enemies dared not enter.

Once Christians decided to build churches, they had to decide where to build them. During Emperor Constantine's time, some wanted to build on sites of pagan temples (to show the change from the old religion to the new) or on sites confiscated from pagan owners. Later on, they built on sites considered sacred by Christians, for example, where martyrs had suffered death for their faith or places in the Holy Land where Jesus himself had walked. As more and more people were baptized and became members of the church, and as more and more regions of Europe were "Christianized," more churches were built at sites with a conspicuous connection to the Christian story in a particular region or where ancient pagan temples had once stood.

Once the process of construction began, churches were built in the style prevailing at the time and place, and so the architecture of churches through the centuries conformed to the styles regnant in society. Posterity then coined labels, such as "Romanesque," "Gothic," or "Baroque," to denote an architectural pattern. Thus, the label "Romanesque," meaning "things Roman," came into usage early in the nineteenth century. It suggested—falsely, as a matter of fact—that this style reflected ancient Roman architecture. Similarly, the term "Gothic," which originally meant "Germanic," was a label given centuries later. People in the fourteenth century would have been stunned to hear their churches described as "Gothic."

The building of churches generally was not an expression of what we call "popular religion," the beliefs and practices of the common people. In fact, the common people had little to do with either the decision to build a church or the complicated issue of how to finance the costly construction. Those decisions were made by the societal elites, secular and ecclesiastical, who often pursued the construction of a new church with the enthusiasm nowadays reserved for alumni supporting a new football stadium (both projects having about the same staggering financial dimension). Someone had to foot the bill, and most of the time the grandiose vision of the would-be builders exceeded their financial resources, regularly forcing construction to languish for years and decades, even centuries. The elites of a community, in short, determined the details of what was proposed, often with bishops planning the construction of an impressive cathedral church, with the result of heavy competition between the community and the bishop.

The proposal to build a new (and expensive) church was hardly welcomed with open arms by everyone in the community, though there were always fervent supporters—as is also the case nowadays when the construction of a center for the arts or aquatics is on the agenda in our communities. Often, the resident bishop was the driving force behind the proposal to build a cathedral, since an imposing edifice (larger and more impressive than the cathedrals of the neighboring dioceses) epitomized authority and power. The cathedral was the bishop's church, after all, and the larger, the more daunting his importance. Accordingly, when the vision of a new cathedral arose, the bishop and his cathedral chapter tended rather magnanimously to decline offers of support from the well-to-do laity in the community—often an easy decision, because a bishop's income came from secular sources. The notion was, of course, that accepting funds from the community would require that the people behind those funds have a say in the cathedral's design and construction. Always, spiritual devotion and civic pride merged.

As the building of churches proliferated throughout the Mediterranean and Europe, theologians began to assign symbolic meaning to the architectural aspects and styles of churches. Everything seemed so engulfed. Even minor architectural details became manifestations of deep symbolic truth, often, one suspects, much to the surprise of those who had built and decorated the churches in the first place. A veritable canon of such symbolic assertions emerged. The footprint of churches, with the nave as torso and the two transepts as outstretched arms, became the cruciform symbol of Jesus' death on the cross; the placing of the nave on a west-east axis with the worshipers facing east became the truth that even as the rising of the sun dispelled the darkness of the night, so the coming of Jesus in the east had dispelled the darkness of sin. The reality appears to have been a bit more prosaic: the cruciform footprint arose not from an effort to replicate the cross of Jesus but from the practical need to add two chambers to the nave, one for the priest and the other for the remains of those buried in the church.

We know little about the kind of places of Christian worship during the church's first three centuries, and so only tentative observations are possible. With a few exceptions, there were no church buildings as we know them today during that time. Prior to the early fourth century, Christians met in the homes of members of the congregation, occasionally in more open places, such as shops or storage rooms. Since Christians were under the steady threat of possible persecution, public worship was not feasible. Since the Christian gatherings were small in number, private homes were altogether sufficient as meeting places. Meeting in the home of a local leader also suited the fellowship character of the gatherings.

This state of affairs changed when the Christian religion was officially recognized and Christians were able to worship publicly. As Christianity gained recognition as well as esteem in society, church membership increased, and ever larger spaces for worship were needed. The disrepute of the old religions made it easy to turn pagan temples into Christian houses of worship. The most notable instance was the Pantheon in Rome, which had been dedicated by Emperor Hadrian to "all gods" but was consecrated as a Christian church early in the seventh century, dedicated to Mary and the saints.

However, pagan temples did present a problem, since they did not offer the kind of sacred space Christians needed for their worship—space sufficiently large to accommodate the entire assembly when gathering for the exposition of Scripture and the celebration of the Eucharist. Greek and Roman temples were built to house divine statues and to encourage individual access, whereas Christians needed a place to gather as a community for worship.

The early churches were modeled after the Roman town halls where citizens gathered to deliberate on community matters. These were the basilicas, which became the first distinctive architectural style employed by Christians, structures with an extended rectangular hall, flat roof, two arcades, or side aisles, and an apse at the end of the nave of the width of the center aisle. The main entrance was opposite the apse. Numerous such basilica churches have survived the centuries in remarkable condition, most notably the church of S. Paoli fueri le Mura in Rome, "St. Paul's Outside the Wall."

Emperor Constantine's espousal of Christianity had entailed his decision to finance the construction of churches in important Christian centers. A concerted building effort got under way, with Roman basilicas serving as models. An important example of Constantine's efforts was the

Church of the Nativity in Bethlehem. The structures provided for a large, hall-like space suitable for Christian worship. The sitings of these first churches differed, and when larger basilicas began to be built, the customary three-aisle arrangement gave way to five aisles, some with transepts, some without. Most of these Constantinian churches (as most churches from those early centuries) have fallen into oblivion. There are hardly any remains.

The important element in the interior of these Christian basilicas was the altar, patterned after the standard Roman dining table. Unlike the arrangement in pagan temples, the Christian altar was placed inside the church. Whenever possible, relics of saints and martyrs were put in or near the altar, and the deposition of relics was the most important aspect of the formal dedication of new churches. The location of the altar in the churches differed. While it was generally in or near the apse, it could also be in the middle of the nave. Accordingly, in some instances, the priest faced the congregation when at the altar, whereas in other churches he did not. Before long, however, the location of the altar and the posture of the priest when praying became important considerations, with the result that the priest officiated in front of the altar so that both he and the congregation faced east when praying.

Churches had a baptismal font, which had to be large enough to allow the immersion of adult candidates for baptism. At first, the baptismal font was not in the church itself, denoting that baptism marked one's entrance into the church. Placing the font inside the church began in the Middle Ages, though there were other arrangements, such as attaching a baptistery to a church or even having a separate building. The cathedral Santa Maria del Fiore in Florence is a medieval illustration of a church with a separate baptistery.

The front portal of the basilica included a narthex, or vestibule, meant for catechumens (members-in-process), who were not yet considered part of the congregation and therefore could not participate in the Eucharist. They needed a place to observe the worship service—and, one suspects, to mill around. Sometimes, a courtyard graced the outside of the narthex entrance, though that space had no liturgical significance.

From these beginnings developed the long history of Christian architecture. In the various forms it took through the centuries, three essential elements were always present: technical competence, cost of construction, and symbolic meaning. Each was important, though perhaps none more than the limitations set by technical competence. Medieval chronicles are full of accounts of the construction of churches where the exuberance of the builders exceeded their competence, with the result that the steeple, nave, or choir collapsed during construction, and the masons and the carpenters had to start all over again. Seeing the massive and grandiose structures of the Gothic cathedrals, not to mention their rich, even excessive, ornamentation in stone and glass, makes clear why the financial side of things was crucial, and why it took decades and centuries to complete the projects.

Above all, of course, there was the symbolism of what the church represented. The building was the place where the newborn was received into the church through baptism, where the mystery of the Mass was celebrated, where the departed were prepared for eternity. Naturally, different eras evoked different symbolic truths, but throughout, the edifice was taken to be a symbol of refuge, a fortress, a haven—and, indeed, a heaven. Churches were anticipations of heaven; after all, what function did the rites of the Christian community have other than to prepare the faithful for eternity and the heavenly abode?

Art was to be *ad majorem gloriam Dei*—to the greater glory of God. Whether in a village in Tuscany or in an imperial free city in Germany, the churches that were built also owed their existence to the invocation of God's glory. Indeed, once the edifice had been completed and squabbles over finances and prestige were largely resolved, it became an object of community pride and power. The cathedral of Speyer, whose construction began in the early eleventh century and was financed by Emperor Conrad II, was not only to be his final resting place but also a testimony to imperial power and authority. He did not live to see it completed.

The second period of church building took place in the early Middle Ages and featured the "Romanesque" style. Its beginnings lay roughly in the middle of the eleventh century, and for two hundred years this style dominated church architecture in France and Germany. There is no agreement as to the reason for the ubiquitous emergence of the Romanesque style other than the reality that by the eleventh century, medieval society had attained a measure of stability. Security had been achieved, and towns were beginning to emerge. Most surviving Romanesque churches were built in places that had a strong Christian presence, though churches built in the style are found all across Europe; there were regional stylistic variations, and the building materials reflected local resources.

From a distance, churches in the Romanesque style are easily taken to be forts or fortresses. The walls are massive, the exterior facades plain, the windows small. The edifice, with its heaviness, seems to hug the earth. Romanesque churches evoke the symbolism of heaven and God's house as places of refuge and security. Given the widespread insecurity and even lawlessness of the early Middle Ages, such symbolism was apt and meaningful. The features of the edifice—thick walls, round arches, sturdy columns, large towers—gave the building a clear form. Frequently, Romanesque churches have a regular, symmetrical outline, so that their overall appearance is one of simplicity, particularly when compared with the Gothic buildings of a later time.

But this simplicity was challenged by carefully chosen decorations. If , for example, sculptures of cows were put on the towers of the stylistically complex cathedral of Laon, France, with its four towers, this reflected the agricultural livelihood of the community. Indeed, the rich imagery of Romanesque churches suggests another, perhaps inadvertent, testimonial to the societal setting of the churches. Not only is the portrayal of Jesus on his Judgment Seat reminiscent of a feudal overlord, but secular themes, such as the four seasons or the signs of the zodiac, intrude prominently among the religious symbols.

Romanesque churches impress with the plainness and the simplicity of their interiors. Most Romanesque churches have three naves—one main and two side naves—separated by rows of massive columns. There is no ornamentation, the exception being the stone carvings on the capitals of the columns in the nave. It is on the capitals that the imagination of the stonemasons found expression. The Benedictine abbey church of Sainte-Marie-Madeleine in Vézelay, Burgundy, France, a UNESCO World Heritage site, is a splendid reminder of the massive grandeur of Romanesque architecture, with its exquisite imagery on the sculpted capitals in the nave and the complex vision of its tympanum.

It is the subsequent architectural style, the Gothic cathedral, however, that more than anything else epitomizes the European Christian tradition of faith. This was not always the case. The very term "Middle Ages" originally conjured up a disparaging judgment about an undistinguished era between and in the "middle" of two more important eras—antiquity and modernity. But such disparagement gave way to deep and profound appreciation, especially by the representatives of the Romantics of the early nineteenth century. They succeeded in sharing their exuberance about style and culture, which has very much been part of the perception of the

High Middle Ages (and the Gothic style) ever since. As noted, the label "Gothic" was a misnomer or a misunderstanding, for it suggested that the style was "strange" and "barbaric." It was coined by none other than the Italian Renaissance Humanist Giorgio Vasari, who saw the Gothic style as a fateful decline from the superb style of antiquity.

Gothic edifices made their appearance in the middle of the twelfth century in the region around Paris, and for four hundred years they dominated sacred as well as secular buildings. During those four centuries, the Gothic style underwent a dynamic development. The center of the style was found in France; the cathedrals of Amiens, Sens, Bourges, and Chartres are classic examples of the Gothic richness one can still find in France today despite the ravages that devastated large parts of the country in two world wars.

The Gothic style has several telling features that include cross-rib vaults, high walls, and large windows. Romanesque churches had featured massive, solid walls with small windows. Now the builders turned the walls into a symphony of columns, which carried the weight of the roof. Large windows, with or without colorful glass paintings, gave lightness to the interior of the structures in a way that had been impossible for Romanesque builders. As a rule, Gothic churches also feature a rosette window above their main western portal. These churches emphasized verticality. The naves of Gothic churches were staggering in their heights, making the worshipers' glance dramatically more upwardly directed than in Romanesque churches. Little by little, Gothic builders had learned how to build closer to the heavens.

The lure of Gothic architecture, perhaps even of the other arts, lies in the ease with which one will find symbolism in just about every aspect of a Gothic church. Whether the builders of these churches were always cognizant of such symbolism and were committed to embracing it is, however, another question. By all odds, in some churches they undoubtedly sought to evoke meaningful symbolism; in others, they merely followed routine.

The cathedral of Chartres, France, is a wonderful illustration of the use of symbols in order to make the edifice a teaching tool. Sited on an east-west axis, it has the worshipers facing east—the direction not only of the rising sun, which brings light into the world, but also the direction of Jerusalem, the heart of the faith. The east-west axis of the nave meant that that the north facade lay in relative darkness: thus, its windows depicted Old Testament scenes and figures who did not enjoy the knowledge of the whole truth, while the south façade, basking in the unhindered brilliance of the sun, depicted the heroes of the New Testament.

In the French towns of Sens, Noyon, and Laon, the Gothic building vision came early, and their early style evolved into the "high" Gothic found in the cathedrals of Chartres, Reims, or Amiens. With increasing size and splendor, churches took on functions both sacred and profane. Churches were not only places where the Mass was celebrated, baptisms performed, and funerals conducted; they also were (at least until the thirteenth century) deeply secular places, serving as warehouses, stables, and places to conduct business. City halls first were built in the course of the thirteenth century, and until that time churches were used as formal and informal gathering places, where the citizens met to discuss communal issues or transact business. Things could easily become very secular: in Strassburg, for example, the city council had to decide on one occasion whether prostitutes could be allowed to meander in the side aisles of the cathedral offering their services.

Nonetheless, the sacred space in a church was clearly marked, for screens or banisters separated the sanctuary and the altar from the openness of the nave. Since pews did not come into use until in the sixteenth century (the celebration of the Mass hardly took any time, in contrast to the hour-long sermons in Protestantism), the nave was wide open—as one can see in seventeenth-century Dutch paintings of church interiors. Moreover, reverential quiet and cleanliness were not considered core values.

In the later Middle Ages, the religious commitment and faith of the well-to-do citizens of a community found expression in their financing of municipal churches, often in outright competition with the bishop's church, the cathedral. In the northwest German town of Münster—infamous in the time of the Reformation for its brief acceptance of Anabaptist rule—the guilds made possible the construction of the Saint Lamberti Church within a stone's throw of the church of the bishop, the cathedral dedicated to the Apostle Paul. This citizen's church was meant as a manifestation of independent civic power and authority, not of the bishop but of the artisans and merchants of the town.

By the late sixteenth century a new style was making its appearance in Europe, notably in countries whose formal allegiance had remained Catholic. The Baroque style, increasingly prominent between 1575 and 1770, has often been described as the style of the Catholic Counter–Reformation. The connection between this flamboyant and brilliant architectural and artistic style and the reassured vitality of the church is obvious.

In Baroque architecture, the complex Gothic and the classicist Renaissance style gave way to myriad complex architectural expressions—cupolas, pillars, convex and concave lines—and of colors that evoked sensuous responses of power and vibrancy. Sculpture, painting, and architecture converged brilliantly in Baroque churches to appeal to the viewer's senses. But the sumptuousness that Baroque churches offered the worshiper was make-believe. To be sure, the brilliance of the colors was real, but the marble columns and the artfully draped red velvet cloth hanging loosely over the balustrades, so impressive in their richness and splendor, were in fact molded of plaster. The worshiper's senses absorbed this splendor of vibrant color and lavish gold in eager anticipation of the future kingdom of heaven. Yet what was seen with one's eyes was anything but real, and in this way, Baroque church decoration served as a poignant reminder that this world, no matter how overwhelming to our senses, is but a vague anticipation of the real world to come.

Relatively few churches were built in the eighteenth century—even church construction reaches a saturation point. But what was built, renovated, or improved followed the classical style then in vogue. "Classical" referred in this case to classical antiquity, so that ancient buildings became the templates for new construction. In their exterior, classical churches such as the Pantheon (formerly the Church of Saint Geneviève) in Paris or Saint Martin-in-the-Fields in London resembled ancient Greek temples. This style of eighteenth-century church building cannot be easily related to themes prevailing in theology at the time unless one sees the heavy wave of secular influences as a testimonial to the novel Deist and Enlightenment reinterpretation of the Christian faith as the universal religion of nature. La Madeleine in Paris, whose construction began in 1777, in its appearance a Greek temple, tellingly became a "general" temple ("of Glory") during the time of Napoleon. In England, the churches and chapels built by the nonconformists, such as Baptists, Congregationalists, and Methodists, adopted the classicist style, undoubtedly to draw a visible distinction to the Anglican parish churches, and to emphasize simplicity of form.

Then came the nineteenth century, and new churches rose up all over Europe in large numbers. It was a century of incessant church construction. The social changes resulting from the Industrial Revolution triggered massive population shifts from rural areas to the cities, which called for building churches in the burgeoning suburban areas of the emerging industrial centers. More churches were built in England in the nineteenth century than in any other century. Since even modern methods of construction required time for completion, time lags were inevitable and meant that working-class suburbs remained without neighborhood churches for lengthy periods.

The architectural styles of the nineteenth century ranged widely, but they mainly imitated the Romanesque and Gothic styles, and thus they were labeled "neo-Romanesque" and "neo-Gothic." There seemed to be good reason to evoke the splendor of medieval Christianity: the Middle Ages were understood by many to have been an age of faith, and the Gothic churches and cathedrals the material manifestations of Christian ideals. This medieval revival was undergirded by the assertion, made by theologians and architects throughout Europe, that the Gothic style was quintessentially Christian and, indeed, was the only proper style for churches.

The churches of the Gothic revival include the chapel of Keble College in Oxford and Saint Patrick's Cathedral in New York City, built between 1858 and 1888. Saint Patrick's Cathedral illustrates yet another aspect of late nineteenth and twentieth-century church building: churches, even magnificent ones, came to be overshadowed by the mammoth high-rise structures of modern cities. Saint Patrick's Cathedral is dwarfed by the gigantic skyscrapers of midtown Manhattan. The skylines of twenty-first-century cities are no longer dominated by magnificent spires attempting to reach heaven.

Little changed architecturally in the opening decades of the twentieth century. The churches built during that time (and until the years after World War I) followed traditional, mainly neo-Gothic lines. It was not until the middle of the century that sacred architecture in Europe and North America began to reject historical styles and brought new modern visions of bewildering diversity. An interesting illustration is the Catholic cathedral in Liverpool, England, in which the pointed verticality of traditional Gothic structures was given a modern, abstract turn, quite in contrast to the neo-Gothic Anglican cathedral. Some of the churches built at that time have become famous for their architecture—Antoni Gaudí's Church of the Holy Family in Barcelona, Spain, for example, or Le Corbusier's chapel at Ronchamp, France. In the latter, all traditional symbolism is done away with and curved walls as well as irregularly placed windows dominate. The best known example in North America may well be the Crystal Cathedral near Los Angeles, a work of the architect Philip Johnson. The "cathedral," the sanctuary of an evangelical, nondenominational megachurch, is a symphony of glass and steel.

A more recent trend in church building, certainly in North America, is that the new church architecture no longer focuses on the proclamation of Scripture and the celebration of the sacraments but instead aims to provide space for the Christian "community." This was anticipated in the late nineteenth century when the church building proper was only part of a larger complex that included a classroom building as well as social space. In evangelical churches of North America, this emphasis on community has brought additional structures, building complexes reminiscent of arts centers and fitness gyms, the incorporation of "Family Christian Life Centers" complete with basketball courts, as well as church souvenir stores, coffeehouses, and Laundromats (if the church is located near a college campus).

In the southern United States, twentieth-century churches have been constructed in traditional architectural styles, particularly the red-brick Georgian colonial style so popular in the American South.

CHRONOLOGY OF THE CHRISTIAN RELIGION

Note: Not all of the personages and events listed here are mentioned in the text.

64	Emperor Nero persecutes Christians; the Apostles Peter and Paul suffer martyrdom
81	Emperor Domitian persecutes Jews and Christians
98	Emperor Trajan establishes policy for how Christians should be treated
107	Martyrdom of Ignatius
115	Irenaeus born
130	Conversion of Justin Martyr
144	Marcion rejects the Hebrew Scriptures (Old Testament) and is expelled from the Christian congregation in Rome
150	Clement of Alexandria born
156	Montanism
160	Tertullian born
165	Justin martyred
185	Origen born
200	Irenaeus martyred
216	Mani, founder of Manichaeism, born
222	Tertullian dies

251	Antony, key figure in Western monasticism, born
253	Origen dies
263	Eusebius of Caesarea, first historian of the Christian religion, born
284	Persecutions under Emperor Diocletian
286	Pachomius, first cenobite (communal) monk, born
297/ 300	Athanasius born
305	End of the Diocletian persecution
310	Apollinaris born
312	Constantine defeats Maxentius in the battle of Milvian Bridge and becomes undisputed Roman emperor
313	*Edict of Milan* gives equal rights to Christian religion
311– 15	Donatist controversy
325	Council of Nicea condemns Arianism
328	Athanasius becomes bishop of Alexandria
328	Constantine revokes condemnation of Arius
340	Eusebius of Caesarea dies

345	John Chrysostom born
347	Jerome born
354	Augustine born
361–63	Persecution under Emperor Julian the Apostate
369	Pelagius born
373	Athanasius dies
379–95	Emperor Theodosius; Christianity becomes the official religion of the Roman Empire
381	Council of Constantinople affirms modified creed of Council of Nicea
382	Council of Rome affirms the authority of the New Testament canon
386	Conversion of Augustine
390	Pope Leo the Great born
395	Augustine becomes bishop of Hippo
411	Pelagian controversy
451	Council of Chalcedon affirms Nicene creed and full humanity of Jesus; beginnings of Monophysite controversy
480	Benedict of Nursia born

540	Gregory the Great born
545	Benedict of Nursia dies
560	Isidore of Seville born
590	Gregory the Great elected pope
604	Gregory the Great dies
622	Mohammed's flight from Mecca to Medina; the beginning of Islam
635	Nestorian Christians reach India
675	John of Damascus born
680	Boniface born
909	Founding of Cluny monastery
988	Christianity made formal religion in Russia
1014	*Filioque* ("and from the Son") inserted into the Nicene Creed in the Western church
1033	Anselm born
1054	Metropolitan of Constantinople is excommunicated by Pope Leo IX; division of Eastern and Western churches
1076	Pope Gregory VII excommunicates Emperor Henry IV

1077	Investiture controversy
1090	Bernard of Clairvaux born
1095	The First Crusade
1100	Peter Lombard born
1109	Anselm dies
1142	Peter Abelard dies
1145	The Second Crusade
1153	Bernard of Clairvaux dies
1181/82	Francis of Assisi born
1184	Waldensians, followers of Peter Waldo, declared heretical
1188	The Third Crusade
1204	The Fourth Crusade; Constantinople sacked by crusaders
1209	Pope Innocent III proclaims a "crusade" against the Waldensians
1209	Order of Friars Minor (Franciscans)
1212	The Children's Crusade

1215	Fourth Lateran Council requires annual Communion and promulgates doctrine of transubstantiation
1215	Order of Preachers (Dominicans)
1217	The Fifth Crusade
1225	Thomas Aquinas born
1226	Francis of Assisi dies
1228	The Sixth Crusade
1249	The Seventh Crusade
1309–77	The "Babylonian Captivity of the Church"; rival papacy moves to Avignon, France
1320	John Wycliffe born
1369	Jan Hus born
1377	End of the "Babylonian Captivity"
1378	Schism of the Western church begins; Pope Gregory XI returns the papacy to Rome
1380	Thomas à Kempis, author of *The Imitation of Christ*, born
1381	Wycliffe suspected of involvement with the English peasants' revolt, and banished from Oxford
1384	Wycliffe dies

1414	Council of Constance condemns Wycliffe, burns Jan Hus
1417	The Council of Constance deposes both popes and elects a new one, ending the Schism in the Western church
1483	Martin Luther born
1492	Muslims expelled from Spain
1497	Philip Melanchthon born
1498	Savonarola burned in Florence
1507	Luther ordained priest
1509	Henry VIII becomes king of England
1509	John Calvin born
1513	Pope Leo X elected
1517	Luther posts *Ninety-five Theses*
1519	Charles elected emperor of the Holy Roman Empire; Leipzig Disputation
1521	Luther excommunicated
1521	Diet of Worms declares Luther a political outlaw
1521	Ignatius of Loyola wounded

1524–25	German Peasants' War
1525	Rise of Anabaptism in Zurich
1526	Diet at Speyer suspends Edict of Worms
1529	Diet at Speyer reintroduces the Edict of Worms; reformers called "Protestants"
1529	The Colloquy of Marburg
1530	Diet of Augsburg; Lutheran Augsburg Confession
1531	Huldrych Zwingli dies in battle at Kappel
1534	Parliament in England declares king "the only supreme head in earth of the Church of England"
1534/35	Anabaptist rule in Münster, Germany
1535	Dissolution of the monasteries in England
1536	Erasmus dies; Calvin arrives in Geneva
1536	Menno Simons emerges as leader of the Anabaptists in north Germany
1536	William Tyndale burned at the stake
1536	Calvin's *Institutes of the Christian Religion*
1539	Act of Six Articles in England

1540	Society of Jesus is approved
1541	Calvin returns to Geneva
1545	The Council of Trent opens
1546	Luther dies
1547	Edward VI becomes king of England
1549	*Consensus Tigurinus*, Zwinglians and Calvinists to agreement on Communion
1549	*Book of Common Prayer* in England
1552	New edition of the *Book of Common Prayer*
1553	Forty-two Articles in England
1553	Mary Tudor succeeds to English throne; Marian persecutions; Servetus burned in Geneva
1555	Peace of Augsburg
1555	Abdication of Emperor Charles V
1556	Ignatius of Loyola dies
1558	Elizabeth succeeds Mary as queen of England
1559	The *Act of Uniformity* makes the 1559 *Book of Common Prayer* the liturgical standard in the Church of England

1560	Jacob Arminius born
1560	Scottish Parliament approves the "Scots Confession," Scotland turns Protestant
1561	Menno Simons dies
1562	First French War of Religion
1563	Final sessions of the Council of Trent
1564	Calvin dies
1567	Vestments controversy, Puritan opposition to 1559 settlement of religion
1571	The *Thirty-nine Articles* approved in England
1572	John Knox dies
1572	Massacre of Saint Bartholomew's Day
1580	(Lutheran) *Book of Concord*
1582	Teresa of Avila dies
1596	René Descartes born
1598	Edict of Nantes promulgated
1604	King James meets with Puritans at Hampton Court

1605	Racovian Catechism
1609	Jacob Arminius dies
1611	The King James (or Authorized) Version of the Bible
1612	The first Baptist congregation established
1618 –19	The Synod of Dort
1620	Plymouth Colony established by English Puritans
1623	Blaise Pascal born
1630	John Winthrop and others migrate to America
1632	John Locke born
1633	The *Book of Sports* reissued
1640	Parliament establishes Presbyterianism in England
1642	Civil War in England begins
1646	Westminster Confession
1647	George Fox establishes the Religious Society of Friends (Quakers)
1654	Conversion of Pascal

1658	Oliver Cromwell dies
1660	Charles II king of England
1661–63	John Eliot publishes the Bible in Algonquin, a Native American language
1662	Pascal dies
1670	John Toland born
1675	Philip Jakob Spener's *Pia Desideria*
1685	Edict of Nantes is revoked
1685	Johann Sebastian Bach born
1695	August Hermann Francke establishes the Pietist "foundations" at Halle, Germany
1703	Jonathan Edwards born
1703	John Wesley born
1707	Charles Wesley born
1734–37	The Great Awakening in New England
1736	Joseph Butler's *The Analogy of Religion, Natural and Revealed*
1738	John Wesley's Aldersgate experience

1759	William Wilberforce born
1761	William Carey born
1770	George Whitefield dies
ca. 1773–75	First African American Baptist church in America at Silver Bluff, South Carolina
1781	"The Countess of Huntingdon's Connexion" established
1784	Thomas Coke, first North American Methodist bishop
1784	Christmas Conference of Methodists in Baltimore
1792	Particular Baptist Society for Propagating the Gospel amongst the Heathen established
1799	Church Missionary Society founded
1799	Friedrich Schleiermacher's *On Religion: Speeches to Its Cultured Despisers*
1800	First camp meeting in Kentucky
1801	William Carey's Bengali New Testament
1813	David Livingston born
1816	African Methodist Episcopal Church founded
1821 –22	Friedrich Schleiermacher's *The Christian Faith*

1824	Charles Finney revivals; the Second Great Awakening
1830	Book of Mormon; founding of the (Mormon) Church of Jesus Christ of Latter-day Saints
1833	The Oxford Movement begins
1834	William Carey dies
1835	David Friedrich Strauss publishes *The Life of Jesus Critically Examined*
1854	Roman Catholic Doctrine of Mary's Immaculate Conception
1855	Søren Kierkegaard dies
1859	Charles Darwin *Origin of Species*
1861	Walter Rauschenbusch born
1864	Catholic *Syllabus of Errors*
1870	First Vatican Council; promulgation of dogma of papal infallibility
1873	David Livingston dies
1879	John Henry Newman elevated to cardinal
1884	Bible Student Movement (later Jehovah's Witnesses) established
1886	Karl Barth born

1890	John Henry Newman dies
1899	Dwight L. Moody dies
1900	Adolf von Harnack's *What Is Christianity?*
1906	Dietrich Bonhoeffer born
1909	Scofield Reference Bible
1910	Edinburgh Missionary Conference
1919	Karl Barth's Romans Commentary
1925	Scopes Monkey Trial over evolution
1930	Adolf von Harnack dies
1934	Barmen Declaration of German Protestants
1939	Pope Pius XII
1940	Taizé (France) ecumenical community founded
1941	Reinhold Niebuhr, *The Nature and Destiny of Man*
1945	Dietrich Bonhoeffer executed
1948	World Council of Churches established

1950	Roman Catholic Doctrine of Mary's Bodily Assumption into Heaven
1958	Pope John XXIII (Angelo Giuseppe Roncalli)
1961	Michael Ramsey becomes archbishop of Canterbury
1962–65	Second Vatican Council
1963	C. S. Lewis dies
1968	Karl Barth dies
1968	Liberation Theology
1978	Pope John Paul II (Karol Józef Wojtyla)
2000	Lutherans and Roman Catholics agree on a common statement about justification
2005	Pope Benedict XVI (Joseph Ratzinger)

GLOSSARY OF TERMS

Allegory	Finding the meaning of a text not in its literal form, by "symbolic" sense
Apostasy	Falling away from the true faith
Asceticism	The understanding that in order to be spiritually committed one must negate physical and bodily needs
Atonement	The teaching of the significance of the life and death of Jesus for the reconciliation of God and humankind
Baptism	The Christian practice of initiation
Benefice	Certain property destined for the support of clergy, or a spiritual office
Canon	The sum of the New Testament writings; also, the pronouncements of a council
Canon Law	The legal code of the Roman Catholic Church and other churches
Catechism	From the Greek, meaning "to instruct"; a primer on the basics of the faith
Cenobitic Monasticism	Monks living in community, rather than in solitude
Christology	The teaching of the life and work of Jesus
Church Fathers	The theologians of the church in Late Antiquity
Coptic	The native Christian church in Egypt. From New Latin Coptus, Cophtus, ultimately referring to Egypt
Council	Gathering of bishops to discuss faith and life of the church
Denomination	A grouping with particular traditions and beliefs
Dispensationalism	A method of interpreting salvation history, dividing God's dealings with humankind into seven stages or dispensations
Ebionites	Jewish Christians who affirmed the continued observation of the Law
Eschatology	Teaching concerning the End Times
Eucharist	Literally "Thanksgiving," the Lord's Supper or Communion

351

Excommunication	Legal action by a church body to sever ties with an individual for reasons of heresy
Fundamentalism	Conservative theological reaction against liberal, nineteenth-century Protestantism
Iconoclasts	Opponents and destroyers of religious art
Icons	Images of Jesus, Mary, and saints as devotional guides
Mendicant orders	Monastic orders in the Catholic Church that rely on begging or on donations
Metropolitan	Diocesan bishop or archbishop of the major city of a historical Roman province, ecclesiastical province, or regional capital
Neo-Orthodoxy (also Dialectic Theology)	A theological movement gathering importance in the 1930s and 1940s, which affirmed traditional Christian tenets and, in particular, rejected any human ability to know God apart from divine revelation
Pope	Bishop of Rome, first of the bishops, thus head of the Roman Catholic Church
Predestination	Teaching that God has predestined the eternal destiny of each human
Revelation	The last book of the New Testament; also the notion of divine self-manifestation
Sacraments	Vehicles of grace; the Catholic Church affirms seven
Scholasticism	The philosophical and theological tool that dominated the Middle Ages; a tool and method for finding the answer to a question or for resolving contradictions; best known for its application in medieval theology
Simony	Obtaining church positions in return for payments of money
Soteriology	The teaching of the redemption of humankind
Trinity	The teaching of the one Godhead, consisting of three persons: Father, Son, and Holy Spirit

BIBLIOGRAPHY

General Surveys and Narratives

Bettenson, Henry. *Documents of the Christian Church*. London: Oxford University Press, 1967.

Bromiley, G. W., ed. and trans. *The Library of Christian Classics*. 20 vols. Philadelphia: Westminster, 1953–69.

Cook, Chris, ed. *The Routledge Companion to Christian History*. New York: Routledge, 2008.

Davies, Noel, and Martin Conway. *World Christianity in the Twentieth Century: A Reader*. London: SCM, 2008.

Duffy, Eamon. *Saints and Sinners: A History of the Popes*. New Haven, Conn.: Yale University Press, 1997.

Gerhart, Mary, and Fabian E. Udoh, eds. *A Christianity Reader*. Chicago: University of Chicago Press, 2007.

Gonzalez, Justo. *Church History: An Essential Guide*. Nashville: Abingdon Press, 1996.

Hillerbrand, Hans J., ed. *Christianity: An Illustrated History*. London: Duncan Baird, 2008.

Marty, Martin E. *The Christian World: A Global History*. New York: Modern Library, 2007.

Norman, Edward R., ed. *The House of God: Church Architecture, Style, and History*. London: Thames & Hudson, 1990.

Pelican, Jaroslav. *Creeds and Confessions in the Christian Tradition*. 3 vols. New Haven, Conn.: Yale University Press, 2005.

Petry, Ray C., and Clyde Manschreck, eds. *History of Christianity*. 2 vols. Englewood Cliffs, N.J.: Prentice-Hall, 1962.

For Early Christianity

Bokenkotter, Thomas. *A Concise History of the Catholic Church*. Rev. ed. Garden City, N.Y.: Image, 1979.

Bredero, Adriaan H. *Christendom and Christianity in the Middle Ages*. Grand Rapids: Eerdmans, 1994.

Brown, Peter. *The Rise of Western Christendom*. Malden, Mass.: Blackwell, 2003.

Frend, W. H. C. *The Rise of Christianity*. Philadelphia: Fortress, 1984.

O'Donnell, J. J. *Augustine: A New Biography*. New York: HarperCollins, 2005.

Ozment, Steven. *The Age of Reform (1250–1550): An Intellectual and Religious History of Late Medieval and Reformation Europe.* New Haven, Conn.: Yale University Press, 1980.

Pelikan, Jaroslav. *The Emergence of the Christian Tradition (100–600).* Chicago: University of Chicago Press, 1971.

Sanders, E. P. *The Historical Figure of Jesus.* New York: Penguin, 1996.

Tellenbach, Gerd. *The Church in Western Europe from the Tenth to the Early Twelfth Century.* Cambridge: Cambridge University Press, 1993.

Ware, Timothy. *The Orthodox Church.* New York: Pelikan, 1993.

Wilken, Robert L. *The Christians as the Romans Saw Them.* New Haven, Conn.: Yale University Press, 1984.

For the Medieval Church

Cunningham, Mary, and Elizabeth Theokritoff, eds. *The Cambridge Companion to Orthodox Christian Theology.* Cambridge: Cambridge University Press, 2008.

Egan, Harvey D. *Christian Mysticism.* Collegeville, Minn.: Liturgical Press, 1991.

Norman, Edward R. *The Roman Catholic Church: An Illustrated History.* Berkeley and Los Angeles: University of California Press, 2007.

Riley-Smith, Jonathan. *The Crusades: A Short History.* New Haven, Conn.: Yale University Press, 1987.

For the Reformation of the Sixteenth Century

Bainton, Roland H. *Here I Stand: A Life of Martin Luther.* Nashville: Abingdon Press, 1990.

Benedict, Philip. *Christ's Church Purely Reformed: A Social History of Calvinism.* New Haven, Conn.: Yale University Press, 2002.

Bernard, G. W., *The King's Reformation: Henry VIII and the Remaking of the English Church.* New Haven, Conn.: Yale University Press, 2005.

Davidson, N. S. *The Counter-Reformation.* Oxford: Blackwell, 1987.

Dickens, A. G. *The English Reformation.* University Park, Pa.: Pennsylvania State University Press, 1991.

Duffy, Eamon. *The Stripping of the Altars: Traditional Religion in England c. 1400–c. 1580.* New Haven, Conn.: Yale University Press, 1992.

Gordon, Bruce. *Calvin.* New Haven, Conn.: Yale University Press, 2009.

Hillerbrand, Hans J. *The Division of Christendom.* Louisville: Westminster John Knox, 2007.

————, ed. *Encyclopedia of Protestantism*. 4 vols. New York: Routledge, 2004.

Matheson, Peter. *Reformation Christianity*. Minneapolis: Fortress, 2007.

O'Malley, John. *The First Jesuits*. Cambridge, Mass.: Harvard University Press, 1993.

Williams, George H. *The Radical Reformation*. 3rd ed. Kirksville, Mo.: Sixteenth Century Journal Publishers, 1992.

For Christianity in the Modern Period

Berryman, Phillip. *Liberation Theology: Essential Facts about the Revolutionary Movement in Latin America—and Beyond*. Philadelphia: Temple University Press, 1987.

Bethge, Eberhard. *Dietrich Bonhoeffer*. Minneapolis: Augsburg Fortress, 2000.

Blaut, J. M. *1492: The Debate on Colonialism, Eurocentrism, and History*. Trenton, N.J.: Africa World Press, 1992.

Cone, James. *A Black Theology of Liberation*. Maryknoll, N.Y.: Orbis, 1990.

Craig, Gerald. *The Church and the Age of Reason*. Harmondsworth, U.K.: Penguin, 1974.

Knight, Douglas. *Methods of Biblical Interpretation*. Nashville: Abingdon Press, 2004.

Livingston, James C. *Modern Christian Thought*. Upper Saddle River, N.J.: Prentice-Hall, 2000.

Neill, Stephen. *A History of Christian Missions*. New York: Penguin, 1986.

Rowland, Christopher, ed. *The Cambridge Companion to Liberation Theology*. 2nd ed. Cambridge: Cambridge University Press, 2007.

Shortt, Rupert. *God's Advocates: Christian Thinkers in Conversation*. London: Darton, Longman and Todd, 2005.

For Christianity in North America

Ahlstrom, Sydney E. *A Religious History of the American People*. 2 vols. Garden City, N.Y.: Image, 1975.

Bowden, Henry W., and P. C. Kemeny, eds. *American Church History: A Reader*. Nashville: Abingdon Press, 1998.

Marsden, George M. *Fundamentalism and American Culture 1875–1925*. 2nd ed. New York: Oxford University Press, 2006.

Marty, Martin E. *Modern American Religion*. 3 vols. Chicago: University of Chicago Press, 1986–96.

For Christianity in the Global Era

Bednarowski, Mary Farrell, ed. *Twentieth-Century Global Christianity*. Minneapolis: Fortress, 2008.

Jenkins, Philip. *The Next Christendom: The Coming of Global Christianity*. Revised and expanded ed. Oxford: Oxford University Press, 2007.

Marty, Martin E. *The Christian World: A Global History*. New York: Modern Library, 2007.

Noll, Mark A. *The New Shape of World Christianity*. Downers Grove, Ill.: IVP Academic, 2009.

Audiovisual Materials

Amazing Grace. Beverly Hills: Twentieth Century Fox Home Entertainment, 2007. The story of William Wilberforce and the prohibition of the slave trade in early nineteenth-century England.

The Apostle. Universal City, Calif.: Universal Home Video, ca. 1998. A Texas preacher on the run from the law establishes his own church.

Becket. Orland Park, Ill.: MPI Home Video, 2007. The encounter between the English king Henry II and Thomas Becket, archbishop of Canterbury.

Black Robe. Toronto: Alliance Communications Corporation, 1991. The encounter between a seventeenth-century Jesuit missionary and Native Americans.

Bonhoeffer: Agent of Grace. Worcester, Pa.: Gateway Films, 2000. The story of the German theologian during the Nazi regime.

Brother Sun, Sister Moon. Hollywood: Paramount [Home Video], 2003. The story of Saint Francis of Assisi.

Cromwell. Beverly Hills: Sony Pictures Home Entertainment, 1970. The story of the seventeenth-century Puritan leader.

Diary of a Country Priest. New York: Criterion Collection, ca. 2004. An idealistic Catholic priest in his first parish.

The Gospel of John. Worcester, Pa.: Gateway Films, 2003. A faithful rendering of the Fourth Gospel.

John Wesley. Worcester, Pa.: Vision Video, 2004. The story of the founder of Methodism.

Kingdom of Heaven. Beverly Hills: 20th Century Fox Home Entertainment, 2005. A film about the Crusades.

Luther. Los Angeles, Calif.: MGM Home Entertainment, 2004. A biographical portrait.

A Man for All Seasons. Culver City, Calif.: Columbia TriStar Home Video, ca. 1998. The story of Thomas More.

The Mission. Burbank, Calif.: Warner Home Video, 2003. A seventeenth-century Jesuit missionary in South America.

Of Gods and Men. Paris: WhyNot Productions, 2010. The semi-historical story of eight Trappist monks caught in the maelstrom of Algerian terrorists.

The Scarlet Letter. Beverly Hills: Hollywood Pictures, 1995. A literary adaptation of Hawthorne's novel about Puritans and Quakers.

Shadowlands. New York: HBO Home Video, 1998. The story of the Christian apologist C. S. Lewis (1898–1963).

The Song of Bernadette. Beverly Hills: Twentieth Century Fox Home Entertainment. 2003. The story of the Marian apparition of Bernadette Soubirous in Lourdes, France, in 1858.

Internet Resources

Not surprisingly, the Internet offers an increasing wealth of materials pertaining to the history of the Christian faith. Some caution is necessary, since a great many materials, for example, the *Catholic Encyclopedia*, are outdated and no longer reflect the current scholarly consensus. By the same token, just about every major figure in Christian history has multiple Internet entries. Note the following:

Christian Classics Ethereal Library. Virtually comprehensive English translations of the "church fathers" together with a sprinkling of more recent texts, www.ccel.org.

The Internet Medieval Sourcebook, www.fordham.edu/halsall/sbook.html.

The Reformation Sourcebook. Major primary texts of the Reformation, www.fordham.edu/halsall/mod/modsbook02.html#Protestant Reformation.

SELECTIONS FROM CHRISTIAN SOURCES

Marcion's God (ca. 110)

Listen, ye sinners; and you who have not yet come to this. Hear that you may attain to such understanding! A better god has been discovered, who never takes offence, is never angry, never inflicts punishment, who has prepared no fire in hell, no gnashing of teeth in the outer darkness! He is purely and simply good. He forbids all delinquency, but only in word. He is in you, if you are willing to pay him homage; for the sake of appearances that you may seem to honor God; for your fear he does not want. They have no fear of their god at all. They say it is only a bad man who will be feared, a good man will be loved. Foolish man, do you say that he whom you call Lord ought not to be feared, whilst the very title you give him indicates a power which must itself be feared?
—Tertullian, *Adversus Marcionem*, vol. 3 of *Ante-Nicene Fathers: Translations of the Writings of the Fathers down to A.D. 325* (Grand Rapids: Eerdmans, 1978–1981), 292–93.

The Witness of Justin Martyr (165)

Rusticus, the prefect, said, "What kind of doctrines do you profess?" Justin said, "I have endeavored to learn all doctrines; but I finally accepted the true doctrines, those of the Christians, even though they do not please those who hold false opinions." Rusticus the prefect said, "Are those the doctrines that please you, you utterly wretched man?" Justin said, "Yes, since I adhere to them with right dogma." Rusticus the prefect said, "What is the dogma?" Justin said, "That according to which we worship the God of the Christians, whom we reckon to be one from the beginning, the maker and fashioner of the whole creation, visible and invisible; and the Lord Jesus Christ, the Son of God, who had also been preached beforehand by the prophets as about to be present with the race of men, the herald of salvation and teacher of good disciples. And I, being a man, think that what I can say is insignificant in comparison with His boundless divinity, acknowledging a certain prophetic power, since it was prophesied concerning Him of whom now I say that He is the Son of God. For I know that of old the prophets foretold his appearance among men."

Rusticus the prefect said, "Where do you assemble?" Justin said, "Where each one chooses and can: for do you fancy that we all meet in the same place? Not so; because the God of the Christians is not circumscribed by place; but being invisible, fills heaven and earth, and everywhere is worshiped and glorified by the faithful." Rusticus the prefect said, "Tell me where you assemble, or into what place do you collect your followers?" Justin said, "I live above Martinus, at the Timiotinian bath, and during the whole time (and I am now living in Rome for the second time) I am unaware of any other meeting than his. And if anyone wished to come to me, I communicated to him the doctrines of truth." Rusticus said, "Are you not, then, a Christian?" Justin said, "Yes, I am a Christian." —Acta S. Justinii et sociorum, vol. 3 of Ante-Nicene Fathers: Translations of the Writings of the Fathers down to A.D. 325 (Grand Rapids: Eerdmans, 1978–1981), 305–6.

The Edict of Emperor Constantine (312)

When I, Constantine Augustus, and I, Licinius Augustus, met near Milan, and considered everything pertaining to the public good and security, we thought that, among other matters pertaining to the common good, the regulations concerning the worship of God surely ought to have priority, so that we might grant to Christians and to all others complete freedom to observe the religion which each preferred. Whence any Deity seated in the heavens may be propitious and graciously disposed to us and to all who are placed under our rule. With this wholesome counsel and honest stipulation we decided that no one should be denied the opportunity to give his heart to the observance of the Christian religion, or to that religion which he considers best for himself, so that the Supreme Deity, to whose worship we freely yield our hearts, may show in all things his customary favor and benevolence. Therefore, it has pleased us to remove all restrictions concerning Christians, which were previously communicated to you in official mandates. Anyone who wishes to observe the Christian religion may do so freely and openly, without any hindrance or molestation. We thought it fit to commend this fully to your care that you may know that we have given to Christians free and unrestricted opportunity of religious worship. When you see that this has been granted to them by us, you will know that we have also conceded to other religions the right of open and free observance of their religion for the sake of the peace in our time, that everyone may have the free opportunity to worship as he pleases.

—Lactantius, *De Mort. Persecutione*, vol. 4 of *Translations and Reprints from the Original Sources of European History* (Philadelphia: University of Pennsylvania, 1897), 29–30.

The Definition of Chalcedon (451)

Therefore, following the holy fathers, we all with one accord teach men to acknowledge one and the same Son, our Lord Jesus Christ, at once complete in Godhead and complete in manhood, truly God and truly man, consisting also of a reasonable soul and body; of one substance with the Father as regards his Godhead, and at the same time of one substance with us as regards his humanity; like us in all respects, apart from sin; as regards his Godhead, begotten of the Father before all ages, but yet as regards his manhood begotten, for us men and for our salvation, of Mary the Virgin, the Mother of God; one and the same Christ, Son, Lord, Only-begotten, recognized in two natures, without confusion, without change, without division, without separation; the distinction of natures being in no way removed by the union, but rather the characteristics of each nature preserved and coming together to form one person and subsistence, not as parted or separated into two persons, but one and the same Son and Only-begotten God the Word, Lord Jesus Christ, as the prophets from the beginning declared concerning him, and the Lord Jesus Christ himself taught us and the creed of the holy Fathers handed down to us.

—*The Seven Ecumenical Councils*, vol. 14 of *A Select Library of Nicene and Post-Nicene Fathers of the Christian Church*, series 2 (ed. Philip Schaff and Henry Wace; Grand Rapids: Eerdmans, 1952), 250.

Augustine. *Confessions* (397–98)

There arose a mighty storm, bringing a mighty shower of tears.... Solitude was suggested to me as fitter for the business of weeping; so I retired so far that even his [Alypius] presence could not be a burden to me. Thus was it then with me, and he perceived something of it; for something I suppose I had spoken, wherein the tones of my voice appeared choked with weeping, and so had risen up. He then remained where we were sitting, most extremely astonished. I cast myself down I know not how, under a certain fig-tree, giving full vent to my tears; and the floods of mine eyes gushed out an acceptable sacrifice to Thee. And, not indeed in these words, yet to this purpose, spoke I much unto Thee: and You, O Lord, how long? How long, Lord, wilt You be angry for ever?

Remember not our former iniquities, for I felt that I was held by them. I sent up these sorrowful words: How long, how long, "to-morrow, and tomorrow?" Why not now? Why not is there this hour an end to my uncleanness? So was I speaking and weeping in the most bitter contrition of my heart, when, lo! I heard from a neighboring house a voice, as of boy or girl, I know not, chanting, and oft repeating, "Take up and read; Take up and read." Instantly, my countenance altered, I began to think most intently whether children were wont in any kind of play to sing such words: nor could I remember ever to have heard the like. So checking the torrent of my tears, I arose; interpreting it to be no other than a command from God to open the book, and read the first chapter I should find. For I had heard of Antony, that coming in during the reading of the Gospel, he received the admonition, as if what was being read was spoken to him: Go, sell all that you hast, and give to the poor, and you shall have treasure in heaven, and come and follow me: and by such oracle he was forthwith converted unto Thee. Eagerly then I returned to the place where Alypius was sitting; for there had I laid the volume of the Apostle when I arose thence. I seized, opened, and in silence read that section on which my eyes first fell: Not in rioting and drunkenness, not in chambering and wantonness, not in strife and envying; but put you on the Lord Jesus Christ, and make not provision for the flesh, in concupiscence. No further would I read; nor needed I: for instantly at the end of this sentence, by a light as it were of serenity infused into my heart, all the darkness of doubt vanished away. Then putting my finger between, or some other mark, I shut the volume, and with a calmed countenance made it known to Alypius. And what was wrought in him, which I knew not, he thus showed me. He asked to see what I had read: I showed him; and he looked even further than I had read, and I knew not what followed.
—Augustine, *The Confessions of Saint Augustine* 8.12.29 (ed. Temple Scott; New York: E. P. Dutton; London: Grant Richards, 1900), 194–95.

Augustine. *The City of God* (411)

The glorious city of God is my theme in this work, which you, my dearest son Marcellinus, suggested, and which is due to you by my promise. I have undertaken its defense against those who prefer their own gods to the Founder of this city—a city surpassingly glorious, whether we view it as it still lives by faith in this fleeting course of time, and sojourns as a stranger in the midst of the ungodly, or as it shall dwell in the fixed stability of its eternal seat, which it now with patience waits for, expecting until "righteousness shall return unto judgment," Ps. 94:15, and it obtain, by virtue of its excellence, final victory and perfect peace. A great work this, and an arduous; but God is my helper....

In the previous book after beginning to speak of the city of God, to which I resolved, Heaven helping me, to devote this entire work, it was my first intention to reply to those who attribute the wars by which the world is devastated, especially the recent barbarian sack of Rome, to the religion of Christ. True enough; the Christian religion prohibits the offering of abominable sacrifices to demons. I pointed out that they ought to rather thank Christ, that for His name's sake the barbarians opened the largest churches as sanctuaries, contrary to all customs and laws of war. In many instances they showed such reverence to Christ, that not only His genuine servants, but even those who in their terror feigned themselves to be so, were exempted from all those hardships which by the custom of war may lawfully be inflicted. Then out of this there arose the question, why wicked and ungrateful men were permitted to share in these benefits; and why, too, the hardships and calamities of war were inflicted on the godly as well as on the ungodly. And in giving a suitably complete answer to this large question, I used considerable space, partly that I might relieve the anxieties which disturb many when they observe that the blessings of God, and the common and daily human casualties, fall to the lot of bad men and good without distinction; but mainly that I might minister some consolation to those holy and chaste women who were outraged by the enemy, in such a way as to shock their modesty, though not to sully their purity, and that I might preserve them from being ashamed of life, though they have no guilt to be ashamed of. I then spoke briefly against those who with a most shameless wantonness insult those poor Christians who were subjected to those calamities, and especially over those broken-hearted and humiliated, though chaste and holy women; these fellows themselves being most depraved and unmanly profligates, quite degenerate from the true Romans, whose famous deeds are abundantly recorded in history, and everywhere celebrated, but who have found in their descendants the greatest enemies of their glory. In truth, Rome, which was founded and grew through the labors of these ancient heroes, was more shamefully ruined by their descendants, even while its walls were still standing, than it is now when they are razed. For in this ruin fell stones and timbers; but in the ruin those profligates effected, there fell, not the mural, but the moral bulwarks and ornaments of the city, and their hearts burned with passions more destructive than the flames which consumed their houses. Thus I brought the first book to a close. And now I go on to speak of those calamities which that city itself, or its subject provinces, have suffered since its foundation; all of which they would equally have attributed to the Christian religion, if at that early period the doctrine of the gospel against their false and deceiving gods had been as widely and freely proclaimed as now. . . .

Accordingly, two cities have been formed by two loves: the earthly by the love of self, even to the contempt of God; the heavenly by the love of God, even to the contempt of self. The former, in a word, glories in itself, the latter in the Lord. . . . In the one, the princes and the nations it subdues are ruled by the love of ruling; in the other, the princes and the subjects serve one another in love, the latter obeying, while the former take thought for all. The one delights in its own strength, represented in the persons of its rulers; the other says to its God, "I will love You, O Lord, my strength. . . ." When these two cities began to run their course by a series of deaths and births, the citizen of this world was the first-born, and after him the stranger in this world, the citizen of the city of God, pre-destinated by grace, elected by grace, by grace a stranger below, and by grace a citizen above. By grace, for so far as regards himself he is sprung from the same mass, all of which is condemned in its origin: but God, like a potter (for this comparison is introduced by the apostle judiciously, and not without thought), of the same lump made one vessel to honor, another to dishonor.

—Augustine, *The City of God* preface, 2.2, 14.28; vol. 2 of *The Nicene and Post-Nicene Fathers*, series 1 (ed. Philip Schaff; Edinburgh: T&T Clark; Grand Rapids: Eerdmans, n.d.), 1, 23–24, 282–83.

Vincent of Lérins. *The Rule for Distinguishing the Truth of the Catholic Faith and Scriptures from Heretical Assumptions* (ca. 445)

But someone perhaps will ask: Since the canon of Scripture is complete, and sufficient of itself for everything, and more than sufficient, what need is there to join with it the authority of the Church's interpretation? For this reason: because of the depth of Holy Scripture, all do not accept it in one and the same sense. One understands its words in one way, another in another. It seems to be capable of as many interpretations as there are interpreters. . . .

Moreover, in the Catholic Church all possible care must be taken that we affirm the faith which has been believed everywhere, always, by all. For that is truly and in the strictest sense "Catholic," which, as the name itself and the reason of the matter express, comprehends all universally. This rule we shall observe if we follow universality, antiquity, consent. We shall follow universality if we confess that one faith to be true, which the whole Church throughout the world confesses; antiquity, if we in no wise depart from those interpretations which were manifestly held by our holy ancestors and fathers. Consent, in like manner, if in antiquity we adhere to the definitions and determinations of all, or at the least of almost all priests and doctors are interpreters. For Novatian expounds it one way, Sabellius another, Donatus another, Arius, Eunomius, Macedonius, another, Photinus, Apollinaris, Priscillian, another, Iovinian, Pelagius, Celestius, another, lastly, Nestorius another. Therefore, it is necessary, on account of so great intricacies of such several errors, that the rule for the right understanding of the prophets and the apostles should be framed in accordance with the standard of ecclesiastical and catholic interpretation.

—*Commonitorium*, vol. 11 of *A Select Library of Nicene and Post-Nicene Fathers of the Christian Church*, series 2 (ed. Philip Schaff and Henry Wace; Grand Rapids: Eerdmans, n.d.), 132.

Constitution of the Apostles (ca. 400)

Deacons stand near at hand, in close small girt garments, for they are like the leaders and managers of the vessel: let the laity sit on the other side, quietly and good order. And let women sit by themselves, also in silence. In the middle, let the reader stand upon some high place: let the books of Moses, Joshua, the son of Nun, of the Judges, and of the Kings and of Chronicles be read, and those written after the Israelites returned from the captivity; and besides these, songs of Job and of Solomon, and of the prophets. But when several lessons have been read, let others sing the hymns of David, and let them join at the conclusions of the verses. Afterwards let our Acts be read, and the letters of Paul, our fellow-worker, which he wrote the churches with the guidance of the Holy Spirit; and afterwards let a deacon presbyter read the Gospels, both those I have delivered to you, and those which Luke and Mark, Paul's fellow-workers received and left to you. And while the Gospel is read, let all the presbyters and deacons, and all the people, stand up in great silence; for it is written: "Be silent, and hear, O Israel."... In the next place, let the elders one by one exhort the people, and finally the bishop, as the leader. But if anyone be found sitting out of his place, let him be rebuked by the deacon, and be removed into the place proper for him. Let the young persons sit by themselves, if there is place for them; if not, let them stand. But let those that are already stricken in years sit in order. Let the younger women sit by themselves, if there is a place for them; if not, let them stand behind the women. Let the married women with children be by themselves; but let the virgins, the widows, and the elder women stand or sit in front of the rest; and let the deacon assign the places, that everyone who comes in may go to the proper place, and not sit at the entrance. In like manner, let the deacon oversee the people, that nobody whisper, slumber, laugh, nor nod; for in the church all ought to stand wisely soberly, and attentively, having their attention fixed upon the word of the Lord. After this, let all rise up with one mind, and looking towards the east, after the catechumens and penitents have left, pray to God eastward, who ascended up to the heaven of heavens to the east.

—*Constitutio apostolorum*, vol. 7 of *Ante-Nicene Fathers: Translations of the Writings of the Fathers down to A.D. 325* (Grand Rapids: Eerdmans, 1978), 421–22.

The Rule of Pachomius (d. 348)

Give each to eat and drink according to his strength; and give labors according to the strength of those eating, and forbid neither fasting nor eating. Appoint difficult labors to the stronger and those who eat, and the lighter and easy tasks to those who discipline themselves more and are weaker.

2. Make separate cells in the same place; and let three remain in a cell. But let the food for all be prepared in one house.

3. They may not sleep lying down, but having made seats built inclining backward let them place their bedding on them and sleep seated.

4. By night let them wear linen tunics, being girded about. Let each of them have a shaggy goatskin, made white. Without this let them neither eat nor sleep. When they go in unto the communion of the mysteries of Christ every Sabbath and Lord's Day, let them loose their girdles and put off the goatskin, and enter with only their long, hooded cloak. . . .

8. When they eat let them veil their faces, that one brother may not see another brother eating. They are not to speak while they eat; nor turn their eyes toward anything other than their dish or the table.

9. And he made it a rule that during the whole day they should offer twelve prayers; and at the time of lighting the lamps, twelve; and in the course of the night, twelve; and at the ninth hour, three; but when it seemed good for the whole company to eat, he directed that each group should first sing a psalm at each prayer.
—Palladius, *Historia Lausiaca* (Westminster, Md.: Newman, 1965), chap. 38.

John of Damascus. *On Holy Images* (ca. 730)

Now, as we are talking of images and worship, let us analyze the exact meaning of each. An image is a likeness of the original with a certain difference, for it is not an exact reproduction of the original. Thus, the Son is the living, substantial, unchangeable Image of the invisible God, bearing in Himself the whole Father, being in all things equal to Him, differing only in being begotten by the Father, who is the Begetter; the Son is begotten. The Father does not proceed from the Son, but the Son from the Father. It is through the Son, though not after Him, that He is what He is, the Father who generates. In God, too, there are representations and images of His future acts—that is to say, His counsel from all eternity, which is ever unchangeable. That which is divine is immutable; there is no change in Him, nor shadow of change.... In His counsels, God has noted and settled all that He would do, the unchanging future events before they came to pass. In the same way, a man who wished to build a house would first make and think out a plan. Again, visible things are images of invisible and intangible things, on which they throw a faint light. Holy Scripture clothes in figure God and the angels, and the same holy man explains why. When sensible things sufficiently render what is beyond sense, and give a form to what is intangible, a medium would be reckoned imperfect according to our standard, if it did not fully represent material vision, or if it required effort of mind. If, therefore, Holy Scripture, providing for our need, ever putting before us what is intangible, clothes it in flesh, does it not make an image of what is thus invested with our nature, and brought to the level of our desires, yet invisible? A certain conception through the senses thus takes place in the brain, which was not there before, and is transmitted to the judicial faculty, and added to the mental store. Gregory, who is so eloquent about God, says that the mind, which is set upon getting beyond corporeal things, is incapable of doing it. For the invisible things of God since the creation of the world are made visible through images. We see images in creation which remind us faintly of God, as when, for instance, we speak of the holy and adorable Trinity, imaged by the sun, or light, or burning rays, or by a running fountain, or a full river, or by the mind, speech, or the spirit within us, or by a rose tree, or a sprouting flower, or a sweet fragrance.

Again, an image is expressive of something in the future, mystically shadowing forth what is to happen. For instance, the ark represents the image of Our Lady, Mother of God, so does the staff and the earthen jar. The serpent brings before us Him who vanquished on the Cross the bite of the original serpent; the sea, water, and the cloud the grace of baptism. Again, things which have taken place are expressed by images for the remembrance either of a wonder, or an honor, or dishonor, or good or evil, to help those who look upon it in after times that we may avoid evils and imitate goodness. It is of two kinds, the written image in books, as when God had the law inscribed on tablets, and when He enjoined that the lives of holy men should be recorded and sensible memorials be preserved in remembrance; as, for instance, the earthen jar and the staff in the ark. So now we preserve in writing the images and the good deeds of the past. Either, therefore, take away images altogether and be out of harmony with God, who made these regulations, or receive them with the language and in the manner which befits them.

—*St. John of Damascene on Holy Images* (London: T. Baker, 1898), 98.

Pope Urban II, Call for a Military Expedition to the Holy Land (1095)

I, Urban, by the permission of God chief bishop and prelate over the whole world, have come to this place as an ambassador with a divine admonition to you, the servants of God. I prayed to find you as faithful and as zealous in the service of God as I had assumed you to be. And if there is in you any defect or lack of honesty contrary to God's law, with divine help I will do my best to remove it. For God has put you as stewards over his family to minister to it. Happy indeed will you be if God finds you faithful in your stewardship. You are called shepherds; see that you do not act as hirelings. But be true shepherds, with your crooks always in your hands. Do not fall asleep, but guard on all sides the flock committed to you. For according to the gospel you are the salt of the earth [Matt. 5:13].... But the man who applies this salt should be prudent, wise, modest, learned, peaceable, watchful, pious, just, equitable, and pure. For how can the ignorant teach others? How can the licentious make others modest? And how can the impure make others pure? If anyone hates peace, how can he make others peaceable? But first correct yourselves, in order that, free from blame, you may be able to correct those who are subject to you. If you wish to be the friends of God, gladly do the things which you know will please Him. In particular you must let all matters that pertain to the church be controlled by the law of the church. And be careful that simony does not take root among you, lest both those who buy and those who sell [church offices] be beaten with the scourges of the Lord through narrow streets and driven into the place of destruction and confusion. . . .

Although, O sons of God, you have promised more firmly than ever to keep the peace among yourselves and to preserve the rights of the church, there remains still important work for you to do. Freshly quickened by the divine correction, you must apply the vigor of your righteousness to another matter which concerns you as well as God. For your brethren who live in the east are in urgent need of your help, and you must hasten to give them the aid which has often been promised them. For, as the most of you have heard, the Turks and Arabs have attacked them and have conquered the territory of Romania [the Greek empire] as far west as the shore of the Mediterranean and the Hellespont, which is called the Arm of St. George. They have occupied more and more of the lands of those Christians, and have defeated them in seven battles. They have killed and captured many, and have destroyed the churches and devastated the empire. If you permit them to continue this with impurity, the faithful of God will be even more widely attacked by them. Therefore, I, or rather the Lord, beseech you as Christ's messengers to publish this everywhere and to persuade all people of whatever rank, foot-soldiers and knights, poor and rich, to carry aid promptly to those Christians and to destroy that vile race from the lands of our friends. I say this to those who are present, it is meant also for those who are absent. Moreover, Christ commands it.

All who die on the way, whether on land or on sea, or in battle against the pagans, shall have immediate remission of sins. This I grant them through the power of God with which I am invested. O what a disgrace if such a despised and base race, which worships demons, should conquer a people which has the faith of omnipotent God and is made glorious with the name of Christ! With what reproaches will the Lord overwhelm us if you do not aid those who, with us, profess the Christian religion! Let those who have been accustomed unjustly to wage private warfare against the faithful now go against the infidels and end with victory this war

which should have been begun long ago. Let those who have been rob-
bers, now become knights. Let those who have been fighting against their
brothers and relatives now fight in a proper way against the barbarians.
Let those who have been serving as mercenaries for small wages now
obtain the eternal reward. Let those who have been wearing themselves
out in both body and soul now work for a double honor. On this side will
be the sorrowful and poor, on that, the rich; on this side, the enemies of
the Lord, on that, his friends. Let those who go not put off the journey,
but rent their lands and collect money for their expenses; and as soon as
winter is over and spring comes, let them eagerly set out on the way with
God as their guide.
—Fulcher of Chartres, *Gesta Francorum Jerusalem Expugnantium* in *A
Sourcebook for Medieval History* (New York: Scribner, 1905), 514–16.

Thomas Aquinas. *Summa Theologica* (1265–74)
Article 3: Whether God exists.
By "God," we mean some infinite good. Therefore, if God existed evil
would not. Evil does exist in the world, however. Therefore God does not
exist.

Furthermore, one should not needlessly multiply elements in an explanation. It seems that we can account for everything we see in this world
on the assumption that God does not exist. All natural effects can be
traced to natural causes, and all contrived effects can be traced to human
reason and will. Thus there is no need to suppose that God exists.

But on the contrary God says, "I am who I am" (Ex. 3:14).

Response: It must be said that God's existence can be proved in five
ways. The first and most obvious way is based on the existence of motion.
It is certain and in fact evident to our senses that some things in the world
are moved. Everything that is moved, however, is moved by something
else, for a thing cannot be moved unless that movement is potentially
within it. A thing moves something else insofar as it actually exists, for to
move something is simply to actualize what is potentially within that
thing. Something can be led thus from potentiality to actuality only by
something else which is already actualized. For example, a fire, which is
actually hot, causes the change or motion whereby wood, which is potentially hot, becomes actually hot. Now it is impossible that something
should be potentially and actually the same thing at the same time,
although it could be potentially and actually different things. For example, what is actually hot cannot at the same moment be actually cold,

although it can be actually hot and potentially cold. Therefore it is impossible that a thing could move itself, for that would involve simultaneously moving and being moved in the same respect. Thus whatever is moved must be moved by something, else, etc. This cannot go on to infinity, however, for if it did there would be no first mover and consequently no other movers, because these other movers are such only insofar as they are moved by a first mover. For example, a stick moves only because it is moved by the hand. Thus it is necessary to proceed back to some prime mover which is moved by nothing else, and this is what everyone means by "God."

The second way is based on the existence of efficient causality. We see in the world around us that there is an order of efficient causes. Nor is it ever found (in fact it is impossible) that something is its own efficient cause. If it were, it would be prior to itself, which is impossible. Nevertheless, the order of efficient causes cannot proceed to infinity, for in any such order the first is cause of the middle (whether one or many) and the middle of the last. Without the cause, the effect does not follow. Thus, if the first cause did not exist, neither would the middle and last causes in the sequence. If, however, there were an infinite regression of efficient causes, there would be no first efficient cause and therefore no middle causes or final effects, which is obviously not the case. Thus it is necessary to posit some first efficient cause, which everyone calls "God." . . .

The fourth way is based on the gradations found in things. We find that things are more or less good, true, noble, etc.; yet when we apply terms like "more" and "less" to things we imply that they are closer to or farther from some maximum. For example, a thing is said to be hotter than something else because it comes closer to that which is hottest. Therefore something exists which is truest, greatest, noblest, and consequently most fully in being; for, as Aristotle says, the truest things are most fully in being. That which is considered greatest in any genus is the cause of everything is that genus, just as fire, the hottest thing, is the cause of all hot things, as Aristotle says. Thus there is something which is the cause of being, goodness, and every other perfection in all things, and we call that something "God."

The fifth way is based on the governance of things. We see that some things lacking cognition, such as natural bodies, work toward an end, as is seen from the fact that they always (or at least usually) act the same way and not accidentally, but by design. Things without knowledge tend toward a goal, however, only if they are guided in that direction by some

knowing, understanding being, as is the case with an arrow and archer. Therefore, there is some intelligent being by whom all natural things are ordered to their end, and we call this being "God."
—Thomas Aquinas, *Summa Theologica* (New York: Benziger Bros., 1947), 1:11–13.

Catherine of Siena. *Dialogue of the Seraphic Virgin* (1370)

How very pleasing to God is the willing desire to suffer for Him.

Very pleasing to me, my dearest daughter, is the willing desire to bear every pain and fatigue, even unto death, for the salvation of souls, for the more the soul endures, the more she shows that she loves me. Loving me she comes to know more of my truth, and the more she knows, the more pain and intolerable grief she feels at the offenses committed against me. You asked me to sustain you, and to punish the faults of others in you, and you did not say that you were really asking for love, light, and knowledge of the truth, since I have already told you that through the increase of love grief and pain increase as well. Therefore he that grows in love grows in grief. I say to you all, that you should ask, and it will be given you, for I deny nothing to those who ask me in truth. Consider that the love of divine charity is so closely joined in the soul with perfect patience; neither can leave the soul without the other. For this reason (if the soul elects to love me) she should elect to endure pain for me in whatever mode or circumstance I may send to her. Patience cannot be proved in any other way than by suffering, and patience is united with love as has been said. Therefore bear yourselves with manly courage, for, unless you do so, you will not prove yourselves to be spouses of my truth, and faithful children, nor of the company of those who relish the taste of my honor, and the salvation of souls.
—Catherine of Siena, *Dialogue of the Seraphic Virgin* (Westminster, Md.: Newman, 1925), 38.

Rule of the Order of Friars Minor (1223)

2. If any, wishing to adopt this life, go to our brothers they shall be sent to the provincial fathers, who alone have the right to receive someone into the order. They shall carefully examine them in the Catholic faith and the sacraments of the church. If they believe these and faithfully confess them and promise to observe them to the end of life, and if they have

no wives, or if they have wives, and the wives have either already entered a monastery or have received permission to do so, and they have already taken the vow of chastity with the permission of the bishop of the area, and their wives are of such an age that no suspicion can rise against them, let the provincial ministers repeat to them the word of the holy gospel, to go and sell all their goods and give to the poor.... Then the ministers shall give them the attire of a novice, two robes without a hood, a girdle, trousers, and a hood with a cape reaching to the girdle. The fathers may add to these if they think it necessary. After the year of probation is ended they shall be received into obedience by promising to observe this rule and life forever. And according to the command of the pope they shall never be permitted to leave the order and give up this life and form of religious faith. For according to the holy gospel no one who puts his hand to the plough and looks back is fit for the kingdom of God [Luke 9:62]. And after they have promised obedience, those who wish, may receive one robe with a hood and one without a hood. Those who must, may wear shoes and all the brothers shall wear common clothes, and they shall have God's blessing if they patch them with coarse cloth and pieces of other kinds of cloth. But I caution and exhort them not to despise or judge other men who wear fine and bright clothing, and have delicious food and drink.

3. The clerical brothers shall perform the divine office according to the rite of the holy Roman church, except the Psalter, from which they may have breviaries. The lay brothers shall say 24 Lord's Prayers at matins, 5 at lauds, 7 each at primes, terces, sexts, and nones, 12 at vespers, 7 at completorium, and then offer prayers for the dead. And they shall fast from All Saints Day [November 1] to Christmas. They may observe or not, as they choose, Lent which begins at Epiphany [January 6] and lasts for 40 days, and which our Lord consecrated by his holy fasts. They shall observe the other Lent. The rest of the time the brothers are obligated to fast only on Fridays. But in times of manifest necessity they shall not fast. But I counsel, warn, and exhort my brothers in the Lord Jesus Christ that when they go out into the world they must not be quarrelsome or con-tentious, nor judge others. They must be gentle, peaceable, and kind, mild and humble, and virtuous in speech, as is becoming to all. They shall not ride on horseback unless compelled by clear necessity or infirmity to do so. When they enter a house they shall say, "Peace be to this house." According to the holy Gospel, they may eat of whatever food is set before them.

4. I strictly forbid the brothers to accept money or property either directly or indirectly. Nevertheless, for the needs of the sick, and for clothing the other brothers, the fathers and guardians may, as necessity requires, provide through spiritual friends, according to the locality, season, and the degree of cold which may be expected in the region where they live. But, as has been said, they shall never receive money or property.

—*Bulla Romanum III*, 220ff in A *Sourcebook for Medieval History* (New York: Scribner, 1905), 499.

Pope Boniface VIII. Bull *Unam Sanctam* (1302)

We are informed by the words of the Gospels that there are two swords; namely, the spiritual and the temporal, in this church and in its power. For when the Apostles said: 'Behold, here are two swords' [Lk 22:38] that is to say, in the church, since the Apostles were speaking, the Lord did not reply that there were too many, but these two are sufficient. Certainly, he who denies that the temporal sword is in Peter's power has not listened well to the word of the Lord: "Put up thy sword into thy sheath" [Mt 26:52]. Both, therefore, are in the power of the church, that is to say, the spiritual and the material sword; the former is to be administered for the church but the latter by the church; the former in the hands of the priest; the latter by the hands of kings and soldiers, but at the will and sufferance of the priest. However, one sword ought to be subordinated to the other and temporal authority subject to spiritual power. For since the Apostle said: "There is no power except from God and the things that are, are ordained of God" [Rom 13:1-2], they would not be ordained if one sword were not subordinated to the other and if the inferior one, as it were, were not led upwards by the other. For, according to the Blessed Dionysius, it is a law of God that the lowest things reach the highest place by intermediaries.

—*Unam Sanctam* in A *Sourcebook for Medieval History* (New York: Scribner, 1905), 314–17.

Saint Francis Preached to the Birds, and All the Creatures Obeyed Him

Francis came to a certain place near Bevagna where a very great number of birds of various kinds had congregated—doves, crows, and some others popularly called daws. When the most blessed servant of God, Francis, saw them, being a man of great fervor and great tenderness toward lower creatures, he left his companions at the side of the road and ran eagerly toward the birds. When he was close to them, seeing that they were waiting expectantly for him, he greeted them in his usual way. Not a little surprised that the birds did not rise in flight, as they usually do, he was filled with great joy and humbly begged them to listen to the word of God. Among the things he spoke to them were these words: "My brothers, birds, you should praise your creator very much and always love him; he gave you feathers to clothe you, wings so that you can fly, and whatever else was necessary for you. God made you noble among his creatures, and he gave you a home in the purity of the air; though you neither sow nor reap, he nevertheless protects and governs you without any solicitude on your part." At these words, Francis himself used to say and those too who were with him, the birds, rejoicing in a wonderful way according to their nature, began to stretch their necks, extend their wings, open their mouths, and gaze at him. And Francis, passing through their midst, went on his way and returned, touching their heads and bodies with his tunic. Finally he blessed them, and after he had made the sign of the cross over them, he gave them permission to fly away to another place. Francis went his way with his companions, rejoicing and giving thanks to God, whom all creatures venerate with humble acknowledgement.

—Thomas of Celano, *The First Life of St. Francis* (Chicago: Franciscan Herald, [1963]), chap. 21.

Grievances against the Church, Presented at the Diet of Worms (1521)

Papal Dispensation and Absolution. Popes and bishops reserve to themselves the absolution from certain sins from which, they claim, only they can absolve us. Whenever such a "case" occurs and someone wants absolution, only money will procure it. Nor does Rome issue a dispensation from canon law except on payment of gold. A poor individual will not have his case properly handled. A rich individual may, moreover, obtain papal letters of indulgence in return for a substantial fee, which will entitle him to priestly absolution for any sin he might commit in the future, murder, for example, or perjury.

Indulgences. We consider it objectionable that the pope should permit numerous indulgences to be sold in Germany, a practice which misleads the common people and cheats them of their savings. When the pope sends nuncios or emissaries to a country, he allows them to offer indulgences for sale and retain a portion of the income for their own travel expenses and salaries.... Bishops and local secular authorities get their share of the proceeds for taking care of practical arrangements. These moneys are obtained from poor and lowly people who do not understand the deceptions of the Roman curia.

Some Clerics Escape Punishment for Their Misdeeds. If a cleric engaged in secular business in secular clothes is brought before a secular court on a criminal charge, he need only say "I am ordained" to be transferred to an ecclesiastical court, where he will go free. His bishop will support him, even if the person was apprehended without tonsure and wearing secular attire....

Many Clerics Operate Taverns and Gambling Joints. Priests frequently set themselves up as tavern keepers. On holidays, they provide gaming tables and invite people to play. They keep the profits, shamelessly claiming that these belong to them.

—Hans J. Hillerbrand, ed, *The Protestant Reformation* (New York: HarperCollins, 2007), 3–10.

Martin Luther, Account of His Conversion Experience (1545)

However irreproachable my life as a monk, I did not feel myself in the presence of God to be a sinner with a most unquiet conscience, nor could I believe him to be appeased by the satisfaction I could offer. I did not love—nay, I hated this just God who punishes sinners, and ... I was indignant against God, as if it were not enough that miserable sinners, eternally ruined by original sin, should be crushed with every kind of calamity through the law of the Ten Commandments, but that God through the gospel must add sorrow to sorrow, and even through the gospel preaching his righteousness and wrath to bear on us. So I raged with a savage and confounded conscience.... I began to understand that the righteousness of God is the righteousness in which a just person lives by God's gift, in other words, by faith. In fact, that is what Paul means: the righteousness of God is revealed in the gospel, it is passive righteousness by which the merciful God justifies us through faith. At this I felt myself born again and to have entered through the open gates into paradise itself.

— *Luther's Works. American Edition.* Vol. 34, *Career of the Reformer IV* (Philadelphia: Fortress, 1960), 7.

Martin Luther. 95 *Theses* (1517)

1. When our Lord and Master Jesus Christ said "Repent" he wanted the entire life of believers to be one of penitence.

2. Therefore, the indulgence preachers err who say that humans are absolved from every punishment [for sins] with papal indulgences.

3. This means not inward repentance only; indeed, there is no inward repentance which does not outwardly work divers mortifications of the flesh.

4. The punishment for sins committed, therefore, continues as long as hatred of self continues; for this is true inward repentance, which continues until our entrance into the kingdom of heaven....

26. The pope does well when he grants remission to souls in purgatory, not by the power of the keys (which he does not possess), but by way of intercession.

27. They preach human doctrine who say that so soon as the coin drops into the money-chest, the soul flies out of purgatory.

28. It is certain that when the coin drops into the money-chest, wealth and avarice may increase, but the result of the intercession of the Church lies in the power of God alone.

29. Who knows whether all the souls in purgatory wish to be redeemed from it, as we read in the legend of Saints Severinus and Paschal.

30. No one is sure that his own contrition is sincere; much less that he has attained full remission.

31. Rare as is the individual who is truly penitent, so rare is also the individual who truly buys indulgences, i.e., such men are most rare. . . .

45. Christians are to be taught that those who see someone in need and pass by, and provide money for indulgence pardons, do not purchase the indulgences of the pope, but the indignation of God.

46. Christians are to be taught that unless they have more than they need, they are bound to keep what is necessary for their own families, and not squander it on pardons.

47. Christians are to be taught that the buying of pardons is a matter of free choice, and not of a commandment.

48. Christians are to be taught that the pope, in granting pardons, needs and desires their devout prayer for him more than the moneys they contribute.

49. Christians are to be taught that the pope's pardons are useful, if they do not put their trust in them; they are altogether harmful, if because of them they lose their fear of God.

50. Christians are to be taught that if the pope knew the doings of the indulgences preachers, he would rather want St. Peter's church go up in ashes, than to build it with the skin, flesh and bones of his sheep.
Adolph Spaeth, L. D. Reed, Henry Eyster Jacobs, et al., trans. and ed., *Works of Martin Luther* (Philadelphia: A. J. Holman, 1915), 1:29–38.

Martin Luther, *Invocavit Sermon* (1522)

We are all called upon to die, and no one will die for the other, but every one of us must fight with death alone. We may well shout into one another's ears, but at the time of death each of us must be prepared. I then will not be with you nor will you with me. Therefore, everyone must fully know and accept the main affirmations which pertain to a Christian.

They are as follows:

First of all, that we are children of wrath, and that all our works, intentions, and thoughts are nothing at all. In this regard we must have a clear strong passage, which testifies to this point, such as the word of Paul in Ephesians 2. Take note of this. Even though there are many such passages in the Bible, I do not wish to drown you with them: "We are all children of wrath."

Second, that God sent us his only begotten son that we might believe in him. And who trusts in him will be free from sin and a child of God, as we read in John 1:12 "to all who believed in his name, he gave power to become children of God." On this point, we should be well versed in the Bible and confront the devil with many passages.

With regard to these two points I sense no error or deficiency among you, for they have been lavishly preached to you, and I should be sorry if it were not so. In fact, I know well that you are more learned than I, and not just one, two, three, or four of you, but surely 10 or more, all enlightened with this understanding.

Third, we must have love, and in love we must do among us what God has done through faith, for without love, faith is nothing, as Paul says in I Corinthians 13:1. "And if I had the tongues of angels and could speak sublimely about faith, and have not love, I am nothing." Dear friends, have you not failed in this regard? I sense no love in you, and find that you have not been grateful to God for his rich treasure and gift.

Let us beware that we do not turn the Wittenberg into Capernaum. I see that you know well how to talk about doctrine, which was preached to you, concerning faith and love. That is no miracle: if an ass can learn how to sing, you should be able to talk and learn doctrine and the little words of Scripture. Listen, dear friends, the kingdom of God, which is us, does not consist in talk or in words, but in doing, and that means in deeds, works, and discipline. God does not want passive listeners or regurgitators, but followers and doers, and that in faith through love. For faith without love is not sufficient, indeed, it is not even faith, but a mere appearance of faith as the face seen in the mirror is not a real face, but a reflection.

Fourth, we sorely need patience. For the person who has faith, trusts God and shows love to the neighbor and practices such love daily, will surely suffer persecution. For the devil does not sleep, but gives that person a lot of trouble. And patience works to bring about hope, which freely gives itself and merges into God. And so faith increases, through much temptation and challenge and is strengthened from day to day.... Therefore, dear friends, we must not do what we are entitled, but observe what is meaningful and attractive to the neighbor....

Love, therefore, demands that you have compassion with the weak. All apostles had that. When Paul came to Athens (Acts 17 [:16–32]), a powerful city, he found in the temple ancient altars. He went from one to the other and looked at them, but he did not even touch a single one with his foot. Rather, he stood in the middle of the market square and said they were nothing but idolatrous things, plead that they would forsake them, but did not forcefully demolish a single one. When the Word captured their hearts, they forsook the temples of their own accord, and the matter took care of itself. Likewise, if I had seen them celebrate Mass, I would have preached to them and corrected them. Had they listened to my admonition, I would have won them over. Even if not, I would not have pulled them away by the hair or used sheer force, but would have simply allowed the Word to act, and I would have prayed for them. For the Word created heaven and earth and all things, and this Word must do it, and not we poor sinners.

In sum: I shall preach, teach, write all this, but will constrain no one by force, for faith must come freely without compulsion. Take me as an example. I opposed indulgences and the papists, but never with force. I simply taught, preached, and wrote God's Word; otherwise I did nothing. And while I slept or drank Wittenberg beer with my friends Philip and Amsdorf the word so greatly weakened the papacy that no ruler or emperor ever inflicted such losses upon it. I did nothing; the Word did everything. Had I desired to cause trouble, I could have brought great bloodshed upon German lands; indeed, I could have started such a game that even the emperor would not have been safe. But what would it have been? Mere fool's play. I did nothing; I let the Word do its work.

—Martin Luther, *Der Kampf um die reine Lehre*, Luther Deutsch. Bd. 4 (Berlin: Evang. Verlagsanstalt, 1950), 57–66 (author's translation).

Thirty-nine Articles (1563)

Article 28—The Lord's Supper

The Supper of the Lord is not only a sign of the love that Christians ought to have among themselves, one to another, but rather it is [also] a sacrament of our redemption by Christ's death: to those who rightly, worthily, and with faith receive it, the bread that we break is a partaking of the body of Christ, and likewise the cup of blessing is a partaking of the blood of Christ.

Transubstantiation (or the change of the substance of bread and wine) in the Supper of the Lord, cannot be proved by Holy Scripture, but is repugnant to the plain words of Scripture, overthrows the nature of a Sacrament, and has given occasion to many superstitions.

The body of Christ is given, taken, and eaten in the Supper, only after a heavenly and spiritual manner. And the means by which the body of Christ is received and eaten in the Supper is faith.

Lord's Supper was not by Christ's ordinance reserved, carried about, lifted up, or worshipped.

Article 29—The Wicked Which Do Not Eat the Body of Christ, in the Use of the Lord's Supper

The wicked and those who are void of a lively faith, although they do carnally and visibly press with their teeth (as S. Augustine said) the sacrament of the body and blood of Christ, yet in no wise are they partakers of Christ, but rather to their condemnation do eat and drink the sign or sacrament of so great a thing.

Article 30—Both Kinds

The Cup of the Lord is not to be denied to the lay people; for both parts of the Lord's sacrament, by Christ's ordinance and commandment, ought to be ministered to all Christian men alike.

—www.tudorplace.com.ar/Documents/the_39_articles.htm. Accessed June 2, 2011.

John Calvin, *Institutes of the Christian Religion* (1559)

The covenant of life is not preached equally among all men, and among those to whom it is preached, it does not gain the same acceptance either constantly or in equal degree. In this diversity the wonderful depth of God's judgment is made known. For there is no doubt that this variety also serves the decision of God's eternal election. If it is plain that it comes to pass by God's bidding that salvation is freely offered to some while others are barred from access to it, at once great and difficult questions spring up. They are inexplicable when proper views concerning election and predestination are not held. To many this is a perplexing topic, because they consider it absurd that of the great multitude of humankind, some should be predestined to salvation and others to destruction....

VII. Though it is sufficiently clear, that God, in his secret counsel, freely chooses whom He will, and rejects others, His gratuitous election is but half displayed till we come to particular individuals, to whom God not only offers salvation, but assigns it in such a manner, that the certainty of the effect is liable to no suspense or doubt....Paul, therefore, justly reasons from the passage of Malachi which I have just quoted, that where God, introducing the covenant of eternal life, invites any people to Himself, there is a peculiar kind of election as to part of them, so that he does not efficaciously choose all with indiscriminate grace. The declaration, "Jacob have I loved," respects the whole posterity of the patriarch, whom the prophet there opposes to the descendants of Esau.

—John Calvin, *The Institutes of the Christian Religion* (Philadelphia: Westminster, 1960), 910–16.

The English Parliament, Supremacy Act (1534)

Be it enacted by authority of this present Parliament, that the king our sovereign lord, his heirs and successors, kings of this realm, shall be taken, accepted, and reputed the only head in earth of the Church of England, called *Anglicana Ecclesia*; and shall have and enjoy, annexed and united to the imperial crown of this realm, as well as the title and style thereof, as all honors, dignities...to the said dignity of the supreme head of the same Church belonging.

—26 *Henry VIII, cap. 1; Statutes of the Realm, iii.* 492. Henry Gee, *Documents Illustrative of English Church History* (New York: Kraus Reprint, 1972), 55.

Ignatius of Loyola, *Rules for Thinking with the Church*

First Rule. All judgment laid aside, we ought to have our mind ready and prompt to obey, in all, the true Spouse of Christ our Lord, which is our holy Mother the hierarchical church.

Second Rule. To praise confession to a Priest, and the reception of the most Holy Sacrament of the Altar once in the year, and much more each month, and much better from week to week, with the conditions required and due.

Third Rule. To praise the hearing of Mass often, likewise hymns, psalms, and long prayers, in the church and out of it; likewise the hours set at the time fixed for each Divine Office and for all prayer and all Canonical Hours.

Fourth Rule. To praise much religious orders, virginity and continence, and not so much marriage as any of these.

Fifth Rule. To praise vows of religion, of obedience, of poverty, of chastity and of other perfections of supererogation. And it is to be noted that as the vow is about the things which approach to Evangelical perfection, a vow ought not to be made in the things which withdraw from it, such as to be a merchant, or to be married, etc.

Sixth Rule. To praise relics of the Saints, giving veneration to them and praying to the Saints; and to praise stations of the cross, pilgrimages, indulgences, pardons, Cruzadas, and candles lighted in the churches.

Seventh Rule. To praise constitutions about fasts and abstinence, such as Lent, Ember Days, Vigils, Friday and Saturday; likewise penances, not only interior, but also exterior.

Eighth Rule. To praise the ornaments and the buildings of churches; likewise images, and to venerate them according to what they represent....

Eleventh Rule. To praise positive and scholastic learning.... it is more proper to the Scholastics, to define or explain for our times the things necessary for eternal salvation; and to combat and explain better all errors and all fallacies. For the scholastic doctors, as they are more modern, not only help themselves with the true understanding of the Sacred Scripture and of the constructive and holy doctors, but also, they being enlightened and clarified by the Divine virtue, help themselves by the councils, canons and constitutions of our holy mother the church.

Thirteenth Rule. To be right in everything, we ought always to hold that the white which I see, is black, if the hierarchical church so decides it, believing that between Christ our Lord, the bridegroom, and the church, his bride, there is the same Spirit which governs and directs us for the salvation of our souls. Because by the same Spirit and our Lord who gave the Ten Commandments, our holy mother the church is directed and governed.

Fourteenth Rule. Although there is much truth in the assertion that no one can save himself without being predestined and without having faith and grace; we must be very cautious in the manner of speaking and communicating with others about all these things.

Fifteenth Rule. We ought not, by way of custom, to speak much of predestination; but if in some way and at some times one speaks, let him so speak that the common people may not come into any error, as sometimes happens, saying: Whether I have to be saved or condemned is already determined, and no other thing can now be, through my doing well or ill; and with this, growing lazy, they become negligent in the works which lead to the salvation and the spiritual profit of their souls.
—Ignatius Loyola, *Spiritual Exercises*, part 2 (www.ccel.org/ccel/ignatius/exercises.xix.v.html. Accessed September 2, 2011.)

Adeline Spicer, A New England Puritan Diary

December 5. I am fifteen years old to-day, and while sitting with my stitchery in my hand, there came a man in all wet with the salt spray, he having just landed by the boat from Sandwich, which had much ado to land by reason of the surf. I myself had been down to the shore and saw the great waves breaking, and the high tide running up as far as the hillocks of dead grass. The man George, an Indian, brings word of much sickness in Boston, and great trouble with the Quakers and Baptists; that many of the children throughout the country be not baptized, and without that religion comes to nothing. My mother hath bid me this day put on a fresh kirtle and wimple, though it be not the Lords day, and my Aunt Alice coming in did chide me and say that to pay attention to a birthday was putting myself with the worlds people. It happens from this that my kirtle and wimple are no longer pleasing to me, and what with this and the bad news from Boston my birthday has ended in sorrow.

December 25. My Cousin Jane coming to-day has told me much of the merry ways of England upon this day, of the Yule log, and plum puddings, till I was fain to say that I would be glad to see those merry doings; but she told me it was far better to be in a state of grace and not given over to popish practices. But I thought she looked sad herself and almost unhappy as she reminded of the coming of John Baily who is to preach to-morrow all day.... The preaching began at ten in the morning, and held until twelve, when a strong prayer was made and I was, I hope, much built up. But when the sermon was preached in the afternoon I would fain sleep, and lost much I fear me of the discourse, and this weighed heavily on my conscience, so that when I went home and found that brother Stephen had received word that he was to be bound to Mr. Bates of Plymouth for five years I wept sore and felt to murmur greatly.

February 2. Yesterday our Indian, George, betrayed much uneasiness after father had read the account of the burning of Sodom and Gomorrah. He has learned to understand English, and sometimes I tremble lest he should betray to the wandering Indians of the Narragansett, who sometimes are found prowling about, what we speak of in the family. Mother after much fearful anxiety has submitted to the will of the Lord, whose strong right arm has gotten us the victory in many sore straits in the past. Mother has counseled Father about many things, and when Father said that women knew naught about such matters she told him how Capt. Underhill's wife saved him in his expedition against the Block Islanders, in 1636, when our country had more straits to pass through than even now when Philip is breathing out threatenings and slaughter. Give me leave to observe two things from hence: first, when the hour of death is not yet come, you see God uses weak means to keep his purpose inviolated: secondly, let no man despise advice and counsel of his wife, though she be a woman. It was strange to nature to think a man should be bound to fulfill the humor of a woman, what arms he should carry: but you see God will have it so, that a woman should overcome a man. What with Delilah's flattery, and her mournful tears they must and will have their way, when the hand of God goes along with the matter. Therefore let the claim be quenched. I daily hear in my ears, that New England men usurp over their wives, and keep them in servile subjection. The country is wronged in this matter, as in many things else. Let this precedent satisfy the doubtful, for that comes from the example of a rude soldier. If they be so courteous to their wives as to take their advice in warlike matters, how much more kind is the tender, affectionate husband to honor his wife as the weaker vessel.

March 5. A very disgraceful thing has happened in our meeting, and much scandal hath been caused. Hannah Smith is married with her husband's brother, and it is declared null by the court of assistants and she hath been commanded not to entertain him further; and she did appear before the congregation on lecture day and make a full confession. A lesson this is to all young women, Mother says, not to act hastily or allow our minds to wander into by or forbidden ways.

March 12. Although it has been pointed out to me that in times of danger I ought not to be merry, I could not help laughing at the periwig

of Elder Jones, which had gone awry. The periwig has been greatly cen-
sured as encouraging worldly fashions, not suitable to the wearing of a
minister of the gospel, and it has been preached about by Mr. Mather and
many think he is not severe enough in the matter, but rather doth find
excuse for it on account of health.

March 16. At afternoon discourse on I am afraid of thy judgments Mr.
Moody prayed an hour, sung the Fifty-first psalm.

March 20. This day had a private fast. Mr. Willard spoke to the second
commandment. Mr. Elliot prayed. While we were ceasing for half an
hour, I saw Samuel Checkly and smiled; this was not the time to trifle,
and I repented, especially as he looked at me so many times after that I
found my mind wandering from the psalm. And afterwards when the
Biskets, Beer, Cider and Wine were distributed he whispered to me that
he would rather serve me than the elders, which was a wicked thing to
say, and I felt myself to blame.

—Adeline E. H. Spicer, "A Puritan Maiden's Diary," *New England
Magazine* 17 (1894): 21–25.

Philip Jakob Spener, *Pia Desideria* (1675)

We must beware how we conduct ourselves in religious controversies
with unbelievers and heretics. We must first take pains to strengthen and
confirm ourselves, our friends, and other fellow believers in the truth and
to protect them with great care from every kind of seduction.

To those we owe, first of all, to pray earnestly that God may enlighten
them with the same light with which he has blessed us, lead them to the
truth, prepare their hearts for it or, having counteracted their dangerous
errors, reinforce the true knowledge of salvation in Christ they still have
in order that they may be saved as a branch plucked from the fire. This is
the meaning of the first three petitions of the Lord's Prayer, that God may
hallow his name in them, bring his kingdom to them, and accomplish his
gracious will in and for them.

Second, we must set a good example and take the greatest pains not to
offend them in any way, for this would give them a bad impression of our
teaching and would make their conversion more difficult.

To this should be added . . . a practice of heartfelt love toward all unbelievers and heretics. While we should indicate that we take no pleasure
in their unbelief or false belief or their practice and propagation, but are
vigorously opposed to them, yet in other things which pertain to ordinary
affairs we should demonstrate that we consider these people to be our

neighbors (as the Samaritan was represented by Christ in Luke 10:29-37 as the Jews' neighbors), regard them as our brothers and sisters according to our common creation and God's universal love.

—Philip Spener, *Pia Desideria* (Philadelphia: Fortress, 1962), 29–30.

Silesian Children's Prayer Revival (1708)

In our town, as well as surrounding towns, Lutheran boys between the ages of 4 and 14 meet to follow a practice they observed in Swedish soldiers who had lodged in their town and they come together to pray twice a day for something like two hours. While initially small in size, attendance at these prayer meetings has swelled to over 200. The City Council dispersed their gatherings three times already, but they moved their meetings to the Fiscal Hill, which is beyond the jurisdiction of the City Council. Wooden barricades have been erected to keep onlookers, some 3 to 4,000, from disturbing the children. They have come to observe the piety of the children of such tender age. The children kneel during the entire meeting; they elected a reader from their midst, who not only selects the hymns and begin this to sing them but also reads the prayers. They typically sing seven hymns, interspersed with the reading of a penitential Psalm and a passage from the Bible. Everything takes place in an orderly fashion, they come and leave in pairs, holding hands. The onlookers are swept away crying and tend to join the singing of the boys so that it is heard as far as the Oder River. Among their intercessory prayers they include the petition that the churches will be restored to them.

—*Quellenbuch zur Geschichte der Evangelischen Kirche in Schlesien* (Munich, 1992), 167–70.

Jonathan Edwards. *Sinners in the Hands of an Angry God* (1741)

Your wickedness makes you as it were heavy as lead, and to tend downwards with great weight and pressure towards hell; and if God should let you go, you would immediately sink and swiftly descend and plunge into the bottomless gulf, and your healthy constitution, and your own care and prudence, and best contrivance, and all your righteousness, would have no more influence to uphold you and keep you out of hell, than a spider's web would have to stop a falling rock. Were it not for the sovereign pleasure of God, the earth would not bear you one moment; for you are a burden to it; the creation groans with you; the creature is made subject to the bondage of your corruption, not willingly; the sun does not willingly shine upon you to give you light to serve sin and Satan; the earth does not willingly yield her increase to satisfy your lusts; nor is it willingly a stage for your wickedness to be acted upon; the air does not willingly serve you for breath to maintain the flame of life in your vitals, while you spend your life in the service of God's enemies. God's creatures are good, and were made for men to serve God with, and do not willingly subserve to any other purpose, and groan when they are abused to purposes so directly contrary to their nature and end. And the world would spew you out, were it not for the sovereign hand of him who hath subjected it in hope. There are the black clouds of God's wrath now hanging directly over your heads, full of the dreadful storm, and big with thunder; and were it not for the restraining hand of God, it would immediately burst forth upon you. The sovereign pleasure of God, for the present, stays his rough wind; otherwise it would come with fury, and your destruction would come like a whirlwind, and you would be like the chaff of the summer threshing floor.

—*Selected Sermons of Jonathan Edwards* (New York, London: Macmillan, 1904), 86.

Thomas Chubb. The True Gospel of Jesus Christ Asserted (1738)

The *great end* and the *professed design* of our Lord Jesus Christ as to his coming into the world, and with respect to what he has revealed to it, performed in it, and suffered from it, and for it is manifestly and apparently this, *viz. to save men souls*; that is, it is to prepare men for, and to insure to them the *favor* of God, and their *happiness* in another world, and to prevent them from bringing *great* and *lasting misery* upon themselves.

...Luke 9:56. For the Son of man is not come to destroy men's lives, but to save them. Chap. 19:10. For the son of man is come to seek and to save that which was lost. John 3:16, 17.... From these and such like declarations which Christ has made, it is most evident and apparent, not only that men by their vices and wickedness had rendered themselves unworthy of God's favor, and had exposed themselves to his just displeasure; but also that the great end and the professed design which Christ came into the world to prosecute was to procure their salvation....

As this was the main or chief end which Christ came into the world to prosecute; so in consequence thereof, and thereby in a secondary and less proper sense, he may be said to come into the world to promote and secure the *present well-being* of mankind; namely, to lead men to *present pleasure*, and to secure them from *present misery*, as the pleasures and pains of this world, are generally *connected* with the pleasures and pains of another; that is, what sits and prepares a man for future felicity, generally *tends* to make him easy and happy here; and what exposes a man to the miseries of another world, generally *tends* to make him unhappy and miserable in this. And in this view of the case Christianity may as truly be said to be subservient to men's *present* as to their *future* well-being; not by investing any Christian with any *temporal power* or *jurisdiction* over his brethren or fellow Christians out of which his present good or temporal advantage might arise; but only by engaging each and every individual to put on *Such* a temper of mind, and *such* a behavior as renders each person a *blessing* to *himself*, and to *society*, and from which temper and behavior the *present temporal good* of each individual generally flows....

As the grand design of Christ and the Christian revelation is to promote the future good and well being of mankind, and not the present interest of any person..., so whenever the *name* or the *revelation* of Christ is made use of to support and carry on the *temporal interest* of any Christian, or any set, or order, or body of men among Christians, by investing them with any the least degree of *temporal power* out of which their *present interest* might arise, this is manifestly an *abuse* of the name and of the revelation of Christ.

—Thomas Chubb, *The True Gospel of Jesus Christ Asserted wherein is shewn what is, and what is not the gospel...humbly offered to publick consideration* (London: Thos. Cox, 1738), 32–33.

Joseph Butler. *The Analogy of Religion, Natural and Revealed* (1736)

Of the Importance of Christianity

Some persons, upon pretence of the sufficiency of the light of nature, avowedly reject all revelation, as, in its very notion, incredible, and what must be fictitious. And indeed it is certain, no revelation would have been given, had the light of nature been sufficient in such a sense, as to render one not wanting and useless. But no man, in seriousness and simplicity of mind, can possibly think it so, who considers the state of Religion in the heathen world before revelation, and its present state in those places which have borrowed no light from it: particularly the doubtfulness of some of the greatest men, concerning things of the utmost importance, as well as the natural inattention and ignorance of mankind in general. It is impossible to say, who would have been able to have reasoned out that whole system, which we call natural Religion, in its genuine simplicity, clear of superstition: but there is certainly no ground to affirm that the generality could. If they could, there is no sort of probability that they would. Admitting there were, they would highly want a standing admonition to remind them of it, and inculcate it upon them.

And further still, were they as much disposed to attend to Religion, as the better sort of men are; yet even upon this supposition, there would be various occasions for supernatural instruction and assistance, and the greatest advantages might be afforded by them. So that to say revelation is a thing superfluous, what there was no need of, and what can be of no service, is, I think, to talk quite wildly and at random. Nor would it be more extravagant to affirm, that mankind is so entirely at ease in the present state, and life so completely happy, that it is a contradiction to suppose our condition capable of being, in any respect, better.

There are other persons, not to be ranked with these, who seem to be getting into a way of neglecting, and, as it were, overlooking revelation, as of small importance, provided natural Religion be kept to. With little regard either to the evidence of the former, or to the objections against it, and even upon supposition of its truth; "the only design of it," say they, "must be, to establish a belief of the moral system of nature, and to enforce the practice of natural piety and virtue. The belief and practice of these things were, perhaps, much promoted by the first publication of Christianity: but whether they are believed and practiced, upon the evidence and motives of nature or of revelation, is no great matter." This way of considering revelation, though it is not the same with the former, yet borders nearly upon it, and very much, at length, runs up into it: and requires to be particularly considered, with regard to the persons who seem to be getting into this way. The consideration of it will likewise further show the extravagance of the former opinion, and the truth of the observations in answer to it, just mentioned. And an inquiry into the importance of Christianity, cannot be an improper introduction to a treatise concerning the credibility of it.

Now if God has given a revelation to mankind, and commanded those things which are commanded in Christianity; it is evident, at first sight, that it cannot in any wise be an indifferent matter, whether we obey or disobey those commands: unless we are certainly assured, that we know all the reasons for them, and that all those reasons are now ceased, with regard to mankind in general, or to ourselves in particular. And it is absolutely impossible we can be assured of this. For our ignorance of these reasons proves nothing in the case: since the whole analogy of nature shows, what is indeed in itself evident, that there may be infinite reasons for things, with which we are not acquainted.

But the importance of Christianity will more distinctly appear, by considering it more distinctly: *First*, as a republication, and external institution, of natural or essential Religion, adapted to the present circumstances of mankind, and intended to promote natural piety and virtue: and *Secondly*, as containing an account of a dispensation of things, not discoverable by reason, in consequence of which several distinct precepts are enjoined us. For though natural Religion is the foundation and principal part of Christianity, it is not in any sense the whole of it.
—Joseph Butler, *The Analogy of Religion, Natural and Revealed* (New York: Nelson and Phillips, 1875), 1–3.

David Friedrich Strauss, *The Life of Jesus, Critically Examined* (1835)

What they [the Gospels] narrate is only thus much: that Jesus caused his small store of provisions to be distributed, and that in consequence of this the entire multitude obtained enough to eat. Here, in any case, we want a middle interpretation, which would inform us how it was possible that, although Jesus had so little food to offer, the whole multitude obtained enough to eat. A very natural middle interpretation is to be gathered from the historical combination of the circumstances. As, in comparison with John 6:4, the multitude appear to have consisted for the greater part of a caravan on its way to the feast, they cannot have been quite destitute of provisions, and probably a few indigent persons only had exhausted their stores. In order then to induce those better provided to share their food with those who were in want, Jesus arranged that they should have a meal, and himself set the example of imparting what he and his disciples could spare from their own little provisions. This example was imitated, and thus the distribution of bread by Jesus having led to a general distribution, the whole multitude were satisfied. It is true that this natural middle interpretation must be first mentally interpolated into the text; as, however, the supernatural middle interpretation which is generally received is hardly stated expressly, and both alike depend upon inference, the reader can hardly do otherwise than decide for the natural one: the alleged identity in the relation of the two middle interpretations to the text does not in fact exist. For while the natural explanation requires us to suppose a new distributing subject, (the better provided among the multitude,) and a new distributed object, (their provisions) together with the act of distributing these provisions, the supernatural explanation contents itself with the subject actually present in the text, (Jesus and his disciples) with the single object given, (their modest provisions) and the described distribution; it only requires us to supply from our imagination the means by which this store could be made sufficient to satisfy the hunger of the multitude, namely its miraculous augmentation with the hands of Jesus (or of his disciples). How can it be maintained that neither of the two middle interpretations is any more suggested by the text than the other? That the miraculous multiplication of the loaves and fishes is not expressly mentioned, is explained by the consideration that the event itself is one of which no clear conception can be formed, and therefore it is best conveyed by the result alone. But how will the natural theologian account for nothing being said of the distribution, called forth by the example of Jesus, on the part of those among the multitude who had provisions? It is altogether arbitrary to insert that distribution between the sentences, *He gave them to the disciples, and the disciples to the multitude* (Matt. 14:19), and, *they did all eat and were filled* (*v. 20*).

—David Friedrich Strauss, *The Life of Jesus Critically Examined* (New York: Macmillan, 1892), 508–10.

Thirteen Articles of Faith of the Church of Jesus Christ of Latter-day Saints (1842)

1. We believe in God, the Eternal Father, and in His Son, Jesus Christ, and in the Holy Ghost.
2. We believe that men will be punished for their own sins, and not for Adam's transgression.
3. We believe that through the Atonement of Christ, all mankind may be saved, by obedience to the laws and ordinances of the Gospel.
4. We believe that the first principles and ordinances of the Gospel are: first, Faith in the Lord Jesus Christ; second, Repentance; third, Baptism by immersion for the remission of sins; fourth, Laying on of hands for the gift of the Holy Ghost.
5. We believe that a man must be called of God, by prophecy, and by the laying on of hands by those who are in authority, to preach the Gospel and administer in the ordinances thereof.

6. We believe in the same organization that existed in the Primitive Church, namely, apostles, prophets, pastors, teachers, evangelists, and so forth.

7. We believe in the gift of tongues, prophecy, revelation, visions, healing, interpretation of tongues, and so forth.

8. We believe the Bible to be the word of God as far as it is translated correctly; we also believe the Book of Mormon to be the word of God.

9. We believe all that God has revealed, all that He does now reveal, and we believe that He will yet reveal many great and important things pertaining to the Kingdom of God.

10. We believe in the literal gathering of Israel and in the restoration of the Ten Tribes; that Zion (the New Jerusalem) will be built upon the American continent; that Christ will reign personally upon the earth; and, that the earth will be renewed and receive its paradisiacal glory.

11. We claim the privilege of worshiping Almighty God according to the dictates of our own conscience, and allow all men the same privilege, let them worship how, where, or what they may.

12. We believe in being subject to kings, presidents, rulers, and magistrates, in obeying, honoring, and sustaining the law.

13. We believe in being honest, true, chaste, benevolent, virtuous, and in doing good to all men; indeed, we may say that we follow the admonition of Paul—We believe all things, we hope all things, we have endured many things, and hope to be able to endure all things. If there is anything virtuous, lovely, or of good report or praiseworthy, we seek after these things.

—Thirteen Articles of Faith, *Encyclopedia of Mormonism* (New York: Macmillan, 1992), 1–3.

The Catholic Dogma of Papal Infallibility (1870)

We teach and define that it is a dogma divinely revealed that the Roman pontiff, when he speaks *ex cathedra*, that is when in discharge of the office of pastor and doctor of all Christians, by virtue of his supreme Apostolic authority, he defines a doctrine regarding faith or morals to be held by the universal church, by the divine assistance promised to him in Blessed Peter, is possessed of that infallibility with which the Divine Redeemer willed that his church should be endowed in defining doctrine regarding faith or morals, and that therefore such definitions of the Roman pontiff are of themselves and not from the consent of the Church irreformable.

So then, should anyone, which God forbid, have the temerity to reject this definition of ours: let him be anathema.
—*The Church Teaches; Documents of the Church in English Translation* (St. Louis: B. Herder, 1955), 102.

The Syllabus of Modern Errors (1907)

The best theory of civil society requires that popular schools open to children of every class of the people, and, generally, all public institutes intended for instruction in letters and philosophical sciences and for carrying on the education of youth, should be freed from all ecclesiastical authority, control and interference, and should be fully subjected to the civil and political power at the pleasure of the rulers, and according to the standard of the prevalent opinions of the age.

48. Catholics may approve of the system of educating youth unconnected with Catholic faith and the power of the Church, and which regards the knowledge of merely natural things, and only, or at least primarily, the ends of earthly social life....

77. In the present day it is no longer expedient that the Catholic religion should be held as the only religion of the state, to the exclusion of all other forms of worship.

78. Hence it has been wisely decided by law, in some Catholic countries, that persons coming to reside therein shall enjoy the public exercise of their own peculiar worship.

79. Moreover, it is false that the civil liberty of every form of worship, and the full power, given to all, of overtly and publicly manifesting any opinions whatsoever and thought, conduce more easily to corrupt the morals and minds of the people, and to propagate the pest of indifferentism.

80. The Roman Pontiff can, and ought to, reconcile himself, and come to terms with progress, liberalism and modern civilization.
—Philip Schaff, *Creeds of Christendom* (New York, 1877), 2:213.

Walter Rauschenbusch. *Christianity and the Social Crisis* (1908)

And how will it be with us? Will that vaster civilization which began in Europe and is now spreading along the shores of all the oceans, as Rome grew from Italy outward around the great inland sea, run through the same stages? If the time of our weakness comes, the barbarians will not be wanting to take possession. Where the carcass is, the vultures will gather.

Nations do not die by wealth, but by injustice. The forward impetus comes through some great historical opportunity which stimulates the production of wealth, breaks up the caked and rigid order of the past, sets free the energies of new classes, calls creative leaders to the front, quickens the intellectual life, intensifies the sense of duty and the ideal devotion to the common weal, and awakens in the strong individuals the large ambition of patriotic service. Progress slackens when a single class appropriates the social results of the common labor, fortifies its evil rights by unfair laws, throttles the masses by political centralization and suppression, and consumes in luxury what it has taken in covetousness. Then there is a gradual loss of productive energy, an increasing bitterness and distrust, a waning sense of duty and devotion to country, a paralysis of the moral springs of noble action. Men no longer love the Commonwealth, because it does not stand for the common wealth. Force has to supply the cohesive power which love fails to furnish. Exploitation creates poverty, and poverty is followed by physical degeneration. Education, art, wealth, and culture may continue to advance and may even ripen to their mellowest perfection when the worm of death is already at the heart of the nation. Internal convulsions or external catastrophes will finally reveal the state of decay.

It is always a process extending through generations or even centuries. It is possible that with the closely knit nations of the present era the resistive vitality is greater than in former ages, and it will take much longer for them to break up. The mobility of modern intellectual life will make it harder for the stagnation of mind and the crystallization of institutions to make headway. But unless the causes of social wrong are removed, it will be a slow process of strangulation and asphyxiation.

In the last resort the only hope is in the moral forces which can be summoned to the rescue. If there are statesmen, prophets, and apostles who set truth and justice above selfish advancement; if their call finds a response in the great body of the people; if a new tide of religious faith and moral enthusiasm creates new standards of duty and a new capacity for self-sacrifice; if the strong learn to direct their love of power to the uplifting of the people and see the highest self-assertion in self-sacrifice— then the entrenchments of vested wrong will melt away; the stifled energy of the people will leap forward; the atrophied members of the social body will be filled with a fresh flow of blood; and a regenerate nation will look with the eyes of youth across the fields of the future.

The cry of "Crisis! crisis!" has become a weariness. Every age and every year are critical and fraught with destiny. Yet in the widest survey of history Western civilization is now at a decisive point in its development. Will some Gibbon of Mongol race sit by the shore of the Pacific in the year A.D. 3000 and write on the "Decline and Fall of the Christian Empire"? If so, he will probably describe the nineteenth and twentieth centuries as the golden age when outwardly life flourished as never before, but when that decay, which resulted in the gradual collapse of the twenty-first and twenty-second centuries, was already far advanced.

Or will the twentieth century mark for the future historian the real adolescence of humanity, the great emancipation from barbarism and from the paralysis of injustice, and the beginning of a progress in the intellectual, social, and moral life of mankind to which all past history has no parallel?

It will depend almost wholly on the moral forces which the Christian nations can bring to the fighting line against wrong, and the fighting energy of those moral forces will again depend on the degree to which they are inspired by religious faith and enthusiasm. It is either a revival of social religion or the deluge.

—Walter Rauschenbusch, *Christianity and the Social Crisis* (New York: MacMillan, 1908), 230.

James Orr. *On the Virgin Birth* (1907)

It is the object of this paper to show that those who take the lines of denial on the virgin birth just sketched do great injustice to the evidence and importance of the doctrine they reject. The evidence, if not of the same public kind as that for the resurrection, is far stronger than the objector allows, and the fact denied enters far more vitally into the essence of the Christian faith than he supposes. Placed in its right setting among the other truths of the Christian religion, it is not only no stumbling-block to faith, but is felt to fit in with self-evidencing power into the connection of these other truths, and to furnish the very explanation that is needed of Christ's holy and supernatural Person. The ordinary Christian is a witness here. In reading the Gospels, he feels no incongruity in passing from the narratives of the virgin birth to the wonderful story of Christ's life in the chapters that follow, then from these to the pictures of Christ's divine dignity given in John and Paul. The whole is of one piece: the Virgin birth is as natural at the beginning of the life of such a One—the divine Son—as the resurrection is at the end. And the more closely the matter is considered, the stronger does this impression grow. It is only when the scriptural conception of Christ is parted with that various difficulties and doubts come in.

It is, in truth, a *very superficial* way of speaking or thinking of the virgin birth to say that nothing depends on this belief for our estimate of Christ. Who that reflects on the subject carefully can fail to see that if Christ was virgin born—if He was truly "conceived," as the creed says, "by the Holy Ghost, born of the Virgin Mary"—there must of necessity enter a supernatural element into His Person; while, if Christ was sinless, much more, if He was the very Word of God incarnate, there must have been a miracle—the most stupendous miracle in the universe—in His origin? If Christ was, as John and Paul affirm and his church has ever believed, the Son of God made flesh, the second Adam, the new redeeming Head of the race, a miracle was to be expected in His earthly origin; without a miracle such a Person could never have been. Why then cavil at the narratives which declare the fact of such a miracle? Who does not see that the Gospel history would have been incomplete without them? Inspiration here only gives to faith what faith on its own grounds imperatively demands for its perfect satisfaction.

It is time now to come to *the Scripture itself*, and to look at the fact of the Virgin birth in its historical setting, and its relation with other truths of the Gospel. As preceding the examination of the historical evidence, a little may be said, first, on the *Old Testament preparation*. Was there any such preparation? Some would say there was not, but this is not God's way, and we may look with confidence for at least some indications which point in the direction of the New Testament event.

One's mind turns first to that *oldest of all evangelical promises*, that the seed of the woman would bruise the head of the serpent. "I will put enmity," says Jehovah to the serpent-tempter, "between you and the woman, and between thy seed and her seed; he shall bruise thy head, and thou shall bruise his heel" (Genesis 3:15). It is a forceless weakening of this first word of Gospel in the Bible to explain it of a lasting feud between the race of men and the brood of serpents. The serpent, as even Dr. Driver attests, is "the representative of the power of evil"—in later Scripture, "he that is called the Devil and Satan" (Rev. 12:9)—and the defeat he sustains from the woman's seed is a moral and spiritual victory. The "seed" who should destroy him is described emphatically as the *woman's* seed. It was the woman through whom sin had entered the race; by the seed of the woman would salvation come. The early church writ-

ers often pressed this analogy between Eve and the Virgin Mary. We may reject any element of over-exaltation of Mary they connected with it, but it remains significant that this peculiar phrase should be chosen to designate the future deliverer. I cannot believe the choice to be of accident. The promise to Abraham was that in *his* seed the families of the earth would be blessed; there the *male* is emphasized, but here it is the *woman*— the woman distinctively. There is, perhaps, as good scholars have thought, an allusion to this promise in 1 Timothy 2:15, where, with allusion to Adam and Eve, it is said, "But she shall be saved through her (or the) child-bearing."
—James Orr, *The Virgin Birth of Christ* (New York: Charles Scribner, 1907), 2–4.

Second Vatican Council, *Declaration on Religious Liberty* (1965)

A sense of the dignity of the human person has been impressing itself more and more deeply on the consciousness of contemporary man, and the demand is increasingly made that men should act on their own judgment, enjoying and making use of a responsible freedom, not driven by coercion but motivated by a sense of duty. The demand is likewise made that constitutional limits should be set to the powers of government, in order that there may be no encroachment on the rightful freedom of the person and of associations. This demand for freedom in human society chiefly regards the quest for the values proper to the human spirit. It regards, in the first place, the free exercise of religion in society. This Vatican Council takes careful note of these desires in the minds of men. It proposes to declare them to be greatly in accord with truth and justice....

This Vatican Council declares that the human person has a right to religious freedom. This freedom means that all men are to be immune from coercion on the part of individuals or of social groups and of any human power, in such wise that no one is to be forced to act in a manner contrary to his own beliefs, whether privately or publicly, whether alone or in association with others within due limits.

The council further declares that the right to religious freedom has its foundation in the very dignity of the human person as this dignity is known through the revealed word of God and by reason itself. This right of the human person to religious freedom is to be recognized in the constitutional law whereby society is governed and thus it is to become a civil right.

—Norman P. Tanner, *The Decrees of the Ecumenical Councils* (Washington, D.C.: Georgetown University Press, 1990), 56.

Dietrich Bonhoeffer. *The Cost of Discipleship* (1937)

Cheap grace is the deadly enemy of our church. Today our struggle pertains to costly grace.

Cheap grace means that grace as cheap merchandise, cheap forgiveness, cheap comfort, cheap sacraments; it is grace as inexhaustible storeroom of the church, emptied by careless hands without thought or limitation. It is grace without a price, without cost. Is it not precisely the meaning of grace that the bill was paid in advance for all eternity? Once the bill is paid, everything may be obtained without cost. Since the cost was infinite, the possibilities of using it are infinite as well. What would grace be if it were not cheap grace?

Cheap grace means grace as doctrine, as principle, as theological system; it means forgiveness of sins as a universal truth, means the love of God as the proper Christian understanding of God. Whoever affirms this love already has the forgiveness of sins. The church which so understands grace claims to have this grace. In this church, the world finds a cheap cover for its sins, which are not repented. Nor does the world wish to be freed of those sins. Therefore cheap grace is the denial of the living word of God, denial of the incarnation of the Word of God.

Cheap grace means justification of sin and not of the sinner. Since grace does everything, everything can remain as heretofore. "All our striving is in vain." The world remains the world, and we remain sinners. "Even in the perfect life." Therefore, the Christian should live as does the world, should follow the values of the world and above all not dare—as did the Reformation radicals with their heresy—to live under grace a different life than under sin. He surely must refrain from agitating against grace, to humiliate great, cheap grace, and to posit a new biblical legalism by attempting an obedient life under the commandments of Jesus Christ. The world is justified by grace, therefore, for the sake of this grace, in order not to resist this irreplacable grace, the Christian lives as does the world. To be sure, the Christian would like to do something extraordinary, it is undoubtedly the heaviest burden not to be able to do this but to live in a worldly fashion....

Cheap grace is proclamation of forgiveness without repentance; baptism without church discipline; the Lord's Supper without the confession of sin; absolution without personal confession. Cheap grace is grace without discipleship, grace without the cross, grace without the incarnate Jesus Christ.

Costly grace is the hidden treasure in the field, for which humans joyfully sell all they have; the precious pearl for which the merchant gives all his property; the kingdom of Christ for which people pluck the eye that offends, the call of Jesus Christ, to which the disciple responds by leaving the nets and following him.

Costly grace is the gospel, which is evermore sought, the gift, which is evermore desired, the door which must be knocked. It is costly grace because it calls for discipleship; it is grace, because it calls for being a disciple of Jesus Christ; it is costly, because it demands one's life. It is grace, because it bestows life if rightly understood; it is costly, because it condemns sin. It is grace, because it justifies the sinner. It is costly grace, above all, because it was costly for God because it cost God the life of his son—"you have been purchased with a precious price"—and because it cannot therefore be cheap for us. Whatever is costly for God, above all his grace, because God did not consider his son too costly for our lives but gave him up for us. Costly grace is the incarnation of God.

—Dietrich Bonhoeffer, *Nachfolge* (Munich: Chr. Kaiser, 1952), 1–3 (author's translation).

José María Vigil. *Getting the Poor Down from the Cross* (2007)

All Theology is an expression of praxis and spirituality, that is to say, of a form of being Christian and of following Jesus. These are the "secondary" and "primary" moments of which Gustavo Gutierrez spoke many years ago. Even if at this stage it may seem self-evident, this simple finding is one of the great contributions of liberation theology to all theology, one of the affirmations that make this theology a "teacher of suspicion" (Paul Ricoeur). It is intolerable, though, for a large part of the theological intelligentsia, whether in Rome or in San Salvador, in Tübingen or in Buenos Aires.

The history of the reception of Vatican II in Latin America is inseparable from the road that the Christian communities of our continent have made, first towards the poor, later together with the poor, and finally originating from the poor. It would be impossible to relate in any other way or by any other roads to theology than through what the Spirit inflamed within us, through the response to Vatican II. The option for the poor with all its implications, ripe and unheard-of fruit of the Council in Latin America, testifies to this.

Although there are some who always wanted to see in such an option a circumstantial "deviation" of the authentic Christian faith perpetrated by the "horizontalizers," what Christians in Latin America express in it is the recovery of an essential dimension of the Gospel of Jesus, many times forgotten, but read in between the lines in the lives of those believers— of whom there will never be a lack—who knew how to express the radicalism of the Gospel at the most diverse moments in history. For however weak it was in many circumstances, the flame of this torch was passing from generation to generation (this is what tradition means!) from the beginning. And so it was that one day John XXIII invited all Christians to "shake off from Peter's seat the imperial dust of Constantine," to turn to the sources, and to make the Church the "Church of the Poor." In our continent, many took this to heart. And they continue to do it.

One has either experienced this perspective, or one has not. And if the latter is the case, one can either open him/herself to the authenticity of the experience of others, or one can negate it obstinately or even ridicule it. I believe that it is worth the effort to review an example of this latter attitude. In the "Instruction on Certain Aspects of the 'Theology of Liberation'" (1984), the Congregation for the Doctrine of the Faith affirms/accuses: "We should recall that the preferential option described at 'Puebla' is two-fold: for the poor and 'for the young.' It is significant that the option for the young has in general been passed over in total silence" (VI, 6). I will only make two brief comments. One point to the conceptual: these two options—one centered on the pain caused by the human being and its structures, the other centered on an age group—cannot command the same theological-pastoral intensity. The other comment is entirely practical: in Latin America, the immense majority of the poor are young and the immense majority of the young are poor. The distinction made in Puebla is often unverifiable in practice. But, since only concepts are evaluated in Rome, major barbarities end up being said without anyone being taken to task for them.

In the following lines, I only seek to share some intuitions that speak to us about the poor as a theological setting, coming from the perspective of faith in the evangelical testimony of Jesus' relationship with the poor.

This is the hermeneutic setting—normative for Christian thought—of the response to the God of the Kingdom and of life in abundance.
—José María Vigil, *Getting the Poor Down from the Cross* (International Theological Commission of the Ecumenical Association of Third World Theologians, 2007), 53–54.

MODERN STATEMENTS OF FAITH AND CONFESSIONS

The Anglican Communion. Lambeth Conference of 1888.

"Lambeth Quadrilateral" of 1888 is a statement by the Anglican bishops that established the parameters of Anglican ability to engage in church unions and mergers. It stated, as basis of the Anglican faith:

The Holy Scriptures of the Old and New Testaments as containing all things necessary to salvation and as being the rule and ultimate standard of faith.

The Apostles' Creed as the Baptismal Symbol; and the Nicene Creed as the sufficient statement of the Christian faith.

The two Sacraments ordained by Christ himself—Baptism and the Supper of the Lord—ministered with unfailing use of Christ's words of Institution and of the elements ordained by Him.

The Historic Episcopate locally adapted, in the methods of its administration, to the varying needs of the nations and peoples called of God into the unity of His Church.

The United Church of Christ (1959)

The United Church of Christ came into being in 1957 through the merger of the Congregational Christian Church and the Evangelical and Reformed Church; the statement of faith was adopted by the General Synod of the United Church of Christ in 1959.

[We believe that God] in Jesus Christ, the man of Nazareth, our crucified and risen Lord, he has come to us and shared our common lot, conquering sin and death and reconciling the world to himself. He bestows upon us his Holy Spirit, creating and renewing the church of Jesus Christ, binding in covenant faithful people of all ages, tongues, and races. He calls us into his church to accept the cost and joy of discipleship, to be his servants in the service of men, to proclaim the gospel to all the world and resist the powers of evil, to share in Christ's baptism and eat at his table, to join him in his passion and victory. He promises to all who trust him forgiveness of sins and fullness of grace, courage in the struggle for justice and peace, his presence in trial and rejoicing, and eternal life in his king-dom which has no end.

Masai Creed (1960)

This creed was composed by (Catholic) missionaries in East Africa in con-junction with the Masai people. It blends local and universal aspects of the faith.

We belief in the one High God of love who created the beautiful world and everything good in it. He created man and wanted man to be happy in the world. God loves the world and every nation and tribe in the world. We have known this God in darkness, and we now know God in the light. God promised in his book the Bible that he would save the world and all the nations and tribes.

We believe that God made good his promise by sending his son, Jesus Christ, a man by the flesh, a Jew by tribe, born poor in a little village, who left his home and was always on safari, doing good, curing people by the power of God, teaching about God and man, showing that the meaning of religion is love. He was rejected by his people, tortured and nailed hands and feet to a cross, and died. He lay buried in the grave, but the hyenas did not touch him, and on the third day he rose from the grave. He ascended to the skies. He is lord.

We believe that all our sins are forgiven through him. All who have faith in him must be sorry about their sins, be baptized in the Holy Spirit of God, live by the rules of love and share the bread together, to announce the good news to others until Jesus comes again. We are wait-ing for him. He is alive. He lives. This we believe. Amen.

—Vincent J. Donovan, *Christianity Rediscovered* (Maryknoll, N.Y.: Orbis, 2003), 200.

SCRIPTURE INDEX

Old Testament

Genesis
1:4 47
3:8 .... 216, 217
14:14 74
47:9 225

Exodus 26
20:2-3 67
32:14 217

Deuteronomy
23:1 26

Joshua
10:12 215

1 Samuel
15 26

Psalms 13
51 228

Isaiah
11:6 138

Daniel 95

Apocrypha

Wisdom of Solomon 13

New Testament

Matthew 27, 34
10:20 174

10:32 52
12:31-32 77
14:13-21 4
16:18-19 .... 104, 106
19:16-30 .... 79–80, 81, 82
26:26 .... 12, 170
26:29 11
28:19 .... 2, 6, 9

Mark 27, 245
14:22 12
16:15 .... 2, 6

Luke 34, 70
2:52 72
14:23 49
18:23 79–80
22:19-20 .... 12, 179

John 29, 34, 73, 74, 181
1:2 74
1:18 216
11:43-44 4

Acts 4, 7, 8, 9, 60, 277, 327
2:5-13 7
6 108
11:26 2
15:6-21 9

Romans
6 11
7 50
8:2 69
10:9 54
13 .... 16, 47, 273
13:13-14 45
16:7 277

1 Corinthians
6:12.. 10
7:9.. 50–51
9:16 208
10:23... 10
11 11
11:24-25 12
12:9-10 10–11

Galatians 69
3:28 304

Philippians
2:10-11 91

Colossians
1:15.. 73
2-3 11

1 Timothy 14
2:11-14 277

2 Timothy.. 14

Titus... 14

Hebrews................................... 29, 70, 73

James....................................... 14, 29, 202

2 Peter... 29
2:1.. 60

1 John
2:15.. 80

2 John.. 29

3 John.. 29

Jude... 29

Revelation .... xvi, 26, 29

SUBJECT INDEX

abbot/abbess (office), 85, 88, 101, 110, 279
abortion, 63, 275, 301, 321
Abraham (patriarch), 55, 75, 216
abstinence, 80, 81, 98. *See also* sexual
   abstinence
Adam, 50, 51, 67, 120, 216, 217
Adeodatus (son of Augustine), 44
adiaphora, 165
Admonition to Parliament (1572), 197
adoptionism, 34
Adrian VI (pope), 275
adultery, 51, 108, 194
Aeternis Patris, 254
Africa, 3, 143, 255, 256, 258, 263, 306, 317
   North, xvi, 7, 14, 33, 38, 40, 45, 78, 79,
   94, 98, 143, 305, 317
African Americans, 256, 294, 302–4, 310
African Methodist Episcopal Church, 304
Akiba ben Joseph, 42
Akko (Acre), Israel, 138
Albert of Brandenburg, Cardinal (arch-
   bishop of Mainz), 151–52
alcohol, 233, 237, 294, 298, 302
Aleander, Cardinal Girolamo, 156
Alexander (bishop of Alexandria), 56, 63,
   72, 73, 74
Alexander VI (pope), 281
Alexandria, Egypt, 33, 41, 56, 60, 71, 74,
   75, 94, 105, 245
Alexius I Comnenus (emperor), 134
Algeria, 44, 136
allegory, 26, 43
alleluia (acclamation), 134
Allstedt, Germany, 171–72
aloofness, 2–3, 12, 15, 16, 47, 83, 174
altar, 313, 316
Amalekites, 26
Amboise, Conspiracy of, 199

Ambrose (bishop of Milan), 31, 37
Ambrose (friend of Origen), 41
American Baptist Churches, 320
American Lutheran Church, 263
American Revolution, 91, 287, 303
Americas, 48, 256, 257, 281, 284, 306
Amiens, France, 330, 331
Amsterdam, Netherlands, 150, 262
Anabaptists, 61, 62, 89, 166, 168, 173–77,
   179, 206, 209, 278, 313, 331. *See also*
   Mennonites
Anchorites, 81, 83
Anglicanism, 5, 87, 169, 201, 203, 209,
   210, 223, 238, 258, 262, 284, 285,
   286, 287–88, 303, 318. *See also*
   Church of England
Anicetus (pope), 30
Anne Boleyn (queen of England), 192–95
anthropology, 6, 49–51, 67, 243, 247, 257,
   314
anti-Catholicism, 150, 221, 298
Antichrist, 95, 139
anticlericalism, 183
Antioch, 8, 14, 60, 94, 105, 137, 142
Antioch, Council of (341), 105
anti-Semitism, 138, 145, 146, 266, 272,
   274, 315
Antitrinitarianism, 169, 181, 209
Antony of Egypt, 82, 116
Antwerp, Belgium, 197
Apocalypse of Paul, 65
Apocalypticism, 119, 139, 175
Apocryphal gospels, 27, 65
Apollinaris (bishop of Laodicea), 143
Apologists, 35–36, 41
Apology (of Augsburg Confession), 161
apostasy, 64, 79
apostle (church office), 11

405

Apostles (the Twelve), 12, 26, 29–30, 32, 53, 256, 277
Apostles' Council, 9
Apostles' Creed, 30, 52, 53, 55, 57, 58, 59, 170, 207, 311
Apostolic authority, 29–30, 35, 68, 104
Apostolic Fathers, 13, 32
Apostolic succession, 29–30, 104, 108
Arabs, 79, 143, 305
Arcadius (emperor), 126
architecture, 324–35
Arianism and Arians, 24, 56, 57, 75, 76, 96, 97, 124, 127, 142, 182, 215, 320–21
Aristotelianism, 119
Aristotle, 121, 201
Arius, 56, 63, 71–76, 182
Arkansas, 253
Arles, Council of (314), 78
Arminius, Jacob, 212
Arndt, Johann, 223–24, 233
  Bücher vom wahren Christentum, 223, 224, 225
Arnold, Gottfried, 61
art(s), 120, 185, 203, 205, 212, 241, 256, 323, 328. *See also* music
Arthur, Prince of Wales, 191
Asbury, Francis, 238, 288
asceticism, 40, 41, 45, 67, 82, 115
Asia, 3, 136, 142, 143, 256, 259, 305
Asia Minor, 1, 3, 16, 35, 39, 82, 94, 142
Assisi, Italy, 115, 116, 119
Assumption (Blessed Virgin Mary), 130, 253, 273
astronomy, 214
Athanasian Creed, 52
Athanasius (patriarch of Alexandria), 31, 37, 56, 57, 72, 73–74, 75, 76
  biography of Antony, 82
atheism, 240, 264, 265
atonement, 73, 181, 242
Augsburg, Germany, 152, 161–62, 165, 166, 184
Augsburg, Peace of, 166, 189
Augsburg Confession (1530), 54, 161, 168, 169
Augsburg Interim, 165

Augustine (bishop of Hippo), 31, 37, 43–51, 79, 84, 99, 109, 146, 288, 291, 321
  Confessions, 43–44, 45
  De civitate Dei, 46–47, 95
  De Trinitate, 46
  Retractions, 43–44
Augustinians (order), 111, 113, 149, 153
Austria, 140, 159, 174, 203, 254
Austria-Hungary, 145, 320
authority, 14, 26, 29–30, 106, 126, 153, 154, 167, 185, 202, 249, 252, 320, 331. *See also under* Bible; papacy
Avila, Spain, 187
Ayyubid dynasty, 138

Babylonian captivity, 129
Bacon, Francis, 215
Balkan Peninsula, 75, 94, 96, 136, 137, 162
baptism, 10, 11, 14, 50, 53, 55, 59, 79, 173, 174, 175, 212, 246, 257, 269, 311, 316, 327, 331
  forced, 140
  infant, 11, 82, 89, 173, 205, 207, 316, 328
  of the dead, 293, 294
Baptist Confession of Faith, 169, 170
Baptist Missionary Society (English), 259
Baptists, 169, 212, 238, 259, 285, 286, 289, 290, 303, 320, 332
Barcelona, Spain, 270, 333
Barmen Declaration, 268, 269
Baroque style, 324, 331–32
Barth, Karl, 268, 270
Basel, Switzerland, 177
Basil (bishop of Caesarea), 37, 84
basilicas, 326, 327
Basilides, 67
Bauer, Bruno, *Kritik der evangelischen Geschichte der Synoptiker*, 245
Baur, Ferdinand Christian, 245
Bavaria, 190, 203, 223
Baxter, Richard
  A Call to the Unconverted, 224
  The Saints' Everlasting Rest, 224
Becket, Thomas à (archbishop of Canterbury), 103

begging and beggars, 111, 112, 115, 117, 118, 185
Belgic Confession, 169
Benedict of Nursia (abbott of Monte Cassino), 85
  Regula, 85–86, 110, 111, 118
Benedict XVI (pope), 31
Benedictines (order), 88, 109, 110, 116, 121
Berlin, Germany, 225, 226, 242, 266, 269, 270
Bernadette, Saint (Marie-Bernarde Soubirous), 251
Bernard of Clairvaux, 146, 250
Bethlehem, Pennsylvania, 232
Bible
  Apocrypha, 29, 42
  authority of the, 106, 122, 123, 126, 130, 153, 156, 157, 159, 167–68, 170, 171, 172, 184, 202, 221, 268, 291, 300, 314
  canon, 28–29, 42, 65, 70, 134
  commentaries, 41, 42, 122
  Epistles (Pauline), 4, 8, 10, 27, 29, 39, 60, 70, 71, 73, 245, 277, 320
  Gospels, 4, 5, 6, 26–27, 28, 29, 39, 68, 69, 73, 244
  inspiration of the, 202, 300, 311
  interpretation of the, xvii, 4–6, 13, 26, 42, 43, 69, 119, 169, 172, 181, 218, 220, 243, 244–45, 255, 274, 276, 290, 295, 300, 301, 319
  New Testament, 7, 13, 29, 30, 39, 52, 65, 70, 71, 104, 245, 246, 277, 287, 321
  Old Testament, 6, 10, 13, 26, 27, 37, 39, 42, 43, 62, 69, 70, 71, 91, 146, 218, 266, 330
  study, 226, 227, 233, 255, 296, 297
  translations, 42, 123, 125, 157, 193, 210, 259
bigamy, 164
bishop(s) (office), 11, 14, 30, 31, 32, 78–79, 84, 96, 99, 100, 101, 103–4, 108, 111, 140, 175, 178, 185, 197, 205, 221, 232, 238, 248, 267, 274, 278, 284, 288, 325, 331

Bismarck, Otto von, 102, 254
Bithynia, 1
Black Death. See Bubonic plague
Black Theology, 309, 310
blasphemy, 49, 62, 90, 91, 181, 220
blood libel, 141–42
body/spirit dichotomy, 51, 68, 81. See also dualism
Bohemia, 203, 204, 231
Bohemian Brethren, 231
Böhme, Jakob, 224, 233
Bologna, Italy, 253
Bolshevik Revolution, 264
Bonaventura, Cardinal, 118, 119
Bonhoeffer, Dietrich, xvii, 269–70
Book of Common Prayer, The, 194, 195, 210, 211, 284, 285, 288
Book of Concord, 54, 169
Book of Mormon, 292
Booth, Catherine Mumford, 299
Booth, William, 299
  In Darkest England..., 299
Boston, Massachusetts, 302
Bourbon family, 199
Bourges, France, 330
Boxer Rebellion (1900), 259
Braunschweig, Germany, 222
Brazil, 261
British East India Company, 259
Brooklyn, New York, 297
Brotherly Union (1527 confession), 168
Bubonic plague, 140
Bucer, Martin, 179
burning (execution), 62, 155, 156, 181, 194, 206, 314
Busskampf, 228
Butler, Joseph (bishop of Durham), 220
  The Analogy of Religion..., 220, 247
Byzantine church. See Eastern church

Caecilian (bishop of Carthage), 77, 78
Cajetan, Cardinal Tomasso de Vio, 152
Calvin, John, xvii, 71, 171, 177–81, 198, 306, 312
  Institutes, 177–78, 180

Calvinism and Calvinists, xvi, 5, 166, 169, 170, 179, 181, 189, 197, 201, 202, 203, 209, 211, 212, 223, 226–27, 233, 265, 285, 306, 312, 313
Cambridge, England, 197, 220, 224
camp meetings, 296
Canada, 282
cannibalism, 12, 16, 38
Canon of Scripture. See under Bible
Canossa, Italy, 102, 254
Canterbury, England, 103, 193
Cape Cod, Massachusetts, 285
Cape of Good Hope, South Africa, 281
Cape Verde Islands, 281
capitalism, 120
Cappadocia, 84
Cappadocian Fathers, 31, 37, 318
cardinal (office), 100, 106–7
Carey, William, 259, 260
    An Enquiry into the Obligations of Christians . . . , 259
Carlstadt, Andreas Bodenstein von, 153, 172, 179
Carmelites (order), 111, 187
    discalced, 185, 187–88
Carthage, 38, 77, 78, 79, 94, 305
Carthage, Councils of, 79
Carthage, Illinois, 293
Cartwright, Thomas, 197
Casas, Bartholomé de las, 257
    Defense of the Indians, 257
castration, 41
casuistry, 203
Câteau Cambrésis, Treaty of, 199
catechesis, 90, 169, 261, 274
Cathari (heretics), 111–12, 145, 314
cathedrals, 325, 328, 329, 330, 331, 333
Catherine de' Medici (queen of France), 199
Catherine of Sienna, 123
Catholic Church, Roman. See Roman Catholicism
Catholic Reform (term), 182
Cavaliers, 211
Celestine I (pope), 98
celibacy, 40, 44, 51, 81, 88, 119, 291
clerical, 101, 108, 134, 169, 193

Celts, 94
Cenobites, 83–84
censorship, 53, 68, 185, 221, 222
Central America, 257, 263, 275, 282, 283, 317
Chalcedon, Council of (451), 58, 94, 106, 132
Chalcedon, Definition of, 58, 132, 143
Chamberlain, Houston Stewart, Foundations of the Nineteenth Century, 266
Champlain, Samuel de, 282
charity, 87, 96, 108, 112, 151, 167
Charles I (king of England), 203, 210, 211, 286
Charles II (king of England), 212
Charles IV (emperor), 147
Charles V (emperor), 155–56, 158, 161, 162, 163–66, 183–84, 192
Chartres, France, 330, 331
Chiapas, Guatemala, 257
Chicago, Illinois, 297, 298, 302
children, xvii, 19, 137, 138, 141, 200, 228, 229, 310
Children's Crusade (1212), 138
Chile, 284
China, 143, 255, 256, 259
Chi-rho (monogram), 22, 89
Christ (title), 2, 4, 6, 9. See also Messiah
Christendom, 48, 88, 109, 135, 309, 316–17
Christian Mission (Salvation Army), 299
Christianity, xv–xvii, 1–2, 3, 4, 7–9, 10, 11, 13, 20, 22, 23, 24–25, 31, 36–37, 38, 44, 46, 51, 89, 95, 125, 219, 220, 222, 241, 242, 243, 245, 249, 268, 287, 302–3, 316–20, 321–22, 323
Christmas, 212
Christology, 34, 36, 52, 54–59, 63, 66, 72–73, 74, 76, 94, 105, 126, 130, 132, 142–43, 179, 181, 305, 311, 314. 320
Christopher, Saint, 33
Christotokos (Marian title), 142
Chubb, Thomas, 219, 222
    The True Gospel of Jesus Christ Asserted, 220

Church, the, xv–xvi, 7, 8, 9, 10, 11, 17, 18, 19, 20, 22, 23, 28, 30, 33, 37, 40, 46, 50, 53, 54, 59, 60, 61, 63, 65–66, 67–68, 79, 82, 84, 95, 96, 120, 150, 154–55, 157, 173, 174, 191, 205, 206, 250–51, 274. *See also* Eastern church
organization and governance of, 10–11, 14, 17, 23, 30, 32, 103, 178–79, 180, 197, 232, 265, 267–68, 270–71, 277, 284, 288, 321
unity of, 128–29, 136, 253, 261–62, 274. *See also* ecumenism
church and society, 16, 18, 47, 48, 49, 62, 86, 87, 89–91, 93, 96, 101, 135, 139, 150, 174, 240, 247, 249, 274, 287, 288, 307, 310, 311, 312, 313, 321, 323
church and state, 15–16, 17–18, 19, 21, 23–24, 47–48, 53, 62, 75–76, 78, 79, 82, 89, 90, 91, 93, 96, 97, 100–103, 105, 135, 144, 146, 150, 158, 165, 172, 173, 184, 189, 193, 199, 207, 240–41, 247, 248–49, 254, 263–65, 269, 271, 272–73, 310, 313, 317, 318. *See also* state religion
separation of, 62–63, 89, 91, 254, 264, 286, 288
church attendance, 207, 246, 247, 317–18
church buildings, 10, 17, 19, 78, 93, 96, 119, 120, 203, 205, 212, 241, 264, 265, 285, 323–34
Church of England, 169, 197, 209, 210–11, 233, 236, 238, 240, 285, 287, 288, 332. *See also* Anglicanism
Church of Jesus Christ of Latter-day Saints. *See* Mormons
Cimabue, Giovanni, 120
circuit riders, 289
circumcision, 9, 10
Cistercians (order), 111
Citeaux, France, 111
Civil Constitution of the Clergy (France), 240–41, 248–49
civil rights (U.S.), 301
Clare of Assisi, 118
Clark, Samuel, 220

classical style, 332
Clement I (pope), 103–4
Clement II (pope), 115
Clement III (pope), 102
Clement VII (pope), 191, 192
Clement XIV (pope), 248
Clement of Alexandria, 41, 43
clergy, 23, 77, 107–8, 183, 207–8, 226, 228, 248, 289, 302. *See also* priesthood and priests *and under* celibacy; marriage
clergy/laity, 14, 86, 107, 108, 320–21
Clermont, France, 134
clothing, 40, 146, 147, 185, 226, 237, 315
Clotilda (queen consort of Clovis), 97
Clovis (king of the Franks), 97
Cluny, France, 109–11
coercion, 49
Coke, Thomas, 238, 288
Cold War, 266, 301
Colet, John, 190, 191
Coligny, Gaspard de, 200
collegia pietatis, 226, 227
collegium philobiblicum, 227
Collins, Anthony, 219
Colored Episcopal Methodist Church, 304
Columbus, Christopher, 214, 281
Columbus, Ohio, 299
commands and counsels, 80–81
common people. *See* laity
communion in both kinds, 165
Communism, 175, 232, 264, 265, 266, 275, 298, 301
community, 36, 83, 150, 173, 334
Confessing Church (Germany), 266, 268, 269, 270
Confessio Augustana. *See* Augsburg Confession
Confessio Tetrapolitana, 161
Confessionalism, 201–2, 204
Confessions of faith. *See* creeds
Congregational Christian Churches, 320
Congregationalists, 212, 238, 288, 332
Conrad II (emperor), 328
consensus, 250–51
conservatism and conservatives, 5, 60, 64, 241, 244, 249–50, 251, 255, 260,

conservatism and conservatives (continued) 262, 265–66, 268, 274, 275, 276, 287, 295, 299, 300–301, 304, 310, 319

Constance, Council of (1414–1418), 156, 252

Constantine I (emperor), 3, 19, 21–23, 29, 35, 47, 53, 56, 57, 68, 73, 74–75, 76, 78, 89, 90, 93, 105, 106, 108, 125, 135, 217, 323, 326

Constantinople (city), 33, 105, 125, 126, 128, 130, 138, 142

Constantinople (patriarchate), 99, 105–6, 125, 126, 128, 130, 169, 253, 262

Constantinople I, Council of (381), 58, 76, 106, 130

Constantinople II, Council of (553), 126, 130

Constantinople III, Council of (681), 130, 132

Constantius II (emperor), 24, 57, 76, 124

consubstantial (term), 57, 58

contemplation, 45, 87

contraception, 274–75

conversatio (term), 88

conversion(s), 116, 177, 227–28, 229, 230, 235–36, 288–89, 294, 296, 297, 298, 301
   forced, 140, 257, 261

Cop, Nicolas, 198

Copernicus, Nicolaus, 215
   On the Revolution of the Heavenly Bodies, 214

Coptic Church, 58, 306

Coptic language, 65

councils, 57, 75, 106, 122, 126, 130, 133, 153, 183, 185, 252, 253

Counter–Reformation, 182, 231, 316

Cranmer, Thomas (archbishop of Canterbury), 169, 193–95

creeds, 3, 30, 52–59, 168–70, 202, 311–12

crisis, sense of, 151, 154–55, 157, 191

Cromwell, Oliver, 210, 211, 212, 213

Crosby, Fanny, 297–98

cross, sign of the, 18, 197, 314

cross, theology of the, 153, 170

crucifixion, 19, 23. See also under Jesus Christ

cruciform (architecture), 325

Crusade(s), 96, 127, 135–36, 138
   First, 134–37, 139, 140, 145
   Second, 137, 140
   Third, 137
   Fourth, 128, 137–38
   Seventh, 138
   Eighth, 138

Crystal Cathedral (Garden Grove, Calif.), 333–34

Cuius regio, eius religio (motto), 166

cursing. See swearing

Cyprian (bishop of Carthage), 31, 79, 104

Cyril (apostle of the Slavs), 124–25

Cyril (bishop of Jerusalem), 37

Cyril (patriarch of Alexandria), 142–43

Czech Republic, 124, 231

Dante Alighieri, Inferno, 46

Dark Ages (term), 95–96. See also Middle Ages

Darwin, Charles, 218, 295, 300
   On the Origin of Species, 247

David (king of Israel), 13, 26, 228

deacon (office), 11, 14, 108, 178–79

death, 154, 220, 261, 322

Decius (emperor), 18, 64

Declaration of Independence (U.S.), 287

Declaration of Sirmium, 57

Declaration of the Rights of Man, 239

Defenestration of Prague (1618), 204

Deism and deists, 219, 220–21, 222, 238, 242, 247, 287, 290, 295, 309, 332

Demiurge, 67, 70

democracy, 239, 251, 266, 288

Denmark, 189, 246

Descartes, René, 215

Desert Fathers, 67, 80, 82, 83

Deus vult (battle cry), 136

Deutsche Christen. See Germanic Christians

development of dogma, 130

"Dialogues of Jesus with his Disciples...," 54

Diaspora, Jewish, 12, 13, 90

Dibelius, Otto, 266
Dictatus Papae, 101
Didascalia Apostolorum, 55
Diego de Acevedo (bishop of Osma), 111
dietary laws, 9
diocese, 104, 105
Diocletian (emperor), 18–19, 20, 75, 76
discipline, 40, 80, 85, 134, 179, 228, 232, 235, 286, 313
dissent, 49, 53, 59–60, 62–64, 68, 89, 90, 145, 153, 181, 196, 208, 210–11, 221, 238, 314
diversity/uniformity, 11, 13, 32, 65–66, 94, 166, 170–71, 173, 189, 239
divorce, 51, 313, 318
Dnieper River, 125
doctor of the church (title), 121, 187, 188, 279
dogma, 223, 243, 250–51, 255
Dominic de Guzmán, 111–13
Dominicans (order), 87, 111–13, 120, 121, 153, 187, 250, 275
Domitian (emperor), 16
Donation of Constantine, 105, 217
Donatism and Donatists, 64, 76–79, 109, 208
Donatus (bishop of Carthage), 77–78
Doopsgezinde (Dutch Mennonites), 177
Dordt, Synod of (1618), 169
Dositheus, Confession of, 169
Dresden, Germany, 226, 229, 231, 232
dualism, 47, 67, 68, 69–70, 81, 112
Duns Scotus, John, 250
Düsseldorf, Germany, 230
Dutch East India Company, 258
Dutch Reformed Church, 258
Dwight, Timothy, 289

East Asia, 259
East Northfield, Massachusetts, 298
Easter, 34–35, 57, 212
Eastern church, 28, 33–34, 41, 55, 60, 73, 74, 75, 76, 84, 94, 96, 106, 120, 124–34, 142, 183
Eastern Orthodoxy, xvi, 58, 64, 87, 128, 143, 169, 262, 264, 306, 324. See also Russian Orthodox Church

Eberlin von Günzburg, Johann, 171
Ebionites, 13
ecclesia (term), 10
Eck, Johann, 153
economics, 119–20, 136, 138, 141, 147, 150, 159, 171, 177, 180, 189, 208, 228, 229, 256, 257, 259, 293, 299, 301, 324–25, 327, 328
eco-theology, 310
ecumenism, 167, 262–63, 319–20
Eden, Garden of, 50, 51, 67, 216
Edessa, 137
Edinburgh, Scotland, 260
education, 84, 87, 96, 112, 113, 119, 121, 123, 124, 185, 186, 207, 228, 242, 247, 259, 261, 264, 277, 282, 297, 298. See also seminaries
Edward VI (king of England), 194, 195
Edwards, Jonathan, 288
Egypt, 27, 54, 67, 80, 81, 82, 83, 94, 136, 143, 305, 306
Eisenhower, Dwight, 208
elder (church office), 11, 104, 178–79, 180, 197
election, 212
Eleutherus (deacon), 30
Elias, Brother, 119
Elizabeth I (queen of England), 169, 195, 204
Emerson, Ralph Waldo, 136
Emperor, Holy Roman (office), 156, 162
emperor worship, 16
End Time, 39, 119, 146, 224, 290
England, xvii, 87, 90, 91, 94, 97, 98, 102–3, 110, 137, 141, 147, 168–69, 180, 190, 191, 196, 199, 202, 203, 204, 208, 209, 210–13, 218, 219, 221, 224, 235–39, 245, 247, 248, 258, 259, 260, 282, 284, 286, 287, 289, 297, 299, 321, 332
English language, 123, 193, 194, 210
English Reformation, 53–54, 90, 91, 189, 191–96
enlightenment, 67, 68
Enlightenment, The, 5, 91, 95, 147, 221, 222, 239, 240, 241, 242, 244, 247, 248, 249, 251, 295, 332

Ephesus, 14, 16
Ephesus, Council of (431), 133
episcopacy. See bishop(s)
epistemology, 122
Erasmus, Desiderius, 150–51, 190, 191, 198
eschatology. See End Time
Essenes, 60
established religion. See state religion
ethics. See morality
Ethiopia, 94, 143, 282, 306
Ethiopian Orthodox Tewahedo Church, 256
Eucharist, 11–12, 14, 32, 34, 62, 123, 133, 167, 178, 179, 195, 205, 232, 233, 237, 238, 246, 262, 303, 316, 326. See also Mass
bread, 128, 178
Eugene III (pope), 124
Eugenikos, Markos (metropolitan of Ephesus), 129
Europe, 3, 86, 89, 93, 136, 144, 177, 190, 239, 240, 241, 247, 255–56, 258, 259, 260, 261, 263, 273, 287, 289, 290, 305, 306–7, 315, 316, 317, 318, 321–22, 323, 333
Eusebius (bishop of Caesarea), 19, 22, 29, 30, 56–57
Eusebius (bishop of Nicomedia), 74
Evangelical and Reformed Church, 327
Evangelical Churches (Germany), 265, 266, 268, 269
Evangelical Synod of North America, 321
Evangelical United Brethren Church, 321
Evangelische Kirche in Deutschland, 262
evangelism, 86, 87, 93, 232, 257, 258, 261, 291, 294, 297, 306
Eve, 51, 67, 216, 217
evolution (theory), 218, 295, 297, 301
excommunication, 35, 61–62, 64, 102, 103, 128, 153, 155, 158, 179, 183, 184, 235, 262
Exsurge domine, 153

faith, 10, 79, 122, 155, 168, 171, 173, 228, 235, 243
Falwell, Jerry, 301
Farel, Guillaume, 177–78

Fascism, 272–73
fasting, 40, 81, 134, 233, 288
Felgenhauer, Paul, 224
Felix (bishop of Aptunga), 77
Fell, Margaret, 278–79
Feminist Theology, 309
Ferdinand I (emperor), 166
Ferdinand II (king of Bohemia), 204
Ferrara, Italy, 129
Festschrift (term), 41
Feti, Domenico, 230
Feuerbach, Ludwig, 247
Field, John, 197
Fifth Monarchy Men, 212
Filioque, 127, 128, 129
Final Judgment. See Last Judgment
Finland, 189, 320
Fitzgerald, Edward Mary (bishop of Little Rock), 253
Flagellants, 140–41
Flanders, 140
Florence, Council of (1438–1445), 129
Florence, Italy, 129, 150, 327
font (baptismal), 327
forgiveness of sins, 54, 59, 151–52, 155, 243, 257
Formosus (pope), 99
Formula of Concord (1577), 169
fornication, 51
Forty-two Articles (1553), 169, 194
Fox, George, 212
Fragments from the Pen of an Anonymous Author, 222
France, 62, 94, 97, 110, 111–12, 136, 137, 140, 141, 162, 164, 177, 178, 179, 180, 184, 185, 189, 190, 198–201, 203, 204, 208, 209, 221, 224, 230, 238, 239, 240–41, 247, 248–49, 254, 264, 282–83, 328, 330. See also French Revolution
Francis I (king of France), 177, 184, 198–99
Francis II (king of France), 199
Francis de Sales (bishop of Geneva), Introduction à la vie dévote, 224
Francis of Assisi, xvii, 113–19, 124, 206, 303

Franciscans (order), 87, 111, 112–15, 117–20, 187, 250, 257
Francke, August Hermann, 227–29, 232, 260
Franckesche Stiftungen, 228–29
Frankenhausen, Germany, 159
Frankfurt, Germany, 150, 158, 225, 226, 227
Frederick I Barbarossa (emperor), 137
Frederick II (elector of Saxony), 152, 156
Frederick William I (elector of Brandenburg), 223, 225
Frederick William III (king of Prussia), 265
freedom, 239, 249, 251
  Christian, 49–50, 168, 193, 257, 275
  religious, 24, 49, 182, 197, 204, 212, 251, 274, 285, 286. See also toleration
French Revolution, 90, 91, 110, 239–40, 248, 249, 251, 263
Fuller, Thomas, Church History of Britain, 240
fundamentalism, 295–96, 300–301
Fundamentals, The, 295, 300
future life, 25, 59

Galen, Cardinal Clemens August von, 271–72
Galerius (emperor), 18, 19, 21
Galileo Galilei, 214, 215
Gaudí, Antoni, 333
Gaul, 97
gender, 10, 205, 269, 310. See also sexuality
Geneva, Switzerland, 171, 177–78, 179, 180–81, 197, 198, 313, 314
Genoa, Italy, 140
gentiles, 8–10, 13, 32
Georgia (American colony), 233
Georgia (Russian republic), 264
Georgian style, 334
Gerhardt, Paul, 224–25
  "Nun ruhen alle Wälder," 225
German language, 157, 203, 260
German Theology, 223
Germanic Christians, 266–68, 269, 270, 271
Germanic tribes, 93–94, 97

Germany, 48, 90, 94, 102, 110, 137, 139, 141, 145, 147, 151, 152, 154, 155–56, 158–59, 160–61, 163, 166–67, 168, 169, 171, 174, 175, 176, 183, 184, 189, 190, 203–4, 209–10, 221, 222, 226, 229, 230, 232–33, 245, 254, 258, 260, 262, 263, 265–73, 295, 302, 320, 328
  territorial rulers of, 155, 156, 158, 160, 162, 165, 166, 189, 207
ghettos, 185
Gibbon, Edward, Decline and Fall of the Roman Empire, 73, 95, 299
Gideons, the, 301
Giotto di Bondone, 120
Gladden, Washington, 299
Glaucha, Germany, 227, 228
globalization, 305
glossolalia, 7, 11, 39
Gnostic gospels, 27–28
gnosticism and gnostics, 28, 37, 38, 64–68, 104, 112
God, 3, 5, 6, 34, 36, 50, 67, 70, 71, 97, 122, 170, 180, 216, 217, 218–19, 298
  kingdom of, 6, 11, 75, 95, 276, 300
  proofs of, 122
God the Father, 6, 9, 34, 52, 54, 57, 58, 59, 72–73, 76
Golden Rule, 81
Gospel, the, xvi, 2, 4, 9, 10, 26, 29, 60, 61, 70, 257, 274, 276
Gospel of Judas, 27
Gospel of Peter, 14, 27
Gospel of Philip, 65
Gospel of Thomas, 4, 14, 27–28, 65
Gospel of Truth, 65
Gospel to the Egyptians, 65
Gothic style, 241, 324, 329–31, 332, 333
Goths, 18, 46, 75, 95, 96, 124
Göttingen, Germany, 270
grace, 49, 99, 155, 167, 170, 171, 180, 212
Graham, Billy, 301
gravamina, 154
Great Awakening (1734), xvi, 288, 296
Great Britain, 7, 299. See also England; Scotland
Greece, 14, 66, 82, 150, 332

Greek language, 7, 33, 39, 42, 60, 66, 72, 73, 227, 233
Greenland, 258
Gregory I (pope), 31, 98–99
Gregory VII (pope), 100–102, 115, 127, 254
Gregory XIII (pope), 200
Gregory XVI (pope), *Il trionfo della santa sede*, 249
Gregory of Nazianzus, 37, 75
Gregory of Nyssa, 37
Gregory of Tours, *History of the Franks*, 97
Guatemala, 257
Guidi, Cardinal Filippo Maria, 253
Guise family, 199, 200
Gustavus I Vasa (king of Sweden), 189
Gustavus II Adolf (king of Sweden), 204
Gutenberg, Johannes, 154, 207
Gutiérrez, Gustavo, *A Theology of Liberation*, 275–76

Habsburg family, 204
Hadrian (emperor), 326
Haeckel, Ernst, 247
Hagia Sophia (Constantinople church), 125, 128
Haile, John, 193
Halle, Germany, 221, 227, 228–29, 260
  orphanage, 228, 230
Hallesche Zeitung, 229
Hamburg, Germany, 221
Hamilton, Alexander, 286
Harnack, Adolf von, 71, 245
Heaven, 328, 329, 332
Hebrew language, 42, 218
Hefele, Karl Joseph von, 252–53, 254
Hegesippus, 30
Heidelberg, Gemany, 197
hell, 55
Helvetic Confessions (1536; 1564), 169
Henriette Marie (queen of England), 210
Henry, Patrick, 286
Henry II (king of England), 102–3
Henry II (king of France), 199
Henry III (emperor), 100
Henry III (king of France), 200

Henry IV (emperor), 101–2, 103, 127, 139, 254
Henry IV (king of France), 199, 200–201
Henry VIII (king of England), 54, 90, 91, 168, 184, 190, 191–94, 195, 199, 207, 248, 315
  Assertio Septem Sacramentorum, 184, 191
Herbert of Cherbury, 1st Baron (Edward Herbert), *De Veritate*, 219
Hercules, 22
heresy and heretics, xv, 3, 13, 37, 38, 53, 60–64, 68, 72, 79, 89, 108, 112, 113, 129, 142, 145, 155, 156, 160, 175, 184, 191, 194, 198, 206, 253, 255, 320
Hernnhut (community), 232, 236
Hesse, 158, 161, 164
Hexapla, 42
Hildebrand. *See* Gregory VII (pope)
Hildegard of Bingen, 123–24
  Scivias, 123–24
Hippo (Africa), 45, 79
Hippolytus, 31, 55
historiography, xv–xvii, 95, 206–7, 217, 218, 251
"history of religions," xvi, 245
Hitler, Adolf, 266, 269, 270, 271
Hodge, Charles, 295
Holland. *See* Netherlands
Holy Club (Oxford), 233, 235, 236, 237
Holy Cross, Congregation of, 254
Holy Family (Barcelona church), 333
Holy Land, 12, 96, 127, 135, 136, 137, 138, 139, 140, 185–86, 215, 324. *See also* Palestine
Holy Roman Empire, 100, 155, 165–67. *See also* emperor; Germany
Holy Spirit, 8, 9, 11, 39, 53, 54, 55, 59, 66, 127, 128, 212
homoiousios/homoousios, 72–73, 75, 127
homosexuality, 275, 318
Honorius I (pope), 132
Honorius (emperor), 126
Hooker, Richard, *Of the Laws of Ecclesiastical Polity*, 202, 209
hours, canonical, 86

Huguenots, 199–200, 201, 203
human nature. See anthropology
Humanae vitae, 274–75
Humanism and Humanists, 95, 150–51, 172, 190, 330
Humbert of Silva Candida, Cardinal, 128
Hungary, 140, 179, 189
Hunne, Richard, 191
Hunt, Robert, 284
Huntingdon, Countess of (Selina Hastings), 279
Huozmann, Rudiger (bishop of Speyer), 141
Hus, Jan, 156
hymns, 224, 225, 229, 289, 296, 297–98. See also music

iconoclasm, 120, 132–33
icons, 132, 133, 264
idolatry, 108, 132, 133
Ignatius (bishop of Antioch), 13, 14, 19, 31, 104
Ignatius of Loyola, 185–86
  Spiritual Exercises, 187
Illinois, 293
images, 132–33, 212, 223
Immaculate Conception (Blessed Virgin Mary), 120, 130, 250–51, 252, 254, 273, 318
imperialism, 258, 260–61, 263, 275, 284
Incas, 257
inclusivity, 61. See also diversity
Index Librorum Prohibitorum, 185, 214, 217
India, 94, 113, 143, 229, 255, 256, 259, 282, 306, 307
Indians. See Native Americans
indulgences, 135, 149, 151–52, 153, 167, 177, 191, 203
Industrial Revolution, 299, 332
Ineffabilis Deus, 250–51
inerrancy, biblical, 300, 311
infallibility, papal, 62–63, 101, 106, 252–54, 318
infanticide, 23
Innocent III (pope), 112, 117–18, 119
Inquisition, The, 49, 113, 214, 217, 314, 315

Inter caetera, 281, 282
intercessory prayers, 21
Interrogatory Creed, 55
intolerance, 3, 90, 91, 145, 174, 248, 291, 293, 314, 315, 322
Investiture Controversy, 100, 101, 127, 207, 248, 254
Iraq, 143, 305, 318
Ireland, 84, 97–98, 219, 302
Irenaeus (bishop of Lyons), 13, 27, 31, 37, 54–55
Isaac (patriarch), 55
Islam, xvi, 79, 94, 125, 127, 128, 130, 132, 133, 135, 136, 137, 138, 139, 140, 141, 143, 162, 186, 187, 256, 258, 264, 305, 316, 317, 318
Israel (people), 36, 70
Italy, 14, 33, 82, 85, 94, 99, 105, 110, 137, 150, 189, 217, 251, 263, 272–73, 302
itinerant ministers, 289

Jacob (patriarch), 26, 55
James, Saint (the apostle), 12
James I (king of England), 210, 211
  Book of Sports, 210
Jamestown, Virginia, 284, 285
Jamnia, Israel, 42
Jane Seymour (queen of England), 194
Japan, 256, 259–60
Jefferson, Thomas, 286, 287
Jehovah's Witnesses, xvi, 294–95
Jerome, 33, 41, 64
Jerusalem, 2, 6, 9, 11, 12, 105, 127, 137, 169, 215, 330
Jerusalem, kingdom of, 137
Jesuits (order), 87, 185–87, 188, 203, 248, 253, 256, 284, 320
  Rule, 186–87
Jesus Christ, xv, xvi, xvii, 2, 4, 5, 6–12, 13, 22, 23, 24, 25, 26, 27–28, 29, 30, 31, 33, 40, 50, 52, 54, 59, 65, 68, 69, 70, 82, 91, 116, 146, 172, 206, 216, 219, 220, 224, 230, 243, 244, 246, 250, 266, 267, 276, 277, 287, 292, 297, 299, 300, 304, 313, 314, 322, 324, 329. See also Christology

Jesus Christ (continued)
crucifixion and death of, 2, 6, 73, 105, 145, 153, 246, 274, 300, 325
and descent to the dead, 28, 55
divinity of, 34, 52, 54, 55, 56, 57–58, 63, 70–71, 72–73, 74, 75, 76, 132, 142–43, 147, 243, 294, 315, 317
historical, 4, 5, 27, 244
humanity of, 34, 58, 63, 68, 94, 132, 142–43
incarnation of, 57, 133, 143, 246
resurrection of, 2, 4, 6–7, 34, 70, 220, 244, 300, 310
return of, 6, 10, 14, 16, 38, 39, 51, 59, 176, 290, 291, 294, 300
as "Son of God," 6, 8, 52, 54, 55, 59, 72–73
virgin birth of, 26, 52, 54, 55, 59, 66, 300
will of, 58
Jewish War, First (66–70), 12
Jewish War, Second (132–135), 90
Jews, 12–13, 90, 137, 138–42, 145–47, 185, 212, 266, 269, 270, 271, 272, 273, 274, 301, 314, 315. See also Judaism
jihad, 135, 136
Joachim of Fiore, 32, 119
Johann Sigismund (elector of Brandenburg), 226
John, Saint (the apostle), xvi, 16
John IV Nesteutes (patriarch of Constantinople), 99
John VIII (pope), 99
John VIII Palaiologos (emperor), 129
John XXIII (pope), 273, 274
John Chrysostom (archbishop of Constantinople), 33, 37
John of Damascus, 133
The Fount of Wisdom, 133
John of the Cross (Juan de Yepes), 188
John Paul II (pope), 250, 261, 273, 275
Johnson, Philip, 333–34
Jonah (prophet), 218
Joseph II (patriarch of Constantinople), 129
Joseph of Cupertino, 88

Josephus, Flavius, History of the Jewish Wars, 60
Joshua, 215
Jovian (emperor), 24, 76
Judaism, xvi, 6, 8–10, 13, 15, 32, 34–35, 42, 60, 66, 69, 70, 125, 245, 266, 267–68. See also Jews
Chrisian hostility and, 90–91, 137, 138
Judas Thomas, 65
Julian (bishop of Eclanum), 50
Julian of Norwich, 123
Julian the Apostate (emperor), 24, 64, 76
Junia (Romans 16:7), 277
"just war," 47–48, 136, 315, 321
justice, 47, 70, 276, 300, 309
justification, 163, 167, 319
by faith, 153, 168, 235
Justin Martyr, 13, 30, 36–37, 54, 55
Justinian I (emperor), 126
Justinian II (emperor), 134

Kant, Immanuel, 242, 243
Katherine of Aragon (queen of England), 191–92, 194
Keble College (Oxford), 333
Kempe, Margery, 123
Kierkegaard, Søren, 245–46
The Moment, 246
Kirchenkampf, 268
Königshofen, Jakob von, 147
Kulturkampf, 254

Lactantius, 19
Laetentur Coeli, 129
laity, xvii, 31, 77, 86, 154, 180, 197, 205–8, 226, 246, 311, 312, 315, 321, 324. See also clergy/laity
Lamentabili sane exitu, 255
language(s), 7, 15, 125, 146, 154, 167, 256, 274, 281, 289. See also particular languages
Languedoc (French region), 112
Laon, France, 329, 331
LaSalle, Robert de, 282
Last Judgment, 8, 10, 53, 59, 119, 175, 219, 329
Last Supper, 11–12, 170, 179

Lateran Council IV (1215), 141
Latin language and culture, 7, 33, 39, 60, 78, 123, 125, 128, 154, 186, 201, 207, 274
Laud, William (archbishop of Canterbury), 286
Law, 6, 8–9, 10, 13, 32, 38, 40, 49, 60, 69, 70, 71
    and Gospel, 9, 10, 70, 170
Law, William, 233
    A Serious Call . . . , 224
lay preachers, 237–38
Lazarus (beggar), 55
Lazarus of Bethany, 4, 220
learning. See education
Le Corbusier (Charles-Édouard Jeanneret-Gris), 333
Lee, Ann, 291
Lefebvre, Marcel (archbishop), 320
Lefèvre d'Étaples, Jacques, 190
Leibnitz, Gottfried Wilhelm, Freiherr von, 243
Leipzig, Germany, 153, 227
Lent, 97–98, 134
Leo I (pope), 94
Leo III (emperor), 133
Leo IX (pope), 100, 115, 128
Leo X (pope), 153
lepers, 145
Lessing, Gotthold Ephraim, 222
Leuenberg, Switzerland, 262
Levelers, 210
Leyden, Jan van (Jan Beukelszoon), 175
Leyden, Netherlands, 197
liberal Christianity, 222, 270, 300, 301
liberalism and liberals, 5–6, 60, 241, 243–44, 246, 250, 251, 262, 266, 274, 275, 276, 287, 295, 299, 304, 310, 318
liberation theology, 275–76, 309, 310, 321
Licinius (emperor), 19
Liegnitz, Germany, 90
Lima, Peru, 282, 284
Lincoln (English diocese), 207
literacy, 120, 150, 207
liturgy. See worship
Liverpool, England, 333

Lives of the Fathers, 84
Livingston, David, 258
Lollard movement, 191
Lombards, 95
London, England, 191, 232, 270, 299, 332
London Missionary Society, 260
Lord's Prayer, 154, 207–8
Lord's Supper. See Eucharist
Louis IX (king of France), 138
Louis XIV (king of France), 201
Louis XVI (king of France), 239
Louisiana, 282
Lourdes, France, 251
love, 36, 70, 112, 168, 224, 298, 314
Lübben, Germany, 225
Luther, Martin, xv, xvi, 61, 71, 147, 149, 151–60, 163, 164, 166, 167, 168, 169, 171–72, 173, 177, 178, 179, 180, 183, 184, 190, 198, 202, 223, 224, 226, 229, 235, 306, 313
    Babylonian Captivity of the Church, 184, 191
    Bible translation, 157
    Commentary on Romans, 235
    Heidelberg Theses, 153
    Ninety-five Theses, 63, 149, 151, 152, 153, 154, 183
    To the Christian Nobility of the German Nation, 171, 278
Lutheran Church in America, 263
Lutheranism and Lutherans, xv, 5, 54, 87, 156–57, 161–62, 163, 164, 165, 166, 168, 169, 170, 179, 189, 190, 198, 201, 202, 207, 209, 222, 223, 224, 225–27, 229, 230, 231, 232, 233, 238, 246, 247, 258, 262, 265, 266, 268, 269, 270, 273, 285, 289, 306, 313, 319–20
Lyons, France, 37
Lyons II, Council of (1274), 111, 128

Macon, Georgia, 249
Madeleine, La (Paris church), 332
Madison, James, 286
Magdeburg, Germany, 141
Magellan, Ferdinand, 214
magic, 16

Mainz, Germany, 139, 151
Maistre, Joseph Marie, comte de, *Du Pape*, 249
Malines, Belgium, 251
Mamelucos, 261
Mameluke Empire, 138
Manes (Mani; Manichaeus), 44, 57
Manichaeism, 44, 45
Manuel I (king of Portugal), 282
Mar Thomas Church, 143, 306
Marcellinus, Ammianus, 57
Marcion, 24, 27, 37, 57, 68–71
Marcionite church, 69
Marcus Aurelius (emperor), 37
Marienthal, Germany, 272
marriage, 40, 51, 138, 154, 164, 191, 231, 254. *See also* remarriage
   clerical, 101, 108, 165, 172, 193
Marseilles, France, 112, 140
Marshall, John, 286
martyrdom and martyrs, xvii, 12, 18, 19, 20–21, 25, 33, 35, 36, 37, 38–39, 40, 174, 195, 196, 205, 249, 264, 272, 322, 324, 327
   theology of, 174
Marx, Karl, 247, 265, 302
Mary, Blessed Virgin, 55, 59, 133, 142, 143, 185, 223, 251, 254, 277, 326.
   See also Assumption; Immaculate Conception
Mary I (queen of England), 194–95
Maryland, 286
Mass, 86, 108, 109, 122, 129, 134, 157, 158, 165, 167, 196–97, 198, 207, 274, 328, 331. *See also* Eucharist
   private, 86, 169
Massachusetts, 285
mathematics, 214, 215, 216–17
Matthijs, Jan, 175
Maurice, Frederick Denison, 245
Maxentius, Marcus Aurelius Valerius (emperor), 22, 89
Maximilla (Montanist), 39
Mayflower (ship), 197, 211, 282, 284, 285, 286
Melanchthon, Philipp, 161, 165
mendicant orders, 111, 113, 117, 119

Menno Simons, 176–77
Mennonites, 48, 177, 202, 285. *See also* Anabaptists
messiah (term and office), 2, 6, 8, 9, 10, 11, 12, 13, 26, 70, 146, 245
Methodism and Methodists, 233, 235, 236–38, 279, 287, 289, 293, 296, 299, 303, 320, 332
Methodist Episcopal Church, 238, 288, 320
Methodist Protestant Church, 320
Methodius (apostle of the Slavs), 124–25
metropolitan (office), 31, 105
Mexico, 263, 283, 284
Mexico City, Mexico, 282, 284
Michael Cerularius (patriarch of Constantinople), 128
Michael VII (emperor), 127
Michelangelo Buonarroti, 120, 185, 216
Middle Ages, 95, 96, 241, 312, 317, 329–30, 333
Middle East, 136, 143, 256, 306
Middleton, Conyers, 219
Milan, Edict of (313), 3, 23, 47, 89
Milan, Italy, 45, 101, 150
military force, 135, 162, 163, 164, 176, 200, 256, 257, 260, 313
Miller, William, 290
   Evidence from Scripture..., 290
Miltiades (pope), 64
Milton, John, 210
   Paradise Lost, 46
Milvian Bridge, Battle of (312), 22, 23, 89
Milwaukee, Wisconsin, 302
Minor Reformed Church, 181–82
miracles, 4, 99, 216, 218, 220, 243, 244–45, 292
Mirari vos, 249
missions and missionaries, 10, 14, 93, 96, 97, 124–25, 144, 186, 229, 252, 255–61, 263, 279, 282, 283, 284, 291, 294, 306
Missouri, 293
Mit brennender Sorge, 271
modalistic monarchianism, 34
Modernism, 255

modernity, 89, 240, 249, 251, 254–55, 266, 318

Monasticism, 33, 79–88, 98, 99, 106, 109–13, 116, 117, 132, 158, 185, 186, 187, 188, 206, 224, 248, 254, 273, 277–78, 279, 313

Monica (mother of Augustine), 44

monophysitism, 58, 94, 130, 132, 143

monotheism, 9, 34, 314

Monothelitism, 132

Montanists, 39–40

Montanus, 39

Monte Cassino, Italy, 85

Moody, Dwight L., 297–98

Moody Bible Institute, 298

morality and moral theology, 9, 14, 17, 23, 25, 32, 40–41, 48, 49–50, 78, 79, 106, 122, 168, 174, 203, 212, 219, 220, 221, 226, 244, 245, 265, 287, 294, 300, 311, 313, 315, 318

Moravia, 124, 231

Moravians, 231, 232, 235, 236, 242, 258, 260

More, Sir Thomas, 191, 192

Utopia, 171, 192

Moritz I (elector of Saxony), 164, 165

Mormons, xvi, 291–94

Moroni (angel), 292, 293

motion pictures, 294, 295, 298

Mount Hermon (Massachusetts school), 298

Muggletonians, 212

Mühlberg, Germany, 164

Munich, Germany, 251, 254

Münster, Germany, 174–76, 271, 272, 331

Müntzer, Thomas, 171–72

murder, 108, 272

music, 71, 99, 124, 224, 237, 256, 297–98, 309. See also hymns

Muslims. See Islam

Mussolini, Benito, 272

mysticism, 33, 123, 188, 224, 230

myth, 244, 276

Nag Hammadi, Egypt, 27, 64

Nag Hammadi papyri, 27–28, 64–65, 67–68

Nantes, Edict of (1598), 201, 203

Napoleon I (emperor of France), 136, 239, 240, 242, 249, 332

National Association of Evangelicals (U.S.), 262

National Baptist Convention, 304

National Council of the Churches of Christ (U.S.), 262

Native Americans, 235, 257, 261, 283, 284, 286, 306, 314

Nativity, Church of the (Bethlehem), 328

natural religion, 219, 220, 221

Nazarenes (early sect), 13

Nazis, 265, 266–69, 270–73, 295

Neo-orthodoxy, 246, 268, 270, 321

Neo-Platonism, 45

Nero (emperor), 17

Nestorianism, 143, 256, 305

Nestorius (archbishop of Constantinople), 142–43, 305

Netherlands, 175, 176, 177, 180, 182, 189, 190, 197, 204, 230, 285

new birth, 227–28, 230, 236. See also conversion

New England, xvi, 212, 282, 288, 296, 317

New Guinea, xvii

New Jerusalem, 176, 286

New Mexico, 284

New York (city), 270, 297, 299, 333

New York (state), 291, 300

Newton, Sir Isaac, 215, 217

Nicaea I, Council of (325), 23, 24, 35, 52, 53, 56–57, 74–76, 93, 94, 105, 127, 130, 132, 181

Nicaea II, Council of (787), 130, 132, 133

Nicene Creed, 52, 57–58, 59, 75, 126, 127, 128, 294, 311

Nicomedia, 74

Niemöller, Martin, 269, 270

Nietzsche, Friedrich Wilhelm, 247

nominalism, 122–23

non-Christian religions, 227, 243, 274. See also Islam; Judaism

nonjurors (France), 249

nonviolence, 174, 176, 327. See also pacifism

Norse (people), 94

North America, xv, xvi, 3, 177, 197, 201, 236, 238, 245, 256, 258, 263, 273–74, 279, 282, 284–85, 286, 288, 290, 295, 297, 299, 302, 303, 305, 306–7, 309, 310, 311, 316–17, 318, 319–20, 321, 323, 333, 334
North Carolina, 284
Norway, 189
Norwich, England, 141
Nostra Aetate, 274
Notre Dame University, 254
novices, 88
Noyon, France, 177, 331
numerology, 290
Nuremberg, Germany, 141, 147, 150, 158, 175, 193

oaths, 16, 18, 255
obedience, 81, 88, 108
Odilo (abbott of Cluny), 110
Odo (abbott of Cluny), 110
Oecolampadius, Johann, 179
Oglethorpe, James, 233
Ohio, 293
Old Catholic Church, 63, 254
Olson, Regine, 245
Olympic Games, 24
Opium Wars, 259
Ora et labora (motto), 87, 313
orders. *See* mendicant orders; Monasticism
ordination, 86, 108–9. *See also under* women
Origen, 33, 41–43, 46, 74, 81
Orlamünde, Germany, 172
Orr, James, 295
Orthodox Church. *See* Eastern Orthodoxy
orthodoxy, 3, 60, 201, 202, 320
Osiander, Andreas, 193
Ostrogoths, 96
Otto I (emperor), 100
Ottoman Empire, 129, 130, 162
Oxford, England, 123, 194, 233, 235, 236

Pachomius, 83–84
pacifism, 12, 16, 36, 47, 48, 174, 176, 291, 295
paganism and pagans, 22, 24, 38, 44, 90

Pakistan, 136
Palestine, 2, 7, 8, 24, 60, 82, 94, 111, 137, 305
Palladius (Irish bishop), 97
Palmyra, New York, 292
pamphlets, 154, 155, 157, 159, 171, 210, 290
Pantheon (Paris), 333
Pantheon (Rome), 326
papacy and popes, 31, 75, 98, 99, 100–102, 106, 112, 115, 130, 135–36, 149, 150, 151, 162, 163, 165, 166, 184, 186, 205, 240, 249, 252, 281–82. *See also* infallibility
  authority of, 101, 110, 111, 122, 169, 185, 217, 248, 249, 252, 320
  elections of, 100, 107, 128
  primacy of, 96, 99, 104–6, 125, 127–28, 129, 136, 253
papal states, 99, 251
Paraguay, 203, 261, 284
Paris, France, 186, 198, 200, 239, 253, 330, 332
Particular Baptist Missionary Society, 260
Pascendi Dominici gregis, 255
Passover, 11, 34, 57
pastor (church office), 178–79
patriarch (church office), 105
patriarchs (Old Testament), 26, 176
Patrick (Irish bishop), 97–98
Paul, Saint (the apostle), 4, 8–11, 12, 16, 32, 42, 51, 70, 71, 73, 146, 235, 245, 252
Paul III (pope), 163, 186, 257
Paul IV (pope), 185
Paul VI (pope), 274
Paul of Samosata (bishop of Antioch), 57
Pax Romana, 7
peasants, 150, 159–60, 171
Pelagius, 49–50, 99
penance, 77, 80, 140, 179
Pentecost, 7
Pentecostals, 263
perfection, 32–33, 50, 67, 80, 84, 278, 313
perjury, 108

Perkins, William, *A Declaration of the True Manner of Knowing Christ Crucified*, 224

persecution(s), 2, 14–21, 23, 25, 33, 38, 39, 61, 64, 75, 76–77, 78, 174, 194, 198, 241, 249, 263, 264, 269, 274, 291, 293, 295, 314–15, 322, 326. *See also* intolerance; suppression

of non-Christians, 24, 91, 139–40, 141, 145, 261, 264–65, 314

Persia, 14, 143, 282, 305

Peru, 257, 275, 284

Perugia, Italy, 115

Peter, Saint (the apostle), 7, 12, 14, 104–5, 106, 245, 252

Peter the Venerable (abbott of Cluny), 140, 147

Pharisees, 60

Philadelphia, Pennsylvania, 287, 297

Philip II (king of Spain), 195

Philip I, Langrave of Hesse, 158, 164

Philo of Alexandria, 43

philosophy and philosophers, 36, 37, 41, 45, 66, 72, 121, 150, 215, 241, 242, 245, 247, 301

Photinus (bishop of Sirmium), 57

physics, 214

Pietism, 223–24, 227, 229, 230, 231, 232–33, 235, 238, 242, 258, 288, 318

pilgrimage, 135, 141, 151

pillar saints, 83

Pius VI (pope), 249

Pius VII (pope), 248

Pius IX (pope), 249–52

Pius X (pope), 255

Pius XI (pope), 271

Pius XII (pope), 272, 273

Pizarro, Francisco, 257, 284

Plague. *See* Bubonic plague

Plato, 242

Pliny the Younger, 1–2, 15, 21

pluralism, religious, 23, 24, 166–67. *See also* diversity

Plymouth Colony, 197, 282, 284

pneumatology, 127, 128, 129

Pocahontas, 284

pogroms, 137, 138, 141, 147

Poissy, France (colloquy), 199–200

Poland, 169, 181, 182, 189, 203, 273, 275, 302

politics, xv, 3, 17, 19, 23, 25, 47, 48, 50, 57, 62, 78, 94, 99, 102, 105, 125, 126, 127, 129, 132, 138, 160, 171, 180, 183, 189, 194, 195, 197, 198–99, 204, 205, 208, 210, 211, 218, 238, 240, 256, 258, 261, 273, 275, 282, 287, 288, 301

Polycarp (bishop of Smyrna), 13

polygamy, 26, 164, 175–76, 293–94

Pontius Pilate, 55, 58, 59

poor, the, 6, 87, 108, 116, 247, 309, 310, 324

Poor Clares (order), 118

Portiuncula, La (church), 116

Portugal, 189, 256, 281–82, 284

Porvoo, Finland, 262

postulants, 88

poverty, 44, 81, 88, 111, 112, 113, 116–18, 119, 121, 275, 322. *See also* simplicity

Prague, 204

prayer, 83, 86, 87, 116, 188, 216, 217, 226, 229

preaching and preachers, 86, 90, 119, 120, 124, 157, 158, 167, 179, 205, 206–7, 223, 225, 226, 236, 238, 261, 274, 278, 282, 289, 296, 297, 298, 301, 303, 304, 326, 331, 334

outdoor, 134, 236

predestination, 170, 180, 212

presbyter (office), 14, 31, 103–4, 179, 180, 197

Presbyterian Church, 63, 240

Presbyterianism, 197, 285, 289, 295, 320

priesthood and priests, 32, 84, 86, 96, 107, 108–9, 150, 219, 221, 274, 277, 327

priesthood of all believers, 278

Primary Chronicle, 125

Princeton Theological Seminary, 295

printing and publishing, 154, 207, 228–29, 295, 298

Priscilla (Montanist), 39

Professio fidei Tridentinae, 169

Prohibition, 312

property, 111, 112, 119, 264, 291
prophet (church office), 11
prophets, 54, 59, 208
Protectorate, The (England), 211, 213
Protestant (term), 161
Protestant Episcopal Church, 288, 318
Protestantism and Protestants, 37, 62, 64, 88, 161–68, 170, 175, 177, 178, 180, 182, 183, 185, 186, 189, 193, 194, 195–96, 198–201, 202, 203, 204, 206, 209, 210, 217, 222, 223, 227, 232–33, 241, 246, 256, 259, 261, 265, 268–69, 270, 273, 275, 278–79, 285, 288, 290, 295, 296, 297, 299, 301, 309, 311, 313, 316–17, 318–19, 320, 321, 331
Protocols of the Elders of Zion, The, 145
Prussia, 201, 223, 226–27, 228, 242
Prussian Union, 265
Pseudepigrapha, 13–14
Ptolemaic system, 214, 215
Pulcheria (empress), 142
Punics (people), 78
purgatory, 99, 168
Puritanism and Puritans, 40, 196–97, 208, 209, 210–11, 212, 224, 286, 288, 295, 317

"Q" (source), 26–27
Quakers, 48, 212, 238, 279, 285, 291
Quanta cura, 251
Quartodecimans, 34
Quebec, Canada, 282, 283
Quinsext Council (692), 133–34
Quintavalle, Bernard de, 116

race and racism, 145, 146, 266, 269, 271, 331
Racovian Catechism, 169
Raleigh, Sir Walter, 284
Ranters, 212
rationalism, 222, 242
Ratzinger, Joseph. *See* Benedict XVI (pope)
Rauschenbusch, Walter, 245, 299–300
real presence (eucharist), 179, 195
reason, 122, 156, 221, 242, 243
reconciliation, 243

redemption, 10, 59, 67, 69, 243. *See also* salvation
reform, 101, 102, 109, 111, 113, 115, 118, 123, 154–55, 157–60, 167, 170–71, 182, 189, 190, 222–23, 225–26, 273, 292, 299, 311, 312
Reformation, The, 43, 90, 91, 112, 149, 158, 160, 165, 166, 167–68, 170, 172, 175, 182, 183–84, 189, 190, 191, 193, 198, 202, 203, 205, 206, 209, 222, 275, 278, 298, 312, 317
Reformed Church (denomination), 320
Reformed tradition and churches, 5, 169, 209, 223, 226, 229, 231, 232, 233, 238, 262, 265, 312
Reimarus, Hermann Samuel, 221–22
    Abhandlungen von den . . . Wahrheiten der natürlichen Religion, 221
    Apologie, 221–22
Reims, France, 331
reincarnation, 42
relics, 327
religionless Christianity, 270
remarriage, 40, 318, 321
Renaissance, The, 217, 332
repentance, 6, 10, 40, 77, 173, 227–28
resurrection of the dead, 55, 59
revelation, 15, 38, 122, 123, 202, 218–19, 220, 221, 224, 242, 243, 268, 291, 292, 295
    private, 39, 224, 291–92, 293
revivals, 288–89, 296–99, 301
rhetoric, 45
Richard I (king of England), 137
Richelieu, Cardinal-Duc de (Armand Jean du Plessis), 204
Ritschl, Albrecht, 245, 321
Roanoke Island, North Carolina, 284–85
Robertson, Pat, 301
Rochester Theological Seminary, 299
Roe v. Wade, 312
Roman Catholicism, xvi, 5, 31, 33, 54, 61, 62–63, 64, 87, 102, 113, 121, 128, 130, 153, 157, 158, 160, 161, 162, 163, 165, 166, 167–69, 171, 175, 179, 182–204 *passim,* 209, 210, 212,

Roman Catholicism (continued)
214, 217, 222, 223, 230, 240–41, 247,
248–55, 258, 259, 262, 264, 266,
270–72, 273–75, 277–78, 282–84,
285, 291, 301, 302, 306, 312, 313,
318–19, 320, 324, 331
Roman Empire, 1, 2–3, 7, 12, 13, 15–25
passim, 31, 38, 39, 46, 47, 49, 59, 62,
68, 82, 89, 90, 91, 93, 95, 96, 126,
138, 146, 305, 312, 321, 323
Eastern, 21, 74, 94, 106, 125–26, 127
Romanesque style, 324, 328–29, 330, 333
Romanticism, 241, 243, 250, 329–30
Rome, Italy, 1, 16, 17, 22, 23, 30, 33, 37,
45, 46, 50, 67, 69, 78, 85, 98, 102,
105, 106–7, 112, 117, 119, 152, 186,
192, 245, 250, 273, 305, 326
Ronchamp, France, 333
Rothmann, Bernhard, 174–75
Roundheads, 211
Rule of Faith (term), 53, 54
Rule of the Master, 85
rules (monastic), 84, 85–86, 87
Russell, Charles Taze, 294
Russia, 125, 248, 264, 314. See also Soviet
Union
Russian Orthodox Church, 125, 264, 265

Sabbath, 34, 90, 210, 237, 291. See also
Sunday
Sabellius, 57
sacraments, 79, 80, 84, 109, 153, 173, 179,
184, 191, 247, 334
Sacrorum antistitum, 255
Sadducees, 60
Saint Bartholomew's Day massacre, 200
Saint Francis Basilica (Assisi), 120
Saint Lamberti Church (Münster), 331
Saint Louis, Missouri, 302
Saint Maria del Fiore (Florence church),
327
Saint Martin-in-the-Fields (London
church), 332
Saint Nikolai (Berlin church), 225
Saint Patrick's Cathedral (New York City),
333
Saint Paul's Cathedral (Münster), 331

Saint Paul's Outside the Walls (Rome
basilica), 326
Saint Peter's (Rome basilica), 23, 105,
151–52
Saint Thomas (Caribbean island), 258
Sainte-Marie-Madelaine (Vézelay church),
329
saints and sainthood, 21, 33, 115, 120, 132,
138, 187, 188, 223, 277, 327
Salem, Massachusetts, 288
Salem, North Carolina, 232
salvation, 8, 11, 40, 54, 55, 56, 57, 68, 73,
99, 155, 170, 171, 180, 212, 220,
235, 291, 292, 300. See also
redemption
Salvation Army, 299
salvation history, 36, 46, 67, 95, 124, 250
Samaria, 36
sanctification, 228
Sankey, Ira, 297
Santiago de Cuba, 284
Santo Domingo, Dominican Republic, 284
Sassanid Empire, 143
Saul (Ireland), 98
Saul (king of Israel), 26
Saul of Tarsus. See Paul, Saint
Saxons, 94
Saxony, 158, 161, 164, 172, 190, 203, 231
schism, 39, 64, 95, 129, 253
Schleiermacher, Friedrich Daniel Ernst,
241–43, 246, 321
Der Christliche Glaube, 242
Über die Religion . . . , 242
Schleitheim Confession. See Brotherly Union
Schmalkald, League of, 163, 164, 165, 168,
207
Schmalkald Articles, 168
Schmolck, Benjamin, 224
scholasticism, 121, 123, 130, 150–51, 201
Schopenhauer, Arthur, 247
science and scientists, xvii, 215, 216–18,
219, 222, 241, 245, 247, 256
Scientific Revolution, The, 213–17
Scopes trial (1925), 295, 301
Scotland, 84, 179, 180, 189, 203, 211
Scripture. See Bible
Secret Book of James, 65

secularism, 265–66, 316
secularization, 240, 247, 275, 316
Seekers, 212
Seljuk Turks, 127, 134
semi-Arians, 76
semi-Augustinianism, 46, 99
seminaries, 185, 226, 252, 298
Sens, France, 330, 331
Seoul, South Korea, 317
Separatists, 285, 286, 288
Septuagint, 42
Sergius (patriarch of Moscow), 264
Sergius I (patriarch of Constantinople), 132
Sergius I (pope), 134
Sermon on the Mount, 12, 47, 81, 117, 174, 313
sermons. *See* preaching
Servetus, Michael, 181, 314
Servites (order), 111
Seven Years' War, 282
Seventh-Day Adventist Church, 290–91
sexual abstinence, 51, 81, 291. *See also* abstinence
sexual perversion, 16, 38
sexuality, 41, 42, 51, 291, 319, 321. *See also* gender
Shakers, 291
Shaw, Anna Howard, 279
Sicily, 98
silence, 81, 86
Silesia, 229
Simeon Stylites, 83
Simons, Menno. *See* Menno Simons
simony, 101, 108
simplicity, 40, 80, 83, 111, 116, 226, 291. *See also* poverty
sin(s), 6, 49, 77, 176, 243, 276, 291, 296, 298, 300. *See also* forgiveness of sins
  cardinal, 108
  confession of, 44
  original, 50, 51, 250
  unforgiveable, 77, 79
Sinope, 69
Sistine Chapel (Vatican), 120, 185, 216
Six Articles (1539), 53–54, 168–69, 193–94

slavery and slaves, 10, 20, 23, 39, 98, 138, 139, 203, 233, 237, 256, 257, 259, 261, 291, 302–3, 309, 314, 320
Slavic language, 125
Slavs, 124
Smith, Hyrum, 293
Smith, Joseph, Jr., 291–93
Smyrna, 37
social class distinctions, 10, 32, 78, 84, 159, 207, 236, 237, 242, 269, 299, 324
Social Gospel, 299–300
society, xv, 16, 24, 49, 63, 81, 84, 86, 117, 149–50, 154–55, 157, 171, 174, 187, 189, 202, 204, 214, 222, 238, 239, 242, 247, 249, 251, 275–76, 287, 296, 299–300, 301, 303, 307, 309, 313, 318–19. *See also* church and society
Society for the Advancement of Protestant Missions among the Heathen, 260
Society for the Propagation of the Gospel, 235
Society of Friends. *See* Quakers
Society of Jesus. *See* Jesuits
Socinians, 182
Socinus, Faustus, 181
  De Jesu Christo Salvatore, 181
Socinus, Laelius, 181
  Brevis Explicatio, 181
Socrates, 36
Söderblom, Nathan (archbishop of Uppsala), 262
sodomy, 108
Sola gratia, sola fide, sola scriptura (motto), 167, 168, 202, 268
Soldier's Catechism, The, 211
Solomon (king of Israel), 13, 26
Soubirous, Marie-Bernarde. *See* Bernadette
Souk, Algeria, 44
South Africa, 258, 260
South America, 257, 261, 275, 282, 283
South Carolina, 286
South Korea, 263, 306, 317–18
Southern Baptist Convention, 320
Soviet Union, 263, 264–65. *See also* Russia
Spain, 48, 94, 135, 139, 141, 147, 158, 161, 162, 164, 177, 184, 185, 186, 188,

Spain *(continued)*
    189, 195, 199, 204, 256, 281–82,
    284, 305
Spener, Philip Jakob, 226–27, 229
    Pia Desideria, 225–27
Speyer, Germany, 139, 141, 160, 328
Spinoza, Baruch, 242
Stalin, Joseph, 264
state religion(s), 47, 62, 68, 74, 89, 91, 189,
    195, 201, 210, 238, 240, 241, 270,
    286, 287, 290, 312, 323, 326. *See also*
    church and state
Stephen (king of England), 102
Stephen III (pope), 133
Stephen VI (pope), 99
Stewart, Lyman, 295
stigmata, 118
Stoicism, 245
Strassburg, Germany, 175, 177, 178, 331
Strauss, David Friedrich, 244–45, 246
Stuttgart Declaration of Guilt, 273
Sublimis Deus, 257
substance (theological term), 52, 57, 58,
    72, 76, 127
Suetonius, 16
suffering, 137, 146, 171, 174, 176, 309,
    313, 314, 322
Sunday, 23, 34, 35, 89, 212, 228, 291
Sunday, William (Billy), 298
supernatural. *See* miracles
suppression, 3, 15, 17, 89, 172, 198, 241,
    263–65, 271, 286. *See also*
    persecution
Supremacy, Act of (1534), 192–93
suspicion, 3, 12, 15, 16, 17, 47, 53, 139,
    174, 312, 315
swearing, 90, 212, 213, 237
Sweden, xvii, 87, 189, 203, 204, 247, 262,
    289, 306, 320
Switzerland, 168, 169, 174, 181, 189, 230,
    254, 270
Syllabus of Errors, 251, 253
symbolism, 179, 195, 325, 327, 328, 329,
    330, 333
synagogue(s), 9, 10, 13, 32
Syria, 14, 35, 55, 81, 82, 83, 133, 142, 143,
    305

Syriac language, 60
systematic theology, 36, 37, 46, 168

Tacitus, Cornelius, 16
taxation, 100, 108, 150, 248
teacher (church office), 11, 178–79
temple (Jewish), 12–13
Ten Commandments, 9, 207
Teresa of Avila, 32, 187–88, 206, 279
    Interior Castle, 188
Teresa of Calcutta, 113
Tertullian, 17, 20, 37, 38–41, 53, 74, 196,
    313
    Apologeticum, 38–39
Tetzel, John, 153
Texas, 284
Thagaste, 44
Theatines (order), 185
Theodosius I (emperor), 24, 126, 138
theology and theologians, 13, 14, 31–32,
    33, 35–36, 39, 41, 43, 46, 54, 75,
    120, 121, 123, 126, 130, 133, 147,
    150, 151, 153–54, 167, 168, 171,
    201–2, 205, 215, 216, 217, 218–19,
    223, 229, 241, 242, 247, 254, 256,
    267, 275, 276, 277, 283, 295, 301,
    306, 309–10, 314, 318–19, 321, 332
Theotokos (Marian title), 133, 142
Thirty-nine Articles, 169, 210
Thirty Years' War, 203–4, 209–10, 224,
    225, 315
Thomas, Saint (the apostle), 14, 143, 256
Thomas à Kempis, *Imitation of Christ*, 223
Thomas Aquinas, 61, 121–22, 123, 250,
    254
    Summa Theologica, 61, 121–22
Thomism, 122–23
Tillotson, John, *The Wisdom of Being
    Righteous*, 224
Time (magazine), 266
Tindal, Matthew, 219–20
    Christianity as Old as the Creation,
    219–20
Titian (Tiziano Vecelli), 164
tobacco, 294
Toland, John, 219
    Christianity not Mysterious, 219

Toledo III, Council of (589), 127, 138–39
Toledo IV, Council of (633), 139
toleration, 2, 15, 47, 90, 94, 137, 139, 145, 181, 201, 232, 265, 314. *See also* intolerance
Toleration, Edict of (311), 19, 21. *See also* Milan, Edict of
tongues, speaking in. *See* glossolalia
tonsure, 107
Torah, 6, 10, 13. *See also* Law
torture, 19, 39, 40, 62, 134
Totalitarianism, 263, 265, 272–73, 275
Toulouse, France, 112
tradition, 126, 167, 168, 184, 202, 215, 217, 253
Traditores, 20, 77
Trajan (emperor), 1, 2
transubstantiation, 123, 169, 193
Trent, Council of (1546–1563), 165, 166, 184–85, 188, 202, 203, 252
Trier, Germany, 139
Trinitarian controversy, xvii, 24, 55, 305
Trinity, 9, 34, 39, 57, 127, 133, 181, 182, 294
Trullo, Council of (692), 133–34
Tübingen, Germany, 245
Tuscany, 328
Twelve Articles of the Peasants, The, 159
Tyre, Council of (335), 76

ultramontanism, 249
Unitarians, 209
Unitas Fratrum (Moravians), 232
United Church of Christ, 320
United Methodist Church, 279, 320
United Society of Believers in Christ's Second Appearance, 291
United States, 48, 238, 240, 256, 260, 262, 283, 287–88, 293, 296, 299, 301, 302, 312. *See also* American Revolution
universals (philosophy), 122–23
universities, 282
Urban II (pope), 134–35, 136, 138
usury, 141, 147
Utah, 293

Valentinian I (emperor), 24
Valentinus, 57, 67
Valla, Lorenzo, 217
Vandals, 95
Vasari, Giorgio, 330
Vatican Council I (1869–1870), 62, 63, 252–53, 254, 274
Vatican Council II (1962–1965), 185, 273–74, 275, 312, 320
vegetarianism, 291
veneration of saints, 21
Venice, Italy, 186
Vermont, 290
vestments, 165, 196, 197, 210
Vézelay, France, 329
via media, 209
Victor I (pope), 35
Victorius (Patrick's vision), 98
Vietnam, 48
Virginia, 284, 286
virtue, 36. *See also* morality
Visigoths, 95, 96
Vitoria, Francisco de, 48
Vladimir the Great, Grand Duke of Kiev, 125
vocation, 278
Voetius, Gisbert, 312
Voltaire (François Marie Arouet), 221
vows, 88. *See also* oaths

Wagner, Richard, 266
Tannhäuser, 156
Waldensians, 145
war, 48, 176, 204, 257. *See also* "just war"
Wartburg (Eisenach castle), 156
Washington, George, 286
Watchtower (magazine), 295
Watchtower Society. *See* Jehovah's Witnesses
weddings, 254. *See also* marriage
Weigel, Valentin, 224
Weimar Republic, 265–66
Wesley, Charles, xvii, 232, 234
Wesley, John, 220–21, 233–38
Wesley, Samuel, 233
Wesley, Susanna, 233

West Indies, 232
Westphalia, 272
Whiston, William, 219
Whitaker, Alexander, 284
White, Ellen G., 290
Whitefield, George, 236
Wilcox, Thomas, 197
will, human, 50, 51, 99, 154, 212, 243
William I (duke of Aquitaine), 109
William I (king of England), 102
William of Occam, 122–23
Williams, Roger, The Bloody Tenent of Persecution, 286
Winthrop, John, 286
witchcraft, 288
Witness of Justin, The, 54, 55
Wittenberg, Germany, 149, 151, 153, 156, 161, 164, 172, 224, 226, 230
Wolfenbüttel, Germany, 222
Wolff, Christian, 221
womanist theology, 309, 310
women, 14, 39, 40, 41, 67, 84, 86, 123–24, 175–76, 187, 188, 205, 261, 277–79, 293–94, 309, 319, 320
ordination of, 63, 275, 279
Woolston, Thomas, 219, 220, 222
Word of God, 157–58, 160
works, good, 151, 155, 167, 168
World Council of Churches, 262, 320
World Missionary Conference (1910), 260, 261
World War I, 246, 269, 301
World War II, 48, 85, 208, 270, 273

Worms, Edict of (1521), 156–57, 158, 160, 161
Worms, Germany, 136, 139, 156, 159, 173, 184
worship, 10, 12, 14, 27, 30, 31, 32, 34, 35, 36, 43, 87, 89, 99, 108, 110, 111, 125, 132, 133, 134, 157, 165, 167, 194, 196, 199, 200, 210, 211, 219, 274, 286, 289, 303, 304, 311, 324, 325, 327
Württemberg, Germany, 158
Wycliffe, John, 123, 191, 206

Yale College, 288, 289
Yazid II (caliph), 133
Yepes, Juan de. See John of the Cross
Young, Brigham, 293
Young Men's (Women's) Christian Association, 301

Zeno (emperor), 94
Ziegenbalg, Bartholomäus, 229
Zinzendorf, Nikolaus Ludwig von (count), 229–32, 235, 260
Zion's Watchtower (magazine), 294
Zion's Watchtower Tract Society, 294
Zollikon, Switzerland, 173
Zoroastrianism, 44
Zurich, Switzerland, 161, 168, 171, 172–74, 175, 181
Zwingli, Huldych, 171, 172–74, 179, 190
Fidei Ratio, 161, 168

CPSIA information can be obtained at www.ICGtesting.com
Printed in the USA
LVOW132147130712

290022LV00002B/1/P